Visit us at

www.syngress.com

Syngress is committed to publishing high-quality books for IT Professionals and delivering those books in media and formats that fit the demands of our customers. We are also committed to extending the utility of the book you purchase via additional materials available from our Web site.

SOLUTIONS WEB SITE
To register your book, please visit **www.syngress.com**. Once registered, you can access your e-book with print, copy, and comment features enabled.

ULTIMATE CDs
Our Ultimate CD product line offers our readers budget-conscious compilations of some of our best-selling backlist titles in Adobe PDF form. These CDs are the perfect way to extend your reference library on key topics pertaining to your area of expertise, including Cisco Engineering, Microsoft Windows System Administration, CyberCrime Investigation, Open Source Security, and Firewall Configuration, to name a few.

DOWNLOADABLE E-BOOKS
For readers who can't wait for hard copy, we offer most of our titles in downloadable e-book format. These are available at **www.syngress.com**.

SITE LICENSING
Syngress has a well-established program for site licensing our e-books onto servers in corporations, educational institutions, and large organizations. Please contact our corporate sales department at corporatesales@elsevier.com for more information.

CUSTOM PUBLISHING
Many organizations welcome the ability to combine parts of multiple Syngress books, as well as their own content, into a single volume for their own internal use. Please contact our corporate sales department at corporatesales@elsevier.com for more information.

Mac OS X, iPod, and iPhone Forensic Analysis DVD Toolkit

Jesse Varsalone Technical Editor
Ryan R. Kubasiak, Sean Morrissey Lead Authors

Walter Barr
James "Kelly" Brown
Max Caceres
Mike Chasman
James Cornell

Disclaimer::

All equipment photos are provided courtesy of Apple® and are intended for informational purposes only. Their use does not in any way constitute endorsement, partnering or any other type of involvement on the part of Apple®.

Elsevier, Inc., the author(s), and any person or firm involved in the writing, editing, or production (collectively "Makers") of this book ("the Work") do not guarantee or warrant the results to be obtained from the Work.

There is no guarantee of any kind, expressed or implied, regarding the Work or its contents. The Work is sold AS IS and WITHOUT WARRANTY. You may have other legal rights, which vary from state to state.

In no event will Makers be liable to you for damages, including any loss of profits, lost savings, or other incidental or consequential damages arising out from the Work or its contents. Because some states do not allow the exclusion or limitation of liability for consequential or incidental damages, the above limitation may not apply to you.

You should always use reasonable care, including backup and other appropriate precautions, when working with computers, networks, data, and files.

Unique Passcode

32750962

PUBLISHED BY
Syngress Publishing, Inc.
Elsevier, Inc.
30 Corporate Drive
Burlington, MA 01803

Mac OS X, iPod, and iPhone Forensic Analysis DVD Toolkit

Printed in the United States of America
1 2 3 4 5 6 7 8 9 0

ISBN 13: 978-1-59749-297-3

Publisher: Laura Colantoni
Acquisitions Editor: Andrew Williams
Developmental Editor: Matthew Cater
Technical Editor: Jesse Varsalone
Project Manager: Andre Cuello

Page Layout and Art: SPI
Copy Editors: Alice Brzovic, Audrey Doyle, Judith H. Eby
Indexer: SPI
Cover Designer: Michael Kavish

For information on rights, translations, and bulk sales, contact Matt Pedersen, Senior Sales Manager, Corporate Sales, at Syngress Publishing; email m.pedersen@elsevier.com.

Library of Congress Cataloging-in-Publication Data
Application Submitted

Technical Editor

Jesse Varsalone, (CISSP, A+, Linux+, Net+, iNet+, Security+, Server+, CTT+, CIW Professional, MCT, MCSA, MSCE 2000/2003, MCSA/MCSE Security, MCDBA, MCSD, CWSP, CWNA, CNA, CCNA, MCDST, Oracle 8i/9i DBA, Certified Ethical Hacker), has served as the director of the MCSE and Network Security Program at the Computer Career Institute at Johns Hopkins University. For the 2006 academic year, he served as an assistant professor of computer information systems at Villa Julie College in Baltimore, MD. He taught courses in networking, Active Directory, Exchange, Cisco, and forensics.

Jesse holds a bachelor's degree from George Mason University and a master's degree from the University of South Florida. Jesse was a contributing author for Syngress's *The Official CHFI™ Exam 312-49 Study Guide: For Computer Hacking Forensics Investigators*, ISBN 978-1-59749-197-6, *Penetration Tester's Open Source Toolkit, Volume 2*, ISBN 978-1-59749-213-3 and Technical Editor for *Microsoft Forefront Security Administration Guide*, ISBN 978-1-59749-244-7. He runs several Web sites, including www.mcsecoach.com, which is dedicated to helping people obtain their MCSE certifications. He currently lives in Columbia, MD with his wife, Kim, and son, Mason.

Lead Authors

Ryan R. Kubasiak, (Apple Certified Support Professional, Certified Computer Examiner, Encase Certified Examiner, Certified Electronic Evidence Collection Specialist, Bachelor of Science in Computer Science), has 10 years of experience in law enforcement and is currently assigned as an investigator in the New York State Police Computer Crime Unit. Ryan specializes in digital examinations as well as network intrusion investigation with his extensive network training through law enforcement and corporate training. He has worked professionally for the State University of New York at Buffalo as a Local Area Network Administrator supporting multi-platform environments including Macintosh, Microsoft and Novell server and desktop operating systems. Ryan is the webmaster for the successful Macintosh forensic website www.macosxforensics.com. In his spare time, Ryan dedicates himself to his family, Michelle, Lucas, Makayla and Marisa.

Sean Morrissey, is presently employed by a U.S. Corporation as a Senior Computer Forensic Professional and is assigned to a contract to provide computer forensic training in nine subject areas, including Macintosh forensics, Windows forensics, and data recovery. Mr. Morrissey received a Bachelors Degree from Creighton University. Mr. Morrissey was a Commissioned Officer in the United States Army, a Law Enforcement Officer in Maryland, and a Trainer for the U.S. Department of State. Mr. Morrissey's experience with Macs dates back to 1984. Mr. Morrissey has also supported companies such as Dell and Hewlett Packard.

Mr. Morrissey would like to thank Dawn Morrissey, whose patience and understanding throughout this process made his contributions possible. Mr. Morrissey would also like to thank Jesse Varsalone for making this book possible and for bringing him into this project.

Mr. Morrissey currently resides on the Eastern Shore of Maryland, and has one son that is presently serving his country in the United States Army.

Contributing Authors

Walter "Wally" Barr, (A+, Network+, MCSE, CTT+), has been involved with computers for nearly twenty years. He has served in various roles including technical support, hardware and software design, Web programming, desktop publishing, graphic design, video and music production, database administration, network administration, and technical training for both the public and private sectors. He has served in the military as an MP and later worked for a computer hardware manufacturer, a Dot.com company, and a contracting firm doing database administration for FEMA.

James "Kelly" Brown, (MCSE, CTT+), is a Senior Computer Forensic Professional with over nine years of experience in the Information Technology field. Mr. Brown is an Instructor and Curriculum Developer at the Department of Defense Cyber Crime Center and holds a Bachelor's Degree in Computer Science from Strayer University. Prior to teaching at the Defense Cyber Investigations Training Academy, Mr. Brown worked for IBM as an Information Security Professional in the Security, Privacy, and Wireless Division Federal Sector. While at IBM his duties included conducting network and database audits, reporting information assurance and compliance activities, and conducting annual security awareness training. Mr. Brown has extensive field experience as a Senior Systems Engineer responsible for the successful development, implementation, and administration of numerous companies' networks in the private sector.

Max Caceres is director of research and development for Matasano Security, an independent security firm specializing in providing software and services to help organizations and vendors improve their security postures. Max has over 14 years of product development and security research experience, and is one of the security industry's leading experts on penetration testing. Before joining Matasano, Max led the team responsible for creating the first automated penetration testing product

CORE IMPACT and co-invented several now-patented technologies including system call proxying and exploit automation.

Max lives in New York City and enjoys spending time with his wife Gabriela and jumping out of airplanes.

Mike Chasman, (MCSE, MCSA Messaging, Security+, Server+, Network+, A+), is Vice President of Sparq Technology Consulting, an information technology consulting company for small to mid-sized businesses head-quartered in Baltimore, MD. His specialties include network security, interoperability in mixed environments such as Apple Mac OS X in Microsoft domains, and network reconnaissance and troubleshooting.

Mike has been a consultant in the field for more than 5 years, supporting companies such as Black and Decker, IBM, and Lockheed Martin. Mike currently resides in Baltimore with his lovely wife, Sera Clara, and three beautiful (and smart) daughters Reena, Abigail, and Sheera.

I would like to thank Sera, my wife, who made my contribution possible (somebody had to watch the kids). I would also like to thank my good friend Jesse for all his hard work in making this book possible. Thanks Jesse.

James "Jim" Cornell is a noted subject matter expert in the fields of Computer Science and Forensics. He started working with Macintosh computers in 1984 and is an Apple Developer. He is currently a government contractor in the National Capital Region, and has consulted on projects with most governmental agencies in the area. His numerous certifications include Certified Forensic Computer Examiner (CFCE), Certified Information Systems Security Professional (CISSP), Certified Technical Trainer (CTT+) and he has been a Licensed Peace Officer since 1981. Jim was a contributing author to Syngress's *OS X Exploits and Defense*, ISBN 978-1-59749-254-6.

Jim would like to send thanks to Tammy for, once again, being there and understanding the creative process. His love to Katy, Danny, Jewell, Hunter and Colin who give me hope for our future. And deep thanks to Henry Vasquez for being a great role model and for saving my life once or twice.

Contents

About the Mac OS X, iPod, and iPhone Forensic Analysis DVD Toolkit DVD

The accompanying Mac OS X, iPod, and iPhone Forensic Analysis DVD Toolkit DVD consists of two DMG images and a handful of tools to help you follow some of the examples in this book.

The first DMG image is a user's profile from a Mac running OS X. This volume is complete with artifacts that can be used in conjunction with some of the exercises in this book. The authors encourage you to use the DMG to practice recovering artifacts. Due to copyright issues, we did not include a complete image of OS X 10.5 "Leopard". However, this image has the entire web, documents, library, and other artifacts from a single user's profile on a Leopard operating system.

The second image is a DMG of a third-generation 4 GB iPod Nano. This DMG also has artifacts that can be used with the exercises in this book related to the iPod. All the artifacts contained in this iPod Nano DMG are files that were either created by the author, or that were obtained as free downloads from iTunes.

The remaining files are tools that can be utilized in conjunction with some of the exercises in the book. These applications are described in this book, and are available for the readers of this book to use. Other tools that are described in this book and not located on this DVD are available for download from the Internet.

Please use the DVD to get the best experience from *Mac OS X, iPod, and iPhone Forensic Analysis DVD Toolkit*. The authors put a lot of time and work into creating the images so the reader would be able to follow the steps of the author. Please do not make illegal copies of the DVD or redistribute it. If you are in the field of forensics, or plan a career in law enforcement, you should never resort to distributing or using illegal copies of pirated software. Enjoy!

MacTracker is the property of Ian Page. Additional information about Mactracker can be found at http://www.mactracker.ca

Chapter 1

Tiger and Leopard Mac OS X Operating Systems

Solutions in this chapter:

- **First Responders and Specialized Examiners**
- **Macintosh History**
- **Macintosh Aspects**
- **Macintosh Technologies**
- **Disk Structure**

☑ **Summary**

☑ **Solutions Fast Track**

☑ **Frequently Asked Questions**

Introduction

Although crimes themselves have not changed, the methodology of committing them is ever changing. Our challenge is to keep pace with the digital aspect of all crimes. Investigations and examinations now must include a digital aspect as well as the traditional methods. Crimes of all levels are being plotted, planned, or perpetrated with computers, PDAs, cell phones, USB flash drives, wrist watches, electronic pens, and other complex electronic devices. The examiner needs to be cognizant of this, and trained to recognize these items. Specialized Examiners need to be continually educated and trained on current forensic techniques to analyze the data on these high tech devices.

First Responders and Specialized Examiners

First responders are critical in initial actions taken such as on-site viewing of evidence and/or the securing of digital evidence. For this person, a checklist is not acceptable. An understanding of what needs to be done so one can adapt to the unique situations that present themselves is necessary. A loss of data or worse, corruption of data, at this point can severely jeopardize any case or situation. Also, an acceptable "touching" of data as a First Responder to get to the heart of a case that could be lost due to encryption in use is not only acceptable, but also imperative at this stage. Recognition of a scene and knowing how to react to the hardware, software, and data transfer methodologies in use are key for any first responder.

Employers need to understand the importance of training, certification, and court presentation. A well qualified examiner, whether a First Responder or Specialized Examiner, will stay up to date in technology advancements and training. For law enforcement, the National White Collar Crime Center offers excellent courses for the perfect price, free. There are many other options for training, most of which will be a financial investment. "Investment" is stressed because taking a course once is not good enough. Repeated training on newly emerging technology is a must. Multiple colleges and universities have recognized and developed digital forensic classes, as well as degree programs. Also, software companies such as Black Bag Technologies, Guidance Software, and Access Data offer classes that concentrate on their specific software, yet teach useful skills in analysis. Courses and certifications that are publicly available vs. law enforcement only classes are preferred. Techniques that can be reproduced by the digital forensic community at large are more revered in a courtroom setting.

There are times that a full analysis of digital media is simply not warranted, requested, or needed for the case at hand.

NOTE

A full analysis could be defined as a complete examination of all digital data on the media being examined, with a report of the relevant findings at the conclusion.

A limited scope analysis can be defined as a narrow look at the digital data on the media being examined for the purpose of answering a quick question.

The conditions, in criminal circumstances, to consider a limited scope examination rather than utilize a full analysis are:

- **Facilitate Arrest** You have a search warrant and need to find evidence at the crime scene to facilitate and arrest of the target.

- **Consent Search** You don't have anything more than permission from the target to look, but the permission is the look on-premises only.

- **Exigent Circumstances** You have a case such as a missing person and a quick look at the most likely useful data sources is warranted.

"Field forensics" is never a substitute for a full-fledged, digital forensic laboratory. Working in an open environment such as a target's home or office presents dangers as well as opportunity for missed information. With that in mind, this book is designed to guide the First Responder or Specialized Examiner to the data in a quick and forensically sound manner.

Digital Examination

Every digital examination should involve the following steps:

- Physically secure evidence or conduct on-site preview (Collection)
- Acquisition of digital media
- Verification of acquired data
- Archive of acquired data with verification
- Analysis of acquired data
- Reporting of results

Only the first two allow for the usage of original evidence. Special care is taken during these steps to insure original evidence is not altered. This book is written entirely based on that care. If you do not wander outside of the scope of this book, you will be conducting a sound digital forensic examination. All techniques outside of this book should be well tested in a controlled environment for expected outcome and actual results before attempting use on evidence.

Limited scope examinations typically will yield only a fraction of the evidence on a target computer. It may yield 0% of the evidence that exists on the target computer. It is not a substitute for a full analysis. Just because it was not found during a limited scope examination, doesn't mean it's not there. The typical full analysis of a personal computer will be conducted in a secure digital laboratory environment. As times have changed, so have the analysis techniques. There are justified reasons why a full examination may actually take place on site and/or on a live machine.

Results from a preview or analysis are only useful if everything has been conducted under forensically acceptable procedures. We must insure that everything done from start to finish guarantees unaltered data or in a worst-case scenario, results that are documentable, known changes to the target machine. The known changes and documentation may include a procedure attempted that did not result in the desired outcome. For instance, if you attempt to boot a target machine with a live CD and instead, the Mac OS boots, you must document what happened.

Another aspect of known changes is the concept of "Live" digital forensics. This is when we actually execute actions or processes on a currently running target machine. This is a decision a First Responder must make at the scene of the investigation. An example is a Macintosh with file vault enabled. If you, as the examiner, choose to copy files from the user's home directory prior to shut down, you have made a decision that results in altered data. You must make note of exactly the actions taken so the altered data has a sound explanation. The changes in this example are minor, known, and expected, and most importantly, justified.

Techniques for Examination

Four techniques are available to examine the target Macintosh: Live look at a powered on Macintosh, Single User Mode, boot CD/DVD methods, and Target Disk Mode. Each of these techniques has benefits as well as pitfalls.

Live Macintosh Examination

Looking at a live Macintosh is many times the first, best way to understand what is happening on the computer being presented. The Mac OS X Desktop, for instance, will present many clues to the steps a First Responder should take at a scene. We will discuss this in detail later in this chapter in the Macintosh Aspects section. A live Macintosh offers a First Responder the ability to asses a situation, gather vital data that may never be available again if the machine is powered off, as well as note other resources in use such as server connections, wireless connections, local external hard drives, and so forth. The live Macintosh tells a story that may not be told again after a shutdown.

Single User Mode

The Macintosh desktop/laptop/server that has Mac OS X installed can be booted into "single-user" mode. This state is initially a forensically sound state, and allows for information to be gathered. In single-user mode, however, a thorough working knowledge of UNIX will be needed. Single User Mode starts out with the system in a read-only state and a limited number of services running. It was designed for system administrators to perform maintenance on a UNIX system. Benefits include an already installed operating system, features established by Apple, and greatest speed of accessing certain types of data. Pitfalls include that it is entirely command line driven, is a manual process to get to many of the areas that our automated tools get us too much faster, and potentially has been shut off or maliciously altered.

WARNING

Using the suspect's own operating system is almost always a bad idea for extended tasks, and can lead to potentially mistaken results. Use Single User Mode carefully.

Boot CD/DVD Methods

Boot CDs and DVDs offer a known boot media with a known operating system each time you start up the Macintosh. They offer a well-known, always available, set of tools for every limited scope examination conducted. They also can be memory intensive, will not always work with the latest hardware, or may not boot at all. BlackBag Technologies offers a subscription for a forensically sound Macintosh boot disk. It is also possible to create your own bootable disk that is both forensically sound and has specific utilities installed. The downside to creating your own disk is the lack of support for future machines. Apple Inc. does tweak the operating to take advantage of newer hardware. The specific changes to software from Apple come on a DVD with the specific computer. For instance, the Mac OS X 10.4 box set available for purchase is for PowerPC Macintoshes only and will not boot Intel-based systems. The only Mac OS X 10.4 Install DVD disks available for Intel-based Macintoshes are the ones that came with the specific model!

That makes boot CDs and DVDs sound nearly impossible or expensive. Fortunately, Linux Live CD's are also abundant on the Macintosh. There are many compilations of Linux on CD available for Intel or PowerPC hardware, but not all will boot a Macintosh. One distribution of Linux, Ubuntu, is available for both the Intel and PowerPC hardware. Even better, forensic compilations of Linux distributions are beginning to show that will boot Intel hardware including SMART from ASR Data built on Ubuntu and Slackware.

Target Disk Mode

Modern Macintosh computers offer a technology not seen on other desktop and laptop computers. The computer can be booted into Target Disk Mode and viewed from a secondary computer. Target Disk Mode offers the greatest flexibility because it essentially turns the Macintosh computer into a firewire-based hard drive. You are able to use your laptop (or desktop) with a choice of operating system to look at the target machine. It yields the greatest speed and the widest variety of tools for examination. Target Disk Mode may not function at all on the suspect computer if it is not supported or has been disabled by Open Firmware Password. This technology is discussed further in the Macintosh Aspects section.

Macintosh History

Apple Inc., formerly Apple Computer Inc. was established in 1976. The company has famously produced many computers, laptops, printers, handhelds, cameras, servers, operating systems, spin off companies, and software over it 30-year history. Apple originally compared to IBM in the "who is better war," but that quickly changed to the current Apple vs. Microsoft that we know today. Apple Inc. has produced computer lines that include the Apple I, Apple II, Apple III, Lisa, and most famously, Macintosh.

Apple Inc. has always been an innovator with technology, many times introducing consumers to products before they knew they wanted them. It has been Apple's best flaw through the years. The first Macintosh to come out was a work of genius with the first Graphical User Interface (GUI) for a personal computer and a commercial turn heads. Publishing companies quickly saw the power of seeing their work on the screen before printing and the "Mac" soon became the computer known for desktop publishing. Apple introduced dot matrix printers such as the ImageWriter and laser printers such as the LaserWriter as they expanded their product lines in desktop publishing. Software was developed such as AppleWorks for all-in-one word processing, spreadsheet, and database functions and was a hit for the company. Operating systems continued to be developed with more user features with System 6 and System 7. But times were not always good for Apple's development team. Apple introduced its first laptop, the Macintosh Portable in 1989. The laptop was nicknamed the "Mac Luggable" because of its size and weight and is likely found in only die-hard Mac fan museums today. In the 1990's, Apple decided it was time to allow for cloning of its hardware architecture and the licensing of its operating system. Sales of the cheaper "clones" cannibalized Apple's market share rather than expand the Mac operating system market share as a whole.

In 1997, the current rebirth of Apple began. Steve Jobs came back to Apple through the acquisition of his company, NeXT and the NeXTSTEP operating system. NeXTSTEP was to form the basis of what is now, Mac OS X. A new outlook, a new team, and new goals all started to come together with the announcement from "Interim" CEO Steve Jobs that Microsoft was investing in Apple and a commitment to share technology was to ensue. The days, months, and years after that admittedly odd announcement to Mac users, have been huge successes for Apple. The consumer market share for Macintosh computers had plummeted to near negligible levels in the 1990's. Today, consumer market share has been reported at levels of 10 percent worldwide and 21 percent in the United States (CNN.com April 1, 2008).

What does that history mean for us as examiners besides a great game of Trivial Pursuit? It means that one in every five computers you encounter are likely to be a Macintosh running the Mac operating system today.

Macintosh Aspects

Apple has always been a very unique company; hence the operating system, file systems, and applications are also unique. Moving from one computer platform to another will always have similarities. Macintosh computers have keyboards, displays, hard drives, and power cords just like their Windows, Linux, UNIX, and other like counterparts. Other similarities that are found in hardware include USB ports, firewire ports, network connectivity, external hard drives, and so forth. Other similarities found in software include an operating system, log files, applications, malware, and so forth. So what sets the Macintosh apart and why do we need a book to understand it all? It is all in the way Apple engineers the hardware and the software to interact to give the end user the Macintosh experience. Consider this simple example to illustrate the point. A simple application such as a Web browser allows a user to access the Internet in a graphical manner. On a Windows-based computer, the likely browser in use is Internet Explorer. On a Macintosh, the likely browser is Safari. One might think that knowing how one browser works means that you will have a good understanding of how the other works. In fact, the two browsers work so differently, that the remnants left behind sometimes can leave you scratching your head wondering if the person was actually using the same Internet as the person using the opposite platform. We will give you a much better understanding of browser history on the Mac in Chapter 8.

Some basics to know and understand before looking at a Macintosh include the following.

Is It a Mac?

Although this might seem like a silly question, not every piece of hardware produced by Apple will look like a standard computer.

Figure 1.1 represents an entire Apple desktop computer, without the keyboard and mouse showing. There is a small pinhole at the top center, which is a built-in iSight high quality camera. At first glance, one could mistake this for the Apple Display with brushed aluminum housing, and potentially leave it behind when looking for "real" computers. This particular computer has a 2.4 GHz Core 2 Duo processor, 4 GB of RAM installed, an ATI Radeon video card with 256 MB of RAM, 320 GB of hard drive, a Dual Layer DVD Super drive, wireless 802.11n Airport Extreme, Gigabit Ethernet, Firewire 800, USB 2.0, and Bluetooth. That is quite a list of features to miss if you were thinking this is just a fancy LCD screen.

Figure 1.1 Is It a Macintosh or a Monitor?

Of course, the easiest way to identify Apple hardware is to look for the typical, large "Apple" on the housing. Apple puts the prominent "bitten Apple" on everything they manufacture somewhere on the case. However, a logo does not identify its function. Always look on the back, side, or bottom for the model information. Apple will typically use machine specifications to name its models of computers. Look carefully for this tag. Some models will show this tag at the bottom of the stand, such as the iMac in Figure 1.1. Other items such as a Macbook Pro, won't show any information on the case, until you remove the battery to reveal the model information. If the model name includes "2.0 GHz Core Duo," you are looking at a computer, not a monitor. I recommend you take the model information and cross-reference it with the Apple Web site (www.apple.com/support) and gather all of the factory information you can about the computer you are examining. There is also a great third-party utility called "MacTracker" that you can run directly from your own Macintosh. MacTracker is a small application that is frequently updated with every model produced by Apple, including yesteryear's clones, listing specifications, factory installed software, and even what the startup chime sounds like. The application has evolved to include AppleTV, iPhone, and iPods. The application can be obtained for free at mactracker.dreamhosters.com and is included on the DVD Toolkit.

File System Overview

MFS, HFS, HFS+. It seems like acronyms never end. The Macintosh originally used the Macintosh File System (MFS). It was a flat file system that was good for a small, floppy disk amount of information. The MFS was innovative in its introduction of resource forks, ability to handle 255-character file names, and simple metadata for a GUI operating system. Its inefficiencies were hidden initially, because going across such a small amount of space "back in the day" was trivial. Very quickly, hard drives came about and the MFS read of large data sources became a time-expensive task. The Hierarchical File System (HFS) was developed and introduced in System 3.0 at the time of the Mac Plus, and was used into System 8 when HFS+ was introduced. As operating systems have continued to evolve, file systems have shown their weaknesses in speed or inability to store enough information about the files themselves. HFS+ is an evolution of the original HFS file system, adding advanced data storage mechanisms such as extended file attributes, UNICODE, larger block sizes, larger file sizes, and larger volume sizes.

HFS+ (and the older HFS) are the two dominant file systems found on any Macintosh. Without "something" to recognize this file system, you will be left looking at a seemingly unallocated drive with raw data only. Tools such as Encase from Guidance Software and BBT Forensic Suite from BlackBag Technologies can appropriately interpret this file system and display the contents in a user friendly way. Free Linux Live CD variants may also have HFS+ recognition. Finally, the Macintosh itself knows how to display its own file system. We use this fact when using the GUI (the Finder) and single-user mode. There is more to come on HFS and HFS+ in Chapter 4: "HFS Plus File System."

A Macintosh may contain other file systems, just as any other computer. With the release of "Boot Camp" from Apple, it suddenly became very easy to install Windows XP and Vista on a Macintosh Intel-based computer. Also, a skilled user can manually partition their hard drive and install any compatible operating system for Intel-based systems. This means as an examiner, you may find NTFS, FAT32, EXT3, and so forth file systems on a Macintosh. The Intel-based Macintosh computers are capable of running multiple operating systems with multiple file systems. Always be aware of this when using techniques, and be aware of the consequences. Also, don't be too quick to exclude the PowerPC-based Macs from partitions and alternate file systems. A very prominent and accepted Linux distribution for the PowerPC Macintosh is YellowDog Linux. There is also Ubuntu Linux for

PowerPC, now in a non-development state, but very possible as an installed operating system. This means you may find file systems such as EXT2 and EXT3 on a PowerPC Macintosh as well. Be very careful during the acquisition and examination phase and don't quickly disregard "unallocated space" as nothing.

What does the future hold for file systems and the Macintosh? This may take a shiny crystal ball or an Apple System Engineer as your best friend for an accurate answer, but we can make some good guesses. First off, Leopard added read-only support for Sun's open source file system, the Zeta File System (ZFS), in its first release. ZFS is a file system that brings with it promises that no other file system has shown thus far. Its speed, reliability, and ability to self-heal are beyond any file system on any personal computer today. Is this the file system of the Macintosh future? Time will certainly tell, but Apple has taken that first step by adding the read-only support.

Figure 1.2 represents a look at the same iMac Aluminum as seen from an application named Disk Utility. Disk Utility is located in the Utilities folder, and we will discuss this application later in detail in Chapter 3.

Figure 1.2 Disk Utility Device Listing

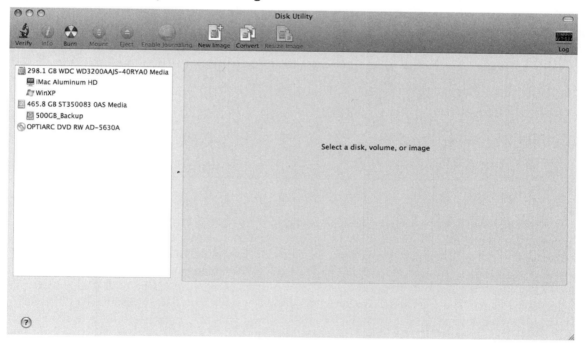

Figure 1.2 represents a typical setup of a home user Macintosh. You are looking at three physical devices: a 298.1 GB hard drive, a 465.8 GB hard drive, and a DVD-RW drive. Looking further into the left pane, we see that the first hard drive has been partitioned into two user partitions, one called "iMac Aluminum HD" and the other called "WinXP." The second physical drive has one user partition called "500 GB_Backup." The DVD-RW is showing no user partitions, which means

there is no disc in the drive (or something is malfunctioning, which is beyond what we are looking into here). Clicking on any of the user partitions will reveal more information about each including their format (file system). Disk Utility is a very powerful application and we will use much of its power throughout this book.

Configuring & Implementing...

Exercise 1.1: What File System Is on Your Hard Drive?

This exercise will familiarize you with the layout of your own hard drive using Disk Utility.

1. From the Finder, click on the **Go** menu and select **Utilities**.
2. Locate Disk Utility and double-click on it to launch it.
3. After Disk Utility gathers information about the attached media, locate the left pane of the window.
4. Locate the user partition of your hard drive and click on it.
5. On the bottom of the Disk Utility window, locate the line that says "Format:." Does it say "Mac OS Extended (Journaled)?"

End of Exercise

Apple uses extra descriptors to describe the specific HFS+ type that is used on the volume. What do I mean by this? Notice in Exercise 1.1 we found the format type to be Mac OS Extended (Journaled). That doesn't say anything about HFS+ in the format. In fact, it is HFS+ with journaling enabled. Three other possibilities are Mac OS Extended, Mac OS Extended (Case Sensitive), and Mac OS Extended (Case Sensitive, Journaled).

Again, Chapter 4 will go much deeper into what all of this means, but suffice it to say, Mac OS Extended is simply another way to say HFS+.

Operating Systems

MacOS X and MacOS 9 are the two dominant operating systems that will be found on any Macintosh. With the release of "Boot Camp" from Apple, any operating system that operates on Intel hardware can be successfully installed and run. Just because an "Apple Logo" is displayed on the side of the computer doesn't mean an Apple operating system will be used. Apple has released Windows XP Service Pack 2 drivers as well as Windows Vista drivers, so expect those more often. Many users have figured out how to use Boot Camp and other means to install other operating systems and successfully boot into them. Just as common will be virtualization software such as Parallels and VMWare Fusion. With these, you will encounter a "file" or series of files that combine to form and contain an entire hard drive worth of data from a different operating system. If you are interested in learning more about these features, both Parallels and VMware Fusion, as well as Boot Camp will be discussed in great detail in Appendix A

With that said, an extremely high percentage of Macs will be running OS X or OS 9. The focus of this book will mostly be on the OS X–based machines. OS X–based PowerPC Macintoshes have the possibility of containing OS 9 within the OS X installation. It is referred to as "Classic" and is run simultaneously to the OS X environment. Some PowerPC Macintoshes also have the option of directly booting into OS 9. An Intel-based Macintosh as well as a PowerPC G5-based Macintosh could not use the classic environment.

It is easy to know exactly which version of the operating system is running on a Mac OS X computer. In the Finder, clicking on the Apple Menu in the upper left corner of the screen reveals a menu. The first choice in the menu is "About This Mac," as discussed in Exercise 1.2. Selecting this choice will reveal the window in Figure 1.3.

Figure 1.3 About This Mac

Figure 1.3 is extremely revealing. At first glance, we get basic information about the Macintosh itself. Two items to note as an examiner might be the operating system version as well as the startup disk in use (the partition that this Macintosh will use by default when powered on). Of even more use here is the button "More Info…," because it will open a very verbose application called System Profiler. We will go into this application later in this book.

Configuring & Implementing…

Exercise 1.2: What Operating System Is on Your Macintosh?

This exercise will familiarize you with the "About This Mac" window.

1. From the Finder, click on the Apple menu and select **About This Mac**.
2. Locate the version number of Mac OS X.
3. Click on the version number. Does it reveal the specific build number for your machine?
4. Click on the build number. Does it reveal the serial number of your Macintosh?
5. Click on the serial number and you will return to the original "About This Mac" window.

End of Exercise

Data Files

This section is probably the oddest section to describe. Think of a file named "moof.doc." It probably makes you think of Microsoft Word. Now think of a file named "moof." What application opens that file? In the Macintosh world, "resource forks" used to take care of this by hiding the ".doc" inside of the file itself with a "Creator Code." Specifically, the same file, "moof.doc" created by MS Word version 6 under Mac OS 9 could save the file as "moof" and that file would open every time with Microsoft Word version 6 by simply double-clicking on the file itself. What Microsoft Word did during the save was embed a Creator Code into the Resource Fork of the file itself of "MSWD." This four-letter word was associated to the application Microsoft Word and would cause the application to launch if the file was opened. Aside from Creator Codes, other data could be put into the Resource Fork as well, including the custom icon for the file. This was a very clean solution on Macintosh that alleviated the user having to remember all of those horrible ".this" and ".that" endings to files. Unfortunately, file sharing between file systems happened. HFS and HFS+ were very capable of saving a file that had a resource fork and Data Fork, but no other file system was (without modification or loading of extensions). What happened when a Mac user saved his "moof" file to a FAT32 volume? The resource fork was simply lost. The first sign of this was that the custom Microsoft Word icon was now missing. The second sign was that double-clicking the file gave a warning that the file was corrupt.

Apple has extremely talented engineers and this problem has to be overcome. How to overcome it? Apple has recommended to developers to discontinue the use of the resource fork. That is not the only answer, but it is the first step. The resource fork is now a deprecated feature that has now been moved to resource files. Macs now also makes use of file extensions, because so many other operating systems found on the Internet use them too. Mac OS X needs to be compatible to be competitive.

As an examiner, this is extremely important to know. The Mac OS X operating system today will handle files copied to alternate file systems quite cleverly. On HFS+, the resource file is never seen, and in fact, the resources are metadata not easily reached by the user. When a user copies a file from one HFS+ location to another, the file and its associated metadata follow along just fine. The clever design of resource files can best be seen on a FAT32-formatted flash drive. When a user copies a Mac file to the destination FAT32 flash drive, the user will see exactly the file that was expected to be copied in the Finder, with no icon oddities, and no loss of application association. However, the way in which it is handled is through a hidden file.

With an example file named "test.doc" placed on a FAT32 flash drive as in Figure 1.4, we can see a single file that will open in Microsoft Word.

Figure 1.4 Finder View of FAT32

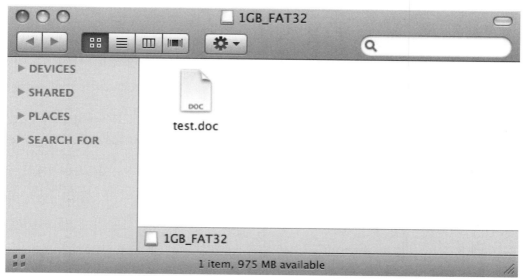

What has occurred on this FAT32 formatted volume "behind the scenes" is best seen through the terminal in Figure 1.5.

Figure 1.5 Terminal View of FAT32

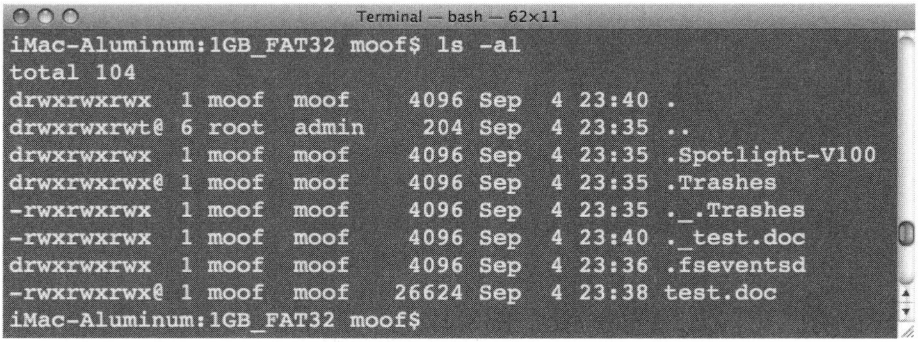

```
iMac-Aluminum:1GB_FAT32 moof$ ls -al
total 104
drwxrwxrwx  1 moof   moof    4096 Sep  4 23:40 .
drwxrwxrwt@ 6 root   admin    204 Sep  4 23:35 ..
drwxrwxrwx  1 moof   moof    4096 Sep  4 23:35 .Spotlight-V100
drwxrwxrwx@ 1 moof   moof    4096 Sep  4 23:35 .Trashes
-rwxrwxrwx  1 moof   moof    4096 Sep  4 23:35 ._.Trashes
-rwxrwxrwx  1 moof   moof    4096 Sep  4 23:40 ._test.doc
drwxrwxrwx  1 moof   moof    4096 Sep  4 23:36 .fseventsd
-rwxrwxrwx@ 1 moof   moof   26624 Sep  4 23:38 test.doc
iMac-Aluminum:1GB_FAT32 moof$
```

You will notice in Figure 1.5 a hidden file in the same directory named "._test.doc." I call this file hidden for two reasons. First, you didn't see it in Figure 1.4. Second, the Finder will not display files whose name begins with the "." (dot) character. It is really that simple to hide a file from the Finder. This "._" file is the resource file. When a file is copied from an HFS+ volume to a file system such as FAT32, the resource fork (metadata) information that would have been lost in the past is now saved into a data file. That data file is smartly associated by the Macintosh operating system to the original file, and combined to show the single file shown in Figure 1.4 thru the Finder. If a user looks at the FAT32 volume from the terminal, as we have in Figure 1.5, or from any other operating system that does not know how to make this association, the two files will be shown. The Macintosh operating system will copy this file from FAT32 correctly when the "test.doc" file is copied back to an HFS+ volume. Mac OS X will also use the metadata contained in the "._" file to properly open the file and utilize the metadata contained therein. Resource forks and resource files can best be equated to alternate data streams in the NTFS world.

Another concept to understand about Macintosh files is the "bundle" and "package." This is a very important concept for an examiner to understand, because you will see very different results depending on the method you are using to look at a "bundle" or "package." Take a look at Figure 1.6 and notice the extensions on each of the Application files listed.

Figure 1.6 Finder View of Applications with Extensions

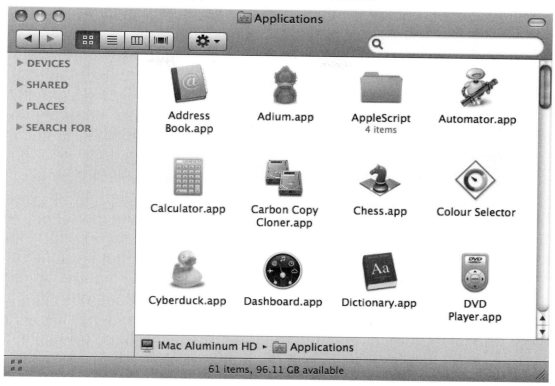

Macintosh application files (or .app files) are actually not a single file at all. They are a folder that is displayed via the Finder as single custom icon, and appropriately launched. If you control-click on an application file you will notice the choice to "Show Package Contents," as in Figure 1.7.

Figure 1.7 Show Package Contents

This will actually open the folder rather than launch the application. The contents have a small chance of being evidentiary in value, but the user data associated with an application is typically in the Home directory. Any folder can be made into an application by simply adding the ".app" extension to the name. However, when you double-click a self-made application, the Finder will likely give an error message, because the application is not a valid application package. Since an application is really just a specialized folder, problems occur if it is copied to a file system and opened within another operating system. Viewing MyApplication.app in a Windows environment will show a folder with the name of MyApplication.app. Further, the folder will open in Windows and the package contents will be seen, much like the "Show Package Contents" command. Be keenly aware of this when you use Windows based tools to examine Macintosh data.

Some applications actually use this package concept to create the data file. iWork has two applications, Keynote and Pages. They each save files in a package format, not a single flat file. Looking at MyDocument.pages on a FAT32 volume through Microsoft Windows will again result in a folder with the name MyDocument.pages, and the folder will open when double-clicked. Be aware of this operation, and expect it when sharing files between operating systems.

Finally, on the Macintosh itself, because "bundles" and "packages" are folders, if you are in the terminal, you will notice that each of these are listed as directories. An application will show as a directory with the "executable" bit set.

Remember, if you are examining a Mac OS-based system with a Windows tool, you will see package files differently than the intended view and functionality. Certain portions of a forensic examination of a Mac OS-based system will require a Macintosh. Plan accordingly.

Macintosh Technologies

Mac OS X has some very robust technologies behind the GUI. The operating system is UNIX-derived, which gives us the power and support of a huge online community. Mac OS X has both a GUI and command line available. Within the OS, Applescript and shell scripting can be done, allowing for both the automation of processes and tasks. In this section, we will attempt to familiarize you with some of the technologies that will affect you as an examiner at the initial approach of a running Macintosh, as well as when examining an imaged system. Here is where it must be said; it would be impossible to note all of the robust technologies that Apple has built into Mac OS X 10.5 or any of its previous siblings. As an examiner, you will be required to learn the technologies that affect your case with some of the many excellent resources available. With that said, here is your introduction to the Macintosh from an examiner's point of view.

The Desktop

Once a Macintosh computer has successfully booted and a user has authenticated, the Finder is presented as the first means of navigation to the data stored on the computer. The interface itself presents to us, as an examiner, many clues to what is happening currently on Mac. The first aspect of the Finder we will look at is the Finder menu bar. It is always present across the top of the screen (or across the top of the main monitor if multiple screens are connected). Aside from the standard menu choices, there are icons that can be presented that will indicate that potential applications or services are enabled or in use. Figure 1.8 shows a Finder menu bar.

Figure 1.8 Finder Menu Bar

The icons represent items that, if we ignore at First Response, could miss huge amounts of data pertinent to the case. Let's go from left to right and look into what each icon is telling us.

Virtual Private Network Virtual Private Network (VPN) is a secure network connection technology. The icon is showing us that the VPN connection is currently inactive. If the connection were active, a timer would be counting like a stopwatch showing connection time.

Time Machine We will talk about Time Machine in detail in Chapter 6. If a Time Machine backup is actually occurring, the clock will appear to be moving "backwards" inside of the arrow-circle as well as the arrow-circle moving counter clockwise.

iChat It represents iChat and shows that the user is currently not logged into his or her account.

Sync Services The fourth icon is the circular, chasing arrows. This represents the Sync service. Here, many items can be synced including MobileMe (formerly .Mac), iPhone, iPod, Cell Phones, and so forth. When a "sync" is occurring, these arrows will be spinning clockwise.

Spaces The fifth icon is Spaces. It appears as a square with a grid and a large number. The number is very important! It shows which "Space" you are working in. A Space is a virtual screen. Spaces allows for 16 virtual screens to occur. You might be looking at the screen that has nothing incriminating. Consider switching to other Spaces to find what else is occurring before turning off the suspect Macintosh.

Bluetooth The Bluetooth icon is currently dimmed, which tells us that the service is disabled. If the icon were a deep black, the service would be enabled. That would mean we should be looking for other devices that might be pertinent to the case at hand that are Bluetooth-enabled. Keep in mind that two popular Apple devices that use Bluetooth are the Apple wireless keyboard and the Apple Mighty Mouse.

Wireless This icon shows us two important pieces of information right away. First, wireless Ethernet communications is enabled on this Macintosh. Second, signal strength is excellent. As the signal gets weaker, the bars get dimmer beginning with the largest bar on the top. We need to be looking to wireless devices pertinent to our case when this is enabled. A popular Apple device that holds digital data is the Time Capsule. It is a wireless 802.11n router and a 500 GB or 1TB wireless hard disk.

Volume This icon simply represents how loud the volume is on this Macintosh. Not necessarily of forensic value, but interesting to note if you are about view a Quicktime video for content and the volume is set to maximum.

Wed 9:06 PM **Clock** Seemingly self explanatory, there are some interesting notes to make here. The clock can obtain its setting by the user, or by a Network Time Server. While I won't go into the difference here, your examination should include noting the date and time, as well as how the Macintosh obtains its time settings.

User This icon is very informative. First of all, it indicates that a feature called "Fast User Switching" is enabled. This means that clicking on this icon will reveal a drop-down menu of the currently logged-in users (shown with a check mark) and allow for a login to other accounts without having to logout of the current user. This is something I recommend you note when you approach a running Macintosh. You should note which account is currently active, and also note which other accounts are currently "logged in."

Spotlight Lastly is the icon for one of the most powerful features built into the operating system. Spotlight is the indexing system that allows for lightning fast access to information contained on this system. By clicking on the magnifying glass icon, a simple dialog box allows text to be typed with live results to show matching the typing. The user can customize spotlight in many different ways to include and exclude areas for indexing. We are going to make great use of this feature throughout this book.

Back to My Mac

Back to My Mac is a great service offered as a part of Mac OS X 10.5 and MobileMe (formerly . Mac). With Back to My Mac enabled and a working Internet connection, a user can reconnect to other Macs the have been registered with the same MobileMe account with a simple click in the Finder. Looking at Figure 1.9, we can see the Back To My Mac options that are available.

Notes from the Underground...

Back to My Mac

A woman in New York had her Mac book stolen and used the Back to My Mac feature to connect to the stolen computer. Using the built in iSight camera, she was able to take a picture of the thieves and have them arrested. It is reasons like these why users love and cannot part with their Macs.

Figure 1.9 Back to My Mac

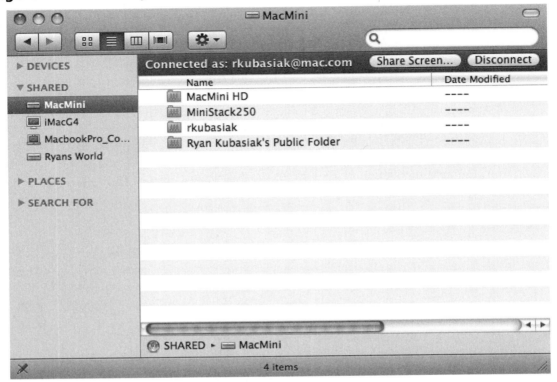

In the Finder, the left pane lists "Shared" resources, including Back To My Mac-registered Macintoshes. In Figure 1.9, MacMini has been clicked on to reveal a connection made as user "rkubasiak@mac.com" as well as the resources available on this computer. You will also notice a button labeled "Share Screen." Here, a simple click will establish a VNC connection to the MacMini and the screen will be seen on our local Macintosh. MobileMe will keep track of all of the connection location information without the end user having to remember their home Internet Protocol (IP) address, their router configurations, and so forth.

Guest Account

The Guest account in Leopard has huge implications for us as examiners. Take a look at Figure 1.10.

Figure 1.10 Guest Account

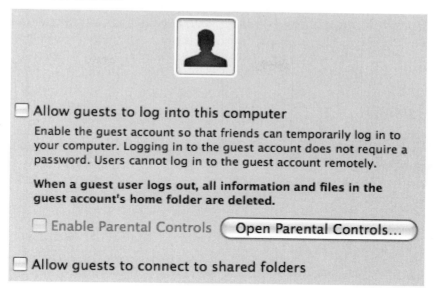

Notice anything that stands out? It's in bold face! Every time the guest user is finished and logs out, all of their files are deleted and the Guest account is clean again. No history for us to look at. The good news is that the delete is not a secure delete. The bad news is it is still a time consuming task to rebuild a deleted account. Keep this in mind when performing forensics, if it seems you are finding all information in unallocated space.

Time Machine

Time Machine is Apple's new way of having everyone back up their files without realizing they are backing up their files. They did a great job of accomplishing this goal. When a user connects a secondary drive (a drive that is not the startup volume), they are presented with a simple question: Would you like to make this a Time Machine drive? When a user turns on Time Machine at this point, they never have to interact with Time Machine again, unless they need to retrieve a lost file or folder. For us as examiners, this is huge. The first run of Time Machine is a complete unencrypted system backup. Every subsequent run backs up the files that have changed, but is done in a clever way which makes it seem that a complete back up was done every day. The Leopard Install DVD has an install option allowing for an install from a Time Machine Backup. If the only item you are able to find is a Time Machine hard drive, you still have found a gold mine of information, because you can rebuild a Macintosh from it.

FileVault

FileVault automatically encrypts and decrypts the contents of a user's home directory on the fly. FileVault is off by default after initial setup or installation, but can be easily enabled. FileVault is not a full disk encryption. It can be enabled for one user, and not another. It uses AES 128-bit encryption as its methodology for security. We will talk about FileVault in more detail in Chapter 5.

UNIX and the FreeBSD System

Mac OS X, all versions, utilizes the UNIX subsystem. This means, that for the first time, the Mac OS is not only a GUI-based system, but also is command-line driven. This brings immense power and flexibility, along with the time-tested stability of UNIX to the operating system. When researching How-To's on the Mac OS X system, you can usually include generic UNIX information, as well as Linux equivalents. Many times, a Linux source code will be able to compile on the Macintosh with little changes.

BootCamp, Microsoft Windows on a Mac?

Yes, if the Macintosh is an Intel-based system running Leopard. "Boot Camp" may be configured and Microsoft Windows XP SP2 or Vista may be installed. In addition, on both PowerPC- and Intel-based Macintoshes, emulation and virtualization software can be run allowing for other operating systems to run. Microsoft VirtualPC (formerly Connectix) is for the PowerPC-based systems. Newer software for the Intel Macintoshes, such as SWSoft's Parallels Desktop or VMWare Fusion, can run multiple, concurrent virtualized operating systems. These technologies will be discussed further in Appendix A.

Target Disk Mode

Target Disk Mode is a technology that allows a Macintosh computer to act as an external, firewire disk. The computer will not access the file system or other data in this state until user interaction causes this. It's an extremely useful tool.

NOTE

Apple tells us: FireWire Target Disk Mode works on internal ATA drives only. Target Disk Mode only connects to the master ATA drive on the Ultra ATA bus. It will not connect to Slave ATA, ATAPI, or SCSI drives.

This means we cannot access multiple installed drives with this method. If you know there are two or more drives in the target computer, consider the Live CD method.

In addition, the following models support the use of Target Disk Mode:

- iMac (Slot Loading) with Firmware version 2.4 or later
- iMac (Summer 2000) and all models introduced after July 2000
- eMac (all models)
- Mac mini (all models)
- Power Mac G4 (AGP Graphics) with ATA drive
- Power Mac G4 Cube
- Power Mac G4 (Gigabit Ethernet) and all models introduced after July 2000
- Power Mac G5 (all models)
- iBook (FireWire) and all models introduced after September 2000
- MacBook (all models)
- PowerBook G3 (FireWire)
- PowerBook G4 (all models)
- MacBook Pro (all models)

Disk Structure

Disk structure on the Macintosh is a very important concept to understand as an examiner. First, we will see from graphical utilities such as Disk Utility, that we can find possible operating system installations by the type of file system that has been used. Second, we can recognize where a hard drive may have been used as a startup device for certain Macintosh hardware. By looking at the physical disk, we gain important evidentiary identifying characteristics that will maintain links between the hard drive and the Macintosh throughout custody.

Apple Partition Map

Macintosh computers will likely use one of two partitioning schemes. From the factory, PowerPC-based Macintoshes come with the Apple Partition Map. An Intel-based Macintosh, however, will utilize the new GUID partition table scheme. GUID stands for "Globally Unique Identifier." If we had to say that Macs use the "Globally Unique Identifier Partition Table Scheme" every time we talked to each other, we would probably stop talking to each other! In fact, the entire scheme has been shortened to GPT for GUID Partition Table. Do not confuse this with the file system of HFS or HFS+. The partitioning scheme is the basic definition of how a hard drive or other media is laid out for a file system to be applied. Figure 1.11 shows the disk structure of a typical PowerPC-based Macintosh.

Figure 1.11 Disk Utility View of Apple Partition Map

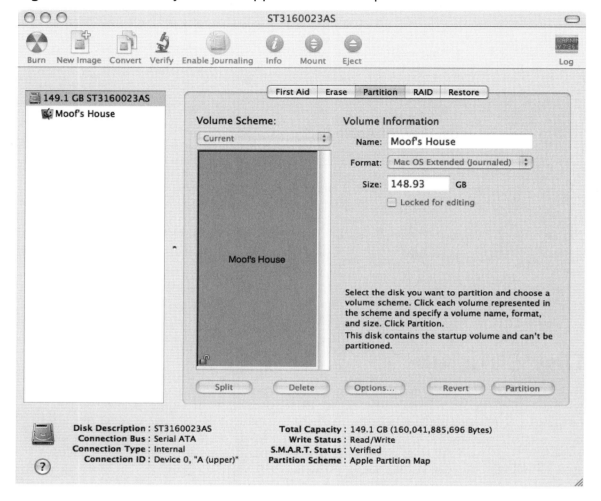

Figure 1.11 is a view from the Apple utility Disk Utility. It shows a 149.1 GB hard drive with model number ST3160023AS with a user given name of "Moof's House." The Volume Scheme shows the drive having only one partition, and the format used is Mac OS Extended (Journaled). Note at the bottom that Apple Partition Map is the partition scheme used.

The left windowpane shows the physical storage devices. Physical storage could also include a DMG that has been mounted. On this computer, only one hard drive is connected. Looking at the lower portion of the window, the drive is a Serial ATA or SATA drive. The Volume Scheme section gives information on the number and types of partitions available. The current partition map shows one large partition across the entire available drive. It has been named "Moof's House" and is formatted using HFS+ with journaling enabled.

Now, let's look at the same disk through the Terminal window using "hdiutil" as shown in Figure 1.12.

Figure 1.12 Terminal View of Apple Partition Map

```
○ ○ ○                          Terminal — bash — 80x24
Moofs-House:~ moof$ hdiutil partition /dev/disk0
scheme:      Apple
block size: 512
 _  ## Type_____ Name_____  Start___  Size____
 +     DDM                   Driver Descriptor Map         0          1
    1 Apple_partition_map    Apple                         1         63
 +     Apple_Free                                         64     262144
    3 Apple_HFS              Untitled                 262208  312319590
 +     Apple_Free                                    312581798        10

 + synthesized
Moofs-House:~ moof$ □
```

Figure 1.12 is a view from Terminal. The command used to give this information was "hdiutil partition /dev/disk0." Notice the extra information we are now seeing as compared to the output of Disk Utility. Sector 0 is the boot sector with a size of 1 sector. Sectors 1 thru 64 are the Apple Partition Map defining the layout of the disk. Apple Free is a "padding" defined as being available for future use. The data section for a forensic analysis finally shows up at the Apple HFS partition starting at sector 262208 and having a length of 3,122,319,590 sectors. There is one more Apple Free partition with a length of 10 sectors, again used as padding.

The Apple Free area is not normally where data will be found. The casual user does not easily access it. However, nothing prevents a savvy user from hiding information there with the right tools. Also, information could be left over in these areas from a previous partition scheme.

GUID Partition Table

Next, let's look at an Intel-based Macintosh. Figure 1.13 shows the Disk Utility information window.

Figure 1.13 Disk Utility View of GUID Partition Table

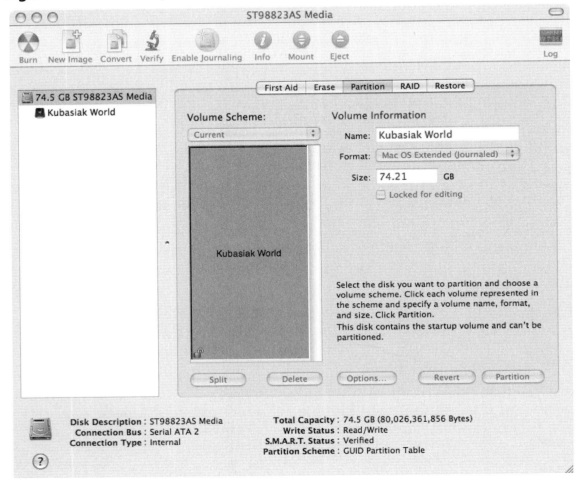

Figure 1.13 is a view from the Apple utility Disk Utility. It shows a 74.5 GB hard drive with model number ST98823AS with a user given name of "Kubasiak World." The Volume Scheme shows the drive having only one partition, and the format used is Mac OS Extended (Journaled). Note at the bottom that GUID Partition Table is the partition scheme used.

The left windowpane shows us physical storage devices. On this computer, only one hard drive is connected. Looking at the lower portion of the window, the drive is a Serial ATA 2 or SATA2 drive. The Volume Scheme section gives information on the number and types of partitions available. The current partition map shows one large partition across the entire available drive. It has been named "Kubasiak World" and has been formatted using HFS+ with journaling enabled.

Now, let's look at the same disk through the Terminal window using "hdiutil" in Figure 1.14.

Figure 1.14 Terminal View of GUID Partition Table

```
  ⊖ ⊖ ⊖                    Terminal — bash — 80x24
Mutara-Nebula:/dev kubasiak$ hdiutil partition /dev/disk0
scheme:      GUID
block size: 512
 _ ## Type_____ Name_____ Start___ Size____
   +   MBR                 Protective Master Boo      0        1
   +   Primary GPT Header  GPT Header                 1        1
   +   Primary GPT Table   GPT Partition Data         2       32
   +   Apple_Free                                    34        6
   1 C12A7328-F81F-11D2-BA EFI System Partition      40   409600
   2 Apple_HFS             Apple_HFS_Untitled_1  409640 155629664
   +   Apple_Free                              156039304   262151
   +   Backup GPT Table    GPT Partition Data  156301455       32
   +   Backup GPT Header   GPT Header          156301487        1

 + synthesized
Mutara-Nebula:/dev kubasiak$ ▌
```

Figure 1.14 is a view from Terminal. The command used to give this information was "hdiutil partition /dev/disk0." Notice the extra information we are now seeing as compared to the output of Disk Utility. Sector 0 is the boot sector with a size of 1 sector. Sector 1 is the Primary GUID Partition Table Header and sectors 2 through 34 contain GUID Partition Table data defining the layout. Notice that these two partitions are replicated at the end of the drive in reverse order. We will recognize the Apple Free partition and the function is similar in nature. The data we are interested in for an exam lies within the Apple HFS partition starting at sector 409,640.

TIP

For a more in-depth look at this topic, read "Technical Note 2166 - Secrets of the GPT" on the Apple Developer Web site.

Summary

This chapter is a warm-up of forensics on a Macintosh. Concepts of analysis have not changed just because we are presented with a new operating system and new hardware. What will change is the technology that needs to be understood. Manufacturers of personal computers today want the customer to be able to access the Internet and get to their e-mail, so we will notice that the Mac OS, Windows, Linux, UNIX, and so forth will have Web browsers and e-mail clients that can do exactly that. It is when the personal computer goes beyond the simple that we need to have a firm grasp on the technology to understand the forensic tracks that get left behind.

Solutions Fast Track

First Responders and Specialized Examiners

☑ Live Examination is a volatile method of gathering information from a running Macintosh computer. Data will be altered in the process, yet sometimes this method is the best choice when encryption or shutdown is not possible.

☑ Single User Mode is a built-in, forensically sound way of looking at the Macintosh when Mac OS X is installed. It is command-line driven, making it cumbersome for some until a comfort level is developed.

☑ Boot CD/DVD offers a safety net when looking at a Macintosh computer. It offers a known, good environment every time you boot the computer from your media.

☑ Target Disk Mode is a technology that allows you to have the Macintosh become an external firewire hard drive.

Macintosh History

☑ Hardware for Macintosh computers has become quite similar to the rest of the personal computer world. There are certainly separating differences that make a Mac a Mac, but a Mac can now run Windows or Linux natively, because of the hardware similarities.

☑ File system possibilities of the Macintosh include the native HFS+, but can also include the many other file systems that come with the multiple operating system a Macintosh can now run. Always be cognizant of the possible NTFS, FAT32, or other file systems on the Mac you are examining.

☑ Operating system possibilities are similar to the above point. Aside from a native install, virtual machines might also be installed with the use of software such as VMWare and Parallels. Always look for the possible Mac with multiple operating systems installed and configured.

☑ Data files are something that is quite different on a Mac if looked at from a foreign operating system. Packages and bundles can confuse an examiner into thinking that odd folders are scattered across the Mac. These folders turn out to be functioning applications to the trained examiner.

Macintosh Aspects

☑ Apple is a unique company that produces unique hardware. Hardware that might look like a simple computer screen could be a full computer. Always look for more when you see an Apple logo!

☑ File systems are an important aspect of the Macintosh as with any other personal computer. Today, HFS+ is the most popular file system installed on a Macintosh.

☑ Mac OS X and System 9 are the two operating systems that are relevant in the Macintosh world today. System 9 is also called "Classic," and has gone to unsupported status from Apple. Mac OS X is current and will be found in versions 10.5 (Leopard) and 10.4 (Tiger).

Macintosh Technologies

☑ The Finder is the GUI to the Macintosh computer. From here, the user is able to perform actions upon the system in a simple way with double-clicks, right-clicks, and so forth.

☑ The Terminal is the command-line utility to the Macintosh computer. It is located in the Utilities folder and is easily accessed from the Finder under the "Go" menu.

☑ The Finder menu bar is a key point to note as a First Responder for clues to the services and applications that the current user might have active upon your approach. Always look for the icons that are across the Menu bar and note when they are in the Active or dimmed mode.

☑ Many technologies are offered with Mac OS X that simply cannot be found elsewhere. Back To My Mac, Time Machine, FileVault, and the BootCamp technology are a few notable, Apple-only features.

☑ Target Disk Mode is an Apple-only technology that can turn a Macintosh desktop or laptop into a firewire hard drive. This allows an examiner to connect the Macintosh to a write-blocked acquisition computer and make an image of the computer safely without ever having to remove a single screw.

Disk Structure

☑ Disk structure on a Macintosh will be one of two supported structures depending on the hardware type. Disk structure on a hard drive can be a key identifying sign to the hardware that it supported.

☑ Intel Macintoshes require the GUID Partition Table scheme in order to boot successfully from a hard drive. Any other partitioning scheme will cause a boot failure.

☑ PowerPC Macintoshes require the Apple Partition Map scheme in order to boot successfully from a hard drive. Any other partitioning scheme will cause a boot failure.

☑ Intel and PowerPC Macintoshes each have the ability to read and write to both GUID Partition Table and Apple Partition Map, which allows for external drives to be easily shared between computers.

Frequently Asked Questions

Q: What is the best tool to use as a First Responder?

A: Every tool you can get your hands on! Although this answer sounds humorous, there is no single tool to do every job. As we have found in this chapter, there are four examination techniques (Live, single user mode, boot CD/DVD, and Target Disk Mode) available. Depending on which technique you choose, there are multiple tools to use. Industry regarded tools such as BlackBag Technologies, ASR Data SMART, Access Data Forensic Toolkit, and Guidance Software Encase are excellent choices, but not your only choices. There are built-in technologies with Leopard (Mac OS X 10.5) that will get you well on your way to a First Responder answer without purchasing anything more than a Macintosh.

Q: Is Target Disk Mode safe?

A: It is as safe as any other firewire hard disk is with the handling policies your business or agency has. There is no "write-protect" on the Target Disk mode, so you will need to apply some form of data protection. Later in this book we will show you a built-in technology on the Mac that is free to give you the write protection you desire.

Q: Is Single User Mode safe?

A: It is initially. You should always remember that Single User Mode is the "root" user, and the potential to bad things is possible if you tell the system to do it. Initially, the system is in a read-only state and is not altering any data.

Q: How do I know more than one operating system is installed?

A: First, look for more than one partition on the hard drive with Disk Utility. For instance, if you see a partition that is a format of NTFS or FAT32, you need to look further. In the case of virtual machines, you should be looking for the application installed as well as the virtual disk file somewhere on the hard drive. We will talk about this in detail later in the book.

Q: Do files from a Macintosh look the same on a Windows-based computer?

A: This question has two answers. Files look quite similar to the end user. Files look quite different to the forensic examiner. Recall the "bundle" and "package" files on the Mac. On Windows, you see the folder instead, because Windows simply does not know what this specialized folder is. This holds true inside of examination software on Windows such as Forensic Toolkit and Encase.

Q: Can Intel Macs use Apple Partition Map? Can PowerPC Macs use GUID Partition Table?

A: Yes and no. Yes, they each recognize and can use the other partitioning scheme for data storage. The requirement is that Intel Macs must use GUID Partition Table on the boot drive and PowerPC Macs must use Apple Partition Map on the boot drive. In other words, Intel Macs will not boot from a drive that has Mac OS X 10.5 installed, but the partition scheme is Apple Partition Map. The same holds true for PowerPC Macs where the partition scheme is GUID Partition Table.

Chapter 2

Getting a Handle on Mac Hardware

Solutions in this chapter:

- MacBooks and Desktop Computers
- iPods
- iPhones
- Other Hardware

☑ Summary

☑ Solutions Fast Track

☑ Frequently Asked Questions

Introduction

The Apple Macintosh was not always a popular platform for criminal activity or for computer forensics. Prior to Apple using an Intel processor that is based on the same instruction set used by Microsoft Windows, many programmers thought the highly proprietary way in which the Macintosh communicated with Apple hardware was too difficult to be bothered with. This, combined with the overwhelming popularity of Windows systems, also made it a matter of numbers. There were simply more Windows systems on the market, and the price dropped on PC's to a reasonable cost, which allowed forensic labs to buy them easily.

But today, a growing number of crime labs are using Intel processor-based Macs as workstations. Of course, criminals are starting to use them as well, and for computer forensic investigators, the race to stay technologically ahead of the bad guys is heating up every day.

Most modern Macs can run today's other popular operating systems such as Windows, and the many versions of Linux, enabling you to access any tool or information you choose to use. Most software today is Mac-compatible as well. Because the Macintosh is now such a popular platform, you'll increasingly be faced with the task of examining one. Therefore, as a computer forensic investigator, you'll need to know how to determine the following:

- The Mac model you are investigating
- What operating system it is running
- The size of the hard disk
- Whether there is more than one drive
- How to get inside the case

To determine the specific model of the machine you're examining, you can choose **About this Mac** from the Apple menu, or look at the model number on the side or bottom of the machine. You can also use the figures in this chapter as a reference. In addition, most systems will allow you to access the hard drive without removing it, by using the FireWire target mode. FireWire Target mode is accessed by holding the T key while powering up a Mac that has a FireWire port built in to it. Connecting a FireWire cable from the system in Target mode to another computer with a FireWire port should allow you to access the primary internal hard drive as if it is a normal external drive.

However, if there is no FireWire port on the Macintosh system, or if FireWire Target mode is disabled in some other way you'll have to remove the hard drive, so, as a computer forensic investigator you'll need to know how to do that without damaging the system. It will also be helpful for you to be able to identify the parts of a Mac in case you are ever asked to testify in a court of law.

Of course, in addition to the Mac, criminals also can store all types of data on their iPhones and iPods, as well as on such Mac hardware as the Apple TV and Time Capsule—the latter two which will require even more complex data recovery techniques.

WARNING

If you are reading this book for general information on your own Macintosh, please note that opening the case will usually void your warranty. Take a moment to consider this before you start.

Most forensic examiners are opening seized computers and are not worried about warranties, just evidence.

Historically, within hours of the official release of a new Macintosh, articles and videos on how to disassemble it have appeared on the Internet. Searching on the model name and the word *disassemble* will return numerous Web sites with detailed, step-by-step instructions on how to take apart that particular device. Within just a few hours after the first iPhone was introduced, several YouTube videos appeared which showed how to take the phone apart and how to override its dependence on AT&T; one video even showed how long the phone would last in a blender.

This disassembly is not limited to hardware. Any vulnerability in security or software is reported in short order as well. In some cases, the information is available before the product is even released. Just prior to Apple's release of its Intel-based Macs a modified version of the prerelease OS X was leaked onto the Internet, which allowed non-Macintosh Intel-based computers to boot the new operating system. This was a clear breach of the agreement that all Apple developers sign, and Apple attorneys quickly went after the source.

Are You Owned?

Do You Know Where Your System Disks Are?

You can use any system boot disk for any version of OS X to gain access or control of a system.

If you boot to the optical drive with the Install disk in the drive, wait until the menus at the top of the screen appear and you will find the drive and password change utilities listed. It is possible to change the password of any account on the system in moments using this method.

Leaving your original system disks next to your computer in an unsecured location is like setting the keys to your car on the hood while you go shopping. So, make sure that you put them in a safe place when they are not actually being used.

In this chapter, we will introduce you to the different versions of desktop and laptop/notebook computers that run Macintosh OS X. Later in the chapter we will look at devices that connect to these systems. This will provide you with a broad overview of the hardware comprising the world of the Macintosh.

NOTE

If you are investigating a particular Mac and you do not see a reference to it in this chapter, check out the Mactracker program included on the DVD that accompanies this book. Mactracker provides a comprehensive list of Apple hardware, complete with pictures and technical information on each system. If you think you are dealing with a new Mac that isn't included on the DVD, you can update the Mactracker database by selecting **Check For Updates** from the MacTracker drop down menu when it is running, then see if the newer Mac or device has been added. You have to be connected to the Internet to update.

We'll start with the most current systems as of this writing and work our way backward to the earliest OS X-compatible Macs.

MacBooks and Desktop Computers

Laptop and notebook Macintosh computers are known as MacBooks if they are equipped with Intel processors and PowerBooks if they are equipped with any of the previous processors, such as the G5 or G4. The MacBook is intended for the entry-level, home, or student market, depending on the configuration. MacBooks feature 13-inch screens and are available in white or black cases (see Figure 2.1).

Figure 2.1 The MacBook, in White and in Black

Courtesy of Apple

MacBooks began shipping in May 2006 and have been selling well ever since. These systems use magnetic latch technology in both the MagSafe power connector and the closure latch to keep the case closed. You can attach the MagSafe connector to the MacBook with either side up, and it will auto-adjust the polarity of the contacts. After years of owners complaining of broken case latches and broken power adapter plugs Apple showed that they listened and the MagSafe connector is the one thing that all veteran Mac owners rejoice about. The magnetic nature of the power connector holds in place until sufficient strain is placed on the power cable and then it releases with no harm done. Likewise, the magnetic case latch means that opening and closing the MacBook is much easier.

MacBooks are true Intel-based systems and will run Apple's Boot Camp, which allows dual or multiple operating system choices at power-up. You can read more about how to install multiple operating systems in Appendix A.

These computers also have a sudden motion sensor built in. While Apple hasn't made commercials about how a sudden shock will send the internal drives into emergency stop and protect mode, it is a safety feature built in to the MacBook. There are some Dashboard Widgets and programs on the Apple site which use the motion sensor in unique ways.

Standard configuration includes Slot Load DVD/CD (right side), Ethernet 10/100/1000, two USB ports, one FireWire port, Video Out, iSight camera, Airport Extreme, and Bluetooth.

Tools & Traps...

Some Disassembly Required?

You may find yourself with a Mac that you need to take apart in order to get to the disk drive or some other part residing inside the case. After you have worked on a few Macs, you will find that most fall into one of two categories: easy to open, or very hard to open. Replacing some things, such as RAM and batteries, are usually fairly easy, but models such as the Mac Mini, covered later in this chapter, can present unique challenges when you want to remove the drive.

There are many good sites on the Internet providing everything from simple modification guides to full-blown videos on how to take systems apart. Also, don't forget to check the Apple Support Site, www.support.apple.com, for the official instructions.
Good hardware sites include:

- www.ifixit.com
- www.macmegasite.com
- www.lowendmac.com
- www.macsales.com

Continued

Here are a few tips to follow when you must disassemble a Mac:

- As you set to work, you may require special tools, such as nylon wedges, paint scrapers, and Torx screwdrivers of various lengths, to take some systems apart. So it helps to have these tools handy.

- Also, heed any instructions that tell you to be gentle or patient. Otherwise, you could easily break a crucial piece of the system hardware that could render your investigation moot.

- Another suggestion is to ensure that you've researched the procedure fully before starting to prevent any unwanted surprises.

MacBook Air

The MacBook Air is Apple's latest entry in the notebook computer market. Not since 1992, when Apple released the PowerBook Duo, has the company offered such a slim and ultra-portable system (see Figure 2.2).

Figure 2.2 The Slim and Portable MacBook Air

Courtesy of Apple

One of the easiest ways to tell whether you are holding a MacBook Air is to notice how thin and light it is. Most Airs weigh only about 3 pounds and are about three-quarters of an inch thick. You also will not find a built-in CD/DVD slot on these systems. You must conduct all data transfers with the Air via WiFi or USB.

One potential wrinkle that the Air presents for computer forensic investigators is its optional solid-state drive. This means there is no drive to remove and image, so you will have to image the solid-state Air via USB.

TIP

You can use USB-bootable Linux-based tools, such as BackTrack 3.0, to start the Air, and you can copy the contents of its internal storage to an external storage device using the *dd* command.

Standard configuration includes one USB port, iSight camera, Airport Extreme, and Bluetooth.

MacBook Pro

Users requiring more power, more RAM, or a larger screen will opt for the MacBook Pro. These laptops are slightly easier to recognize due to their size. With a screen size of either 15 or 17 inches, the MacBook Pro doesn't fit well in most computer bags, but the screen size and sheer portable power cause computer envy at meetings or coffee shops.

Figure 2.3 shows the 15-inch and 17-inch versions of the MacBook Pro.

Figure 2.3 The 15-Inch and 17-Inch Versions of the MacBook Pro

Courtesy of Apple

One other quick way to recognize the MacBook Pro is via its CD/DVD slot on the front of the computer.

NOTE

The external video connectors for the MacBook Pro and the smaller MacBook are not the same. The Pro version uses the more standard DVI-style connector and the MacBook uses the MiniDV connector.

Standard configuration includes Slot Load DVD/CD (front), Ethernet 10/100/1000, three USB ports, two FireWire ports, Video Out, iSight camera, Airport Extreme, and Bluetooth.

Mac Mini

The smallest desktop computer Apple has ever made is aptly named the Mini. When it was introduced in 2005 it was an immediate hit, bringing small size and power to the desktop. Apple designed the system for people who wanted to switch from a PC to the Mac for the least amount of money. You could reuse your PC monitor and even your PC USB keyboard with this system. Because of its size, the amount of RAM you can add is limited to 1 or 2 gigabytes in one RAM slot. Figure 2.4 shows the stylishly Spartan Macintosh Mini.

Figure 2.4 The Macintosh Mini

Courtesy of Apple

Standard configuration includes Slot Load DVD/CD (front), Ethernet 10/100/1000, four USB ports, one FireWire port, Video Out, Airport Extreme, and Bluetooth.

iMac

The iMac has gone through many physical changes over the years. The original "Bondi Blue" iMac shipped in 1998 and will technically run OS X, but it will be a frustrating experience. The 2008 model, shown in Figure 2.5, is the state of the art in form and function for a desktop computer.

Most flat panel iMacs have an access door to make it easy to add more RAM. Hard drives are another matter altogether, ranging from mildly annoying to downright frustrating to get to.

Figure 2.5 iMac (2008 Model)

Courtesy of Apple

Standard configuration includes Slot Load DVD/CD (on side), Ethernet 10/100/1000, three USB ports, two FireWire ports, Video Out, iSight camera, Airport Extreme, and Bluetooth.

Mac Pro and PowerMac

It is hard to find a computer with more processor power than the eight core model of the Mac Pro. It is possible to configure this system with any number of processors and cores up to eight dual core Intel processors running at over 3 GHz.

The good news about this model is that it is easy to get to the internal parts. One lever on the back releases the side panel and everything is right there for you. Having said that, the power supply is one of the few items in which removal may require disassembly of the case.

Figure 2.6 shows a typical MacPro/PowerMac.

Figure 2.6 Typical Mac Pro/PowerMac

Courtesy of Apple

WARNING

If you need to work on a running PowerMac and must plug in a USB device to the front connector panel, make sure you use grounding straps! It is a known issue that any static may reboot or power down the system if an arc occurs at the front panel.

Standard configuration includes Tray Load DVD/CD (front), two Ethernet 10/100/1000, five USB ports, four FireWire ports, two Video Outs, Airport Extreme (optional), and Bluetooth.

iPods

The iPod isn't so much a device as it is a lifestyle. All iPods, with the exception of the Shuffle, share a common concept. Internally they consist of a hard disk drive, logic board, and screen. You can access the drive through the iPod's FireWire or USB connector, and most current operating systems will mount the drive depending on the way it was formatted.

iTunes is intended to be the primary interface for keeping track of files on the various iPod devices, but several open source programs like Floola and YamiPod allow many of the same functions that iTunes offers.

iPod Classic

For the iPod purist, the Classic is the "real" iPod. For these folks, a larger screen and larger hard drive provide the best iPod experience. Inevitably, when two of these folks get together, the question of "How many songs do you have on yours?" comes up. Anyone with fewer than 2000 songs is considered a novice.

You can store any type of file on most iPods, and view any graphics file, including movie files. You can access the iPod's internal drive as you would any USB storage device, and it will mount as a volume in most operating systems seamlessly. If you are investigating an iPod and it does not mount as a volume, you should be wary that encryption and other file obfuscation techniques may have been used on the device.

Notes from the Underground…

Sure You Can, but Why Would You?

Linux users are an interesting bunch. They never seem to get tired of looking for new places to run their favorite operating system. So, it is no surprise that there are Linux distributions for the iPod. For example, there is an iPodLinux distribution.

The Linux OS replaces all the functions of your iPod with open source versions. Granted, this will get you lots of Geek Points from your friends, but other than that, we aren't sure of the rationale for using a Linux OS on an iPod with so few controls.

Figure 2.7 shows a Sixth-generation iPod Classic. Some older–generation iPods had additional buttons and a different scroll wheel.

Figure 2.7 Sixth-Generation iPod Classic

Courtesy of Apple

The earliest iPods were not Windows-compatible, although users could reformat them for use with Microsoft products. If you use any current version of iTunes to reinstall or repair an iPod, you will overwrite any special data residing in custom partitions, and you may lose evidence.

iPod Nano

Answering the consumer demand of smaller electronics, the iPod Nano is twenty-percent smaller than the classic iPod. All the standard iPod concepts and concerns apply to the Nano, which, because of its size, can be even harder to open than the full-size iPod.

Figure 2.8 shows one of the Third-generation versions of the iPod Nano.

Figure 2.8 Third-Generation Version of the iPod Nano

Courtesy of Apple

In late 2008, Apple released the fourth-generation of the iPod Nano, which comes in eight color choices (shown in Figure 2.9). The accelerometer that is built into the MacBooks and the iPhone is new in the Nano as well. Turning it on its side will rotate the display screen orientation. Over the years Apple has had a problem with Nano's identity crisis. It started out slim and tall, went to short and fat, and now it's back to slim and tall.

Figure 2.9 Fourth-Generation iPod Nano

Courtesy of Apple

iPod Shuffle

The iPod Shuffle uses solid-state memory and may require special software to access its internals. The earliest Shuffle was white and rectangular. When you pulled the bottom cap off you could access a normal USB connector. You can read this Shuffle with any program used to image a USB drive.

The second-generation iPod Shuffle, shown in Figure 2.10, features a clip on the back to allow you to attach it to your clothing or backpack easily. A docking base for the clip-on Shuffle allows a USB connection as well. Here again, use any program you like for drive imaging.

Figure 2.10 Second-Generation iPod Shuffle

Courtesy of Apple

iPod Touch

For recognition purposes, there is little difference visually between the iPod Touch and the iPhone. You may have to look at the back of the device to see which it is. Or you can look at the upper-left corner of the screen if the default screen settings haven't been changed. It is possible to use the iPod Touch to make phone calls if you use a Touchmod mic which connects the iPod Touch via WiFi to VoIP providers like Skype. For the full story on the iPod Touch and the iPhone, please see Chapters 13 Through 16 in this book.

Figure 2.11 shows the first-generation iPod Touch. Note that there is no speaker slot at the top of the screen, differentiating it from the iPhone.

Figure 2.11 First-Generation iPod Touch

Courtesy of Apple

iPhones

iPhones come with either 8GB or 16GB of storage. See Chapter 15 for more information on the iPhone.

The first-generation iPhone is a GSM phone which uses a SIM card for programming. All iPhones come configured to work only with the AT&T service provider. Programs like JailBreak can be used to allow the iPhone to communicate on any GSM network.

The second-generation iPhones are now 3G network compatible, while still being GSM quad band devices. There is even a new white 16GB iPhone for those who like to be different. The firmware in the second-generation is even more stringently tied to the AT&T service, which is the one strong negative point in most users' minds.

As noted in other devices, the iPhone has an accelerometer and a proximity sensor built in. The accelerometer will orient the screen tall or wide depending on the way the user is holding the device. The proximity sensor detects when the user is holding the phone to his/her face and disables the touch screen to prevent input errors.

The iPhone and iPod Touch are both multimedia devices which can play music and videos like the classic iPods, since they have iTunes built in. This also means that they can be used like an external storage device for files.

Figure 2.12 shows the Second-generation iPhone. Here you can see the speaker slot above the screen.

Figure 2.12 Second-Generation iPhone

Courtesy of Apple

Other Hardware

Some of the devices we discuss in this section are not capable of running the OS X operating system, but we've included them to give you a complete picture of the Apple hardware lineup. Some will have no direct storage capability, whereas other could contain logs or other setting information that could be of use in an investigation.

AirPort Express and AirPort Extreme

The AirPort devices, at a minimum, allow for wireless networking. The device can act as a Wireless Access Point, using normal WiFi connections or via the Apple proprietary Bonjour method. Bonjour does not require the setup or configuration that WiFi does. In September 2008, Apple released a Microsoft Windows driver for Bonjour.

Bonjour is the open network architecture built into OS X allowing Macintosh computers to find, connect and easily share with each other.

Different AirPort devices allow for different capabilities, but they all allow you to connect to hardwired Ethernet access. Some allow you to connect a USB printer for remote printing, and others allow you to connect your stereo system and play your iTunes library through your sound system. Still others allow you to connect external drives and create network storage.

The AirPort Express, shown in Figure 2.13, allows for remote printing and remote playing of iTunes media.

Figure 2.13 The AirPort Express

Courtesy of Apple

The AirPort Extreme, shown in Figure 2.14, allows for remote network storage as well. Keep in mind that you may want to perform a wireless scan for this device as it is capable of being used for storage.

Figure 2.14 The AirPort Extreme

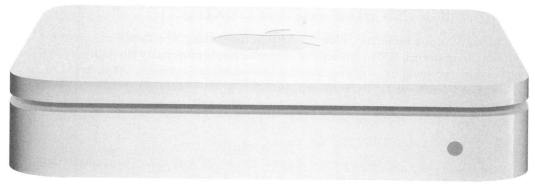

Courtesy of Apple

Apple TV

Many people have a hard time defining the Apple TV in a few words. It is an Intel processor-based system, and it can run OS X amongst other modifications that can be found at www.appletvhacks. net, but what is it for?

The original Apple TV had an 80GB drive inside, and later versions had a 120GB drive. You're meant to connect the system to a network so that you can draw iTunes media from your computer, or use it as a form of external media storage that you can play on your TV using either the composite or the HDMI connectors on the back of the unit. Keep in mind that some individuals may opt to store data on devices such as the Apple TV because they are inclined to believe that these devices are much less likely to be confiscated in a raid. If you come across one of these devices and seizing it is within the scope of your warrant, be sure to get an image of the device and send it to the lab for analysis. Figure 2.15 shows the Apple TV.

Figure 2.15 Apple TV

Courtesy of Apple

Although the Apple TV does feature a USB port, it is meant for service only and not for general use, however, patches from appletvhacks will allow you to use the port for connecting additional external storage. If you want to image the internal drive you should take it out of the case rather than trying to image it through the USB port.

Time Capsule

Don't let the case fool you: Apple's Time Capsule, shown in Figures 2.16 and 2.17, is a full-featured appliance that you should be aware of. This unassuming little box is a wireless router, a three-port Ethernet switch, a network-attached storage device, *and* a remote print server. Apple designed the device to work with the Time Machine system backup feature of Leopard, which we describe in

Chapter 6. Keep in mind that you may want to perform a wireless scan of this device, as it is capable of being used for storage. Also keep in mind that Time Machine backups are unencrypted, so backup information may help you if the original system is utilizing FileVault.

The default configurations included either a 500GB or a 1 TB Hitachi drive, touted as "server grade," since they have a very low failure rate.

Figure 2.16 Front View of Apple's Time Capsule

Courtesy of Apple

Figure 2.17 Rear View of Apple's Time Capsule

Courtesy of Apple

Summary

We have seen that the Macintosh is growing in the forensic community both as an investigative platform and as a target of the investigation. Both the desktop and portable versions are able to run multiple operating systems well, which gives the user a much wider range of available programs and tools.

When gathering evidence from an Apple computer or peripheral you may not have to open the case and remove the disk drive. Most Macintoshes support FireWire target mode, and iPods easily appear as external drives, making data access much easier.

Most other Apple peripheral devices provide some level of access and/or storage on the network which makes them potentially valuable in the evidence collection process.

Solutions Fast Track

MacBooks and Desktop Computers

- ☑ Desktop Macintoshes are known as MacPros or PowerMacs.
- ☑ Laptop Macintoshes are known as MacBooks or PowerBooks.
- ☑ Notebook Macintoshes are known as the MacBook Air or PowerBook Duo.
- ☑ Most Macintosh computers support FireWire target mode, which allows you to connect the computer to your forensic capture machine, such as an external drive for imaging and access.
- ☑ A locked Macintosh running OS X can be accessed using any OS X install disk and the password change utility.

iPods

- ☑ All iPods, except the Shuffle, have internal hard disks.
- ☑ The Shuffle can be read using normal USB drive utilities.
- ☑ The iPod Touch features the same case and logic as the iPhone, but without the cell phone technology.

iPhones

- ☑ First-generation iPhones are quad-band GSM devices (850/900/1800/1900).
- ☑ iPhones use a standard SIM card for programming.
- ☑ White iPhones are 16 GB only as of Generation 2.

Other Hardware

☑ AirPort devices are Wireless Access Points supporting both traditional wireless and Apple's Bonjour protocols.

☑ Some AirPort devices allow remote printing and remote iTunes access.

☑ Time Capsule has an internal hard disk and can act as an Ethernet switch, remote print server, and network attached storage.

☑ Apple's Boot Camp utility allows you to partition the drive for multiple operating systems, and supports boot time menus for selecting OS X, Windows, Linux, or other supported operating systems.

Frequently Asked Questions

Q: Can you boot a Mac from an iPod?

A: Yes and no. It is difficult to boot an Intel Mac to OS X from an iPod. You can boot other operating systems from an iPod easily, however. A Power PC-based Mac will boot Classic Mac OS from an iPod when it is mounted, and set as the boot device in the Control Panel.

Q: Will G5 and G4 Macintosh computers boot from a Windows CD?

A: No. These systems are based on the Power PC chip and they do not support the instruction set for Windows. Several different emulators allow you to run Windows in an OS X window on these systems.

Q: How do I start a Mac in FireWire target mode?

A: Hold down the **T** key while powering up the Mac and you should see the FireWire icon on the screen. You can then connect to the FireWire port and image the internal drive with another system.

Q: How do you force the Mac to boot from a CD/DVD?

A: Hold down the **C** key while powering up to boot from the optical drive.

Q: A CD/DVD is stuck in the drive. How do I get it out?

A: Hold down the **mouse button** while powering up the Mac and the disk should eject. If that doesn't work, look for the small hole in the front of the drive area that allows you to use a paperclip to manually eject the drive *with the system powered down*.

Q: Is it true that the AirPort Express security is easy to break into and allow access to my network?

A: That depends. If you have not changed the default setting on any Wireless Access Point, you are running a large risk of being attacked. On the other hand, if you use the strongest settings available, you are as safe as the technology allows.

Q: Has there ever been a Macintosh clone?

A: Yes! From 1995 to 1997, three companies—Motorola, Power Computing, and UMAX—were granted licenses to build Macintosh clones. Power Computing built the largest number of Mac clones in its assembly plant near Austin, Texas, the building is now owned by Dell.

Chapter 3

Mac Disks and Partitioning

Solutions in this chapter:

- **Disk Utility**
- **First Aid**
- **Erasing a Disk**
- **Partitioning**
- **RAID**
- **Restore**
- **Changing the Startup Disk**

- ☑ **Summary**
- ☑ **Solutions Fast Track**
- ☑ **Frequently Asked Questions**

Introduction

As a computer forensics investigator, it is extremely important to know how to manage disks and partitioning. The Disk Utility tool within the OS X operating system allows users to easily format, delete, and repair disks and partitions. Many people use USB and Firewire mass storage devices to store additional data or backups. The Disk Utility program makes it easy for the average user to partition and format disks. Many of the choices users make in the Mac Disk Utility may have forensic implications, such as the ability for users to zero out data on drives or perform a complete 7 or 35 pass erase. Other choices that can play a role in the investigation include what type of file system the user formats the disk with, such as MS-DOS or Case Sensitive File system.

With added features such as Boot Camp, users may have multiple disks or partitions on a system. The Mac also gives the user the option to set up mirrored, stripped, and concatenated RAID sets. You can use the Mac Disk Utility to determine whether the user has RAID (Redundant Array of Inexpensive Disks) enabled. It is essential that you are able to view the number of disks and partitions in a Mac system, so you can accurately analyze where data is located on the system. Also be aware that if you come across a situation where a Mac is at the Disk Utility screen, there is a chance that the person at the computer could have recently formatted a disk or partition. In summary, it is important to know how to use the Disk Utility so you are able to make informed decisions about what types of disks and partitions exist in the system, so you can use the appropriate tools and procedure to recover data from them.

Disk Utility

The Disk Utility is the primary utility used by the Mac OS X operating systems to conduct many different disk management tasks. The version of OS X that is used will affect the options that are available in the Disk Utility. The Disk Utility can be used to configure many different types of hard drive configurations, mount and unmount disk images, repair disk file permissions, configure RAID on multi hard drive systems, and it's also capable of erasing, formatting, and burning CD's and DVD's.

While conducting an investigation on a MAC system, it's important to be able to determine the disk configuration on the target machine. Depending on how the system is configured, it may have an affect on the best course of action to forensically conduct an investigation of the target machine.

The default location for the Disk Utility is in the Utilities folder under the Applications folder. One way to open the disk utility application is, while in the Finder navigate to **Go | Utilities | Disk Utility**. This will open the Disk Utility application as shown in Figure 3.1. As with any operating system, there are many ways to accomplish the same task. Therefore, you can choose to open the application by whatever way you prefer.

Figure 3.1 Disk Utility

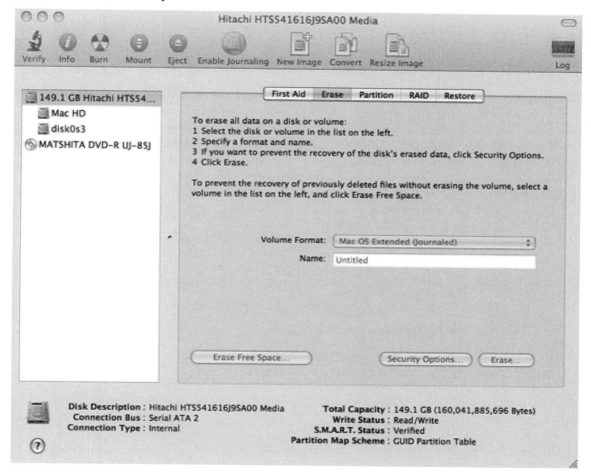

The Disk Utility application is also available on the Mac OS X installation DVD media. The system can be booted to the install DVD by holding down the "c" key on the keyboard when the system is turned on to instruct the system to boot to the CD/DVD drive. This will allow you to view, manage, and attempt to repair a corrupted drive without needing to boot into the operating system installed on the disk. Booting to the installation DVD may be required to complete certain tasks, for example, to repair the boot drive.

Disk Info

The disk info feature within the Disk Utility can be used to retrieve hardware information that is valuable to any investigator. This can give important information that should be recorded in your investigation notes. This feature can be used to retrieve information about all drives connected to the system as well as each individual partition. To view the desired information, click the device or partition displayed in the left pane in the Disk Utility. Then click the Info button in the upper menu bar. Figure 3.2 shows the information for the actual hard drive. Notice the information given, such as media name, connection type, total capacity, disk number, and so forth.

Figure 3.2 Hard Drive (disk0) Information Details

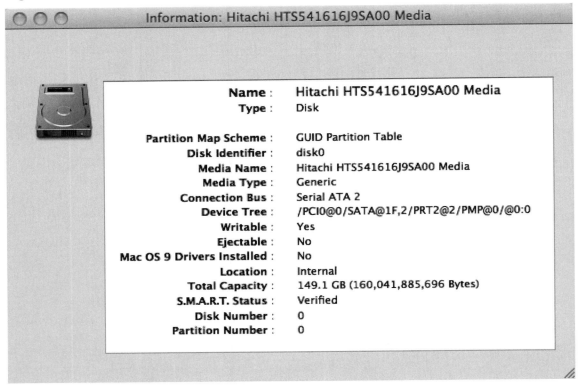

Other important detailed information can be retrieved from selecting an actual partition that is configured on the hard drive. Figure 3.3 is an example of the details displayed for the partition on the primary hard drive. This information will be extremely valuable while conducting an investigation. The information displayed includes the disk identifier, file system type, partition size, used and free space, number of files and folders, partition number, and so forth. Remember the information detailing the number of files and folders is referring to the logical data on the drive that the operating system recognizes. This doesn't mean that other valuable evidence can't be recovered at the physical level. More details about retrieving data at the physical level will be discussed in greater detail in later chapters.

Figure 3.3 Disk Volume (disk0s2) Information Details

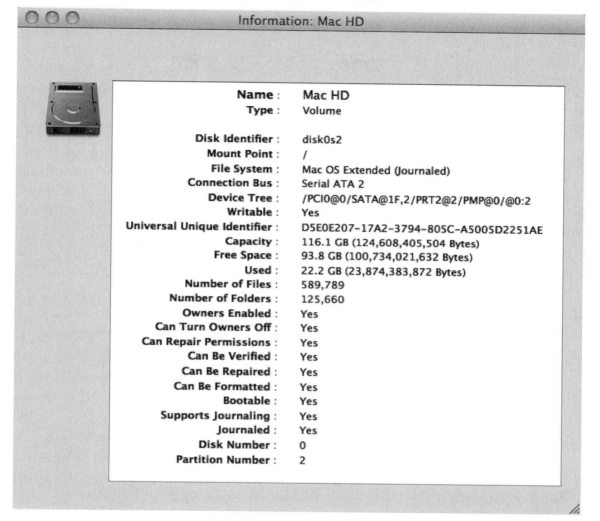

Mounting

OS X is a variant of the BSD operating system named Darwin. In all UNIX, BSD, and Linux distributions, a device or network share must first be "mounted" before it can be utilized by the local operating system. Devices can be configured in any number of ways: MS-DOS, Mac OS Extended, SMB, and so forth. This mounting process will determine the correct type of file system the device is configured with and mount it so it's usable by the operating system.

DMG Files

The Macintosh OS X Disk Copy Disk Image File (DMG) is a mountable disk image file that is commonly used in OS X. The DMG files are created to store groups of files and folders into one easy-to-manage file. These files are commonly used to distribute OS X operating system updates, create backups and restore, to send multiple files to another OS X user, and so forth. There are several options available to you when creating a DMG file: compressions, encryption (AES-128), password protection, and so forth.

These disk images are used by double-clicking the file. This will cause it to "mount" on the desktop as a virtual drive. From there you can work with the image as if it were any other hard drive partition, depending on the options that were used during the image creation process. For example, the image could be created with read/write access giving you the ability to add and delete files from the disk image. Or the disk image could be created with read-only access to prevent any files from being altered.

Info

A DMG file is a single file that has properties like a separate hard drive or CD device. To view the drive info screen highlight the mounted virtual drive (Drive-1) and select **File | Get Info**. Figure 3.4 shows an example of the properties for a mounted DMG file named Drive-1. You can notice from the picture below the differences in the info screen for the actual disk image file (Drive-1-Image.dmg) vs. the info for the mounted Drive-1. The size of the actual file is only using 204KB of disk space on the system, but the mounted image is showing 20.5 MB used out of a 5.68 Gig Volume.

Figure 3.4 Comparing Mounted DMG and File Level DMG Info

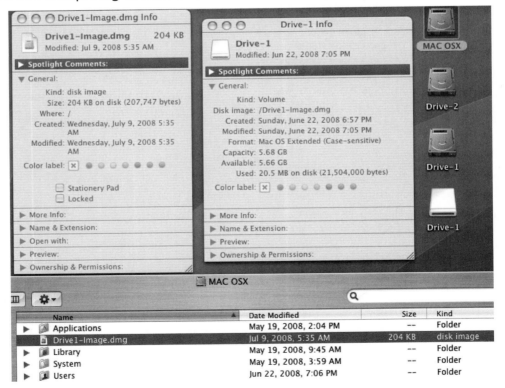

Locking

If we take another look at Figure 3.4 you will notice the "Locked" check box option in the Drive1-Image.dmg file properties window. Selecting this option is supposed to prevent the image from being edited (files copied to or deleted from) and prevent it from being deleted from the system. The Finder provides for "locking" a Macintosh file to prevent it from being deleted, moved, or altered by users accidentally or maliciously. As examiners, we can take advantage of this by clicking on the "Lock" button in the Get Info box of a DMG (or any file) we have created. A caveat to the Lock is the Owner of a file still retains permission to alter the content of the file, even with the Lock applied. To remain forensically sound, an examiner should apply the Lock property to an image file, and then do all actions from a separate user account to guarantee that no operations have the ability to alter evidence in any manner.

Un-mounting

Once the disk image is no longer needed, it can be un-mounted. This will remove the virtual device from the desktop. The term "un-mounting" is commonly used when referring to hard drives or shared folders across the network. Either way, it is talking about the disconnection of the mounted item.

A DMG file can be un-mounted from within the disk utility by selecting the mounted disk image and clicking either the "Unmount" or the "Eject" button. Also, the mounted disk image on the desktop can be highlighted, then select **File | Eject "Disk Image"**. Another easy way to un-mount the device is to simply click and drag it to the trash. Once the mounted device has started to drag, the trash icon will automatically change to an eject icon. Any method will successfully disconnect from the media.

Ejecting

Since DMG files and mountable media can be referring to CD/DVD drives, the disconnection of the media is also commonly referred to as "ejecting." Ejecting and un-mounting is somewhat used interchangeably throughout OS X and accomplishes the same task. To eject a DMG file, hold down the control button and select the Eject option. To unmount or eject the DMG file from the Disk Utility application, select the mounted DMG and select unmount or eject from the menu bar, as seen in Figure 3.5.

Figure 3.5 Ejecting or Un-mounting a DMG File with Disk Utility

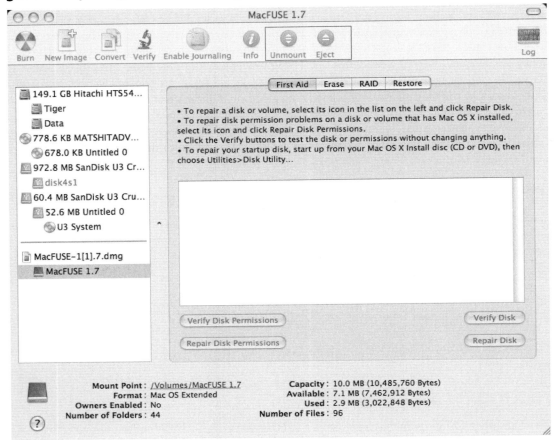

First Aid

Mac OS X has a built-in feature to help correct disk, permission, and file system errors as well as improving the overall stability and performance of the system. These options are available in the First Aid tab in the Disk Utility application. This may be necessary if the system is running slow, crashing frequently, displaying strange errors, or simply behaving in an unusual way. The First Aid Utility can also be used as preventive maintenance by preventing smaller errors from developing into larger system-wide problems.

To perform this preventive maintenance on the drive, select the desired partition to check. Then click the Verify Disk button to begin the analysis. If errors are found, the Repair Disk button will become active. Also note that if the startup disk requires repair, it will be necessary to run the repair procedure from the bootable Mac installation DVD. The process may need to be repeated several times to fix all of the errors. If errors are found that the First Aid Utility is unable to fix, you may have to back up all your data, reformat, and then restore the data back to the drive.

Repairing Disk Permissions

Many software applications installed in OS X are installed using a package file with the extension of ".pkg." When an application is installed, a ".bom" file, which stands for Bill of Materials, is also stored in the packages receipt file. The receipt file is saved in /Library/Receipts/. This file contains a list of all the files that were installed for that specific application and the proper permissions associated with each file. When you run "Repair Disk Permissions" on the disk, all of the "bom" files are reviewed and checked against the actual permissions on the files. If the file permission doesn't match, it will be reported and automatically fixed. Since Mac OS X software can be updated, it's best to always repair the permissions while booted to the hard drive volume instead of using the bootable OS X installations DVD media. This will insure that the latest correct permissions are correctly applied to the files.

NOTE

Only files that are installed with the OS X package installer will be checked for correct permissions. Some software applications may be installed by some other method and those files will not be checked during this process.

Verifying Disk Permissions

The Verify Disk Permissions feature works in the same way as the Repair Disk Permissions does, with one major difference. The Verify Disk Permissions will only report the differences without actually fixing them. It takes approximately the same amount of time to run the verify process as it does to run the repair process and it's not required to execute a verify process prior to running the repair. Therefore, there is no specific reason not to only run the Repair Disk Permission task instead of the Verify Disk Permissions, since any errors should be fixed anyway.

Erasing a Disk

It's become a well-known fact that when a file is deleted the system only removes the references to the file and the deletion doesn't actually remove or overwrite the deleted files with zeros or ones. This is why it's often possible to recover deleted files from a system with certain software tools. OS X has several options available to securely erase (wipe) data from the drive.

There are many different situations where a disk should be erased. As an investigator, if you are imaging a suspect's drive, your evidence storage media should be wiped before you use it to store an image or any other digital evidence. The reason media is wiped (all zeros only) before you use it, is to avoid possible contamination that could occur if the media is not properly forensically sanitized. Never assume you can skip the wiping step, even if your agency just purchased a new disk. It is an industry standard to always forensically prepare your collection media prior to use and document the date, time, utilities, and commands executed during the process. Any negligence in this process could potentially cause the collected media to become inadmissible in court, which could be devastating to a case containing digital evidence.

There are also other various reasons that people use the Mac OS X Disk Wiping Utility. In some instances, it may be for a suspect to attempt to forensically remove evidence from the system and other instances may merely be good computer usage practices by the user. It is also good security practice to wipe the drives before the system is sold or donated. Some agencies mandate such a procedure. Also, a user may want to backup their data and zero out the free space before the system is sent out to be serviced. Either way, it's important to understand some of the options available to users that are integrated directly in the operating system.

Security Options

The Mac OS X operating system has physical layer data security built directly in the operating system. Users are now more aware of issues related to the security of the data on their computers due to items like better security training as well as the number of Information Technology (IT) security-related incidents being broadcast on nationwide news. These items, along with the scare of the potential for identity theft have helped encourage users to better understand the potential risks associated with utilizing computer systems, and more users than ever are beginning to take more precautions. The Mac OS X operating system addresses those concerns without the need for third-party software, unlike other commercial operating systems.

OS X has the ability to forensically wipe the "free space" on the drive while leaving current files intact. This is a great security option for users that don't want to disturb the files currently stored on the system, but want to make sure that all files that have been deleted on the system are not forensically recoverable. When this feature is used, three options, discussed in more detail later, are available to wipe the free space of the system. These options are: zero out deleted files, 7-pass erase of deleted files, and 35-pass of deleted files.

To use this feature open the Disk Utility application, choose the desired disk or volume displayed on the left side of the window, select **Erase Free Space** to open the Options windows, choose the desired erase free space option shown in Figure 3.6 (1, 7, or 35 passes), and click **Erase Free Space**.

Figure 3.6 Erase Free Space Options

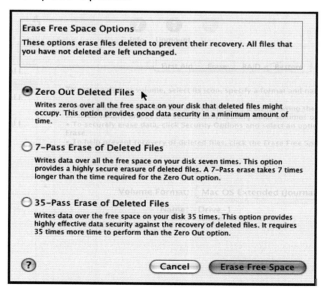

Don't Erase Data

Mac OSX has several different security options available for erasing the entire disk or volume structure. These options are shown in Figure 3.7. To view this option open the Disk Utility and select the desired disk or volume, select the **Erase** tab, and click **Security Options** to display the Secure Erase Options. The first option available is the "Don't Erase Data" option. It's important to note that this is the default erase option that will be used if no other option is specifically selected. This is the fastest and least secure option available. The Don't Erase Data option only erases directory information on the disk so the operating system can no longer access them. This is similar to the quick format feature in Microsoft Windows systems. The data is left untouched and will only be over written when that space is requested to be used for storage. Therefore, there is the possibility that files may be forensically recovered when this option has been used.

Figure 3.7 Secure Erase Options

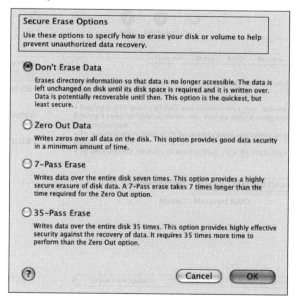

Zero Out Data

The zero out data option will over write the entire disk or volume with zeros one time. This is the fastest available option and is theoretically secure enough to prevent the data from being forensically recoverable using today's most current software methods. This is also the best option for forensically preparing a drive to be used to store digital evidence, since the entire drive will contain all zeros.

WARNING

Prior to using any storage media to store investigative digital evidence, the media must first be forensically wiped to prevent any possibility of cross contamination. The only acceptable secure erase option in OS X is the Zero out Data option.

To forensically zero out the current system drive of the computer, you must first boot to the Mac OS X installations DVD and run the Disk Utility from there (see Exercise 3.1). This is due to the fact that you can't zero out or delete the drive that you are currently booted to.

Configuring & Implementing...

Exercise 3.1: Forensically Wiping a Disk

This exercise will walk you through forensically wiping a disk. This process will zero out all data at the physical layer and will be ready to store digital evidence.

1. Open Disk Utility.
2. In the left pane, highlight the desired disk to be wiped.
3. In the right pane, click the **Erase** tab.
4. Click the **Security Options** button.
5. Select **Zero Out Data** and click **OK**.
6. Click the **Erase** button.
7. Confirm the erase action by clicking the **Erase** button in the Erase Volume pop-up window to begin the disk wiping process.

End of Exercise

7-Pass Erase

The 7-Pass Erase will overwrite the entire disk seven times. This option meets the DoD 5220 22-M specification for data storage sanitization. Unlike the zero out data option, each pass will vary the data written to the physical disk. Notice in Table 3.1 that the last pass will overwrite the storage media with random data. Therefore, this is an excellent option to provide a high degree of security against data recovery, but isn't an option to be used to prepare digital evidence collection media.

Table 3.1 7-Pass Data Overwrite Scheme

Pass #	Binary Notation	Hexadecimal Notation
1	11110110	0xF6
2	00000000	0x00
3	11111111	0xFF
4	Random	Random
5	00000000	0x00
6	11111111	0xFF
7	Random	Random

35-Pass Erase

The 35-Pass Erase provides the highest degree of security against data recovery. This option uses the Gutmann algorithm to write 35 patterns to the disk to overwrite data. This is a highly secure option and will take 35 times as long to complete than the zero out data option. The last four passes in this method will write random data to the disk. Therefore, just like the 7-pass secure erase option, it also is not an option for preparing storage media to collect digital evidence, but is an excellent option to prevent data from being forensically recovered. However, the disadvantage of using the Gutmann wipe is that it is extremely time consuming.

Volume Format Options

Mac OS X provides many different volume-formatting options to its users. Each available option has its own unique features and functions that could be beneficial in optimizing the storage media in different environments. Not all formats are directly readable by other types of operating systems.

Mac OS Extended

The Mac OS Extended (previously HFS+) volume format is compatible with both OS X and Mac OS 9. This allows for users to use capitalization in file names.

Mac OS Extended (Journaled)

The journaling feature was added to the Mac OS Extended in Mac OS X Server 10.2.2. The purpose of journaling is to help protect the file system during unexpected system failures such as power outages, hardware failures, and so forth. This additional protection is possible because the journal feature keeps a log of all disk transactions such as copy, move, delete, and so forth. When the system is restarted after an incident, the log is used to help repair the structure of the disk, thus helping to keep a functional operating system.

Mac OS Extended (Case-Sensitive)

This format provides all the functionality of the Mac OS Extended format with the addition of being case-sensitive. This means that files can be stored in the same folder with the same name with different upper and lower cases. Therefore, "File1" and "file1" are considered two completely different files on this volume format.

Mac OS Extended (Case-Sensitive, Journaled)

This format combines the functions and features of both the previously discussed volume formats. While providing the extra protection of journaling, it also allows for saving files with the same name in different cases.

MS-DOS File System

This format is used by Microsoft Windows operating systems. It may not be as interesting as that OS X is capable of creating an MS-DOS formatted partition, but it does reveal its ability to read those types of formatted media. This can be particularly useful in most environments where there are both Microsoft Windows and Mac operating systems being used.

When the Disk Utility is used to create an MS-DOS volume, it is created with FAT 32. It is important to remember that MAC OS X is running a distribution of BSD called "Darwin under the hood." This means that you must be aware of the possibilities of the extremely powerful terminal. By using the terminal, it's possible to create a FAT 16 volume, among numerous other tasks. This could be useful in instances where a device may only be able to read FAT 16 like some hardware that use SD cards. The following command will format a volume with FAT 16:

```
diskutil partitionDisk /Volumes/test 1 MBRFormat "MS-DOS FAT16" "hoot" 2M
```

This command will partition the mounted volume "test" and format it with FAT 16 and name it "hoot." The "1" represents the number of partitions and the 2M represents the size of the partition. If it is the last or only partition, it will automatically use the rest or all of the drive. This is just one simple example of using the terminal. If you want to take your knowledge to the next level, it is highly recommended that you learn to become comfortable utilizing the terminal in any operating system.

Unix File System

The underlying system of Mac OS X is BSD, which is a derivative of UNIX. Therefore, it only makes sense that it is capable of creating and supporting a UNIX File System.

Notes from the Underground...

Using NTFS Drives on Mac OS X

Most mass storage devices you purchase from the store come formatted with the FAT 32 file system. These drives are compatible in almost all Linux, Windows, and Mac OS X systems. Sometimes, Windows users will convert these drives to NTFS because of the 4GB file size limitation of the FAT 32 file system. Unfortunately, by default, your Mac OS X operating system will not be able to write to external drives that are formatted with NTFS in a Windows operating system. However, you can load drivers that will allow you to read and write to NFTS drives within the Mac OS X operating system. If you download the MacFUSE driver and the NTFS-3G driver for Mac, you will be able to read and write to drives that were formatted with the NTFS file system. You can use the search engine Google to find both the MacFUSE and NTFS-3G DMG packages on the Internet.

Partitioning

Partitioning is when a hard disk is broken up into more than one logical drive. There are many reasons why you may want to create varying sizes of partitions on a drive. One example may be to set up one or more partitions to be about 4.7 Gigs in size to temporarily store files that you want to backup to DVD's. Then as you downloaded pictures from your digital camera or created videos and so forth, you could store them on these partitions. Once the partition was full, you could then easily back up the entire contents of that partition onto a DVD. In this situation, the reason for this may be to simply make it easier to manage the files you want to back up. This is just one example of any number of possible reasons why a user may want to partition their drives.

TIP

While setting up the partitions in the disk utility, changes are not physically made to the drive until the "Partition" button has been clicked. Clicking the partition button will prompt the user for confirmation to apply the current changes to the disk by displaying a warning message stating that all data on the disk will be destroyed. Only after confirming the warning message will the actual configurations be committed to the hard drive.

Volume Schemes

The Mac OS X disk utility makes is easy for you to set up different types of volume schemes. The volume scheme allows you to define how many partitions you want to create on the drive. (See Figure 3.8 for an example of possible volume scheme configurations.) This example displays a drive that has been configured with four partitions. Below the Volume Scheme pull-down menu will be a visual representation of the partitions on the drive. By default, selecting a number of partitions from the pull-down menu will split the drive into equally sized partitions. Therefore, selecting four partitions on the 6 GB drive will result in the drive being broken down into four partitions of 1.5 GB each. From this point, the partitions can be manually edited by using the buttons in the lower section of the disk utility screen.

Figure 3.8 Volume Scheme Menu

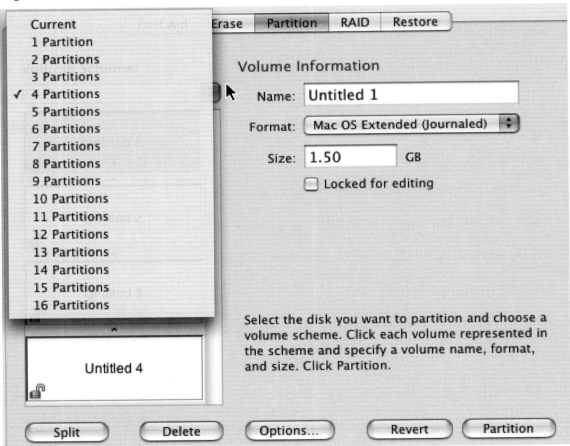

The sizes of the partitions can be edited in a couple of different ways. You can use the visual representation window to click and drag the line between the partitions and move it up and down to change its size. This will dynamically alter the size of the partition above and below the line that you selected. Another option is to select a partition and type in the desired size in megabytes into the "Size" section and hitting the **Enter** key.

Volume Labels

The Volume labels can be edited in the Volume Information section of the utility. The chosen name will be displayed as the name of the drive when it is mounted on the desktop. It is generally considered good practice to label your Volumes to avoid confusion when you are performing any type of operation between disks or partitions.

Splitting a Partition

An easy way to divide a single partition into two new partitions is to use the "Split" button. This will split the selected partition into two new partitions of equal size. From that point, you can continue on and adjust the sizes of those two partitions however you may choose. This is useful when you want to have more partitions than what the drive is currently configured for, without disturbing any of the other partitions. The delete button is used in the same manner as the Split button. It will simply delete the selected partition.

Locked for Editing Setting

While you are setting up the desired partitions on your hard drive, you may want to use the "Locked for editing" feature as shown in Figure 3.9. This feature allows you to lock the partition(s) once you have it the way you want. Then you can go ahead and change other partitions without worrying about it automatically changing when other partitions are manually edited using the buttons at the bottom of the disk utility.

WARNING

It is important to note that if you use the pull-down menu to change the Volume Scheme (the number of partitions you want on the drive), any and all locked partitions will be unlocked and the volume scheme will be changed to the default layout determined by the number of partitions that you selected.

Figure 3.9 Volume Information Pane

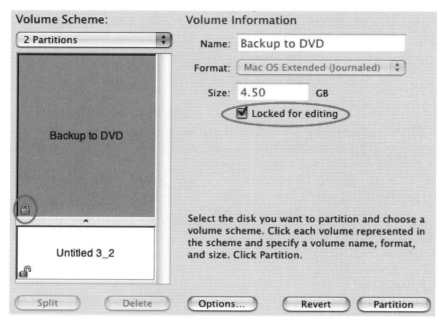

Reverting to a Previous Volume Scheme

As mentioned in an earlier note, the configurations are not actually committed to the disk until the Partition button is clicked and the action is confirmed. At any point up until then, the Revert button can be used to revert back to the current partition layout. This can be useful if at any time you wish to cancel all changes you've made.

RAID

RAID (Redundant Array of Inexpensive Disks or Redundant Array of Independent Disks) is a technology that uses multiple hard drives to provide improved performance, fault tolerance against hardware failures, and/or provide larger data volumes. The OS X operating system provides these advanced abilities from within the Disk Utility. Since the operating system software is controlling and managing the RAID functions, there will be some loss of overall performance on the system. This is the same as with any software RAID implementations, when compared to any dedicated hardware RAID solutions.

RAID Sets

There are several different RAID sets available that can be utilized in Mac OS X, with each having its own pros and cons. All of these options will be configured in the Disk Utility under the RAID tab.

When creating a RAID set, all data on all of the drives configured to be used in the RAID set will be deleted. This is because all the drives will be formatted with the volume format that you choose during the setup process.

To configure the RAID set, open the Disk Utility, click the **RAID** tab, input the RAID Set Name, select the desired Volume Format, and choose the desired RAID Type, as shown in Figure 3.10.

Figure 3.10 RAID Types

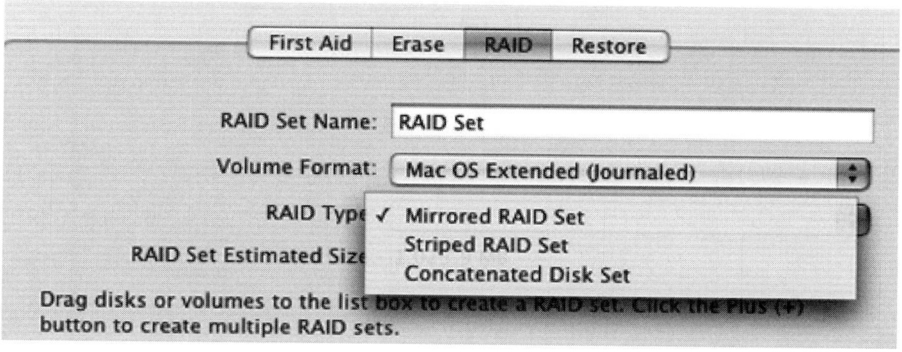

Next, click the **Options** button below the list box and select the "RAID Mirror AutoRebuild" option and click **OK** (see Figure 3.11). The default RAID block size can be customized from the default 32K. A smaller block size will increase transfer speeds but will create more fragmentation. A larger block size will decrease transfer speeds but will be less fragmented. The default 32K block size should be sufficient in most cases.

Figure 3.11 RAID Options Pane

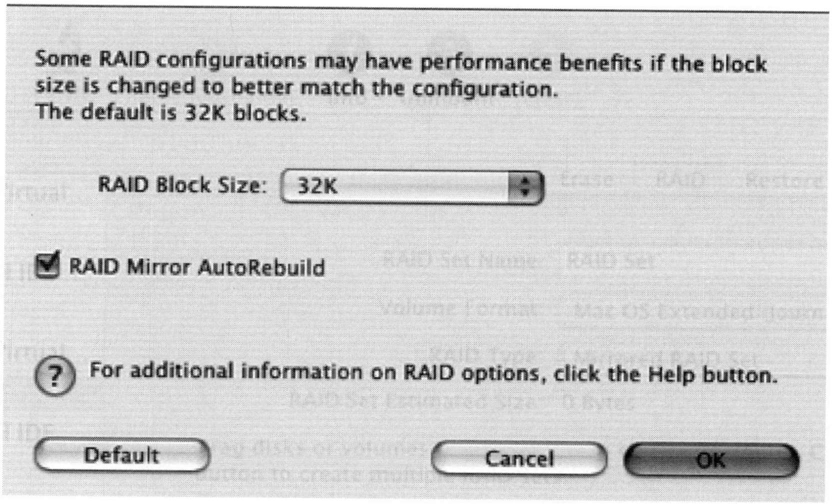

Then drag the drives to be used in the RAID Set from the left side of the utility over to the list box on the right. At this point, a window similar to Figure 3.12 should be shown.

Figure 3.12 Mirrored RAID Set Members

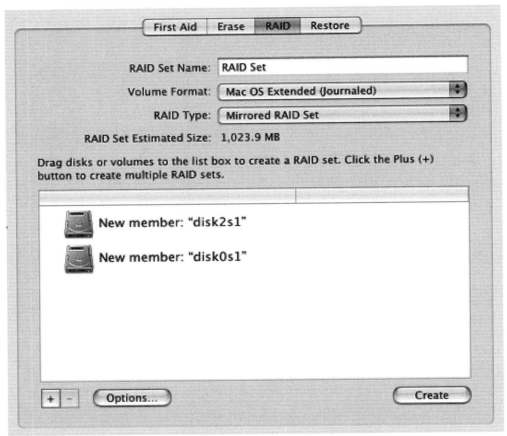

Once all the drives are selected and the options have been configured, click the **Create** button. The "Creating RAID" confirmation window will be displayed asking you to verify that you wish to use the selected disks in the RAID Set. Click **Create** to continue. The RAID Set Name that you chose will be automatically mounted and displayed on desktop. All the functions and features of the RAID will happen behind the scenes and be transparent to the user. Figure 3.13 shows an example of a completed mirrored RAID configuration setup.

Figure 3.13 Online Mirrored RAID Setup

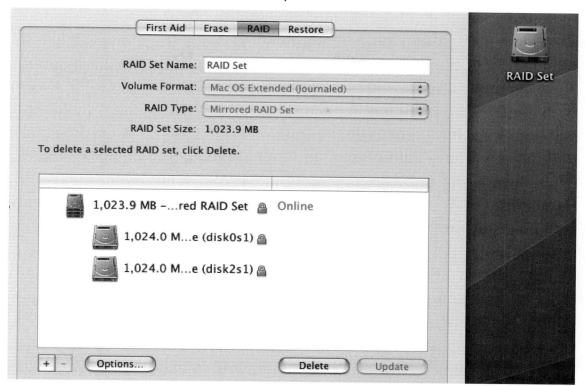

Mirrored RAID Set

The mirrored RAID set (also known as RAID 1) is probably the most common of the RAID types, which could partly be because it only requires two hard drives. This is commonly found being used on the system volumes, because it provides excellent fault tolerance in the event of a hard drive failure. If one of the drives fails, the system will continue to operate correctly without any disruptions or data loss. Then the failed drive can be replaced and the mirror set rebuilt.

The RAID set will show a status of "Degraded" when one of the drives fails. Figure 3.14 illustrates when a drive has failed and a new drive has been added to the RAID set. With the new drive in place, click **Rebuild** to recreate the RAID Set without loosing any data and to regain the benefits of the RAID.

Figure 3.14 Degraded Mirrored RAID Set

NOTE

Since the same data is constantly being written to each of the drives in the mirrored set, files that are deleted from the system can be recovered from either of the drives in the set.

Striped RAID Set

A striped RAID set (also known as RAID 0) provides greater performance for applications, such as video processing that requires accessing large amounts of data on the drive. The striped set stores files across all of the drives in the set and is able to improve the performance by reading and writing to all the drives simultaneously without the need to buffer the data. The downside to this RAID set is that it does not provide any fault tolerance. If one of the drives fails, the data on the entire set will be lost. Therefore, it's highly recommended to back up the data frequently.

Concatenated RAID Set

A concatenated RAID set is the oldest of the available RAID sets and isn't used very often anymore. This could simply be because there isn't as much need for it due to the current size of hard drives and there is no real benefit except for creating a single large volume from multiple drives or volumes of different sizes. This RAID set is also called JBOD or simply "just a bunch of disks." One unique feature of this set is that it does allow you to expand the set by adding volumes or devices to the RAID set without loosing the data already stored on the rest of the set. Concatenated RAID set doesn't provide any greater performance or fault tolerance. Therefore, if any drive fails that is part of this set, all the data stored on this set will be lost.

RAID Options

Different types of RAID setup software can have very complex options that may be more than a normal end user would want to tackle. Mac OS X helps to keep the setup very minimal and easy to configure, by only providing the most basic options.

RAID Mirror AutoRebuild

This option can be set in the options window during RAID setup, as displayed in Figure 3.11. With this option set, when the system notices that the RAID is out of sync, it will automatically start rebuilding itself. It is possible for the set to become degraded even without a hardware failure. This AutoRebuild operation takes place without any notification to the user.

RAID Block Size

The RAID block size is another option the user has the ability to control. This setting controls how many pieces a file will be broken down to. Smaller block size will allow the files to be broken down into smaller pieces allowing the file to be spread over more drives. Theoretically, this will improve the transfer performance, but will also cause more fragmentation to occur on the drives. Setting the size to a larger size will decrease the transfer performance, but will also reduce the fragmentation of the drives.

Restore

The Restore function allows you to restore files, volumes, or drives from an image file created with the Disk Utility. This can be a good way to back up data in compressed and even encrypted (AES-128 encryption) password protected files that can be used to restore your data in the case of accidental deletion or hardware failure. The encryption and password protection helps keep your data secured while stored in any safe and convenient location.

Creating a Disk Image

The Disk Utility makes it easy for you to be able to backup or store all the data into a single easy-to-manage file. Once the image has been created, it can be stored on another system, burned to CD/DVD, and so forth. Figure 3.15 displays the three different options for creating a new image, including creating a blank or empty image from a folder or from a disk. Once you select the desired option, you will be asked to input the name of the new image and a location to save the image. You will have the option to choose what format you want the image saved as: read-only, compressed, read/write, or DVD/CD master.

Figure 3.15 Creating Disk Image

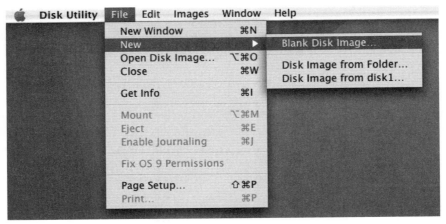

When you choose to protect your image by using encryption (see Exercise 3.2), you will be required to enter a password to securely protect your image, as displayed in Figure 3.16. This password is not recoverable and will be required to open the image. If you happen to forget the password, you will not be able to recover the data stored within the image. Once you enter a password and click OK, the image creation process will continue.

Figure 3.16 Setting Password for Encrypted Image

Converting an Image

This feature allows you to convert an already created image into another image format, as shown in Figure 3.17. Therefore, an image that was created in the read/write format can be converted to a read-only image format to prevent any changes to the file. The same goes for the encryption options. If you wish to add encryption to your image then you can convert the image into an encrypted image and vice versa.

Figure 3.17 Convert Image Formats

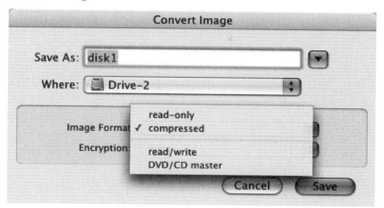

Configuring & Implementing...

Exercise 3.2: Creating an Encrypted DMG Image

This exercise will walk you through creating an encrypted 40 MB DMG image file. This will allow you to securely store files within the encrypted DMG image.

1. Open **Disk Utility**.
2. Navigate to **File | New | Blank Disk Image**.
3. The New Blank Image window will be displayed, as shown in Figure 3.18. Complete the following fields.
   a. Save As: **Junk_Files**
   b. Where: **Desktop**
   c. Size: **40 MB**
   d. Encryption: **AES-128**
   e. Format: read/write disk image

Continued

Figure 3.18 Creating the Encrypted DMG Image

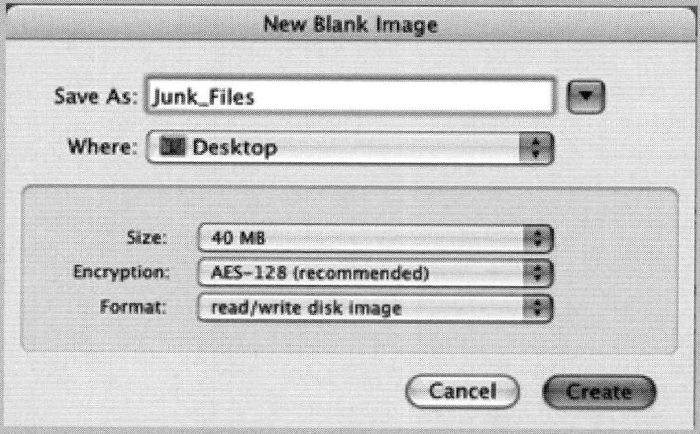

4. Click **Create** to continue the process
5. The Authenticate window will be displayed requesting input.
   a. Uncheck **Remember password**. This will cause the user to be prompted each time the image is mounted.
   b. Enter **mypassword** into the password field.
   c. Enter **mypassword** again in the verify field.
6. Once the desired password has been entered, click **OK** to continue.
7. Once the file creation process has been completed, the file will be saved to the Desktop and automatically mounted and ready to use. Double-click the mounted image and copy/create files as normal.
8. The image can then be un-mounted and will require the password to reopen the image to view its contents. Highlight the mounted image, then click **File | Eject "Junk_Files"**.

End of Exercise

Verifying a Disk Image

The Verify option makes it easy for you to check the CRC32 or Message Digest 5 (MD-5) checksum, as shown in Figure 3.19. MD-5 is a hashing function commonly used in the forensics field. This allows you to verify the hash value of the contents of the disk image. This can be used to compare the hash value for an image with the hash value of the drive after a restore has been completed, to verify that all the files were in fact copied successfully and as intended.

Figure 3.19 Verify Disk Image

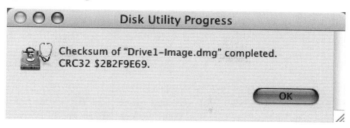

Restoring an Image File to a Disk

If an image can be created to back up files and drives, then there must also be a way to restore those files contained in the image back to a drive. This can be accomplished by using the Restore section of the Disk Utility. This is done by simply selecting the source image and the desired destination. Also note the Erase Destination option in Figure 3.20. When this option is not selected, this procedure will add the contents of the image file to the destination. On the other hand, if this option is selected, all of the files and folders on the destination drive will be erased prior to copying the data from the image to the destination, thus leaving only the data contained in the image on the destination.

Figure 3.20 Restoring an Image File to Drive

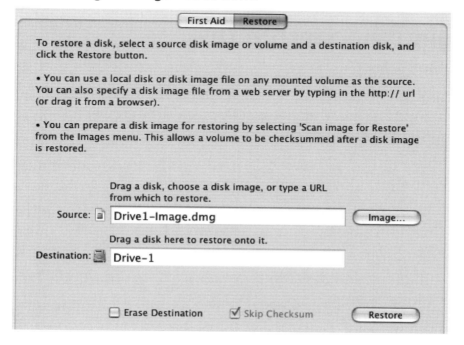

Restoring a Disk from a Web Server

OS X allows images that are stored on a network Web server to be restored to disk over the network. This can be useful for situations where a disk image needs to be restored to multiple systems by allowing the image to be stored in one centralized, easy-to-manage location on the Web server.

To accomplish a Restore from a web server, simply insert the Uniform Resource Locator (URL) to the location of the image stored on the Web server. Figure 3.21 shows an example of the image "Drive1-Image.dmg" being stored on an internal Web server called "backup.com."

Figure 3.21 Restoring Image from Web Server

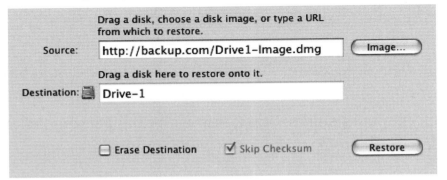

Changing the Startup Disk

The startup disk refers to the media that the hardware will use as its boot device. This could be a CD/DVD drive, a network boot, an internal drive, or external USB drives formatted with a Globally Unique Identifier (GUID) (only supported on Intel-based Macs with OS X 10.4.5 or later), and so forth. You can format a USB drive with the GUID partition table (see Figure 3.22), by clicking the options button when you are partitioning with the Disk Utility.

Figure 3.22 Changing the Partitioning Scheme

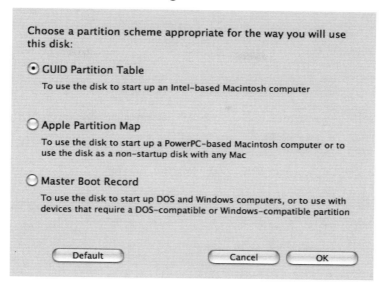

There are many reasons why an individual may want or need to change the startup disk. Possibly, to boot to the OS X DVD install media to perform system maintenance on the system drive, or to boot from a NetBoot server. There may also be multiple Mac OS X System folders installed on separate drives in the system. For example, it could be possible that booting to Disk0 would start up OS X 10.4 and booting to Disk1 could start up OS X 10.5, as seen in Figure 3.22. Although it is possible to boot from many different devices, there can be only one device selected as the startup disk in the Startup Disk pane of the system preferences.

To specify a Startup Disk open the System Preferences and select Startup Disk. This will open the Startup Disk window, as shown in Figure 3.23, which will allow you to set the device that you wish to boot to by default each time the system is started. Simply select the desired system and click restart to set that device as the startup device and reboot your system to that device.

Figure 3.23 Selecting Startup Disk

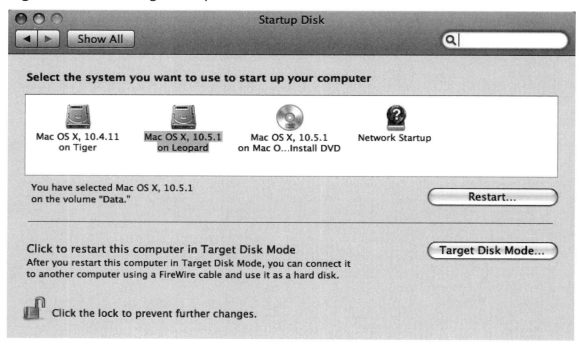

As with all previous versions of Mac, they have continued with the tradition of allowing you to specify individual keys or key combinations on the keyboard to select a startup device during the system boot. The primary utility to select the boot device during boot is the Startup Manager. The Startup Manager is accessed by pressing and holding the "Option" key immediately after the system is restarted or first powered on. The Startup Manager will scan the system for all available boot volumes and display each as an option on the screen. Depress the desired volume and click the arrow button on the lower right to boot to the selected volume.

TIP

To scan for a NetBoot Server volume that may be on the network, you will need to click the rescan button on the lower left side of the Startup Manager.

Target Disk Mode

Target Disk Mode allows you to start a Mac computer to use its internal hard drive as an external device on another system over FireWire. The computer started in Target Disk Mode is considered the "target" and the computer the target is connected to over FireWire is considered the "host." Once the target system has been started in Target Disk Mode, the host computer can then transfer files to and from the target drive as it would any other external storage device. Target Disk Mode will only work on internal ATA drives and will only connect to the drive that is configured as the Master on the channel. Target Disk Mode does not support ATA devices configured as Slave, ATAPI devices, or SCSI drives. Target Disk Mode can be a useful when you are trying to acquire a system's drive. However, you definitely want to practice using this feature on your own system before you try it out in the field.

There are two ways to start a system in Target Disk Mode. First, it can be done by using the Startup Disk pane in the System preferences, as shown in Figure 3.23. Simply open the Startup Disk pane and click **Target Disk Mode**. The computer will then be restarted into Target Disk Mode and be available to a host system connected by FireWire. Second, the "T" key can be pressed during boot to instruct the system to start in Target Disk Mode.

NOTE

A computer that has been configured with an Open Firmware Password will not be able to boot into Target Disk Mode. The Open Firmware Password secures the system by preventing the system from being able to boot to the DVD drive, NetBoot, Target Disk Mode, and so forth. It also prevents resetting the PRAM, starting up into safe mode or single user mode, and so forth. The utility to add the password is found on the OS X Install DVD in the Utilities folder and is called "Open Firm-ware Password." It can also be copied to the local hard drive for use.

The Open Firmware password, as seen in Figure 3.24, is used by both PPC- and Intel-based Macintoshes. Don't be confused by the name. The "Open Firmware Password" name is simply retained from the PPC-based Macs, and does not reflect that Open Firmware is used on Intel-based Macs.

The Open Firmware Password can be circumvented with physical access to the machine. This is done by adding or removing RAM from the system, resetting the PRAM by holding Command + Option + P + R, and then restarting the system.

Figure 3.24 Setting an Open Firmware Password

Terminal Window – Apple Partition Map

Most people feel more comfortable using Graphical User Interface (GUI) tools, but disks can also be viewed and managed from the command line. One of the most helpful commands to use in the terminal window is "hdiutil." In order to use this command, you need to open a terminal window. The terminal window can be opened from the Utilities folder. You may want to increase the font size because the print is small by default. After opening the terminal window, type **sudo su**, and then type the password for the root account for your system. Analyzing and managing disks is something that often requires root level access.

Figure 3.25 Viewing a Partition Map Using the hdiutil Command

```
Terminal — bash — 80x24
Moofs-House:~ moof$ hdiutil partition /dev/disk0
scheme:       Apple
block size: 512
  ## Type                   Name                   Start     Size
+     DDM                    Driver Descriptor Map      0         1
   1 Apple_partition_map    Apple                      1        63
+     Apple_Free                                       64    262144
   3 Apple_HFS              Untitled              262208 312319590
+     Apple_Free                                 312581798        10

+ synthesized
Moofs-House:~ moof$ []
```

The command used to give this view is **hdiutil partition /dev/disk0**, as seen in Figure 3.25. Notice the additional information displayed as compared to the output of Disk Utility. Sector 0 is the boot sector with a size of 1 sector. Sectors 1 through 64 are the Apple Partition Map, which defines the layout of the disk. Apple Free is a "padding" defined as being available for future use. The data section for a forensic analysis finally shows up at the Apple HFS partition starting at sector 262208 and having a length of 3,122,319,590 sectors. There is one more Apple Free partition with a length of 10 sectors, again used as padding.

The Apple Free area is not normally where data will be found, as it is not easily accessed by the casual user. However, nothing prevents a more savvy user from hiding information there with the right tools. Also, information could be left over in these areas from a previous partition scheme.

Summary

This chapter covered many of the different possible configurations available to all users that are running Mac OS X. All of these topics are important to any forensic investigator working on a case that involves a Mac computer. Also, these topics are relevant to investigators who decide to use a Mac OS as a platform for their forensic workstation. (More information about creating a Mac forensic workstation is discussed in Chapter 7.) Either way, it is important to take note of the possible configurations that could be used to either store, secure, hide, or forensically remove evidence from the workstation.

Solutions Fast Track

Disk Utility

☑ The Disk Utility is the primary tool used to configure hard drives, virtual devices, conduct disk maintenance, erase disks, partition drives, create RAID sets, and backup and restore disk images.

☑ The Disk Utility can be used to view the current disk setup on a suspect system.

☑ The Disk Utility can be used to forensically remove evidence from a device as well.

First Aid

☑ The first aid feature allows you to verify and repair the file structure on the drive.

☑ Permissions are used to help prevent accidental damage to important operating system files. The permissions can become unstable and the first aid feature will allow you to verify and repair disk permissions.

☑ You will have to boot to the Mac OS X install disk to repair permissions on the startup disk.

Erasing a Disk

☑ There are several options available to all users for erasing disks. Some options may only delete files while others may actually forensically wipe data from the device.

☑ The erase free space option allows for the user to zero out data on the device while leaving the current file intact.

☑ There are options for a 1-pass, 7-pass, and 35-pass erase functions. Only the 1-pass will leave the drive marked with all zeros. The 7-pass and 35-pass will write the final passes with random characters.

Partitioning

☑ Drives can be partitioned with many different size and format configurations using the Disk Utility.

☑ Partition sizes can be adjusted manually by inputting values into the size box or by dragging the partitions up and down in the visual representation screen.

☑ Just editing the partitions on a drive may leave evidence from previous configurations on the physical disk.

RAID

☑ The RAID configuration on a workstation may determine the best route to processing the drives.

☑ RAID 1 creates an exact duplicate of the disk on both drives. Deleted files will be recoverable from either drive.

☑ A physical disk can actually be configured in multiple RAID configurations simultaneously. The disk can be configured as part of a mirrored RAID and Striped RAID set to gain the benefits of both technologies.

Restore

☑ Data can be securely stored in encrypted and password-protected files, and easily restored when necessary.

☑ The restore process can be used to add the data in the backup image to the destination, or to erase the destination prior to the restore process.

☑ Data can be restored from a disk image stored on a Web server by using the URL to the disk image file as the source location.

Changing the Startup Disk

☑ OS X supports booting to several different devices by pressing and holding an individual key or a combination of keys during startup.

☑ Only one device can be set as the default startup device by using the Startup Disk pane in the System Preferences.

☑ A computer can be started in Target Disk Mode to allow its internal hard drive to be used by another system as an external device using a FireWire cable.

Frequently Asked Questions

Q: Is it possible to recover deleted files from a mirrored RAID set if you only have one of the drives?

A: Yes, it is possible to recover deleted files from a mirrored RAID set from either of the drives, because all the data is written to and deleted from both the drives simultaneously.

Q: Can the boot drive be wiped?

A: Yes, but this requires you to boot to the OS X installation DVD and then run the disk utility from there.

Q: Can you verify or repair disk permissions of the boot drive without using the installation DVD?

A: Yes, you can just use the Disk Utility in the operating system while the system is booted.

Q: When repairing permissions, are their any files that won't have their permissions repaired?

A: Yes. Only the files that were installed using the the OS X package installer will be verified and/or repaired.

Q: Should you verify a drive before running a repair?

A: There is no real benifit from running verify on a disk prior to running a repair. They take almost the same amount of time and there isnt any reason why you wouldn't want to repair what needs to be repaired.

Q: Will there be any way for a forensic analyist to determine if a wipe procedure has been conducted on a drive?

A: There may potentially be evidence of a drive being wiped. If the drive contains all zeros in the free space then a wipe may have been performed. Also, if the entire drive contains random characters, then a 7-pass or 35-pass wipe may have been performed on the drive.

Q: Can I use my computer's USB connection with Target Disk Mode?

A: No. Only a FireWire connection is supported.

Q: Does Mac OS X Support Raid 5?

A: No. OS X supports Raid levels 0, 1, and JBOD.

Q: Why is it important for a forensic investigator to understand the Disk Utility?

A: During investigations it's common to create forensic images of the evidence drives. Due to this, it is important to understand the possible ways a disk can be configured to help determine the best procedures to process the suspect drives.

Q: Is it possible to forensically wipe the boot drive?

A: Yes, but you must first boot to the OS X installation DVD. Then run the Disk Utility from the DVD.

Q: Can .dmg files be created on OS X and then sent to a windows machine?

A: Windows cannot use .dmg files without the use of third-party utilities.

Q: When repairing disk permissions, what permissions will not be repaired?

A: Permissions will not be repaired for any software that was not installed using the OS X package installer.

Q: Should I run a verify to see if anything needs to be repaired before running a repair?

A: Both processes take about the same amount of time, so there isn't any benefit in running a verify first.

Q: Is it possible to securely wipe external USB or FireWire drives?

A: Yes. The disk utility can securely wipe any drive that it's able to detect.

Q: Why should I use a journaling file system?

A: Journaling file systems are more resilient to sudden power losses. Once the system is brought back online, it will use the journal to help keep the file system current and in good working order.

Q: How is it possible to tell if the mirror (RAID 1) is currently in the rebuild process?

A: There will not be any user notification in the event of a rebuild process being started. The only way to tell would be to start the Disk Utility and check the current condition of the RAID. It may be possible to notice the system performance drop while the RAID is being rebuilt.

Q: What is the "secure empty trash" option in the finder?

A: This option will securely delete the file by overwriting the file(s) and folder(s) with random data. This will prevent all items in the trash from being recovered. To securely wipe data from files that have previously been emptied from the trash you must use the "erase free disk space" feature in the Disk Utility.

Q: Is it possible to restore from a disk image stored on a Web server over the Internet?

A: Yes. The system must be able to connect to the Web server regardless of its physical location.

Q: Can I copy files from all the hard drives from a system by booting into Target Disk Mode?

A: No. Only the hard drive configured as the Master on the Ultra ATA channel will be available when booting into Target Disk Mode. Also, non-ATA devices are not supported.

Chapter 4

HFS Plus File System

Solutions in this chapter:

- **HFS Plus Volumes**
- **Boot Blocks**
- **Volume Header**
- **Allocation File**
- **B*-trees**

☑ **Summary**

☑ **Solutions Fast Track**

☑ **Frequently Asked Questions**

Introduction

It is important for computer forensic investigators to understand how an operating system stores data on the file system. Many investigators are familiar with the FAT and NTFS file systems, which they come across routinely when doing forensic examinations on computers with Microsoft Windows. If you are going to perform computer forensics on a Mac, an iPod, or an iPhone, however, you have to have an understanding of the HFS Plus file system.

HFS Plus was developed by Apple to help overcome some of the limits imposed by their HFS file system. As disk size increases, limitations imposed by earlier file systems such as HFS tend to become a problem. The default setting for HFS Plus is to use journaling. Journaling is a mechanism by which transactions to the disk are logged; in the case of an unclean shutdown, the log can help the file system determine which changes to the disk were made. The journaling feature helps prevent file system corruption.

This chapter will cover the most important components of the HFS Plus file system as used by Macs today so forensic examiners can understand how data is stored. For those readers looking for additional details, Apple provides an extensive technical reference for the file system in its *Technical Note TN1150* at http://developer.apple.com/technotes/tn/tn1150.html. The Technical Note does not cover some of the most recent changes, such as extended attributes. For more details on those a review of available HFS Plus source code is recommended.

HFS Plus Volumes

Broadly, a volume represents an instance of the given file system on a storage medium. A single physical disk may contain a single volume or multiple volumes through disk partitioning. One single logical volume may span multiple physical disks. The file system in general, and HFS Plus in particular, is indifferent to where this logical volume sits, and treats the logical volume as a single logical entity that can be randomly accessed.

In this book, when referring to disk tools such as Mac OS's Disk Utility, the HFS Plus format will be called the *Mac OS Extended format*. Similarly, *Mac OS Standard format* will be used to refer to the older HFS format. The HFS Plus format allows for both case-sensitive and case-insensitive name comparisons, and optional journaling features. File and folder name case is preserved regardless of whether name comparisons are case-sensitive or not.

Specifications

In HFS Plus the basic allocation units are called *allocation blocks*. The size of an allocation block is always a multiple of the storage medium sector size (the minimum block size addressable by the storage hardware). Allocation block numbers are stored as 32-bit integers, with 4Kb as a common block size. Some other key characteristics of an HFS Plus file system include:

- Support for file names in the Unicode format (allowing for the use of international characters) with up to 255 characters in their name

- A maximum file size of 263 bytes

- Support for multiple data streams associated with the same file

The actual allocation block size is selected automatically by the implementation, depending on the disk geometry. A large block size may increase the amount of spaced wasted to overhead in a volume, as data can only be stored in block-sized chunks. For example, with a block size of 8,192, a file of length 24,580 will allocate 4 blocks, even though only 4 bytes of the last block will be in use. HFS Plus does not allow blocks to be shared between multiple files.

Structures

The HFS Plus file system is composed of a number of structures that combined provide the information necessary to manage data within a volume. Each volume contains a volume header at offset 1,024, a second copy of this header (the alternate volume header) 1,024 bytes before the end of the volume, and a number of user and special files. The first 1,024 bytes of a volume are reserved as boot blocks. The last 512 bytes are also reserved for legacy reasons. Figure 4.1, illustrates these structures.

Figure 4.1 HFS Plus Volume Format

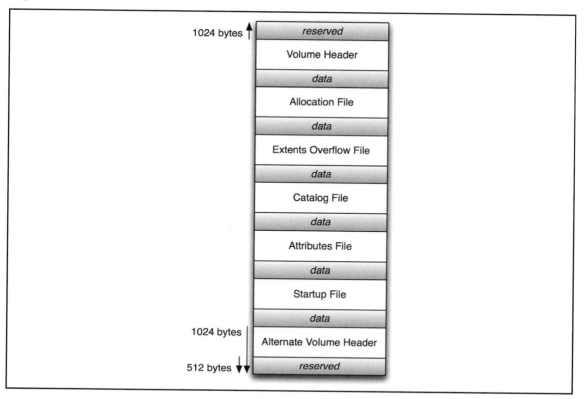

The volume header and five special files—allocation, extents overflow, catalog, attributes, and startup—contain additional structures used to manage volume data.

> **NOTE**
>
> With the exception of the two reserved regions and the two volume header copies at the beginning and end of a volume, the location and order of each special file varies with each volume instance, and can only be determined by inspecting the volume header.

The volume header defines fundamental information about the volume, including the size of each allocation block, the number of used and unused blocks, and the size and location of each special file. The allocation file provides a bitmap of used and unused blocks in the volume. The catalog file describes the directory structure of the file system and is used to find the location of specific files and folders. The extents overflow file contains pointers to additional extents (see below) for files that require more than 8 contiguous groups of blocks to be stored. The attributes file contains custom file attributes. Finally, the startup file can be used to hold information required at boot time. Each one of these special files is described in more detail in the sections that follow. In addition, user file data shares storage space with the special files, in between the two headers.

Both special and user files are stored in *forks*, a collection of allocation blocks. Space is typically reserved in *clumps*, where the size of a clump is a multiple of the allocation block size. The default *clump* size is specified in the volume header. Contiguous allocation blocks for a given file are grouped into *extents*. Each extent has a starting allocation block, and a block count, indicating how many blocks from the starting block contain file data (see Table 4.1 for a description of the *extent descriptor* structure).

Table 4.1 The Extent Descriptor Structure

Field	Size	Description
startBlock	4 bytes	The first allocation block for this extent.
blockCount	4 bytes	The total number of blocks starting at *startBlock* containing data in this extent.

The starting offset of a file can then be determined by finding its first extent, and multiplying its *startBlock* by the allocation block size, which is defined in the volume header. Because files cannot always be completely stored in contiguous blocks and can be fragmented on disk, HFS Plus defines a *fork data* structure, designed to track the location and size of a file's fork. Each fork data structure lists up to 8 extents containing the fork's payload. The fork data structure is described on Table 4.2. When a file requires more than 8 extents of storage, the *extents overflow* file comes into play, associating additional extents to the file. Since special files are stored in the same way as regular files no specialized code is required to access them, and they can grow or shrink as necessary.

Table 4.2 Fork Data Structure

Field	Size	Description
logicalSize	8 bytes	The actual size of the complete file, in bytes.
clumpSize	4 bytes	The size, in bytes, of the default clump size for the file.
totalBlocks	4 bytes	The total number of allocation blocks containing file data.
extents	64 bytes	An array of 8 extents.

The HFS Plus format relies on *B*-trees* as its data structure for storing key–value pairs so that they can be searched efficiently. These B*-trees are used in the catalog, extents overflow, and attributes special files.

User files can have multiple forks, each containing a different payload related to the file. (HFS Plus forks are very similar in concept to NTFS alternate data streams.) All files have at least two forks: the resource and the data fork. The resource fork can be used to store information associated with the file, such as icons and other metadata. The data fork holds the actual file contents. Additional forks can be defined via the attributes special file.

File and folder names are stored as Unicode strings in fully decomposed canonical form, to ensure key comparisons yield the desired results when using multiple languages and character sets. Names have a maximum length of 255 Unicode characters, and are stored with a preceding 16-bit unsigned integer describing their length. All integers are stored in big-endian format. Dates are stored as 32-bit unsigned integers, indicating the number of seconds elapsed since January 1, 1904, GMT, with the exception of the creation date stored in the volume header, which is stored in local time for legacy reasons.

Size Limitations

HFS Plus volumes have a maximum volume and file size of 8 exbibytes (2^{63} bytes). Each file or folder name can have up to 255 Unicode characters. In addition to the standard data and resource forks, each file can have an arbitrary number of additional named forks.

In contrast, HFS volumes have a maximum volume size of 2 tebibytes (2^{41} bytes) and a maximum file size of 2 gibibytes (2^{31} bytes). A single HFS volume can also store a maximum of 65,535 files, each with up to 31 characters in its name in the MacRoman encoding.

NOTE

Gibibytes, tebibytes, and exbibytes are information units based on powers of 2. In 1999, the International Electrotechnical Commission (IEC) adopted these prefixes to differentiate these units from the more commonly used gigabyte, terabyte, and exabyte, which are based on powers of 10. For example, a terabyte refers to 10^{12} bytes (1,000,000,000,000 bytes), while a tebibyte refers to 2^{40} bytes (1,099,511,627,776 bytes).

Forks

Each file in an HFS Plus volume can have multiple payloads or data streams associated with it. In HFS Plus parlance, each one of these streams is called a fork. All files have at least a data fork and a resource fork, any or both of which may be empty.

Data Fork

The data fork holds the actual file contents. This is the data stream you interact with most of the time when opening the file for read or write access. No special operations, other than the usual file I/O system calls, are required to access a file's data fork.

Resource Fork

The resource fork holds additional information associated with a particular file or directory, such as icons, the preferred application used to open the file, the size and location of application windows, and so on.

Resource forks are not supported on file systems other than HFS and HFS Plus. When copying files from an HFS volume to a volume that does not support resource forks, Mac OS X will, by default, create additional files with the "._" prefix and include the contents of the resource fork. With the introduction of Mac OS X application resources became part of the application *bundle*, limiting the applicability of resource forks.

A file's resource fork can be accessed by utilizing the *..namedfork* suffix along with the special name "rsrc". For example, opening **foo/..namedfork/rsrc** would open the resource fork for the file named *foo*. Obviously, doing the same without the suffix would open the data fork instead.

Additional Forks

HFS Plus allows for associating an arbitrary number of forks to a file or folder, beyond the standard data and resource forks. These additional forks are identified by name and are managed through the attributes special file. Mac OS X 10.4 introduced the concept of extended attributes for both files and folders, and provided a concrete use case in its new support for access control lists (ACLs). ACL information for a file or a folder is stored as extended attributes. ACLs are described in more detail in the "Permissions" section.

Beyond access control lists, extended attributes are used for a variety of purposes by Mac OS X, often to store metadata associated with the file or folder they reference. For example, when downloading a potentially dangerous file from the Internet, metadata about the file's origin is stored as extended attributes. This information is later used by **Launch Services** to display an alert before the file is opened. The **xattr** tool can be used to look at some (but not all) of the extended attributes associated with a file. See Figure 4.2 for an example of the **xattr** tool in action.

Figure 4.2 Metadata Stored as Extended Attributes after Download

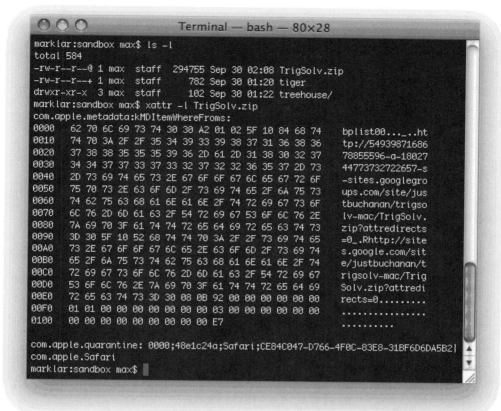

Permissions

HFS Plus supports UNIX-style permissions for its files and folders. Each file and folder in the volume embeds a *BSD Info* structure within its entry in the catalog file, detailing these permissions. Table 4.3 describes the structure.

Table 4.3 The BSD Info Structure

Field	Size	Description
ownerID	4 bytes	The user id of the file or folder owner.
groupID	4 bytes	The group id associated with the file or folder.
adminFlags	1 byte	The BSD flags for the file or folder.
fileMode	2 bytes	The BSD style type and mode bits.
special	4 bytes	Varies with the type of file.

In addition to UNIX-style permissions, Mac OS X 10.4 introduced access control lists (ACLs) for files and folders. Through ACLs it is possible to grant or revoke access to certain files to specific users. An ACL is a list of rights that can be attached to a file or folder. Each entry in the list is called an Access Control Entry (ACE).

Access control list support on a volume must be enabled for the ACLs to be active. The **fsaclctl** tool, which must be run as root, controls whether ACL support is enabled or disabled for a given mount-point. Once enabled, ACLs can be managed through extensions to the familiar **chmod** command. Figure 4.3 shows an example using both tools.

Figure 4.3 Enabling and Setting ACLs

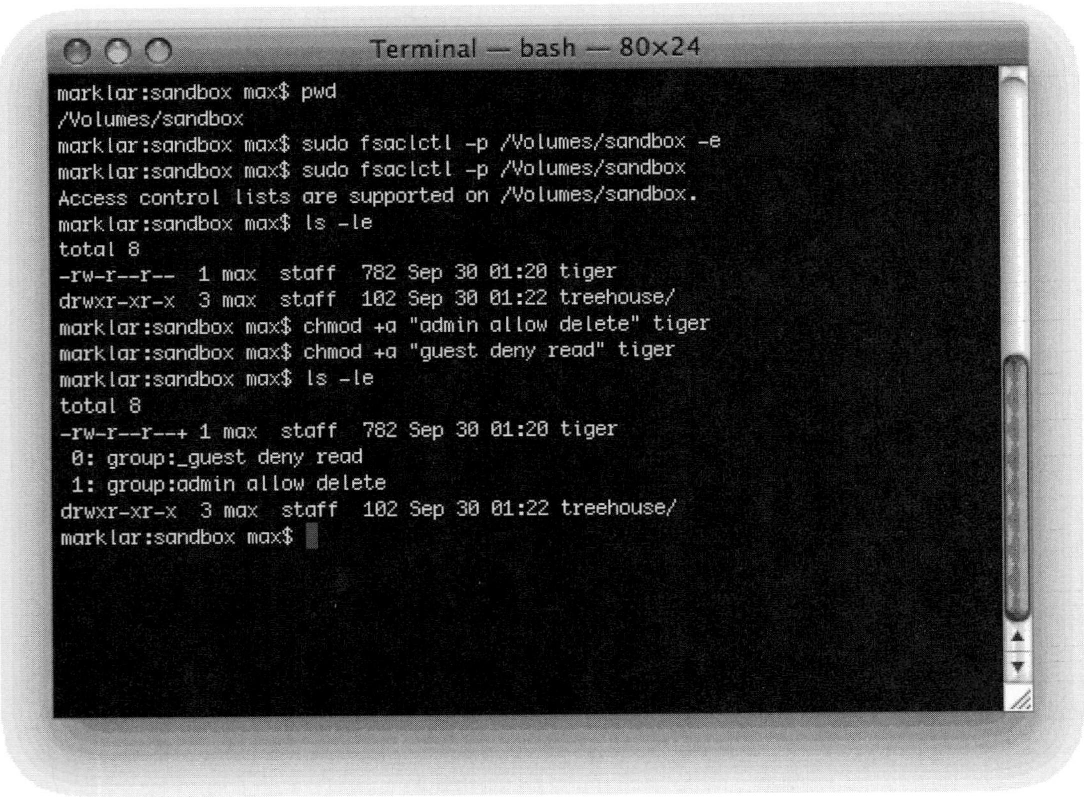

HFS Wrapper

To allow older systems that do not have HFS Plus support in ROM, Apple developed the HFS wrapper. When using this wrapper, an HFS Plus volume is contained within an HFS volume, making it look like an HFS file system to systems that don't understand HFS Plus.

NOTE

On systems with HFS support but no HFS Plus support, the presence of the HFS wrapper can lead to displaying an empty volume, even though it mounted cleanly. This is by design, and aimed at providing an improved user experience where the volume is mounted without errors and can optionally include documentation to explain why the rest of the volume is unavailable.

The HFS wrapper, as seen in Figure 4.4, is laid out in a way that it allows Mac OS 9 systems to find the correct loader code during boot up, and ultimately load HFS Plus support.

Figure 4.4 HFS Wrapper Layout

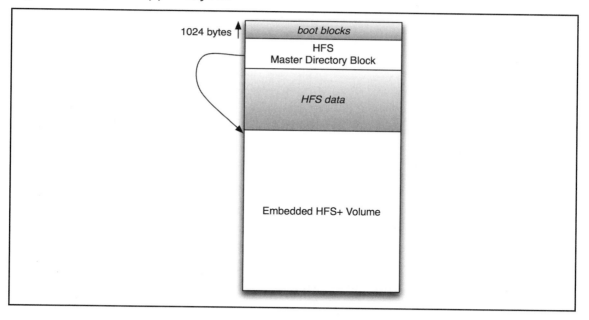

The HFS wrapper contains a Master Directory Block (MDB) at offset 1,024, which is the HFS equivalent to the volume header in HFS Plus. A few fields in the standard HFS MDB have a different meaning when used within an HFS wrapper. Table 4.4 contains a description of the MDB used by the HFS wrapper.

Table 4.4 Master Directory Block within an HFS Wrapper

Field	Size	Description
drSigWord	2 bytes	The volume signature.
drCrDate	4 bytes	The date and time when the volume was created.
drLsMod	4 bytes	The date and time when the volume was last modified.
drAtrb	2 bytes	Volume attributes.
drNmFls	2 bytes	The total number of files in the volume.
drVBMSt	2 bytes	Starting block for volume bitmap.
drAllocPtr	2 bytes	The start of the next allocation search.
drNmAlBlks	2 bytes	The total number of allocation blocks in the volume.
drAlBlkSiz	4 bytes	The size in bytes of each allocation block.
drClpSiz	4 bytes	The default clump size for the volume.
drAlBlSt	2 bytes	The first allocation block in the volume, in 512-byte sectors.
drNxtCNID	4 bytes	The next unused catalog node ID (CNID).
drFreeBks	2 bytes	The number of unused allocation blocks.
drVN	28 bytes	The name of the volume. The first byte holds the length of the name, which cannot be more than 27 bytes.
drVolBkUp	4 bytes	The date and time of the last volume backup.
drVSeqNum	2 bytes	Volume backup sequence number, used internally.
drWrCnt	4 bytes	The number of times the volume has been written to.
drXTClpSiz	4 bytes	The clump size for the extents overflow file.
drCTClpSiz	4 bytes	The clump size for the catalog file.
drNmRtDirs	2 bytes	The number of folders in the root directory.
drFilCnt	4 bytes	The total number of files in the volume.
drDirCnt	4 bytes	The total number of directories in the volume.
drFndrInfo	32 bytes	An array of eight 32-bit values used by the Finder.
drEmbedSigWord	2 bytes	The two-byte signature of the embedded HFS Plus volume (for example, "H+").
drEmbedExtent	4 bytes	The extent descriptor describing the start of the embedded volume. The embedded volume must always be contiguous.

Continued

Table 4.4 Continued. Master Directory Block within an HFS Wrapper

Field	Size	Description
drXTFlSize	4 bytes	The size of the extents overflow file.
drXTExtRec	12 bytes	The extent record describing the size and location of the extents overflow file.
drCTFlSize	4 bytes	The size of the catalog file.
drCTExtRec	12 bytes	The extent record describing the size and location of the catalog file.

When created by the Mac OS, an HFS wrapper volume contains five files in its root folder, including:

- A Read Me file, sometimes called "Where_have_all_my_files_gone?", which explains that the files are not visible because the system does not have support for HFS Plus.

- A System file containing code to find and mount the contained HFS Plus volume and to continue booting from it. The data fork for the file is empty but its resource fork points to code needed to boot.

- An empty Finder file to prevent older Finder versions from disabling the volume as bootable.

- An empty Desktop DF file.

- A Desktop DB file for legacy reasons.

NOTE

Some of the fields found on a traditional HFS MDB changed meaning when used within an HFS wrapper. The *drEmbedSigWord* and *drEmbedExtent* fields in the HFS wrapper replace fields in the regular MDB format. A now deprecated document, at http://developer.apple.com/documentation/mac/Files/Files-102.html, contains additional information about the Master Directory Block found in the original HFS format.

Figure 4.5 shows the contents of an HFS Plus volume embedded within an HFS wrapper, as created by the **newfs_hfs** tool bundled with Mac OS X 10.5.

Figure 4.5 An HFS Plus Volume with an HFS Wrapper Mounted as HFS

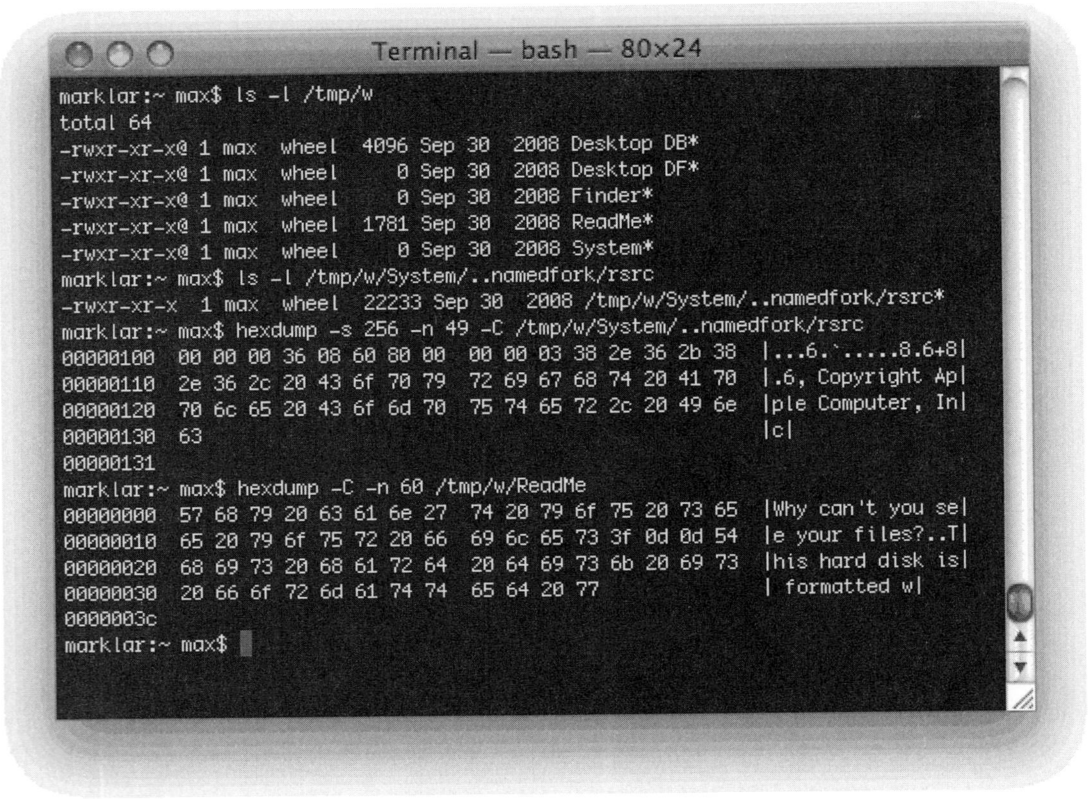

```
marklar:~ max$ ls -l /tmp/w
total 64
-rwxr-xr-x@ 1 max   wheel   4096 Sep 30   2008 Desktop DB*
-rwxr-xr-x@ 1 max   wheel      0 Sep 30   2008 Desktop DF*
-rwxr-xr-x@ 1 max   wheel      0 Sep 30   2008 Finder*
-rwxr-xr-x@ 1 max   wheel   1781 Sep 30   2008 ReadMe*
-rwxr-xr-x@ 1 max   wheel      0 Sep 30   2008 System*
marklar:~ max$ ls -l /tmp/w/System/..namedfork/rsrc
-rwxr-xr-x  1 max   wheel  22233 Sep 30   2008 /tmp/w/System/..namedfork/rsrc*
marklar:~ max$ hexdump -s 256 -n 49 -C /tmp/w/System/..namedfork/rsrc
00000100  00 00 00 36 08 60 80 00  00 00 03 38 2e 36 2b 38  |...6.`.....8.6+8|
00000110  2e 36 2c 20 43 6f 70 79  72 69 67 68 74 20 41 70  |.6, Copyright Ap|
00000120  70 6c 65 20 43 6f 6d 70  75 74 65 72 2c 20 49 6e  |ple Computer, In|
00000130  63                                                |c|
00000131
marklar:~ max$ hexdump -C -n 60 /tmp/w/ReadMe
00000000  57 68 79 20 63 61 6e 27  74 20 79 6f 75 20 73 65  |Why can't you se|
00000010  65 20 79 6f 75 72 20 66  69 6c 65 73 3f 0d 0d 54  |e your files?..T|
00000020  68 69 73 20 68 61 72 64  20 64 69 73 6b 20 69 73  |his hard disk is|
00000030  20 66 6f 72 6d 61 74 74  65 64 20 77              | formatted w|
0000003c
marklar:~ max$
```

The **hinfo** tool included in the accompanying DVD (see the "Inspecting a Real HFS Plus Volume with hinfo" sidebar in the "Volume Header" section) can parse and display the fields in the Master Directory Block of a volume with an HFS wrapper. Figure 4.6 shows sample output from running **hinfo** against a simple volume with the wrapper.

Figure 4.6 Using hinfo to Inspect an HFS Wrapper Header

Notice that *drFreeBks* is 0. This is because all the space in the volume is occupied by the embedded HFS Plus volume and marked as allocated to prevent any accidental overwrite or deletion when mounted as HFS. To prevent file system checking tools from complaining about the allocated space not being in use by any actual files, the embedded volume is also included in the bad block file, even though no blocks are really bad. In this example volume, **hinfo** reports that the embedded volume starts at offset 45,056, which is calculated by adding the starting offset (*drAlBlSt* x 512) to the embedded starting block times (*drEmbedExtent.startBlock* x *drAlBlkSiz*). In the example: 8 x 512 + 10 x 4,096 = 45,056.

TIP

To keep the embedded HFS Plus volume isolated from the wrapper, all offsets referenced within it are relative to its beginning. Using the numbers from the previous example, if the volume header for the embedded volume indicates that the allocation file starts at offset 4,096, the absolute offset from the beginning of the HFS wrapper volume would be 4,096 + 45,056.

HFSJ

The HFS Plus format allows for the use of an optional journal, to minimize the risk of file system corruption. Journaling file systems keep a log of changes in a journal file before committing them to the actual file system. When changes to the file system require multiple changes to the system's metadata (for example, copying a file may require creating new entries in several B*-trees), a system failure between changes may leave the file system in an inconsistent state. When journaling is enabled, all these related changes are grouped together in the journal before being written completely to their final location. If a system failure occurs before the changes are committed, they are simply ignored and the file system is left uncorrupted.

Setting a bit in the *attributes* field of the volume header enables journaling for an HFS Plus volume. The volume will then provide three additional data structures to keep track of the journal: the journal info block, the journal buffer, and the journal header. These structures are stored in the volume as regular files within the root folder. The journal info block is stored in the .journal_info_block file, with the header and buffer stored together in the .journal file. The file system implementation is supposed to hide the existence of these files from the user. The **hinfo** tool can reveal the existence of these files as it parses the catalog file directly:

```
$ ./hinfo.rb /dev/disk2s1 -c
Opening HFS+ volume at /dev/disk2s1
== Reading b*-tree from Catalog File at offset 8527872
- at node 3
- at node 2
  \- leaf node: Catalog Folder (parentID = 1, nodeName = 'sandbox')
  \- leaf node: Catalog Thread (parentID = 2, nodeName = '')
  \- leaf node: Catalog File (parentID = 2, nodeName =
  '.com.apple.timemachine.supported')
  \- leaf node: Catalog File (parentID = 2, nodeName = '.DS_Store')
  \- leaf node: Catalog Folder (parentID = 2, nodeName = '.fseventsd')
  \- leaf node: Catalog Folder (parentID = 2, nodeName = '.HFS+ Private
  Directory Data')
  \- leaf node: Catalog File (parentID = 2, nodeName = '.journal')
  \- leaf node: Catalog File (parentID = 2, nodeName = '.journal_info_block')
```

```
\- leaf node: Catalog Folder (parentID = 2, nodeName = '.TemporaryItems')
\- leaf node: Catalog Folder (parentID = 2, nodeName = '.Trashes')
\- leaf node: Catalog File (parentID = 2, nodeName = 'tiger')
\- leaf node: Catalog Folder (parentID = 2, nodeName = 'treehouse')
\- leaf node: Catalog File (parentID = 2, nodeName = 'TrigSolv.zip')
...
```

HFSX

HFSX defines extensions to the HFS Plus format. One such extension is case-sensitiveness for file and folder names. By default, HFS Plus preserves the case of file and folder names but performs comparisons in case-insensitive fashion. HFSX volumes can then treat case differences as name differences.

The signature for HFSX volumes is "HX" (or 0x4858 in hexadecimal), with a version number of 5.

Boot Blocks

The first 1,024 bytes of the volume are reserved to be used as boot blocks, which can contain information required at system startup. HFS Plus boot blocks are often not required by modern operating systems.

Startup File

HFS Plus supports a special startup file, which can be used as a replacement for traditional boot blocks or as a secondary boot loader. As with the other special files in HFS Plus, the startup file allows for storing large blocks of variable size. However, a startup file that occupies more than 8 extents, although technically supported by HFS Plus, would be hard to reconstruct upon system restart and, thus, its use is discouraged.

The startup file is not required to be present for the HFS Plus volume to be valid. When not required, the file's extent in the header will be empty.

Volume Header

Every HFS Plus volume contains a header describing its structure and contents. This header starts 1,024 bytes from the start of the volume and has 512 bytes of length. The structure of the HFS Plus volume header is described in Table 4.5.

Table 4.5 Volume Header Structure

Field	Size	Description
signature	2 bytes	The volume signature. "H+" in the case of HFS Plus, or "HX" in the case of HFSX.
version	2 bytes	The version of the format. Currently 4 for HFS Plus and 5 for HFSX.
attributes	4 bytes	Several volume attributes represented as individual bits. For example, bit 13 indicates whether the volume has a journal or not.
lastMountedVersion	4 bytes	A *creator code* identifying the software that last mounted the volume for writing. Example values are "10.0" by Mac OS X for non-journaled volumes and "HFSK" for journaled ones. If the volume was last mounted by fsck, this field would have a value of "fsck".
journalInfoBlock	4 bytes	The allocation block containing the *JournalInfoBlock* structure. Only valid if the volume has a journal as indicated by its attributes.
createDate	4 bytes	Volume creation date.
modifyDate	4 bytes	Volume modification date.
backupDate	4 bytes	The last time the volume was backed up.
checkedDate	4 bytes	The last time the volume was checked.
fileCount	4 bytes	The number of files on the volume, excluding special files.
folderCount	4 bytes	The number of folders in the volume, not including the root folder.
blockSize	4 bytes	The size, in bytes, of an allocation block.
totalBlocks	4 bytes	The total number of allocation blocks in the volume.
freeBlocks	4 bytes	The number of free allocation blocks in the volume.
nextAllocation	4 bytes	A hint to improve searching for free allocation blocks.
rsrcClumpSize	4 bytes	The size, in bytes, of the default clump size for resource forks.
dataClumpSize	4 bytes	The size, in bytes, of the default clump size for data forks.
nextCatalogID	4 bytes	The next unused catalog ID.

Continued

Table 4.5 Continued. Volume Header Structure

Field	Size	Description
writeCount	4 bytes	The number of times the volume has been mounted.
encodingsBitmap	8 bytes	A bitmap indicating the text encodings used in file and folder names.
finderInfo	32 bytes	An array of 32-bit attributes used by the Finder.
allocationFile	80 bytes	The fork data structure describing the location and size of the allocation file.
extentsFile	80 bytes	The fork data structure describing the location and size of the extents overflow file.
catalogFile	80 bytes	The fork data structure describing the location and size of the catalog file.
attributesFile	80 bytes	The fork data structure describing the location and size of the attributes file.
startupFile	80 bytes	The fork data structure describing the location and size of the startup file.

The starting location of each special file can be computed by multiplying *blockSize* by the starting block of the first extent in the fork data structure of the file. The volume header includes a fork data structure for each one of the special files that contain important metadata about the file system, as each special file can be located anywhere within the volume.

Tools & Traps…

Inspecting a Real HFS Plus Volume with hinfo

To illustrate some of the key structures discussed in this chapter, the author has put together a simple tool called **hinfo** that can open an HFS Plus volume and navigate its contents.

Continued

The tool can be found on the DVD. It is written in the Ruby language, which makes its source instantly available to you for review. It requires **Ruby** 1.8.6 with **RubyGems,** and the **bindata** gem installed. If you are running OS X 10.5, you already have most of its dependencies and are only missing the **bindata** gem. To install it, type the following command in a terminal window:

```
$ sudo gem install bindata
```

A simple HFS Plus volume for testing purposes can be created with standard Mac OS X tools. To create and mount an HFS Plus volume for testing, type the following commands in a terminal window:

```
$ hdiutil create -size 16 m -fs HFSJ -volname sandbox sandbox.dmg
.............................................................
created: /Users/max/sandbox.dmg
$ hdiutil attach -nomount sandbox.dmg
/dev/disk1        GUID_partition_scheme
/dev/disk1s1      Apple_HFS
```

Note that we attach the image to obtain a valid device file, but we don't mount it. In this way we can access the volume data stored in the disk image as if it were a physical device, without having to worry about the DMG format. Make a note of the assigned device file /dev/disk1s1 in the example above. The **hinfo** tool can now inspect the volume in the device:

```
$ ./hinfo.rb /dev/disk1s1 -i | head
Opening HFS+ volume at /dev/disk1s1
Volume Header
   - signature          = H+
   - version            = 4
   - attributes         = 00000000000000000010000100000000
   - lastMountedVersion = HFSJ
   - journalInfoBlock   = 2
   - createDate         = Tue Sep 30 02:15:26 -0400 2008
   - modifyDate         = Tue Sep 30 08:24:59 -0400 2008
   - backupDate         = Fri Jan 01 00:00:00 -0500 1904
```

Keep in mind that **hinfo** was written to help you interact with some of the concepts discussed in this chapter on your own, and it is not intended to be a complete HFS Plus inspection tool. It will most certainly fail to understand otherwise normal HFS Plus volumes you may run against it.

By utilizing the **hinfo** tool from the DVD (see sidebar) we can inspect the actual volume header of a sample volume:

```
$ ./hinfo.rb /dev/disk1s1 -i
Opening HFS+ volume at /dev/disk1s1
Volume Header
  - signature          = H+
  - version            = 4
  - attributes         = 00000000000000000010000100000000
  - lastMountedVersion = HFSJ
  - journalInfoBlock   = 2
  - createDate         = Tue Sep 30 02:15:26 -0400 2008
  - modifyDate         = Tue Sep 30 08:24:59 -0400 2008
  - backupDate         = Fri Jan 01 00:00:00 -0500 1904
  - checkedDate        = Tue Sep 30 06:15:26 -0400 2008
  - fileCount          = 11
  - folderCount        = 8
  - blockSize          = 4096
  - totalBlocks        = 4086
  - freeBlocks         = 1862
  - nextAllocation     = 2532
  - rsrcClumpSize      = 65536
  - dataClumpSize      = 65536
  - nextCatalogID      = 44
  - writeCount         = 60
  - encodingsBitmap    = 00000000000000000000000000000001
  - finderInfo = 0000000000000000000000000000000, 00000000000000000000000000000000,
00000000000000000000000000000000, 00000000000000000000000000000000, 000000000000000
0000000000000000, 00000000000000000000000000000000, 11101111101010110010011011111
00, 11110111111010101011011100100110
Allocation File
        - logicalSize  = 4096
        - clumpSize    = 4096
        - totalBlocks  = 1
        - extents
          - startBlock = 1
          - blockCount = 1
Extents File
        - logicalSize  = 126976
        - clumpSize    = 126976
        - totalBlocks  = 31
```

```
      - extents
         - startBlock = 2051
         - blockCount = 31
Catalog File
         - logicalSize = 126976
         - clumpSize = 126976
         - totalBlocks = 31
         - extents
            - startBlock = 2082
            - blockCount = 31
Attributes File
         - logicalSize = 122880
         - totalBlocks = 30
         - extents
            - startBlock = 2423
            - blockCount = 30
Startup File
         - logicalSize = 0
         - clumpSize = 0
         - totalBlocks = 0
```

From the output of **hinfo** it is possible to see important volume information, including the format and version of the volume, the allocation block size (4,096), and information about the first extents for the five special files. This volume has no startup file, as evidenced by its fork data structure having a *logicalSize* size of 0. By multiplying the allocation block size by the *startBlock* of a file's first extent, we can obtain the byte offset of the file in the volume. For example, the attributes file for this volume is contained in one single contiguous extent, starting at offset 9,924,608 (4,096 x 2,423), and has 122,880 bytes in size.

Alternate Volume Header

To allow for the recovery of a volume with a corrupted header, a copy of the volume header is stored starting at 1,024 bytes from the end of the volume. This header copy is called the alternate volume header and is generally only used by disk repair tools.

TIP

When inspecting a corrupted disk or a disk that has been partially deleted, keep in mind that this copy of the header exists at the end of the volume, as it may prove useful in data recovery.

Allocation File

The allocation file is used by HFS Plus to keep track of used and unused allocation blocks. The format of the file is a bitmap containing one bit for every available allocation block in the volume. When a bit is set it means that its associated block is used. When a bit is not set it means it is empty and available for use.

> **NOTE**
>
> The complete volume is represented in the allocation file, including the first 1,024 bytes and the last 512. These reserved areas along with the header and the areas occupied by special files are marked as used in the allocation file.

The *—a* option of the **hinfo** tool can be used to inspect a volume's allocation file:

```
$ ./hinfo.rb -a 50 /dev/disk1s1
Opening HFS+ volume at /dev/disk1s1
== Showing first 50 bytes of Allocation File at offset 4096
1111111111111111111111111111111111111111111111111111111111111111111111111111111111
1111111111111111111111111111111111111111111111111111111111111111111111111111111111
1111111111111111111111111111111111111111111111111111111111111111111111111111111111
1111111111111111111111111111111111111111111111111111111111111111111111111111111111
11111111111111111111111111111111111111111111111111111111111111111
```

The volume bitmap is the HFS equivalent to the allocation file in HFS Plus, and has largely the same format. The *drVBMSt* field within the Master Directory Block determines the location of the volume bitmap within an HFS volume. Refer to the "HFS Wrapper" section for a detailed description of the HFS MDR structure.

B*-trees

Three of the special files found in an HFS Plus volume contain a special tree-like structure called a B*-tree. This structure allows for fast searches based on an arbitrary key, which can be a string (as in a file or folder name) or a number (as in a catalog node ID). B*-trees are built in a way so that they stay "balanced" as new nodes are inserted and old ones deleted. This perpetual balanced state guarantees that key searches will be as short as possible. Each B*-tree is composed of nodes of fixed-size, each node containing a number of records specific to each node type. These records can be accessed by navigating the list of record offsets at the end of every node. Records offsets are stored in reverse order as 16-bit integers denoting the number of bytes, from the beginning of the node where the record starts. Figure 4.7 shows the layout of a sample B*-tree node.

Figure 4.7 B*-tree Node Structure

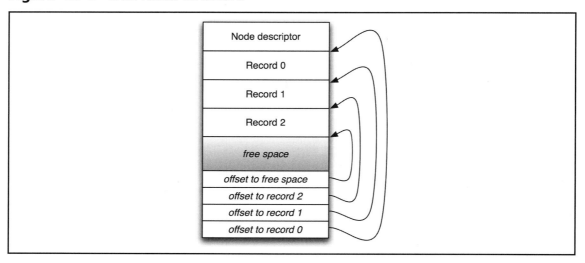

Each node begins with a 14-byte node descriptor, whose fields are described in Table 4.6.

Table 4.6 Structure of a Node Descriptor

Field	Size	Description
fLink	4 bytes	The next node of this type.
bLink	4 bytes	The previous node of this type.
kind	1 byte	The type of node. It can take one of four values:
		■ −1, for Leaf nodes
		■ 0, for Index nodes
		■ 1, for Header nodes
		■ 2, for Map nodes
height	1 byte	The depth of this node within the tree.
numRecords	2 bytes	The number of records in this node.
reserved	2 bytes	Reserved.

The very first node in a B*-tree is a header node (node number 0 with *kind* 0), which contains important information about the tree, such as the location of the root node, the node size, and the maximum size of the key used for searching. The header node contains header, user data, and map records, with the header record being the most important of the three in order to navigate the tree. Table 4.7 illustrates the structure of a header record.

Table 4.7 Structure of a Header Record

Field	Size	Description
treeDepth	2 bytes	The depth of the B*-tree.
rootNode	4 bytes	The root node's number. The root node can be an index or a leaf node, depending on the number of nodes in the tree.
leafRecords	4 bytes	The total number of records contained in all leaf nodes.
firstLeafNode	4 bytes	The first leaf node's number.
lastLeafNode	4 bytes	The last leaf node's number.
nodeSize	2 bytes	The side in bytes of a node in the tree.
maxKeyLength	2 bytes	The maximum size in bytes of a key.
totalNodes	4 bytes	The total number of nodes in the tree.
freeNodes	4 bytes	The number of free nodes in the tree.
reserved	2 bytes	Reserved.
clumpSize	4 bytes	Ignored in HFS Plus, replaced by the *clumpSize* field in the related fork data structure.
btreeType	1 byte	0 for B*-trees in special files, 128 for user B*-trees, such as the hot file B*-tree.
keyCompareType	1 byte	0xCF to indicate case-insensitive key comparison and 0xBC for case-sensitive. Only HFSX volumes honor this field.
attributes	4 bytes	Bit mask for tree-specific attributes. The most important bits are: ■ 1 indicates that the tree was not closed properly. ■ 2 indicates that they *keyLength* field in nodes is 16-bits long, or 8-bit long if not set. ■ 4 indicates that keys in index nodes as many bytes as specified in their *keyLength* fields or *maxKeyLength* if not set.
reserved	64 bytes	Reserved.

From the header record it is possible to find the root node of the tree. This root node can be an index node or a leaf node. Both node types start with *keyLength*, which can be 8-bit or 16-bit depending on the *attributes* field in the header record, followed by the actual *key*, and the record data. Index nodes contain pointers to other nodes in the tree, while leaf nodes contain records with the actual data stored in the tree. The index records are used to find the leaf nodes containing the information we are looking for using a key.

Catalog File

The catalog file is the B*-tree that stores the actual hierarchy of files and folders in the volume. Every file and folder in the catalog file has a unique identifier called the catalog node ID (CNID). The CNID is a 32-bit number, which can take any value as long as it doesn't repeat. Apple defines a set of reserved CNIDs used for important files in a volume (see Table 4.8).

Table 4.8 Reserved Catalog Node IDs

CNID	Description
1	The *parentID* of the root folder.
2	The *folderID* of the root folder.
3	The extents overflow file.
4	The catalog file.
5	The bad block file.
6	The allocation file.
7	The startup file.
8	The attributes file.
14	The repair catalog file, used by **fsck_hfs** when repairing a volume.
15	The bogus extent file, used temporarily during *ExchangeFiles* operations.
16	The first available CNID for files and folders.

Nodes in the catalog B*-tree can include four different types of data records:

- A folder record, which describes a particular folder in the volume.

- A file record, which describes a particular file in the volume.

- A folder thread record, which links a folder with its parent and provides the means to search for folders by their CNID.

- A file thread record, which links a file with its parent folder and provides the means to search for files by their CNID.

As mentioned in the previous section, a key precedes each record. Within the catalog file, keys follow the structure described in Table 4.9.

Table 4.9 CatalogKey Structure

Field	Size	Description
keyLength	2 bytes	The length of the key, not including the *keyLength* field itself.
parentID	4 bytes	The CNID of the parent.
nodeName	Variable	The Unicode representation of the node's name, preceded by a 16-bit length. Empty for thread records.

The **hinfo** tool can be used to navigate the catalog file in simple HFS Plus volumes with its *–c* switch:

```
$ ./hinfo.rb /dev/disk2s1 -c
Opening HFS+ volume at /dev/disk2s1
== Reading b*-tree from Catalog File at offset 8527872
- at node 3
- at node 2
  \- leaf node: Catalog Folder (parentID = 1, nodeName = 'sandbox')
  \- leaf node: Catalog Thread (parentID = 2, nodeName = '')
  \- leaf node: Catalog File (parentID = 2, nodeName = '.com.apple.timemachine.
  supported')
  \- leaf node: Catalog File (parentID = 2, nodeName = '.DS_Store')
  \- leaf node: Catalog Folder (parentID = 2, nodeName = '.fseventsd')
  \- leaf node: Catalog Folder (parentID = 2, nodeName = '.HFS+ Private
  Directory Data')
  \- leaf node: Catalog File (parentID = 2, nodeName = '.journal')
  \- leaf node: Catalog File (parentID = 2, nodeName = '.journal_info_block')
  \- leaf node: Catalog Folder (parentID = 2, nodeName = '.TemporaryItems')
  \- leaf node: Catalog Folder (parentID = 2, nodeName = '.Trashes')
  \- leaf node: Catalog File (parentID = 2, nodeName = 'tiger')
  \- leaf node: Catalog Folder (parentID = 2, nodeName = 'treehouse')
  \- leaf node: Catalog File (parentID = 2, nodeName = 'TrigSolv.zip')
  \- leaf node: Catalog Folder (parentID = 2, nodeName = 'HFS+ Private Data')
  \- leaf node: Catalog Thread (parentID = 16, nodeName = '')
  \- pntr node: nodenumber = 2
- at node 1
  \- leaf node: Catalog Thread (parentID = 17, nodeName = '')
  \- leaf node: Catalog Thread (parentID = 18, nodeName = '')
  \- leaf node: Catalog Thread (parentID = 19, nodeName = '')
```

```
\- leaf node: Catalog Thread (parentID = 20, nodeName = '')
\- leaf node: Catalog Thread (parentID = 21, nodeName = '')
\- leaf node: Catalog File (parentID = 21, nodeName = '0000000005ab37be')
\- leaf node: Catalog File (parentID = 21, nodeName = '0000000005ab3f0e')
\- leaf node: Catalog File (parentID = 21, nodeName = '0000000005ab6b64')
\- leaf node: Catalog File (parentID = 21, nodeName = 'fseventsd-uuid')
\- leaf node: Catalog Thread (parentID = 22, nodeName = '')
\- leaf node: Catalog Thread (parentID = 24, nodeName = '')
\- leaf node: Catalog Thread (parentID = 25, nodeName = '')
\- leaf node: Catalog Thread (parentID = 31, nodeName = '')
\- leaf node: Catalog Thread (parentID = 32, nodeName = '')
\- leaf node: Catalog File (parentID = 32, nodeName = 'raven')
\- leaf node: Catalog Thread (parentID = 33, nodeName = '')
\- leaf node: Catalog Thread (parentID = 35, nodeName = '')
\- leaf node: Catalog Thread (parentID = 36, nodeName = '')
\- leaf node: Catalog Folder (parentID = 36, nodeName = 'folders.502')
\- leaf node: Catalog Thread (parentID = 37, nodeName = '')
\- leaf node: Catalog Folder (parentID = 37, nodeName = 'TemporaryItems')
\- leaf node: Catalog Thread (parentID = 38, nodeName = '')
\- leaf node: Catalog Thread (parentID = 41, nodeName = '')
\- leaf node: Catalog Thread (parentID = 42, nodeName = '')
\- leaf node: Catalog Thread (parentID = 43, nodeName = '')
\- pntr node: nodenumber = 1
```

The file record for a given file includes information about the file's characteristics including extent information for its data and resource forks. Once this record is found, it is possible to then use its extent records along with the block size in the volume header to locate the actual file offset of the data fork. The **hinfo** tool can perform a file search and display the contents of the file record, along with the first 128 bytes of its data fork when the −*f* switch is specified, as illustrated in Figure 4.8.

Figure 4.8 Searching the Catalog File for a Filename

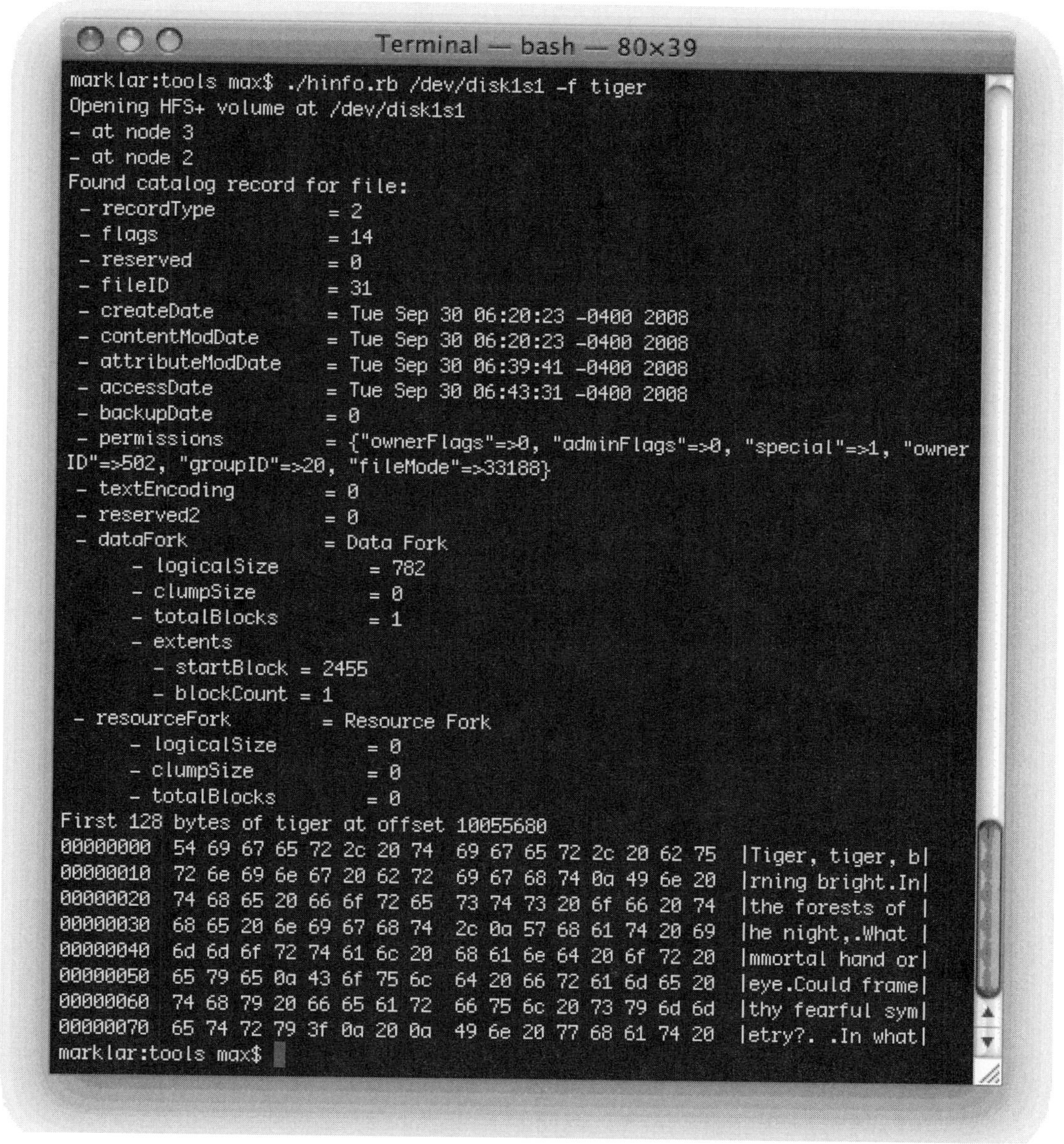

```
marklar:tools max$ ./hinfo.rb /dev/disk1s1 -f tiger
Opening HFS+ volume at /dev/disk1s1
- at node 3
- at node 2
Found catalog record for file:
  - recordType        = 2
  - flags             = 14
  - reserved          = 0
  - fileID            = 31
  - createDate        = Tue Sep 30 06:20:23 -0400 2008
  - contentModDate    = Tue Sep 30 06:20:23 -0400 2008
  - attributeModDate  = Tue Sep 30 06:39:41 -0400 2008
  - accessDate        = Tue Sep 30 06:43:31 -0400 2008
  - backupDate        = 0
  - permissions       = {"ownerFlags"=>0, "adminFlags"=>0, "special"=>1, "owner
ID"=>502, "groupID"=>20, "fileMode"=>33188}
  - textEncoding      = 0
  - reserved2         = 0
  - dataFork          = Data Fork
      - logicalSize      = 782
      - clumpSize        = 0
      - totalBlocks      = 1
      - extents
        - startBlock = 2455
        - blockCount = 1
  - resourceFork      = Resource Fork
      - logicalSize      = 0
      - clumpSize        = 0
      - totalBlocks      = 0
First 128 bytes of tiger at offset 10055680
00000000  54 69 67 65 72 2c 20 74  69 67 65 72 2c 20 62 75  |Tiger, tiger, bu|
00000010  72 6e 69 6e 67 20 62 72  69 67 68 74 0a 49 6e 20  |rning bright.In |
00000020  74 68 65 20 66 6f 72 65  73 74 73 20 6f 66 20 74  |the forests of t|
00000030  68 65 20 6e 69 67 68 74  2c 0a 57 68 61 74 20 69  |he night,.What i|
00000040  6d 6d 6f 72 74 61 6c 20  68 61 6e 64 20 6f 72 20  |mmortal hand or |
00000050  65 79 65 0a 43 6f 75 6c  64 20 66 72 61 6d 65 20  |eye.Could frame |
00000060  74 68 79 20 66 65 61 72  66 75 6c 20 73 79 6d 6d  |thy fearful symm|
00000070  65 74 72 79 3f 0a 20 0a  49 6e 20 77 68 61 74 20  |etry?. .In what |
marklar:tools max$
```

Tools & Traps...

Creating an HFS Plus Volume for Testing

Sometimes the best way to learn a new topic is to get our hands dirty with it. As mentioned before, the **hinfo** tool that accompanies this book can be used to inspect the contents of an HFS Plus volume and see all these structures in action. But having access to simple HFS Plus volumes we can play with may not be as straightforward. Fortunately, Mac OS X comes bundled with a set of useful tools that can be used to create simple HFS Plus volumes for our tests. Here's how you can create your own.

The **hdiutil** tool can be used to create disk images in various formats and sizes. To create a journaled 16 Mb HFS Plus volume, use the following command:

```
$ hdiutil create -size 16m -fs HFSJ -volname sandbox
sandbox.dmg.............................................................
created: /private/tmp/sandbox.dmg
```

The command created a new HFSJ volume within a disk image file in the /tmp folder. Disk images are very useful for testing: they contain fully-fledged file systems as a real device would; yet they can be stored as regular files. The newly created disk image can be mounted by issuing the following command:

```
$ hdiutil attach sandbox.dmg
/dev/disk3      GUID_partition_scheme
/dev/disk3s1  Apple_HFS /Volumes/sandbox
```

We can now create as many files and folders as desired for our testing by writing to /Volumes/sandbox. When we are done, we can detach from the image and analyze the file system directly via its device object. To create a device object associated with an image, run the following command:

```
$ hdiutil detach /Volumes/sandbox
"disk3" unmounted.
'disk3' ejected.
$ hdiutil attach -nomount sandbox.dmg
/dev/disk3      GUID_partition_scheme
/dev/disk3s1  Apple_HFS
```

The last device file can now be used as if it were an HFS Plus partition on a physical disk. For example, here's how you can use the **hexdump** tool to dump the first 64 bytes of the volume header for the image:

Continued

```
$ hexdump -s1024 -n64 /dev/disk3s1
00000400 48 2b 00 04 00 00 21 00  48 46 53 4a 00 00 00 02
00000410 c5 08 32 19 c5 08 6a 5a  00 00 00 00 c5 08 6a 59
00000420 00 00 00 02 00 00 00 02  00 00 10 00 00 00 0f f6
00000430 00 00 07 96 00 00 09 77  00 01 00 00 00 01 00 00
00000440
```

Extents Overflow File

As we've seen in the "B*-Tree" section, each file has an associated extent record, which references the first eight contiguous allocation blocks for each one of its forks. When more than eight extents are required, the extra extents are stored in the extents overflow file. Also a B*-tree, the extents overflow file uses an extent key structure as key, as described in Table 4.10.

Table 4.10 The Extent Key Structure

Field	Size	Description
keyLength	2 bytes	The length of the key, not including the keyLength field itself.
forkType	1 byte	The type of fork for this record. 0 for data forks or 255 for resource forks.
pad	1 byte	Padding.
fileID	4 bytes	The catalog node ID (CNID) of the file.
startBlock	4 bytes	The offset into the fork for the first extent described by this record, in allocation blocks.

If the volume is very fragmented, multiple extent key structures for the same file can be linked together in the correct order by using the *startBlock* field of the key record. The data records within the B*-tree for this file are of the type *extent record*. (An array of eight extent descriptors are covered in Table 4.1.) Each one of these records can reference eight additional extents for the particular fork.

Entries in the extents overflow file referencing the reserved CNID 5 constitute the bad blocks file. This file is not a regular file per-se, but a collection of extents that demark all the bad blocks within the volume. These blocks are also marked as unavailable within the allocation file, as file system verification tools will ensure that all allocated space is assigned to a file or produce errors otherwise.

Attributes File

The attributes file allows for the implementation of named forks within an HFS Plus volume. A named fork associates a data stream with a particular file or folder. Starting with Mac OS X 10.4, named forks are used for storing extended attributes, as described in the "Forks" section of this chapter.

Extended attributes are implemented as name-value pairs, where names follow the same rules as file names (fully decomposed Unicode characters in canonical order), and values can be arbitrary data. Table 4.11 describes the *HFSPlusAttrKey* used to store keys in this B*-tree.

Table 4.11 The HFSPlusAttrKey Structure

Field	Size	Description
keyLength	2 bytes	The length of the key, not including the *keyLength* field itself.
pad	2 bytes	Padding.
fileID	4 bytes	The catalog node ID (CNID) of the file associated with the attribute.
startBlock	4 bytes	The first allocation block number for extents.
attrNameLen	2 bytes	The number of Unicode characters in the attribute name.
attrName	254 bytes	The attribute name in fully decomposed Unicode characters in canonical order.

To optimize the storage of small and medium-size attributes, the attributes file B*-tree supports three different data records for its leaf nodes. An *HFSPlusAttrData* (described in Table 4.12) with *recordType* 0x10 is used for small attributes whose values can be stored in-line in the same record.

Table 4.12 The HFSPlusAttrData Structure

Field	Size	Description
recordType	4 bytes	0x10 for *HFSPlusAttrData* records.
reserved	8 bytes	Reserved.
attrSize	4 bytes	The size of the attribute data in bytes.
attrData	Variable	The attribute's value.

An *HFSPlusAttrForkData* structure (described in Table 4.13) is used for larger attributes. The data stream for these attributes can be stored across multiple extents.

Table 4.13 The HFSPlusAttrForkData Structure

Field	Size	Description
recordType	4 bytes	0x20 for *HFSPlusAttrForkData* records.
reserved	4 bytes	Reserved.
theFork	80 bytes	The fork data structure describing the size and location of the attribute's data stream.

Finally, an *HFSPlusAttrExtents* structure (described in Table 4.14) is used for overflow extents for large, fragmented attributes. Each one of these records references eight additional extents containing attribute data.

Table 4.14 The HFSPlusAttrExtents Structure

Field	Size	Description
recordType	4 bytes	0x30 for *HFSPlusAttrExtents* records.
Reserved	4 bytes	Reserved.
Extents	64 bytes	The extent descriptor, describing eight additional overflow extents for the fork.

Summary

In this chapter we've covered the basic components of HFS Plus, along with details on the most important data structures in use by the format. In combination with standard tools available in Mac OS X, and the **hinfo** tool accompanying this chapter, these details should help you get started with examining HFS and HFS Plus volumes in use by Apple computers and devices.

Solutions Fast Track

HFS Plus Volumes

- ☑ The HFS Plus format is an extension of the HFS format.
- ☑ Allocation blocks are the basic allocation unit of the file system.
- ☑ The format defines a header along with a series of special files to manage its structure.
- ☑ Files and folders can have multiple data streams associated with them, called *forks*.
- ☑ HFS Plus volumes can be wrapped in an HFS wrapper to allow older systems to read them.

Boot Blocks

- ☑ The first 1,024 bytes of a volume are reserved to be used as boot blocks.
- ☑ A special file called startup file can be used as a replacement for the traditional boot blocks.
- ☑ Non-bootable volumes may have blank boot blocks and an empty startup file.

Volume Header

- ☑ Every HFS Plus volume has a standard header at offset 1,024.
- ☑ The header defines important information, such as the format version, the allocation block size, and the location of all the special files.
- ☑ A copy of the volume header, called the alternate volume header can be found starting at 1,024 bytes from the end of the volume.

Allocation File

- ☑ The allocation file keeps track of used and unused allocation blocks in the volume.
- ☑ The file is a bitmap where every bit represents an allocation block.
- ☑ The allocation file has a bit for every block in the volume, including the reserved sectors at the start and the end.

B*-trees

☑   Three of the five special files in an HFS Plus volume have a B*-tree structure, which allows for fast searches on arbitrary keys.

☑   The catalog file contains the file and folder hierarchy and information to locate every file and folder in the volume.

☑   The extents overflow file contains overflow extents for fragmented files and the bad blocks file.

☑   The attributes file allows for the implementation of named forks for files and folders, which in turn are used to implement extended attributes.

Frequently Asked Questions

Q: What is HFS Plus?

A: HFS Plus (or HFS+) is a file system developed by Apple for its family of computers running Mac OS.

Q: What is a special file?

A: Special files are otherwise regular files used by the HFS Plus format to manage the file system.

Q: What is the HFSJ format?

A: HFSJ is the HFS Plus with journaling enabled.

Q: What is the HFSX format?

A: HFSX is HFS Plus extended, currently used to support case-sensitiveness for file and folder names.

Q: What is a fork?

A: A fork is a data stream associated with a file or folder. Most files and folders have at least two forks: the data fork and the resource fork.

Q: What are extended attributes and how can I access them?

A: Extended attributes are name-value pairs associated with a particular file or folder. They can be accessed in a somewhat limited fashion using the **xattr** command line tool.

Q: What is a B*-tree?

A: B*-trees are a data structure composed of balanced trees used by HFS Plus to provide efficiency when searching for files or file metadata.

Chapter 5

FileVault

Solutions in this chapter:

- **FileVault Overview**
- **Acquiring an Unlocked FileVault**
- **Decrypting a Locked FileVault**

☑ **Summary**

☑ **Solutions Fast Track**

☑ **Frequently Asked Questions**

Introduction

Securing data has become one of the biggest concerns among home and corporate computer users. Not too long ago we would transfer files by carrying our most precious financial information on a 3.5-inch floppy disk in a shirt pocket or purse. Some referred to this method of transfer as "sneaker net." That disk offered no protection against data theft. Many times, we accepted a password-protected Excel file to be good enough security. With today's tools, such as AccessData's Password Recovery Toolkit, a simple password such as the one we used for our Excel spreadsheets can be cracked in seconds! In a worst-case scenario, a file offering password protection may still have its raw contents viewable by a separate application, defeating the password altogether. Today, we need solutions to data theft that protect not just a single file, but also our entire realm of personal information. We don't leave our home unlocked with the doors wide open, and lock only the jewelry box sitting on the dresser! Homeowners know that it's a great idea to close the door to their home and lock it when they leave. This is the same idea behind implementing security for our data using encryption.

Encryption is the answer to keeping prying eyes away from your most precious data while you are away, yet easily allowing you access to the data you need when you are there. Apply this concept to the personal computer. If you are sitting at your laptop, you should be able to access all of your data. That is a very simple concept and a computer has always allowed this to happen. If you are away from your laptop, there should be a mechanism to guard against others accessing your data in any useful manner, even if they gain physical control of the machine! This idea is new to the desktop operating system world. In the past, to offer this level of protection required more processing power than most desktop or laptop computers could offer. This is not true today. You now have options for files and folders, user home directories, and entire hard disks to be encrypted. Each of these offers a new level of protection to your data that keeps prying eyes away. Encryption occurs by applying a mathematical equation to the digital data that needs to be secured in combination with a key that only the user should know. When the data is to be decrypted, the user supplies the key; the reverse calculation is completed on the digital data, and the result is the original data, intact. Of course, I have just greatly simplified encryption in this sentence, but the concept holds true.

Microsoft offers encryption at the file and folder levels in Windows XP with the Encrypted File System (EFS), and introduced whole-volume encryption with Windows Vista with its BitLocker encryption technology. Third-party products are also available that offer file-level through whole-disk encryption, with TrueCrypt, dm-crypt, and Loop-AES.

When it comes to the Macintosh, Apple decided to use User Home folder encryption. Apple's choice comes in the form of FileVault. In this chapter, we will focus on how FileVault functions, how to deal with FileVault once you know it is in use, and what you can do once you have been locked out.

FileVault Overview

FileVault, which has been around since OS X Version 10.3 (Panther), is Apple's proprietary name for its encryption answer to data theft. FileVault uses Advanced Encryption Standard (AES) 128-bit encryption for its security. This is the "mathematical equation" through which the data is run in order to encrypt and decrypt the data, and is considered a very secure encryption standard with no known flaws. FileVault is enabled for individual users, not the entire disk. This means a Macintosh with two users may have one with an encrypted Home folder and one with an open Home folder. Figure 5.1 shows how FileVault is initially activated on a Mac running OS X 10.5.

Figure 5.1 FileVault System Preference Window

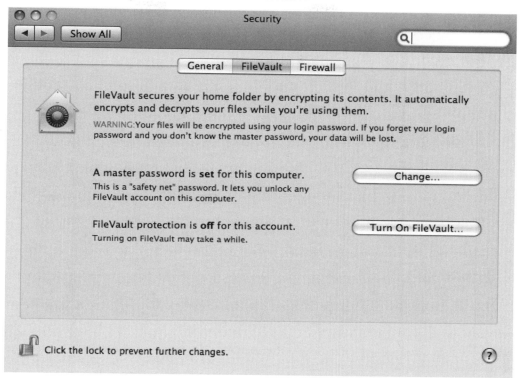

Figure 5.1 shows the System Preference window where an administrator can configure FileVault or a user can enable FileVault for his or her own account (with administrator assistance). Let's discuss each option. First, the *"Master Password* is an extremely important concept to understand on a Mac. You cannot enable FileVault until you set a Master Password, and for good reason: The Master Password is one of two passwords that are used during the encryption process in creating a user's FileVaulted Home folder. Second, to activate FileVault for this user you need to click **Turn On FileVault**. When you click this button, a warning dialog is presented, as shown in Figure 5.2.

Figure 5.2 FileVault Warning Dialog

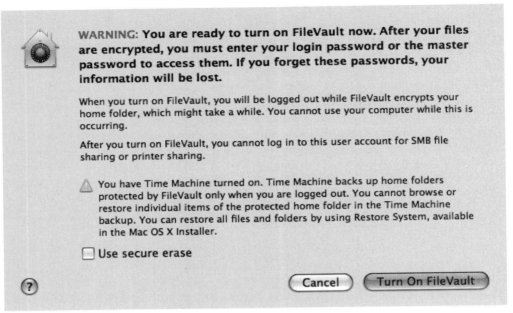

Figure 5.2 shows a significant warning to the user, that also has meaning to us as examiners. Four items stand out as noteworthy to keep in mind:

- First, FileVault allows for two passwords to access the encrypted data: the user's password and the Master Password. The Master Password does *not* provide direct access to unencrypting the data, though. It is used in changing a password, not in directly decrypting the data.

- Second, any account with FileVault enabled will not be using Server Message Block (SMB) (Windows) file sharing.

- Third, there is a significant change in the way Time Machine functions with FileVault enabled.

- Fourth, there is a secure erase option to securely delete the user's entire Home folder after it is placed into FileVault and encrypted.

Let's discuss each point, as they are significant in your understanding exactly how FileVault works. The first point deals with the encryption process and the keys that are available to decrypt the data. FileVault offers two sets of keys to unlock the data: one to the user who owns the data, and one to the Master Password holder. The user is an obvious choice to hold a set of keys, but the Master Password holder is one to explore a bit more.

On a Mac OS X system, there are administrators, or users with privileges to almost anything on the system. There is also a single user named "root" that has privileges to do anything. The system engineers at Apple realized that it is possible to have multiple administrators on a Mac system. It would be a security flaw if all of these administrators were also Master Password holders. Similarly, even the root user is not the Master Password holder. In fact, the Master Password is a separate password, devoid of any account, that is entrusted to someone in the event that a recovery needs to take place. This person does not need to be a Macintosh user at all! The Master Password holder simply needs to know the password and be able to produce it when the Macintosh asks for it during a recovery. We will discuss how the Home folder is encrypted later in this section.

Next, it's noteworthy that with FileVault in use, Windows SMB file sharing and printer sharing will not be available. This is excellent to note for any case as one less possible method of file transmission when you know FileVault has been enabled. It would be impossible to connect to this user's Home folder via Windows SMB and copy a file if FileVault is enabled.

The next point concerns Time Machine and FileVault, a subject we will cover in detail in Chapter 6. But for now, it's important to note that when a user enables FileVault the warning dialog in Figure 5.2 is stating that Time Machine will not act as a simple, single file recovery utility. Time Machine will begin to back up the user's Home folder only after the user logs out. This is a significant change in functionality. Again, Chapter 6 will detail these changes in greater depth.

The last point to understand is the secure erase option. FileVault creates a secure user Home folder by creating either a *sparseimage* or a *sparsebundle*, depending on the version of Mac OS X that is running. Each of these is similar to a Disk Image or DMG, just like the RonaldCarter.DMG that we have distributed with this book. When the operating system creates the Disk Image for the new user Home folder, it copies the entire current User Home folder into the Disk Image. The secure erase option offers the user the ability to securely delete all remnants of the old Home folder that was copied into the Disk Image so that no recovery utilities can locate sensitive data.

NOTE

DMG is a file format that Apple has used as a means of distributing files easily. A Disk Image is a virtual disk that acts just like a real disk. You can mount it on the Desktop, copy files to and from it, and eject it when you're finished. The latest form of the Disk Image file is composed of a series of files (*bands*) and is called a *sparsebundle*. A sparsebundle still functions as a single disk on the Desktop. Disk Utility is the application that can create and customize various Disk Image file types.

Creating a FileVault user Home folder is a process that is similar to creating a Disk Image, with a few small changes. FileVault uses a sparseimage with Mac OS X 10.3 and 10.4 or a sparsebundle with Mac OS X 10.5 for the Disk Image type. A sparseimage is a Disk Image file that can grow as needed, which means you do not have to allocate space upfront for it. As an example, if a user Home folder is 5GB when FileVault is enabled, a sparseimage is created to hold the 5GB of data. If the user adds additional files, the size of the sparseimage will grow to meet the user's needs. A sparsebundle is a Disk Image folder that functions as a single file. A sparsebundle folder is composed of several additional folders and files called "bands". A sparsebundle will grow just like a sparseimage, but it has several efficiency advantages because of the banding. Figures 5.3 and 5.4 show how the sparseimage and sparsebundle look from the Finder and the Terminal.

Figure 5.3 Sparseimage and Sparsebundle from the Finder

In Figure 5.3, notice the two Disk Images and how they appear as a single icon, giving the appearance that each is a single file. Each Disk Image has been named to match its type, but the file extension is given by the Macintosh when the Disk Images are created. These images were created using the Disk Utility application. Later in this section, we will look at the FileVault Disk Image that is created and how it has a slight difference.

Figure 5.4 Sparseimage and Sparsebundle from the Terminal

```
iMac-Aluminum:Examples moof$ ls -al
total 12296
drwxr-xr-x  4 moof  moof      136 Oct  1 22:23 .
drwxr-xr-x  7 moof  moof      238 Oct  1 22:25 ..
drwxr-xr-x@ 6 moof  moof      204 Oct  1 22:22 sparsebundle.sparsebundle
-rw-r--r--  1 moof  moof  6295552 Oct  1 22:22 sparseimage.sparseimage
iMac-Aluminum:Examples moof$
```

Figure 5.4 again shows the Disk Image files, but this time with differences. The first notable difference is the UNIX notation of *d* for *directory* on the *sparsebundle.sparsebundle*. The second notable difference is the @ at the end of the UNIX properties indicating that "extended attributes" are associated with this file. We can learn what these extended attributes are by using Apple's Developer Tool, GetFileInfo, as shown in Figure 5.5.

Figure 5.5 Sparsebundle Extended Attributes

```
iMac-Aluminum:Examples moof$ GetFileInfo sparsebundle.sparsebundle/
directory: "/Users/moof/Desktop/MacOS X Forensics Development/Syngress Book/Chap5/Examples/sparsebundle.sparsebundle"
attributes: avBstclinmedz
created: 10/01/2008 22:22:47
modified: 10/01/2008 22:22:47
iMac-Aluminum:Examples moof$
```

The output shown in Figure 5.5 is very useful. The "created" and "modified" dates and times are the dates and times when this sparsebundle was created. As soon as the sparsebundle is modified in any way, the modified date will change. More interesting, though, is the attributes list. A single letter is used for each attribute. A capital letter indicates that the attribute is *true*. For our Disk Image, the *B* attribute indicates that this is a bundle. You know from earlier chapters that a bundle is a specialized folder that contains data. This attribute is exactly why the Finder is showing the "folder" as a "file."

At this point, you have learned that FileVault can use a sparseimage or a sparsebundle when creating a FileVaulted user Home folder. FileVault in Mac OS X 10.3 and 10.4 will use the sparseimage format, whereas Mac OS X 10.5 will use the newer sparsebundle format. You saw how a sparseimage is truly a flat file, and a sparsebundle is actually a directory with extended attributes, or more specifically, a bundle. You need to go further into the sparsebundle itself and find out what the bundle comprises. Figure 5.6 looks inside the sparsebundle directory from the Terminal.

Figure 5.6 Inside the Sparsebundle Directory

```
● ● ●              Terminal — bash — 59×10
iMac-Aluminum:Examples moof$ cd sparsebundle.sparsebundle/
iMac-Aluminum:sparsebundle.sparsebundle moof$ ls -al
total 16
drwxr-xr-x@ 6 moof   moof   204 Oct   1 22:22 .
drwxr-xr-x  4 moof   moof   136 Oct   1 22:23 ..
-rw-r--r--  1 moof   moof   496 Oct   1 22:22 Info.bckup
-rw-r--r--  1 moof   moof   496 Oct   1 22:22 Info.plist
drwxr-xr-x  5 moof   moof   170 Oct   1 22:22 bands
-rw-r--r--  1 moof   moof     0 Oct   1 22:22 token
iMac-Aluminum:sparsebundle.sparsebundle moof$
```

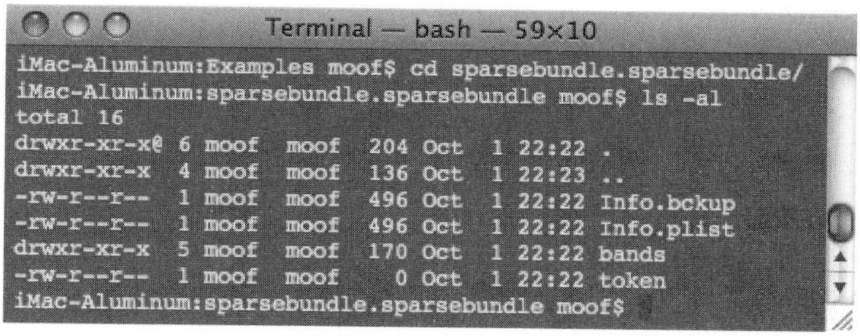

In Figure 5.6, Info.bckup and Info.plist are property list files. Info.plist contains the entries that define how the sparsebundle will be set up, including the maximum size each band file can be. These files contain no user data. Info.bckup is a duplicate of Info.plist. The file named "token" actually contains the key to the encryption, if this sparsebundle is encrypted. It's not easy to get because the key itself is encrypted using Triple Data Encryption Standard (3DES) encryption, so don't get too excited. Lastly, the directory named "bands" contains the data. Figure 5.7 shows this structure.

Figure 5.7 Sparsebundle Bands

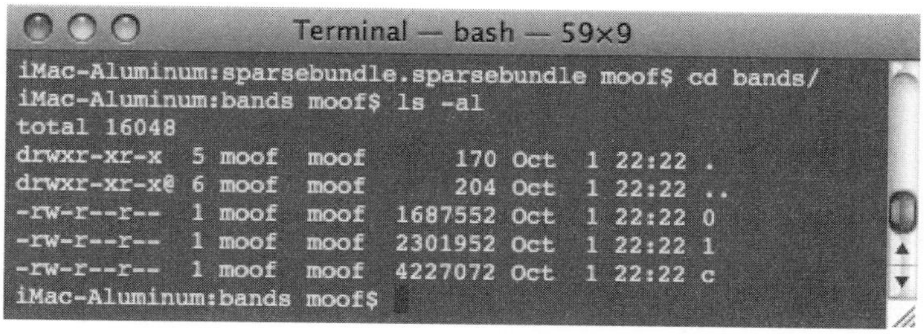

```
● ● ●              Terminal — bash — 59×9
iMac-Aluminum:sparsebundle.sparsebundle moof$ cd bands/
iMac-Aluminum:bands moof$ ls -al
total 16048
drwxr-xr-x  5 moof   moof       170 Oct   1 22:22 .
drwxr-xr-x@ 6 moof   moof       204 Oct   1 22:22 ..
-rw-r--r--  1 moof   moof   1687552 Oct   1 22:22 0
-rw-r--r--  1 moof   moof   2301952 Oct   1 22:22 1
-rw-r--r--  1 moof   moof   4227072 Oct   1 22:22 c
iMac-Aluminum:bands moof$
```

Figure 5.7 shows three bands that comprise the data portion of the Disk Image. The bands have a huge efficiency impact for backup purposes, especially in terms of Time Machine. When data changes inside a sparseimage, the entire flat file has changed, causing the entire sparseimage to be backed up by Time Machine or some other backup utility. With sparsebundle and bands, data can now change inside a single band, causing only a single band to require the backup. When you consider that a user Home folder can be 20GB and a band might be only 8MB, this is a huge timesaver.

Now that we have looked at the sparseimage and sparsebundle in detail, let's look at how they function in FileVault. We'll specifically look at the sparsebundle, since it is the current format used with Mac OS X 10.5. When a user's Home folder is FileVaulted, the following occurs:

- A sparsebundle is created using the user's username for the name of the file. The sparsebundle has AES-128 encryption applied to it using the current Master Password and the user's password as the two available keys for decryption.

- All files and folders from the user's Home folder are copied into the newly created sparsebundle.

- Optionally, the user's old Home folder is securely deleted.

Once FileVault has been applied to a user's Home folder, two significant visual changes occur from all other user's points of view. Figure 5.8 shows a user's Home folder after FileVault has been applied from the Finder.

Figure 5.8 FileVault User Home Folder

Figure 5.8 shows a view of the current user's Home folders on this Macintosh. Currently, user "moof" is logged into this system. Notice that user "aloof" has a folder with a slashed red circle in the bottom right. This is the Finder's notation of "Restricted Access." Double-clicking the folder for "aloof" will show you a dialog stating that you have insufficient privileges and denying you access. Note that user "moof" is an administrator; nonetheless, the Finder will not let "moof" access this folder. However, it is possible to get further inside this data. Figure 5.9 shows a Terminal view of the contents of the "aloof" folder.

Figure 5.9 Terminal View of User Home Folder of "aloof"

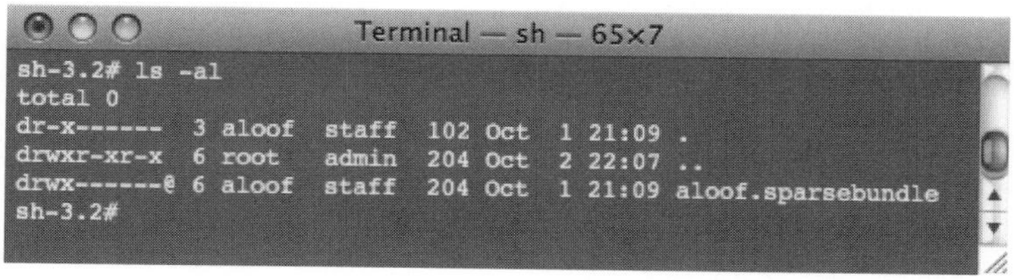

```
sh-3.2# ls -al
total 0
dr-x------   3 aloof   staff   102 Oct  1 21:09 .
drwxr-xr-x   6 root    admin   204 Oct  2 22:07 ..
drwx------@  6 aloof   staff   204 Oct  1 21:09 aloof.sparsebundle
sh-3.2#
```

Figure 5.9 shows a sparsebundle, which is exactly what we were expecting, including the name. We accessed this folder with root privileges. The root user is a Super User and has unquestioned ability to do anything on the system, including accessing protected folders. Recall the earlier note regarding encryption, however. A Super User such as root cannot access FileVault data! By accessing this folder, we have simply made it to the Disk Image, not to the encrypted data. Before we proceed further, let's practice with the concept of Super User access to data. Grasping the Super User concept will be necessary to access FileVaulted user Home folders. This leads us to Exercise 5.1.

Configuring & Implementing...

Exercise 5.1: Obtaining Root Privileges in the Terminal

This exercise will familiarize you with Super User or root privileges in the Terminal.

1. Launch the Terminal application by opening your **Utilities** folder and double-clicking **Terminal**.

2. Type the **whoami** command and press **Return**. The results should be your username.

3. Type the **sudo pwd** command and press **Return**. The results should be a password authentication and then the display of your present working directory. "sudo" is a means of executing a single command as a Super User and then returning your privilege level back to your current user status. "sudo" literally comes from *Super-User-do*. The *pwd* command does not actually require this level of privilege; we are using it here only for demonstration purposes.

4. Type the **whoami** command and press **Return**. The results should be your username again.

Continued

5. Type the **sudo sh** command and press **Return**. The results should be a new prompt. But instead of indicating your username with a *$*, it will now show *sh-3.2#*, indicating that you are now running a shell as root.

6. Type the **whoami** command and press **Return**. The results should be "root". By accessing a shell as root, you now have the ability to access areas of the system without any further authentication.

End of Exercise

Exercise 5.1 walked you through the simple steps of accessing Super User or root privileges when necessary, whether it is once during a single command or for a series of commands through a root-level shell. Continuing with FileVault, to access a user's FileVaulted Home folder, you will need to enter a root-level shell in the Terminal before you can change into that user's Home directory.

Now that you understand the concept of a Super User and how you can access all areas of the system without any further authentication issues, you need to review the security that FileVault provides. FileVault would be a rather lousy encryption technique if, after everything you just learned regarding its encryption ability, it turned out that the Super User could access the data this easily. In fact, the Super User does have a problem. Even though the Super User is able to gain access to the directory where the sparsebundle resides, the Super User cannot do anything further with this file because the Super User does not have the user's password or the Master Password that was used to encrypt that data. So, how do you get to this data? There are two methods, and we'll discuss both of them in the next section.

Acquiring an Unlocked FileVault

Once you have enabled FileVault for a user, getting to that user's data becomes much more difficult. You can use one of two methods to access the data: access it when the door is open (unencrypted), or access it when the door is closed (encrypted). When the user who has enabled FileVault logs in, FileVault decrypts the user's Home folder and all of his or her data becomes accessible for the duration of the login session. This is your best chance of gathering the user's data: accessing it when the door is open. When the user has logged off the system, FileVault encrypts the user's Home folder, and the door is closed again.

Let's begin by looking at the Finder window of a currently logged in user who has FileVault enabled. Figure 5.10 shows user "aloof" with FileVault enabled.

Figure 5.10 FileVault Enabled for User "aloof" As Seen in the Finder

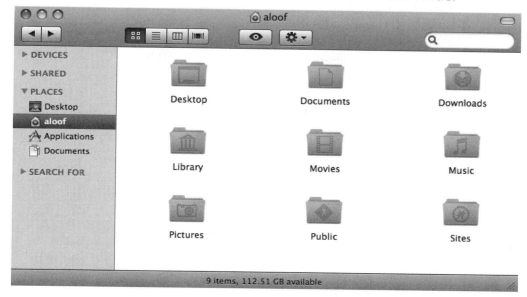

In Figure 5.10, notice how the folder structure looks like a normal folder structure for any user account on a Macintosh system. However, there is one *very* key difference to note in Figure 5.10 that no examiner should ever miss. Notice the blue highlighted "aloof" and the icon for the Home folder. The "house" icon has a lock icon right in the middle of it. Figure 5.11 shows a closer look at this icon.

Figure 5.11 FileVault Icon

The Home folder icon shown in Figure 5.11 could be one of the most important indicators that you as an examiner need to recognize. This icon is the single outward sign that you will receive that FileVault is enabled and that all of the data in the Home folder will be encrypted as this user is

logged out. There is only one good way to gather this user's Home folder now that FileVault is in use; copy everything! Exercise 5.2 will show you the steps in collecting a user's Home folder.

Configuring & Implementing…

Exercise 5.2: Collecting a User's Home Folder with FileVault Enabled

This exercise will walk you through the necessary steps for collecting a user's Home folder when FileVault is enabled. Note that to complete this exercise, you need your own external HFS+ formatted hard drive for data collection.

1. Open a new Finder window or observe a currently open Finder window to view the current user's Home folder. Look at the left pane under the Places section and note the House icon for the current user. If you see a Locked House, *go to step 5*. It is important to note that a user could configure his or her Finder to *not* show this icon in the left pane. If you do not see the House icon, *go to step 2*.

2. When a user has configured his or her Finder to hide the House icon from the left pane, you must look slightly further. In the same Finder window you have open navigate directly to the user's Home folder and look at the icon there. At the top center of the open Finder window is the name of the current folder that is being displayed. While holding down the **Command** key (or **Apple** key), click this **name**. A drop-down menu will appear, giving you a direct way to navigate to the Macintosh computer.

3. Select the **item** that is "lowest" in the list, as this will be the Macintosh computer every time. The contents of the window will change to show all connected drives to this Macintosh. Double-click the **boot drive** for this Macintosh.

4. Double-click the **Users** folder. This folder will contain a folder for each user on this system. In this folder will be the currently logged in user and the House icon. If you see a Locked House icon, go to step 5, as you have properly recognized that FileVault is enabled.

5. At this point, you have recognized that FileVault is enabled. Now you must gather the contents of the user's Home folder prior to shutting down this Macintosh, or the data could be lost forever. First, navigate inside the

Continued

user's Home folder by either clicking once on the **Locked House icon in the left pane** or double-clicking on the **Locked House icon in the Finder Window**, depending on how you got to this step.

6. You need a destination for this information, so connect your external HFS+ formatted evidence collection hard drive. Verify that it appears on the Desktop of the Macintosh with the name you expect to see. Your evidence hard drive should be well named for collections, such as "Evd_Collection_HD".

7. Double-click your **hard drive** to open a Finder window. Verify that it is presenting the contents of your drive and not any other possible drive. Then create a folder on *your* evidence hard drive and name it "Evidence_Collection".

8. At this step, you are ready to copy. You cannot simply copy with the Finder, though. You must use the Terminal to copy the most user data possible. To access the Terminal, select the **Go** menu in the Finder menu bar and select **Utilities** in the menu. The window that was displaying your evidence collection hard drive will change to display the Utilities on this Macintosh. Scroll up or down to find the Terminal and double-click it to launch it.

9. In the window where the Terminal was launched, click the **left navigation arrow** in the upper left of the window itself. This will bring back the contents of your evidence collection hard drive. Verify this by looking at the top center of the window and noting the name that appears. It should be the name of your evidence collection hard drive.

10. In the Terminal window, type the command **cd /Users** and press **Return**. This will change your current location on the file system to the directory that holds the user Home folders.

11. In the Terminal window, type the command **ls –la** and press **Return**. This will list the current directory contents. You should be able to locate the Home folder of your FileVaulted user in this list.

12. Begin copying the user's Home folder to the evidence collection drive by typing the command **cp –R /Users/<username>**. Notice that the switch is a capital *R* for the -*R* portion of the command. Also note that in place of <*username*> you should enter the name of the FileVaulted user Home folder from step 11. Do *not* press Return. To complete the command with a destination, drag the Evidence_Collection folder from your evidence collection hard drive to the Terminal window. The action of dragging the folder to the Terminal window will auto-type the destination for you. Do *not* press Return!

13. Verify that the command in your Terminal follows this format: *cp –R / Users/<username> /Volumes/<EvidenceCollectionDrive>/Evidence_Collection*.

Continued

14. Add a single / (slash) character to the end of this command line. Your command should now look like this: *cp –R /Users/<username> /Volumes/ <EvidenceCollectionDrive>/Evidence_Collection/*. Note the new / after *Evidence_Collection*. This will ensure a more organized copy.

15. Press **Return** to initiate the copy of the user Home folder. You will likely receive a few error messages indicating which files could not be copied. You should note these files as a part of your case notes.

16. When the copy is finished, the prompt will return and a cursor will flash, waiting for the next command. You have now successfully copied a FileVaulted user's Home folder!

End of Exercise

In Exercise 5.2, there are a few points to discuss further. The first point concerns how you copy the user's Home folder. You have copied all of the data through the Terminal and not the Finder. This is for very good reasons. The Finder does not show hidden files; hence it will not allow you to select hidden files. With this limitation, anything that the system or user has hidden would be missed in a Finder copy. In a Terminal window, when you use the *cp* command, you are copying everything in the user's Home folder aside from the few files that did not copy (for reasons that are beyond the scope of chapter). It is a much more complete copy of the evidence you seek.

The second point from Exercise 5.2 to discuss is the evidence collection hard drive. We noted that it should be an HFS+ formatted drive for collection. *If you chose to do this same copy to a FAT32 formatted drive, you would wind up with different information because of how Macintosh files are handled by a FAT32 file system. This would make your task more difficult because of the altered data.* If you later need to access the collected data from an HFS+ formatted drive on a Windows machine (a common reason for using FAT32 for evidence collection), you can perform a second copy in your own lab from your evidence collection drive to a FAT32 volume. A second option for Windows machines is to use an application such as MacDrive7 from Mediafour (www.mediafour.com/products/macdrive).

The last point regarding Exercise 5.2 again concerns your evidence collection hard drive. *Never* connect an evidence collection hard drive that contains other case data! We cannot stress this enough. When you connected your own hard drive, you introduced a method for cross-contamination of cases. Your evidence collection hard drive should be clean and devoid of any data to guarantee that you have not introduced data to the suspect Macintosh.

When you encounter a FileVault-enabled user Home folder, there is no better way to collect data than to complete the steps in Exercise 5.2. Practice these steps many times on your own test system. You should become experienced and well versed with each step prior to encountering a scene. Collecting evidence from a live machine is one of the very few times that you *are* able to *change* evidence. This is quite different from using a write blocker of some sort that prevents any form of mistake on the examiner's part. Live evidence collection will leave behind traces that data was accessed at the exact time you made the copy. This is an acceptable change to the Macintosh system, as you have no other way to gather this user's Home folder before it becomes encrypted. This may require not only education and practice on your part, but also education on your superiors' part regarding why you are working with live systems.

Decrypting a Locked FileVault

As noted earlier, FileVault is encrypted with AES-128 encryption. This standard has no known vulnerabilities, but there are attack vectors to the manner in which FileVault is implemented. There are techniques you can use if you encounter a user Home folder that has already been encrypted. The technique you choose depends on whether you encounter a sparseimage or a sparsebundle. The other options you have depend on how the Mac you've encountered is set up.

First, let's look at what options you have if you have imaged a Macintosh and have a user's Home folder that was encrypted with FileVault. In this case, you are looking at a file named "username. sparseimage" or a folder named "username.sparsebundle". In either case, the data inside is useless at this point. For the sparseimage format, applications are available that perform automated dictionary attacks. One of the freely available applications, MacKrack (http://fsbsoftware.com/macKrack.html), can attack a FileVault user Home folder. For the sparsebundle format, it is a different story. Cracking applications haven't been written yet to efficiently attack against the sparsebundle format. A utility named Spartan (www.macosxforensics.com/), which is written in AppleScript, attempts manual mounts of the sparse-bundle with a given dictionary file until a successful password is found. This utility is quite slow, making the process cumbersome. Other cracking applications are available via a simple Internet search. Always look to see what is currently available and what the clever minds have come up with.

Likely the best method for opening the FileVault user Home folder is with the Mac OS X system itself. Of course, to do this you need a password! On a single-user system, there is little chance you will be able to obtain the Master Password if you are unable to obtain the user's password. In this case, you are stuck until you can obtain a password. Resetting a user's password does *not* change the FileVault password. On a Macintosh on which you can obtain the Master Password, you have a key to get into the House. With the Master Password, you can reset the user's account password and FileVault password in one pass. Figure 5.12 shows an example of how the password reset dialog box looks.

Figure 5.12 Resetting a User Account Password with the Master Password

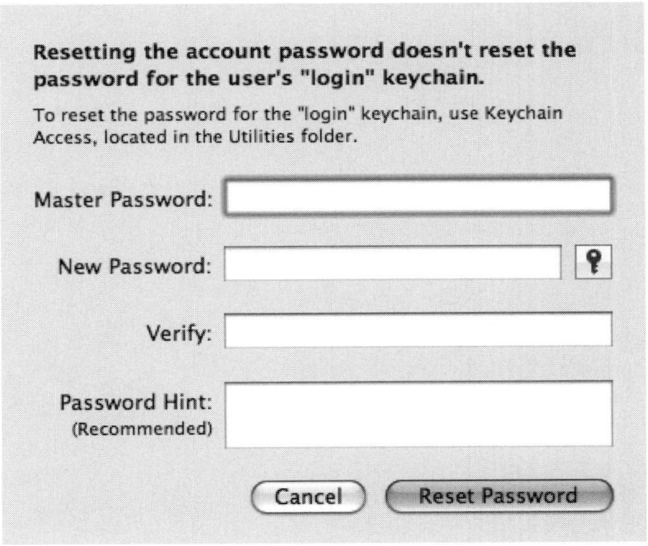

Figure 5.12 shows the dialog box from the System Preferences – Accounts window when Reset Password is selected. By entering the Master Password into this dialog box, you can assign a new password that will not only be the login password for this account, but also will be the new FileVault password. If the user's password is reset in any other manner, the FileVault password is *not* changed, creating a situation in which the user will be prompted for his or her FileVault password in order to log in. Once you have completed this process, you now know the FileVault password for this account! Don't log in, though. You should copy the encrypted Home folder before you attempt to log in so that you always have a copy of the decrypted but untouched Home folder to return to.

Encrypted FileVault is not easy to defeat, and there are not many forms of attack. What happens when someone leaves the password laying around for you to discover with a few simple commands? This is the case with two files that exist on the Macintosh under Mac OS X. Two technologies are used to keep your Macintosh "happy". One file, the page file, located at /var/vm/swapfile0, is used to give a Macintosh the ability to operate with higher memory requirements than the physical RAM installed in the machine. If a user has not enabled Secure Virtual Memory, this file will contain clear text of many of the activities on this Macintosh, including passwords entered into Web sites. An even better source of information is the sleep image file. It will exist if the Macintosh has entered sleep mode. The file is located at /var/vm/sleepimage. If the user has not enabled Secure Virtual Memory, this file *will* contain the user's login password, among others. The contents of each of these files are not useful to look at with the human eye. However, they are immensely useful in creating a dictionary to be used for cracking FileVault! To create a dictionary using either of these files, you simply use the Terminal and the *strings* command. For example, in the Terminal, entering the command *sudo strings /var/vm/swapfile0 > ~/Desktop/dictionary.txt* would yield a text file on your Desktop of your current swap file. As an experiment, open this text file and see whether you can find any of your own passwords.

We have outlined a few FileVault cracking techniques in this section, and others will likely develop over time as people continue to look at the encryption technique used. Continue to refresh your knowledge of the most current attack vectors for FileVault so that you are prepared when your case depends on decrypting FileVault.

Summary

Apple developed FileVault as a method of protecting users' data from the prying eyes of others. FileVault encrypts the user's Home folder, only allowing individual users of a Mac OS X system to have FileVault on or off. Although there are no know direct vulnerabilities to the encryption method used, there are techniques to attack the encryption scheme itself. In this chapter, we outlined how FileVault uses either a flat file or a directory structure, depending on the operating system version installed. Mac OS X 10.3 and 10.4 each use the sparsebundle flat file format for FileVault, and Version 10.5 uses the newer sparsebundle directory and bands format. Decrypting any encryption scheme will always remain a "cat and mouse" game as the community minds try to figure out and reverse-engineer what the corporate developers tried to create.

Solutions Fast Track

FileVault Overview

☑ FileVault uses AES-128 encryption to encrypt users' data.

☑ When FileVault encrypts a user's Home folder, two keys are used to unlock the encrypted Home folder: the user password and the Master Password. The user password is the key to "enter" and the Master Password is the key to "reset".

☑ FileVault uses two types of file formats: sparseimage and sparsebundle. Mac OS X 10.3 and 10.4 use the sparseimage format, whereas Mac OS X 10.5 uses the sparsebundle format.

Acquiring an Unlocked FileVault

☑ Acquiring an unlocked user's Home folder is a key to getting data before it is encrypted and lost. You can do this by copying the contents of the user's Home folder to your own external, HFS+ formatted evidence collection hard drive.

☑ Copying the contents of a user's Home folder is a live action on a live Macintosh system. This means system changes are occurring with every action you take. These changes are acceptable, as without the copy, the data will be encrypted and lost.

☑ Because you are working on a live Macintosh system, you should practice these steps and be well versed in them in order to properly copy a user's Home folder. You should avoid following these steps on a live system so that you affect the least amount of data during the process.

Decrypting a Locked FileVault

☑   You can decrypt FileVault with various tools on the Internet that use dictionaries in their attack.

☑   You can reset the passwords of FileVaulted user Home folders using the Master Password if it is known, granting you access to the data.

☑   Utilities available on the Internet for FileVault attacks are typically for use against the sparseimage format.

☑   The best dictionaries available for attacking FileVault are created from the Macintosh that the user Home folder came from.

Frequently Asked Questions

Q: When first approaching a Macintosh, how do I know whether FileVault is on?

A: Always look for the Locked House icon. The user's Home folder will show the lock when the FileVault service has been enabled for that account.

Q: Does AccessData's Password Recovery Toolkit recognize FileVault?

A: No. The sparseimage and sparsebundle file formats are not recognized for decryption in that application.

Q: Does Guidance Software's EnCase recognize FileVault?

A: No. EnCase will show a folder structure with useless data inside.

Q: Do I need a Macintosh to decrypt FileVault?

A: Yes! This might be one of the best arguments to get a new Macintosh into your office. Every utility available for attempting FileVault decryption is a Macintosh utility.

Chapter 6

Time Machine

Solutions in this chapter:

- **Configuring and Using Time Machine**
- **Restoring Files from Time Machine**
- **Forensic Implications**

☑ **Summary**

☑ **Solutions Fast Track**

☑ **Frequently Asked Questions**

Introduction

Time Machine, a new feature available only in the Macintosh Leopard operating system, is an automatic backup tool that enables Mac users to back up all of their system files, or back up only the files they specify. With Time Machine, users can retrieve deleted files or folders, as well as restore their entire system to a previous point in time. Users can designate an HFS+ formatted FireWire or USB drive connected to their Mac as the Time Machine backup drive, or they can back up to another Mac running Leopard with Personal File Sharing, Leopard Server, or Xsan storage devices. As an alternative, users can back up to Apple's Time Capsule, a wireless device that was designed to work with Time Machine.

Time Machine has tremendous implications for forensic investigators. If you as an investigator receive a suspect drive that was configured with Time Machine, you can retrieve artifacts the user deleted as well as rebuild the entire system when the only item you have is the Time Machine drive. You also can restore the system and view what files and folders the user was accessing at a certain point in time. In Figure 6.1, Time Machine has been configured to display the files and folders the user accessed "today" at "10:08 P.M."

Figure 6.1 Time Machine Displaying Files and Folders Accessed at a Certain Point in Time

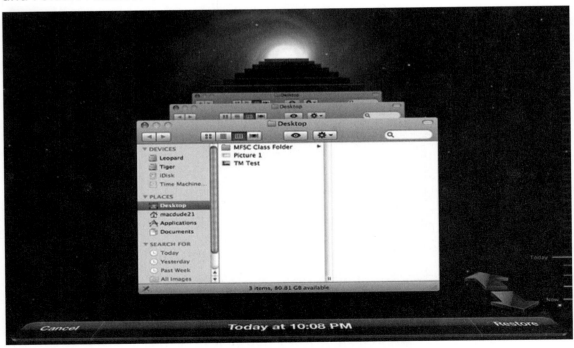

In this chapter, you will learn how to configure and use Time Machine as well as how to restore files from Time Machine. You will also learn how Time Machine can be an important tool to forensic investigators.

Configuring and Using Time Machine

Compared to the backup capability in Microsoft Windows and other third-party backup programs, Time Machine is more straightforward and easier to use. Apple designed Time Machine, as it did many other Mac programs, to be user-friendly. It is probably the easiest, and certainly the flashiest, way to keep track of files in case of accidental deletion or worse. Figure 6.2 shows the Time Machine icon.

Figure 6.2 The Time Machine Icon as Seen in the Dock

As mentioned earlier, to use Time Machine you need either Apple's Time Capsule or an external hard drive, which can be any USB or FireWire drive. If you want your Time Machine backup device to operate as quickly as possible, keep in mind that USB 2.0 will provide you with a slightly faster speed than FireWire 400. FireWire 800 will provide an even faster speed than a USB 2.0 device.

Apple markets Time Capsule as a device that will sync with Time Machine. Time Capsule is essentially an external storage device that is both wired and wireless, with four internal 10/100/1000 Ethernet ports and a Wi-Fi (802.11a/b/g and draft n) Airport Router. According to Apple, Time Capsule can support 50 users and comes in 500GB and 1TB variants. Figures 6.3 and 6.4 show front and rear views of Time Capsule.

Figure 6.3 Front View of Time Capsule

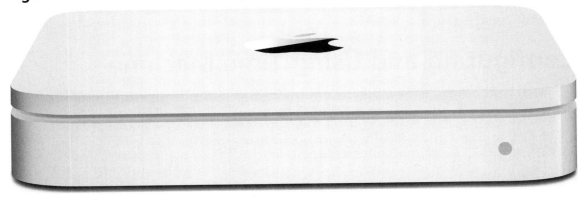

Courtesy of Apple

Figure 6.4 Rear View of Time Capsule

Courtesy of Apple

Customizing Time Machine

When you initially select Time Machine from the task bar or from System Preferences, a pop-up Window appears, as shown in Figure 6.5. Click the **Set Up Time Machine** button to configure a location for the Time Machine backups.

Figure 6.5 The Pop-Up Window to Set Up the Backup Service

Next, the Time Machine configuration window will appear. During the initial setup phase, the Time Machine "switch" will be set to the OFF position, as shown in Figure 6.6. To configure Time Machine properly, you need to select a backup disk by clicking the **Choose Backup Disk** button, as shown in Figure 6.6.

Figure 6.6 The Time Machine Configuration Window

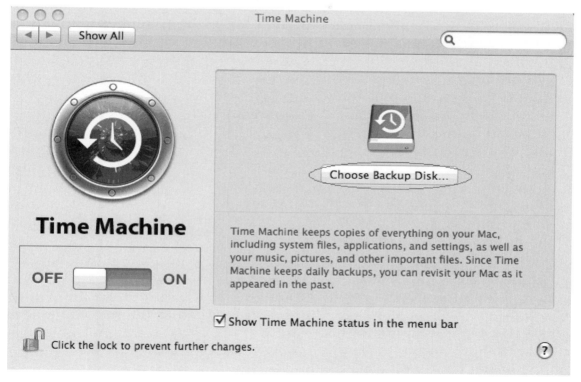

At this point, Time Machine will scan your system for any external hard disk devices, and once it's done, it will provide a list of available drives that you can utilize as Time Machine backup devices. Select from this list the device you want to use as your Time Machine device, and click **Use for Backup**, as shown in Figure 6.7. If "(reformat required)" appears next to the device you've selected, be careful because that means you must reformat the device, a process which will erase all of the data on that drive!

Figure 6.7 Selecting the Destination Volume for Time Machine

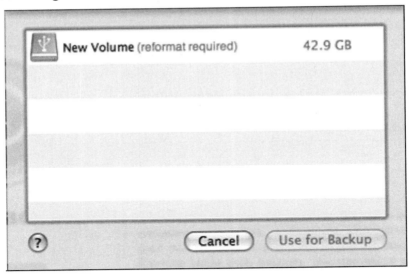

If the backup drive is something other than a Time Capsule device, the dialog box will report that the drive you selected will require reformatting with the HFS+ file system. In Figure 6.7, for example, the "New Volume" drive requires reformatting. You can reformat the drive by selecting the drive and clicking the **Use for Backup** button. Time Machine will ask whether you want to erase the disk or choose another drive. If you choose to erase the disk, Time Machine will automatically reformat the drive so that it can use it during the backup process. Once you designate a disk for Time Machine to use, the icon representing the attached drive will change to a green icon with the Time Machine logo, as shown in Figure 6.8.

Figure 6.8 Time Machine Volume

If you plan to utilize the full capabilities of Time Machine, you must purchase an external drive that is larger than the hard drive in your system; otherwise, Time Machine will fail. You can reduce the size of the backup by selecting the **Preferences** button and choosing to back up only certain items instead of the entire drive.

NOTE

By default, Time Machine will back up a system's entire drive each time it runs. However, although the initial Time Machine backup is time-consuming, subsequent backups will require much less time because when Time Machine is enabled for the first time, it backs up the entire contents of the computer; subsequent backups include only the files that you have modified since the initial backup. Network administrators refer to this as a *differential backup*.

To reduce the size of a backup due to hard drive limitations or because you want to reduce the amount of time the backup will require, choose **Options** from the main Time Machine window and then select which items you do not want to back up on the Time Machine volume. This is demonstrated in the "Do not back up" window, shown in Figure 6.9.

Figure 6.9 The "Do not back up" Window

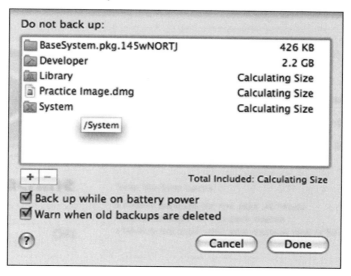

Time Machine backs up certain items by default, grouped into four subfolders listed under Time Machine Backups: Applications, Developer, Library, and System Files and Applications, as shown in Figure 6.10. You can choose what to include in a backup by selecting the subfolders of interest from this list. You can add items to and remove items from the "Do not back up" list by clicking the + and − buttons at the lower-left side of the window. You can control the backup at an even more granular level by clicking the + button within any of the four subfolders and choose what to back up from the list that appears.

A particularly cool feature of Time Machine is that it designates how much space each backup subfolder will occupy on the drive. As shown in Figure 6.10, the System Files and Applications folder, at 21.9GB, occupies a large percentage of this Time Machine backup.

Time Machine can contain a treasure-trove of information, even if the suspect has deleted items from his or her User folder. If he or she has been diligent in their backups, you can retrieve historical items of value. For example, property lists from his or her domain and the domains of other users can contain valuable information of which the suspect is normally not aware of, such as deleted documents, images, emails, calendars, etc.

Also notice in Figure 6.10 the "Warn when old backups are deleted" checkbox. We strongly recommend that you leave this box checked, because the Time Machine application will not provide any type of warning when the backup drive reaches its capacity. Instead, the system will remove previous backups, starting with the oldest, to make room for the new backup. It is nice to have sufficient warning before any backup items are deleted, and checking this box will make you aware of when this is happening.

Figure 6.10 Exclusions from Your Backup

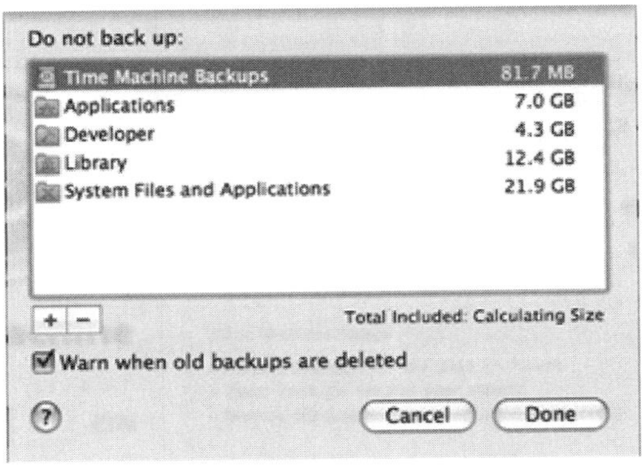

Once you have designated which items you want backed up, click **Done**. Time Machine will attempt to perform the backup. Sit back and wait, if doing a full system backup as this will take many hours, but not as much time as a subsequent backup would require, which could only be around 10 minutes. After the backup is complete, Time Machine will attempt to do hourly, daily, and weekly backups, based on frequency that the Time Machine backup device is mounted.

Issues of Importance to Investigators

As we noted earlier, Time Machine will work with any external USB or FireWire drive. Users also can store Time Machine backups to a network drive, if they own more than one Mac running Leopard or if they have a Leopard server running within their organization. As an investigator, it is important to know that a suspect can create multiple Time Machine backups on numerous external devices.

Also, Time Capsule was specifically designed to be used in tandem with Time Machine. Although storage products from different vendors can be used for external storage, Time Capsule is the only authorized wireless device capable of working with Time Machine. However, be aware that articles on the Web explain how to create a custom wireless backup storage device. Time Capsule has also a USB port, but does not have the ability to use a FireWire connection.

In addition, Time Capsule can use common wireless encryption mechanisms, including Wi-Fi Protected Access (WPA), WPA2, and 64- or 128-bit Wireless Encryption Protocol (WEP). We recommend that you use WPA2 with a very strong passphrase. WPA2 uses Advanced Encryption Standard (AES) encryption and is FIPS 140-2 compliant. From a security standpoint, WEP is the weakest of the wireless security protocols, and hackers are able to penetrate WEP with little effort.

Restoring Files from Time Machine

Restoring either single or multiple files from Time Machine is simple, as you'll see as you work your way through Exercise 6.1.

Configuring & Implementing...

Exercise 6.1: Restoring Files from a Time Machine Volume

This exercise will walk you through the process of restoring files from a Time Machine volume.

1. Launch Time Machine. You can activate Time Machine by clicking the **Time Machine icon** in the **Finder** and selecting **Enter Time Machine**, clicking the **Time Machine icon** in the **Dock**, as shown in Figure 6.11, or double-clicking the **Time Machine** application in the **Applications** folder.

Figure 6.11 Time Machine Icon in the Dock

2. Once inside Time Machine, browse for the files you want to back up by searching in the Finder and using Spotlight, a robust searching tool that is based on indexing all volumes, or by "flying through time" with navigation arrows directing you to a particular point in time, as shown in Figure 6.12.

Continued

Figure 6.12 "Flying through Time" with Time Machine

3. When you have located the file or files that were previously deleted, press the **Spacebar** or double-click it to activate Quick Look to view the files' contents.

4. Confirm that the files found in Time Machine are the ones you were looking for. Then restore them to your Macintosh by clicking the **Restore** button on the right-hand side of the toolbar at the bottom of the Time Machine interface (see Figure 6.13).

5. The operating system will restore the files back to their original location. You may receive a system message noting that a version of one or more of these files already exists in the same location, and asking you what to do about this conflict. Otherwise, you will have successfully restored files from the past to your current Macintosh.

End of Exercise

Figure 6.13 The Time Machine Toolbar, with the Restore Button on the Right

Restoring System Settings

In addition to restoring files, you also can use Time Machine to restore your system settings to the state they were in when you last backed up (see Exercise 6.2). You may want to do this if, for instance, you had to replace your hard drive or purchase a new Mac. All you have to do is place the drive into the new Leopard installation, and the system will ask you whether you want to restore your Mac from Time Machine.

TIP

It's considered a best practice to back up your system on a daily basis. That way, you will always have the latest versions of all of your files, as well as your system settings, in case of system failure.

Configuring & Implementing...

Exercise 6.2: Restoring the Entire System from a Time Machine Volume

In this exercise, you will restore an entire system from a Time Machine volume.

1. Attach the Time Machine external device to the Mac being restored.
2. Power on the Mac.
3. Place the Leopard installation disk into the disk drive.
4. During the installation, select **Utilities** in the menu bar, and then select **Restore System from Backup**.
5. Continue to follow the instructions from the installation until completion.

End of Exercise

Forensic Implications

The new robust backup programs that come with operating systems such as Leopard and Windows Vista provide an important benefit for forensic investigators. Although users may utilize encryption schemes such as FileVault to prevent you from reading their data, their backup drives will be in clear text and may provide access to data that they encrypted or deleted from their system. Even better, a Time Machine backup drive is indexed and you can search it with Spotlight. Time Machine keeps track of files that have been modified through the FSEvents API. Only files that have changed since the last Time Machine run will be in the latest archive. Files not modified will have a hard link set in each archive pointing to the actual file which resides in the previous backup.

A Time Machine backup is not complicated to work with. The way Time Machine archives information makes it easy for forensic examiners to locate files. In addition, the process of imaging the Time Machine drive is no different from that of imaging a normal drive and you can do it using open source tools such as dcfldd and dc3dd. You can also image a Time Machine drive using such proprietary tools as AccessData's FTK Imager and BlackBag's BBT Imagerlite. After they create an image, many investigators feel that the best platform on which to view this information is the Mac; the Mac does a great job of analysis and requires no additional software.

NOTE

If you don't have a Mac, you still can read a Time Machine volume. I have tested several forensic tools, and I feel that X-Ways Forensics, maker of Win-Hex, is the best Windows forensic platform that can read the Time Machine file structure. For more information, visit www.x-ways.net/forensics/.

When you examine a Time Machine volume and the syncing Mac can be located, you need to find the property list associated with Time Machine. In the local library is a Preferences folder, in which you will find a Time Machine property list (property lists are like the Registry items in Microsoft Windows; see Figure 6.14). Navigate to /local/library/preferences/com.apple.TimeMachine. plist. Here you can see the settings for Time Machine.

Figure 6.14 The com.apple.TimeMachine.plist File

Property List	Class	Value
▼ Root	Dictionary	10 key/value pairs
AlwaysShowDeletedBackupsWarning	Boolean	Yes
AutoBackup	Boolean	Yes
BackupAlias	Data	<00000000 013e0002 00010c54 696d6520 4d616368 696e6500 00000000 0000
▼ ExcludeByPath	Array	4 ordered objects
0	String	/Users/seanmorrissey/Library/Calendars/Calendar Cache
1	String	/Users/seanmorrissey/Library/Safari/Webpagelcons.db
2	String	/Users/seanmorrissey/Library/Mail/Envelope Index
3	String	/Users/seanmorrissey/Library/Icons/Webpagelcons.db
▼ IncludedVolumes	Array	2 ordered objects
0	Data	<00000000 012e0002 00010a55 6e746974 6c656420 31000000 00000000 0000
1	Data	<00000000 010e0002 00010649 6d616765 73000000 00000000 00000000 0000
▼ IncludedVolumeUUIDs	Array	2 ordered objects
0	String	2886DADF-0986-369E-AD24-FC92378D430F
1	String	AC173E27-215A-3D20-A074-8553FB0A7642
MaxSize	Number	0
RequiresACPower	Boolean	No
▼ SkipPaths	Array	0 ordered objects
SkipSystemFiles	Boolean	No

The settings in Figure 6.14 indicate that Time Machine is being used. Normally, a property list does not get populated until an application is used. The property list includes alarms for warning that the drive is reaching capacity and that files are going to be deleted. The .plist file also shows whether Auto Backup is on. If Auto Backup is on, that means Time Machine was automatically performing backups. If you see the com.apple.TimeMachine.plist file and Auto Backup is set to on, this indicates that someone has been using Time Machine.

TIP

If you do not currently have the Time Machine volume, you may want to consider filing for another search warrant. And if you can interview the suspect, question him in regard to the location of a drive either overtly or covertly placed.

After your forensic image is created, get the hash value of the dd. If you are using the Mac as your analysis platform, it is best to turn disk arbitration off and then use an open source tool such as dcfldd or dc3dd, or a proprietary tool such as BlackBag's Imager Lite or SubRosaSoft's Mac Forensics, to get the hash value. Turning off disk arbitration in Tiger and Leopard is covered in Chapter 7.

When creating the image using dcfldd or dc3dd, create one single dd file. For example, from the command line using Terminal, type the following:

```
sudo dc3dd conv-sync,noerror if =/dev/rdisk1 of=/Volumes/[data volume name]
/imagename.dd hashwindow=1000000 hash=md5,sha1 hashlog=/Volumes/[data volume name]
/hashfilelogname_log.md5.
```

This will be helpful when bringing that volume into the Mac. When using any imaging tool, create one single dd or .dmg file. Either way, make sure that when you bring the volume into the forensic Mac workstation the dd extension is changed to .dmg by right-clicking the image and choosing **get info**; Then change the extension to .dmg and lock the volume. Figure 6.15 shows that the image was created as a .dmg file and that the volume is locked.

Figure 6.15 Locking the DMG File

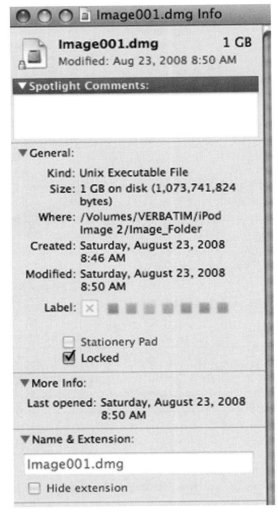

Time Machine Volumes

Usually only one volume is used for a Time Machine backup drive. However, you can use several different drives to back up items. Time Machine does not have to use the same drive every time to complete a backup. All it requires is a properly formatted Time Machine volume to use as a drive. So, as an investigator, keep in mind that a suspect could be using multiple physical drives to complete Time Machine backups.

You will see the following files and folders, also shown in Figure 6.16, in the Time Machine volume:

- **fseventsd** Used by the file system event frameworks.
- **HFS+Private Directory Data** Where the real data lives.
- **.Spotlight –V100** The Spotlight index. The Mac can index the Time Machine volume and then utilize Spotlight.
- **.SymAVAQSFile** A file created by Norton Antivirus.
- **.Trashes** The trash folder.
- **Backups.backupdb** Many subfolders created each time Time Machine backs up the system.
- **Desktop DB** Classic Mac OS desktop database files.
- **Desktop DF** Classic Mac OS desktop database files.

Figure 6.16 Time Machine Folder Structure

Normally an examiner will go straight to the Backups.backupdb folder to look for evidence. You may also want to pay close attention to the symbolic links, as shown in Figure 6.17.

Figure 6.17 Symbolic Links within the Time Machine Image

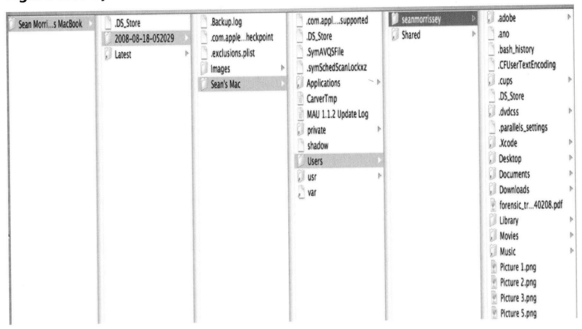

The items are listed by date and time in the folder structure of the backup folder. In Figure 6.17, the folder labeled "2008-08-18-052029" indicates the date and time of the backup; the folder labeled "Sean's Mac" indicates the computer that was backed up. Opening the Sean's Mac folder will reveal its contents, as shown in the figure. From here you can navigate to where you want to go.

You will see folders that are hard linked. If you have located a file of interest, highlight and right click and then select "Get Info." Here you will see exactly where that file actually lives on the drive. Figure 6.18 shows the information from an actual recovered document.

Figure 6.18 Information about a File from a Time Machine Backup

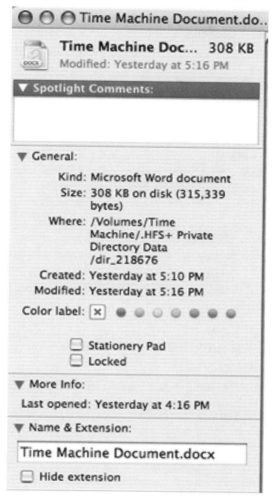

The full path for the Word file seen in Figure 6.19, is really at /.HFS+ Private Directory Data/ dir_218676, as shown in Figure 6.19. Time Machine saves files in the HFS+ Private Directory Data folder and has a naming convention as dir_XXXXXX. Time Machine uses these "dir" files to create its incremental backups. You will have a trace for every file whose parent folder has a link symbol.

Figure 6.19 HFS+ Private Directory Data Folder

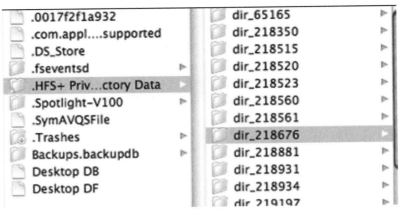

Within each backup are log files that show exactly what Time Machine is doing during the backup procedure. Within each backup is an exclusion property list, as shown in Figure 6.20. The exclusion property list is located at /backup.backupdb/[ComputerName]/Date & time of Backup/.exclusion.plist, and it shows all items that were excluded from the backup. The exclusion paths are also provided.

Figure 6.20 The Exclusion Property List, Indicating
Which Files Were Excluded from the Backup

Property List	Class	Value
▼ Root	Dictionary	4 key/value pairs
▼ sourcePaths	Array	1 ordered object
0	String	/
▼ standardExclusionPaths	Array	0 ordered objects
systemFilesExcluded	Boolean	No
▼ userExclusionPaths	Array	5 ordered objects
0	String	/Developer
1	String	/Practice Image.dmg
2	String	/Library
3	String	/System
4	String	/BaseSystem.pkg.145wNORTJ

Time Machine with FileVault Enabled

Now that you know how both Time Machine and FileVault work, you need to understand how they work together when both technologies are enabled on a user's Mac. Time Machine is enabled for the entire Macintosh, but FileVault is enabled per user account. For our scenario, we will have two user accounts, named "goof" and "aloof", as shown in Figure 6.21. User account "aloof" represents the user who is smart enough to turn on FileVault. User account "goof" represents the poor fool who left FileVault off. (User account "moof" represents the account from which I'm typing all of this, and will not participate in this exercise!)

Figure 6.21 User Accounts "goof" and "aloof"

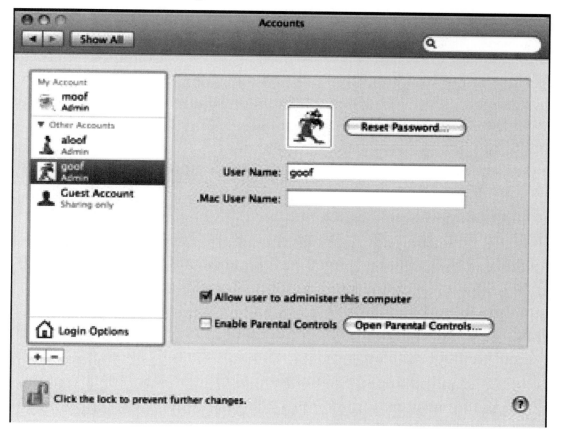

When user "aloof" turns on FileVault for his account, he will see the warning shown in Figure 6.22.

Figure 6.22 FileVault Warning

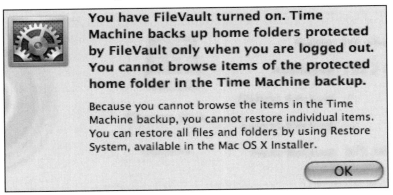

> **You have FileVault turned on. Time Machine backs up home folders protected by FileVault only when you are logged out. You cannot browse items of the protected home folder in the Time Machine backup.**
>
> Because you cannot browse the items in the Time Machine backup, you cannot restore individual items. You can restore all files and folders by using Restore System, available in the Mac OS X Installer.
>
> OK

This warning indicates that Time Machine works quite differently for a FileVaulted account. First, Time Machine does not back up the user's Home directory files while the user is logged in! A user *must* log out first. Second, a user does not restore a single file from Time Machine; rather, a user restores an entire instance of his Home directory! That means that if user "aloof" needs to bring back a file he deleted yesterday, he is going to bring back *everything* (the entire sparse bundle) from yesterday.

Figure 6.23 shows what Time Machine looks like on the external USB drive for "goof" and "aloof".

Figure 6.23 Time Machine on an External USB Drive

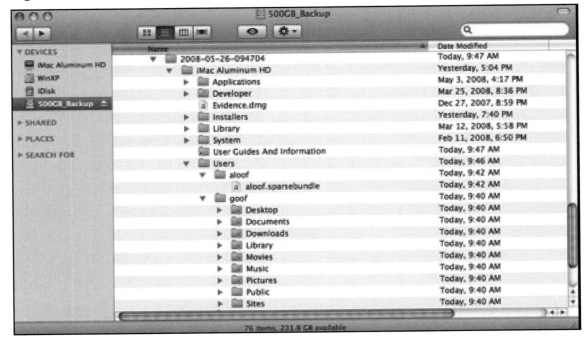

Summary

Developed by Apple, Time Machine is a versatile and ingenious solution. However, its incident response and forensic implications are challenging. It is important to remember that there could be multiple copies of Time Machine backups, some hidden and others wireless. It is important for any investigator to scan an area for hidden wireless devices, if you see an active Time Machine icon in the sidebar, and you can't locate the actual storage drive. You can find a plethora of information in Time Machine, as we discuss in this book—from Internet history and e-mail, to documents and pictures. Indeed, anything a user can save you can locate using Time Machine.

Solutions Fast Track

Configuring and Using Time Machine

☑ Time Machine allows the user to go back and restore files.

☑ Time Machine requires an additional storage device.

☑ Old backups will be deleted when the Time Machine drive runs out of space.

Restoring Files from Time Machine

☑ A user can restore a single file.

☑ An entire system can be restored by booting to the Mac DVD.

☑ Time Machine gives users the ability to "fly through" time.

Forensic Implications

☑ Time Machine volumes can be easily analyzed on a regular Mac.

☑ Time Machine volumes are formatted with the HFS+ file system.

☑ Time Machine volumes can provide you with a user's deleted files and folders.

Frequently Asked Questions

Q: What is Time Machine?

A: Time Machine is an automatic backup tool available with the Macintosh Leopard operating system. With Time Machine, users can restore deleted files and folders.

Q: What does Time Machine require?

A: Time Machine requires Mac OS X Leopard or any external storage device. For instance, it can be a USB or FireWire device from any vendor.

Q: What File System does Time Machine use?

A: Time Machine volumes must be formatted with the HFS+ file system.

Q: Can an entire system be restored by using Time Machine?

A: Yes, if you boot to the Mac Install DVD, you can restore an entire system with Time Machine.

Q: Can each user have his or her own time machine volume?

A: Yes. Time Machine backs up all users, and when it is activated, only that user's volume will be shown to the user.

Q: What is Time Capsule and how many users can it support?

A: Time Capsule is a wired and wireless storage device offered by Apple. It can be configured to support up to 50 users.

Q: Aside from an external drive or Time Capsule, can Time Machine back up to anyplace else?

A: Yes. Time Machine can use a Mac OS X server as a Time Machine backup device if the service has been configured. An examiner should always be aware of this when in a corporate environment.

Chapter 7

Acquiring Forensic Images

Solutions in this chapter:

- **Setting Up an Analysis Mac**
- **Imaging a Mac with a Mac**
- **Imaging a Mac with a Live CD**

☑ **Summary**

☑ **Solutions Fast Track**

☑ **Frequently Asked Questions**

Introduction

Acquiring a forensic image of any piece of digital evidence is possibly the most important step in the forensic process. If the digital image is obtained poorly, it will be inadmissible in court. If you obtain the digital image of a logical partition when you should have gathered the physical device, you may lose a large amount of evidence forever. Worst of all, if you acquire the forensic image in a manner that taints the evidence you will skew the results or render them useless during the examination process. It is incumbent upon you as an examiner to understand how to properly gather the information you seek to analyze. If you do not understand how to gather it, there is no way you can analyze and explain it.

Traditionally, digital evidence comprised a simple copy of the files you needed as evidence for a case. As the digital forensics profession grew, this became unacceptable and methods were developed that enabled examiners to obtain the files they sought without changing the original evidence. Software write blockers and hardware write blockers have come into prominence to aid examiners in obtaining data without altering content or metadata. Each solution blocks "writes" to the data while allowing the examiner to see the existing data.

Available on the Macintosh is a method for blocking all writes to data that results in a forensically sound acquisition of evidence. Mac OS X has its operating system roots in UNIX, which has always treated devices much differently than Windows. As you will see in this chapter, you can have complete control over individual devices using Mac OS X Version 10.5 or 10.4.

As a variant of this idea, the Linux operating system gives the same control over devices that UNIX allows. Furthermore, many Linux operating system variants are available on bootable CDs. Some of these have even been compiled and altered to be what examiners would consider "forensically sound" because they do not auto-mount any device at boot time. We will explore this in greater detail in this chapter as well.

Setting Up an Analysis Mac

The Apple Macintosh is a user-friendly system that is so easy to set up, you may be wondering why I've devoted a section to discussing it. However, forensic examiners must consider certain issues when deploying an analysis Mac. The OS X DVD that came with your Macintosh is invaluable. The boxed version of Mac OS X 10.4 contains only PowerPC code and *will not* install to an Intel-based system—you need the disc that came with your particular system (and sometimes locating this DVD is the hardest step of the setup process).

Once you have located the appropriate boot DVD for your system, however, the process becomes very easy and can be accomplished with the tools that are provided on the Mac OS X disc. Mac OS X 10.5 offers the first single DVD installation for either Intel- or PowerPC-based Macs. However, the currently stated requirements are an 867MHz or faster G4 processor, so don't jump for joy if you miss that mark. I am *not* an advocate of "hack" techniques for installing the OS on lesser machines when the primary use will be forensics. Always stay with the factory recommendations, as this will make your life easier.

WARNING

Before you do anything else, you should back up your Mac hard drive. The analysis process is destructive and will result in the inability to recover anything afterward. Even if you are using a new, out-of-the-box Mac, consider making a copy of the drive just so you have everything the factory supplied, including installed applications that may not be on any other media in the box.

The Setup Process, Step by Step

Apple has made the installation process easy. To begin, insert the installation DVD into your Mac and double-click the **Install Mac OS X icon**. This will restart your Mac and will boot from the DVD.

Next, you need to partition the hard drive using Disk Utility. Disk Utility is included on the installation DVD and you can find it in the Finder menu prior to starting the actual operating system installation. I highly suggest that you use the Disk Utility option to securely erase the contents of your analysis Mac. This guarantees that you know exactly what is on your hard drive before you start.

After the secure erase has completed, you will need to choose a partition scheme that suits your work. Do you want one partition (the entire drive)? Or do you want two partitions, one for the operating system and one for data? The choice is entirely up to you. Once you have chosen the partition scheme, you need to choose the file system. For an internal hard drive, each partition should be initialized as "Mac OS Extended (Journaled)".

The rest of the installation process is straightforward. Once you've completed all of these basic steps, the Macintosh will restart and you will have a running system. However, the setup process isn't complete, because the operating system installation does not install the iLife application suite that comes free with every Macintosh. You want this suite available to you for the included applications, so insert your installation DVD again and look for the **Install Bundled Apps Only icon**. This will only be on DVD discs that came with your Mac. Double-click this icon to install the iLife suite.

As with all systems, updates have come out since the installation media was released. So, this means you'll need to update your Mac at this point. With a valid Internet connection in place, go to the Apple menu and select **Software Update**. Figure 7.1 shows the Software Update selection from the Apple menu in the Finder.

Figure 7.1 Apple Menu Software Update

Software Update will cause your analysis Mac to check with Apple for all available updates to the software you just installed. You should install all of the updates Apple makes available to you. Then you should check Software Update a second time to see whether any secondary updates are available. Once you are satisfied that you have downloaded all available software updates for your analysis Mac, disconnect it from the Internet. A network connection is a vector through which unwanted data can enter your analysis Mac, and you have no control over the Internet.

Next, you need to secure your Mac. It is likely that Bluetooth and Wireless network connectivity are active. Both of these are vectors of unknown data that you must shut off until you need them. You can shut off each of these services in the System Preferences. Figures 7.2 and 7.3 show the Bluetooth and Wireless network services and how to shut off each of them.

Figure 7.2 Bluetooth System Preference on Mac OS X 10.5

In Figure 7.2, the On checkbox is not checked within the Bluetooth System Preference. This disables Bluetooth connectivity entirely. Bluetooth is a short-range wireless access method that could result in someone accessing your evidence inadvertently or maliciously. Within your laboratory, you should not use this service until you need it for a case.

Figure 7.3 Wireless Network System Preference on Mac OS X 10.5

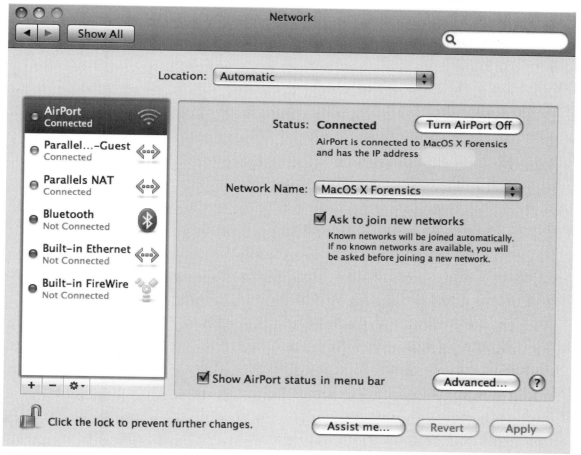

Figure 7.3 shows the Network System Preference and all of the available services. Click the **AirPort service** in the window on the left and a button will appear on the right reading "Turn AirPort Off". Clicking on this button will immediately turn off the wireless network service for your Macintosh.

At this point, you can install any of your favorite forensic applications; once you are done, the system will be configured for use. If any of your applications you typically use are available as Internet downloads, consider obtaining them from a different Mac and copying the applications to your clean analysis Mac via a Flash drive. With your analysis Mac you should minimize outside connectivity to unknown data. Without any further installation of applications, your Mac is now fully capable of performing forensically sound acquisitions and verifications of evidence.

Imaging a Mac with a Mac

Imaging a Mac with a Mac is likely one of the easiest methods of forensically acquiring the physical contents of an evidentiary system. Macs can be some of the most cumbersome laptop computers to disassemble to gain access to a hard drive. Similarly, some Mac desktop models can leave an examiner wishing he or she had a hammer as he or she scavenges for the internal hard drive. Fortunately, for many years the Macintosh has offered a feature called Target Disk Mode (TDM), which allows the Mac to become an external FireWire hard drive. This gives you the benefit of acting on the Mac as you would any other FireWire-connected hard drive.

According to Apple's Support Web site, Article HT1661, you can use the following models as target computers:

- iMac (Slot Loading) with Firmware Version 2.4 or later

- iMac (Summer 2000) and all models introduced after July 2000

- eMac (all models)

- Mac mini (all models)

- Power Mac G4 (AGP Graphics) with ATA drive

- Power Mac G4 Cube

- Power Mac G4 (Gigabit Ethernet) and all models introduced after July 2000

- Power Mac G5 (all models)

- iBook (FireWire) and all models introduced after September 2000

- MacBook (all models)

- PowerBook G3 (FireWire)

- PowerBook G4 (all models)

- MacBook Pro (all models)

If the Macintosh you need to acquire is included in the preceding list, you are in luck: You will not need to take it apart. Interestingly, the Mac Pro and XServe are not on the preceding list. Each of these will boot into TDM, but with a catch: According to Article HT1661, "FireWire Target Disk Mode works on internal ATA drives only. Target Disk Mode only connects to the master ATA drive on the Ultra ATA bus. It will not connect to Slave ATA, ATAPI or SCSI drives." This note applies to all Macs that support multiple internal hard drives. It is in your best interest to check the inside of any Power Mac, Mac Pro, or XServe for multiple hard drives when you are performing an acquisition. You may need to consider removing the hard drives and imaging each one individually if they do not properly present during TDM.

If you have a Macintosh that is not included in the preceding list of supported machines for TDM, you will need to resort to imaging with a Live CD, or physically removing the hard disk from the Macintosh for imaging. If you choose to physically remove a hard disk for imaging, you can still image it using all of the techniques discussed in this section. You will need to supply your own cables to connect the hard drive to your analysis Macintosh, however. You will also need an external USB or FireWire connection kit for the drive you wish to acquire to continue with this section.

WARNING

Never connect a drive that is to be acquired as an internal drive to your analysis Mac. You will have no control over when it gets mounted if you do this.

TDM is not always available, even if your Macintosh is on the preceding list! If the user has applied an Open Firmware Password, this Macintosh will not boot into TDM. This is a problem if you do not check for this. To check for an Open Firmware Password simply boot the Mac by holding down the **Option key**. If the Mac presents a Lock icon with a password dialog box, you have an Open Firmware Password Mac. If, however, you are presented with icons of the bootable partitions available, you have a Mac with no password applied. We will reference this again later, in Exercise 7.1.

NOTE

You can bypass an Open Firmware Password by removing it permanently. Apple has a Technical Note on their support website that describes the process of removing an Open Firmware Password. The downside for computer forensic examiners in performing this procedure is that the current date and time as noted by the Mac will be lost in the process. Weigh this pitfall against the gain in access to TDM if you encounter an Open Firmware Password.

Physical Disks and Slices

Once you have determined that TDM is available, or you have removed the hard drive for imaging, you can continue with the imaging process using the built-in tools of your Mac OS X system. First, I will show you some characteristics of how devices are handled. Figure 7.4 is a look at the Terminal displaying the physical disks that are currently connected to this Macintosh.

Figure 7.4 Terminal Window Showing Devices Connected to This Macintosh

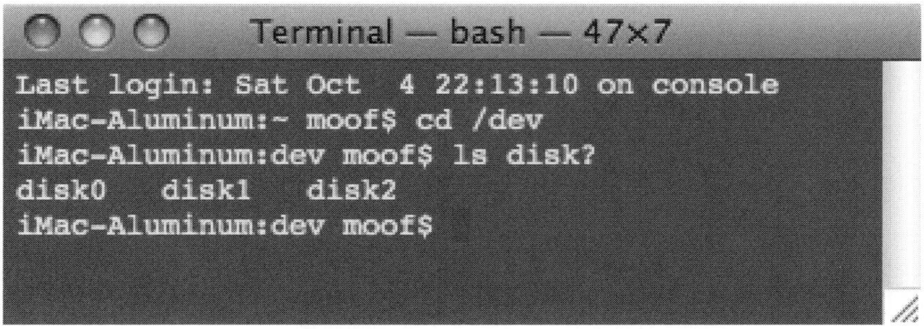

```
○ ○ ○              Terminal — bash — 47×7
Last login: Sat Oct  4 22:13:10 on console
iMac-Aluminum:~ moof$ cd /dev
iMac-Aluminum:dev moof$ ls disk?
disk0    disk1    disk2
iMac-Aluminum:dev moof$
```

In Figure 7.4, you can see that three physical disks are connected to this Mac. To get to this result, you have to execute two commands. First, notice the *cd /dev* command. This command will change the current directory to the dev directory, where device files are stored. Device files are kept for every device on this Macintosh and the directory will update as new devices are introduced or detached. Second, notice the *ls disk?* command, which is a relative path command that lists the entries in the present working directory that match the criteria of the word *disk* followed by any character. Anytime a physical disk is connected to a Macintosh it is assigned a device file, starting with disk0, the boot drive. The result of the *ls disk?* command shows that three disks are currently attached to this Macintosh.

You also can achieve the results shown in Figure 7.4 through the use of *absolute paths*. To do this, type into the Terminal window the exact location for the execution of the desired command. For example, the same *ls* command in Figure 7.4 using an absolute path would look like this: *ls /dev/disk?*. You can execute this command from any location because the path is included in the command itself. When no path is included in the command, the command acts upon the present working directory, which is not always the desired location. As the examiner, you choose which manner suits your needs.

At this point, you have determined that three disks are attached, but this does not show any further information. You do not know whether these disks are mounted, whether they contain multiple partitions, or how large each disk is. To find out more information, you need to use another command from the Terminal. Figure 7.5 shows you how you can gather more detail regarding a particular disk.

Figure 7.5 Terminal Window Showing
Detailed Information of disk0 Using *diskutil*

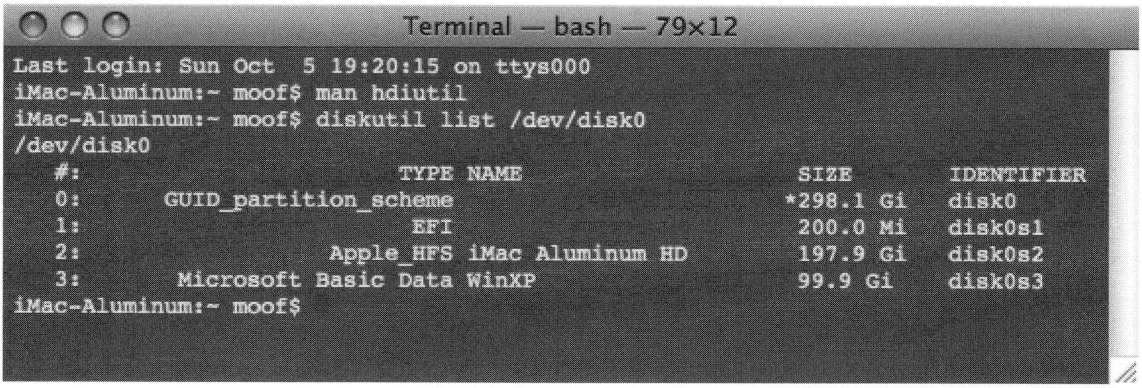

```
○ ○ ○                  Terminal — bash — 79×12
Last login: Sun Oct  5 19:20:15 on ttys000
iMac-Aluminum:~ moof$ man hdiutil
iMac-Aluminum:~ moof$ diskutil list /dev/disk0
/dev/disk0
   #:                       TYPE NAME               SIZE        IDENTIFIER
   0:      GUID_partition_scheme                   *298.1 Gi    disk0
   1:                        EFI                    200.0 Mi    disk0s1
   2:          Apple_HFS iMac Aluminum HD           197.9 Gi    disk0s2
   3:      Microsoft Basic Data WinXP               99.9 Gi     disk0s3
iMac-Aluminum:~ moof$
```

You can see in Figure 7.5 how the *diskutil* command can get you detailed information about a physical disk. Issuing the *diskutil list /dev/disk0* command has resulted in one physical disk with three "slices," which is the Macintosh (or UNIX) way of referring to partitions. The columns denote the following: 0 refers to the physical disk, 1 is the Extensible Firmware Interface (EFI) slice, 2 is a Hierarchical File System (HFS) slice, and 3 is a Windows Basic Data (NTFS) slice. Notice in the reference line for the physical disk how "298.1Gi" has an asterisk. The asterisk notes that the size is being reported and differs from the actual size. This is why it is extremely important that you always have a larger drive on hand when you perform an acquisition! The *diskutil* command is available to you while you have *DiskArbitration* turned on (you will learn more about this daemon later in this section). When DiskArbitration is turned off, you need to get disk information in a different manner. Figure 7.6 shows how you can get information about a disk with an alternative command.

Figure 7.6 Terminal Window Showing Detailed Information of disk0 Using *hdiutil*

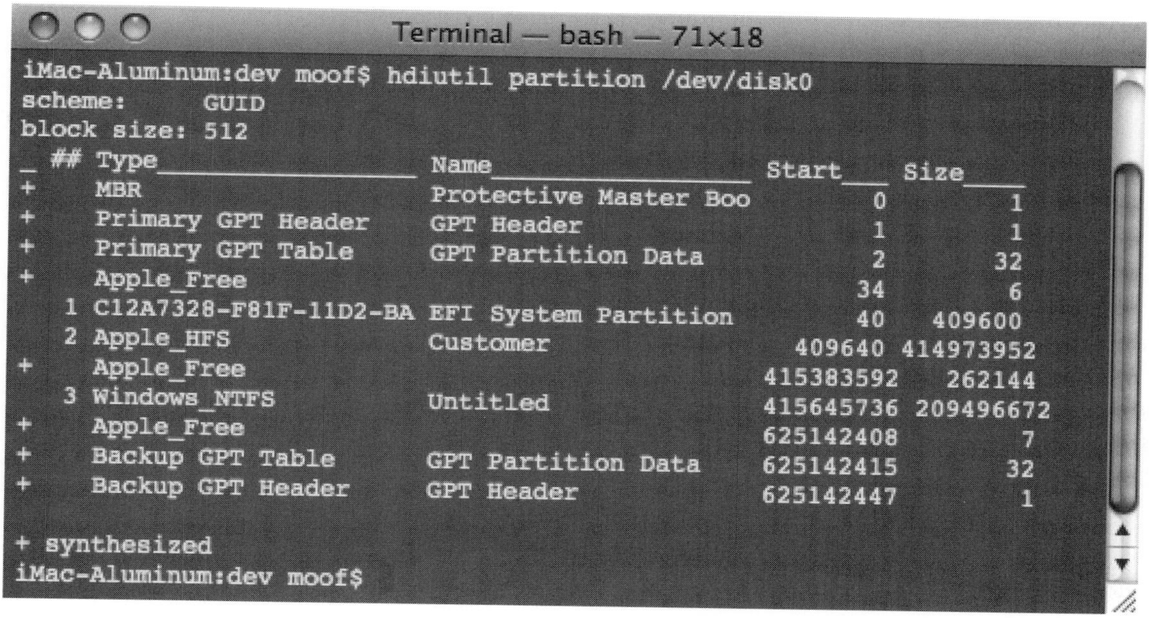

```
iMac-Aluminum:dev moof$ hdiutil partition /dev/disk0
scheme:      GUID
block size: 512
_ ## Type_____ Name_____ Start___ Size____
 +    MBR                    Protective Master Boo        0        1
 +    Primary GPT Header     GPT Header                   1        1
 +    Primary GPT Table      GPT Partition Data           2       32
 +    Apple_Free                                          34        6
   1 C12A7328-F81F-11D2-BA  EFI System Partition         40   409600
   2 Apple_HFS              Customer                 409640 414973952
 +    Apple_Free                                   415383592   262144
   3 Windows_NTFS           Untitled             415645736 209496672
 +    Apple_Free                                   625142408        7
 +    Backup GPT Table       GPT Partition Data  625142415       32
 +    Backup GPT Header      GPT Header          625142447        1

+ synthesized
iMac-Aluminum:dev moof$
```

Notice in Figure 7.6 how you now have even more detailed information about the same device. You still have three slices, but you also see detailed manufacturer-assigned slices and their locations. You as the examiner should determine how to use the commands available in the Terminal. If you prefer to always use *hdiutil* because it always works whether DiskArbitration is on or off, that is acceptable. Alternatively, you may prefer the simple output of *diskutil* when DiskArbitration is enabled. In either case, you will need to know the devices that are connected to your analysis Mac so that when you introduce a Mac to be imaged, you know right away which device it is in the list. The information in Figure 7.5 and Figure 7.6 is similar in output to what you might see from another Mac that has been set up in a similar manner.

> **NOTE**
>
> Devices in the Mac OS X operating system can seem complicated. However, you can minimize the complication by having a single hard drive in your own analysis Mac. The boot hard drive is always assigned "disk0". If you know you have only one hard drive in your system, it is easy to discern any attached devices later as the suspect attached devices.

Now that we have looked at physical disks and slices, we can continue with the process of forensically sound imaging on a Mac. In the next section, we will discuss the DiskArbitration daemon and how it functions.

The DiskArbitration Daemon

You can think of a "daemon" as a service that continuously runs in the background, either waiting to perform a task or performing tasks without user interaction. DiskArbitration is a daemon that runs in the background, and one of its tasks is to mount and unmount disks as they are introduced to your Mac. As an example, when your Mac is running and you insert a USB Flash drive, DiskArbitration immediately recognizes that this disk has been introduced and mounts the available partitions. When you select to eject the device from the Mac, DiskArbitration performs the necessary tasks to perform a clean unmount for the disk.

This daemon makes external disk usage extremely convenient for standard users, but computer forensic examiners are not standard users. We need to control what happens to devices as they are introduced if we wish to be able to use our Mac for forensic imaging. Unfortunately, you cannot control DiskArbitration on a per-disk basis. You can only choose to enable it or disable it. The operating system version you are running will determine what steps you need to take to disable and enable DiskArbitration. It is by far much simpler to control the daemon in Mac OS X 10.5 than in other OS versions. So that's the version we'll discuss here:

- To disable DiskArbitration in Mac OS X 10.5, launch the terminal and type **sudo launchctl unload /System/Library/LaunchDaemons/com.apple.diskarbitrationd.plist**.

- To enable DiskArbitration in Mac OS X 10.5, launch the terminal and type **sudo launchctl load /System/Library/LaunchDaemons/com.apple.diskarbitrationd.plist**. Then type **killall Finder**.

Those simple commands give you complete control over the daemon. We will use this later as we begin the imaging process. But first, let's look at how to control the DiskArbitration daemon in Mac OS 10.4:

- To disable DiskArbitration in Mac OS X 10.4, launch the Terminal and type **sudo cp /etc/mach_init.d/diskarbitrationd.plist /Backup/**. Then type **sudo rm /etc/mach_init.d/diskarbitrationd.plist**. Reboot your Macintosh and DiskArbitration is now off.

- To enable DiskArbitration in Mac OS X 10.4, launch the terminal and type **sudo cp /Backup/diskarbitrationd.plist /etc/mach_init.d/**. Reboot your Macintosh and DiskArbitration is now on.

The enable/disable process in Mac OS X 10.4 is a bit more complicated, and it has a *huge* pitfall. If you skip the copy step and decide not to back up the diskarbitrationd.plist file, you will *not* be able to reenable DiskArbitration later! You can save yourself some headaches by getting a copy of this file from someone else, however, so all is not lost.

Connecting the Mac to Be Acquired

With DiskArbitration successfully under control, you can now move on to connecting a Mac to be acquired. Whether you are using TDM or you had to use the more laborious method of removing the hard drive and connecting it via USB/FireWire, the procedure here is the same.

In Figure 7.4, when we used the *ls disk?* command in the /dev directory, we found out what devices were currently attached to the Mac. Specifically, in Figure 7.4 I showed how disk0 through disk2 were used. You could hypothesize that the next external disk connected to this Macintosh would be assigned the device file disk3, and you likely would be correct. I say "likely," though, because in some instances the sequence won't follow your logic.

Figure 7.7 shows the Terminal window with a new device connected to the analysis Mac.

Figure 7.7 Terminal Window Showing a New Device Connected to This Macintosh

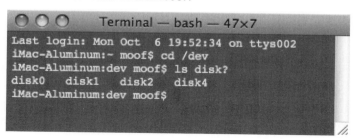

Figure 7.7 shows a perfect example of the sequence not following the preceding hypothesis. For this example, I connected a MacBook Pro in TDM to my analysis Mac. Because I have DiskArbitration disabled, the *diskutil* command is not available to me.

Let's now take a look at the connected physical device using the *hdiutil* command (see Figure 7.8).

Figure 7.8 Terminal Window Showing
Detailed Information of disk4 Using *hdiutil*

```
 ○ ○ ○                Terminal — bash — 71×19
Last login: Mon Oct  6 19:53:36 on ttys002
iMac-Aluminum:~ moof$ hdiutil partition /dev/disk4
scheme:      GUID
block size: 512
  ## Type_____  Name_____  Start___ Size____
+    MBR                    Protective Master Boo      0        1
+    Primary GPT Header     GPT Header                 1        1
+    Primary GPT Table      GPT Partition Data         2       32
+    Apple_Free                                       34        6
   1 C12A7328-F81F-11D2-BA  EFI System Partition      40   409600
   2 Apple_HFS              Untitled              409640 282853376
+    Apple_Free                                  283263016   262144
   3 Windows_NTFS           Untitled            283525160 107196768
+    Apple_Free                                  390721928        7
+    Backup GPT Table       GPT Partition Data  390721935       32
+    Backup GPT Header      GPT Header          390721967        1

+ synthesized
iMac-Aluminum:~ moof$
```

Figure 7.8 shows the partitioning of the physical disk inside the MacBook Pro. Notice the three slices, along with the manufacturer partitions. You also can figure out the approximate size of this hard drive through computation. Notice that the last sector of the physical drive must be 390,721,967 because the Backup GPT Header starts at physical sector 390,721,967 and has a size of 1 sector. Since the hard drive sector numbering starts with 0, we know there is a total of 390,721,968 sectors on this drive. Now, notice in the upper left where it states the block size is "512". On a Mac, a block is a sector. Here you can see that the block or sector size is reported as 512, meaning 512 bytes.

With this information, you can calculate drive capacity. The equation to calculate the approximate drive size in megabytes looks like this:

(Number of Sectors) multiplied by (Block Size) divided by (1,048,576)

Specifically for our example:

(390,721,968) * (512) / (1,048,576) = 190,782 megabytes

If you want gigabytes, divide this number by 1,024:

190,782 megabytes / 1,024 = 186 gigabytes

Remember, this number is an approximation and not an exact representation of the drive capacity. To acquire this MacBook Pro uncompressed you should have 200GB available on your evidence collection drive.

Acquisition Process, Step by Step

Believe it or not, you are now ready to begin an acquisition of a Mac using a Mac. You have determined whether TDM is available, or whether you need to connect the Internet hard drive using some other means. You have taken control of DiskArbitration so that you can control when the Mac operating system can mount a connected hard drive, and you have learned how to determine the relevant information regarding each connected device to the analysis Macintosh itself. Now it is time to bring all of this together. Exercise 7.1 will take you through the steps of performing a forensically sound acquisition of a Mac using a Mac.

Configuring & Implementing...

Exercise 7.1: Acquiring a Macintosh Using a Macintosh

This exercise details the steps necessary to forensically acquire a Macintosh using the built-in tools of the Macintosh operating system.

1. If you are using Mac OS X 10.4, disable DiskArbitration and reboot your system. Launch the Terminal and type the command **cd /dev**. Then type the command **ls disk?**. Note the results here. These are the disks currently attached to your system.

2. If you are using Mac OS X 10.5, disable DiskArbitration by typing the following command: **sudo launchctl unload /System/Library/ LaunchDaemons/com.apple.diskarbitrationd.plist**.

3. Boot the Macintosh to be acquired to TDM. Make certain you perform your first boot by pushing the **Power button** and then immediately holding down the **Option key** to check for an Open Firmware Password. If no Open Firmware Password has been applied, power off the Macintosh by holding down the **Power button**, power it back on, and immediately hold down the **T key** to cause the Mac to go into TDM.

4. Using a FireWire cable, connect the cable end to the TDM Mac.

5. Connect the opposite end of the FireWire cable to your analysis Mac that has DiskArbitration disabled. If you are connecting a removed hard drive, connect it to your analysis Mac now via the appropriate connection (USB or FireWire).

Continued

6. In the Terminal window, type the command **ls disk?**. Note the results here. You should have one additional "disk" noted that was not listed in step 1. This is the Mac you attached in TDM (or the external drive attached via some other means).

7. Type the command **hdiutil partition /dev/disk#**, where # represents the number of the disk of the Mac you connected.

8. From the output of step 7, calculate the size of the internal hard drive of the Mac you will acquire. You need this information to determine whether you have enough room on your analysis Mac to acquire or whether you will need to connect a larger external drive to properly contain the image.

9. Assuming your analysis Mac has sufficient space to perform the acquisition, create a folder on your desktop as a destination for the image by typing the following command: **mkdir ~/Desktop/Evidence_Collection**.

10. Calculate an MD5 hash of the suspect Mac. You do this as the integrity reference of the image you will create. To calculate this, type the following command: **md5 /dev/disk# > ~/Desktop/Evidence_Collection/SuspectMac.md5.txt**, where # represents the number of the disk of the Mac you connected. This command calculates the MD5 hash and saves it to a text file in your Evidence_Collection folder.

11. Begin the acquisition of the Macintosh by typing the following command: **sudo dd if=/dev/disk# conv=noerror,sync of=~/Desktop/Evidence_Collection/SuspectMac.dmg**, where # represents the number of the disk of the Mac you connected. During the acquisition, you will receive no feedback from the dd utility.

12. When the dd utility has finished, you will have your cursor back, ready for the next command to be typed. You will also see a message on the screen regarding the number of "Records In and Records Out". With the imaging process done, hold down the **Power button** of the suspect Mac to power it off (or power off the hard drive that you connected for acquisition).

13. Disconnect the FireWire cable from your analysis Mac as well as the suspect Mac. Properly secure the suspect Mac as original evidence.

14. In the Terminal, validate the image you just created by calculating an MD5 hash of it. Type the following command: **md5 ~/Desktop/Evidence_Collection/SuspectMac.dmg > ~/Desktop/Evidence_Collection/SuspectMac.dmg.md5.txt**. This command calculates the MD5 hash of the image file and saves it to a text file in your Evidence_Collection folder.

15. Close the Terminal and navigate in the Finder to your Desktop; double-click the **Evidence_Collection folder** to open it.

16. *Single-click* the **SuspectMac.dmg file**. Absolutely *do not* double-click this file. The Mac will mount this file and changes will immediately occur to the data.

Continued

17. From the Finder menu bar, click the **File** menu and select **Get Info**.

18. In the Get Info window, click the **Locked** checkbox to lock the file so that changes cannot be made to it.

19. Close the Get Info window. In the Evidence_Collection folder, open the two text files you created as a result of calculating the MD5 hash of your original drive and the image file. Compare the values. If they are not the same, errors occurred. This is not always a bad thing. We will discuss how MD5 values may not match later.

20. Close your text files. Your acquisition is complete and the image file is ready for archive or analysis.

End of Exercise

The steps in Exercise 7.1 are likely not going to work for you on the first try. Do not get frustrated. Some of the commands require exact typing with no sympathy for error. It is in your best interest to practice these steps many times with a few different Macs to become proficient in the task and to understand exactly what you are accomplishing with each step.

NOTE

Calculating the hash value of your original Mac and your image file can result in different values. Although this is certainly undesirable, it is possible. If this occurs, first you should check your acquisition process and start from the beginning. Consider using a different FireWire cable this time in case your first cable is flawed. If a second acquisition results in mismatched MD5 hash values, you likely have a suspect hard drive that is having "read errors". As a part of your dd, you told the acquisition *noerror,sync* as an option, meaning to pad a bad read with spaces. Because your image will now have areas that have data that is not the same as the original, an MD5 hash will not calculate to the same value. The image itself is still a usable image in that the data is the best that was attainable.

Pitfalls and Benefits of Imaging Using the dd Utility

The file you created in Exercise 7.1 is a "raw" image of the original, meaning it is uncompressed and is a bit-for-bit duplicate of the original. Let's discuss some of the pitfalls of imaging using this method, and then point out the benefits.

Pitfalls of imaging using dd include a lack of compression, no user feedback during the imaging process, and a lack of verification such as MD5 during the imaging process. The lack of compression results in an image file that is equal in size to the original drive. In our example, I would need 200GB of free space to acquire the internal drive of the MacBook Pro that was connected. If compression were used, this likely would have been reduced by 75 percent as I know my hard drive was less than half full. Also, during the imaging process, dd gives no feedback regarding how far along it is in the process. Although this is a simple inconvenience, this sometimes causes users to think the process has locked. Lastly, we had to take a separate step to calculate the MD5 hash. It would be much more efficient to calculate this value as the data was being read the first time through.

Despite the pitfalls associated with dd, there are many benefits to using it for forensic acquisitions. Probably the best reason is the bit-for-bit copy that it creates along with its tested results. Many agencies and neutral authorities in the forensic arena have validated this utility. The dd utility is included with every Mac OS X version from 10.0 to 10.5. That makes it always available no matter what system you happen to be at. Also, a variety of forensic utilities can read the uncompressed image it creates, including AccessData's Forensic Toolkit, BlackBag's BlackBag Macintosh Forensic Suite, ASR Data's SMART, and Guidance Software's EnCase, as well as the Mac system itself. This is a huge benefit in terms of compatibility. You should become more familiar with this command by executing the *man dd* command in the Terminal and reading about all of the options available.

Before closing this chapter, I would be remiss if I excluded a few of the free imaging utilities that are available for the Macintosh that have addressed the shortcomings of dd. You can find open source versions of more robust versions of dd under the names "dcfldd" (http://dcfldd.sourceforge.net/) and "dc3dd" (http://dc3dd.sourceforge.net/). Each of these compilations has addressed the downfalls that I mentioned earlier.

I caution you in using one feature with each of these, however: compression. Always remember that when you choose to compress your acquisition, you will lose the ability to use the data with many of the other forensic tools, including the Macintosh operating system itself. You will need to decompress the data before it becomes useful again.

Imaging a Mac with a Mac is a technique you will perfect and revise as you read more about the tools available and the options they offer. You likely will add additional steps to Exercise 7.1 to customize your own routine for a sound image every time that suits your needs. As with every tool, always test your techniques prior to using them in a case scenario.

Imaging a Mac with a Live CD

No two acquisition scenarios are exactly the same. Some acquisitions will be similar with the procedure matching each and every step, and only the MD5 hash values and the computer models will be different. Other times, you will simply not be able to use the same tools you would typically choose. Imaging a Mac with a Mac allows for a certain amount of convenience, familiarity, and comfort because it is your analysis Mac. But at times you simply cannot set up two Macs in a small area, such as a suspect's home.

For times when you would like to be able to boot a suspect Mac using only a CD, you have Linux bootable CDs available. Much like the bootable floppy disk of yesterday, the bootable CD offers a full operating system on a disc, many times with a full complement of applications. Forensic examiners have many Live CD offerings to choose from as well. Beyond the free offerings of the

Linux CDs, proprietary products are also available specifically for the Mac. In this section, we will take a general look at some of the tools available and how you can use them if you need to take this course of action for imaging a Mac.

We'll begin by talking about a few of the offerings of bootable Linux Live CDs available for the Mac. Before mentioning any of them specifically, it is important to note that *no single Linux distribution will boot every Macintosh!* This is true in the PC world as well. It is impossible to include every single driver necessary, for every revision and model of Macintosh, on a single disc, especially when the computer is newer than the CD itself. This means you will likely need to carry a few different bootable Live CDs with you in case one will not work on the particular model Mac you intend to boot. When you find a Live CD that works with a particular model, save that disc for future use!

Live CD compilations are available depending on the "distribution" of Linux on which they are based. *Linux* is a general term for an operating system, but it is incorrect to think that Linux *is* the operating system. Linux is actually at the core, or more accurately, the kernel of the distribution. Distributions come in variations such as Knoppix, Ubuntu, and Slackware. Numerous distributions to boot a typical PC are available; however, fewer are available to boot the Mac.

Of keen interest to us are the reworked distributions that have been specifically modified to be forensically sound. Available for free are distributions such as Raptor from Forward Discovery (www.forwarddiscovery.com), and Helix from e-fense (www.e-fense.com/helix). Both of these distributions are based on the Ubuntu Linux distribution and will successfully boot Intel-based Macintosh computers. Raptor also offers a PowerPC Ubuntu-based Live CD that will boot many of the PowerPC G4 and G5 Macs as well. Choosing a distribution is as easy as downloading the ISO or disc image of the CD itself. If you choose to download Raptor from Forward Discovery, you will find it has a few specific options that have been added to the Raptor Toolbox that make imaging a Macintosh especially easy. Both Raptor and Helix have support for the HFS+ file system, meaning you will be able to conduct a "preview" of the contents of the Mac you have just booted. Helix contains several excellent search and viewing utilities for images, a key point for any "preview" being conducted (e.g., child pornography searches). Both Raptor and Helix will successfully boot PCs and can be used for PC acquisitions and limited forensics as well.

Also available, for a fee, is SMART from ASR Data (www.asrdata.com). This Live CD comes in two distributions—Slackware and Ubuntu—and offers even greater compatibility across a wider variety of PCs and Macintoshes. SMART is a much more robust application environment that you can use for a full forensic analysis, not just imaging. The developer of this distribution is a Macintosh developer and likely will make certain that it continues to function on all future Macintoshes.

Moving away from the Linux environment, Macintosh-bootable environments are available for forensics as well. BlackBag offers the Macquisition DVD and Subrosasoft offers its bootable DVD as a part of its MacForensicsLab suite. Each of these solutions is a bootable Mac OS X-based DVD that offers a familiar Mac environment. Each program is an excellent choice to add to your Macintosh forensic toolkit as your budget allows.

Now that I have mentioned a few of the available bootable CD or DVD options, let's discuss in general terms what you should expect when you use any of these Live CDs. First, as with TDM, you will need to make certain that the Mac you wish to boot with a Live CD does not have an Open Firmware Password applied. If an Open Firmware Password has been applied, the Mac will not boot from media other than the assigned boot drive. To check for the presence of an Open Firmware Password and boot your Live CD, follow the steps in Exercise 7.2.

Configuring & Implementing...

Exercise 7.2: Boot a Live CD (or DVD) in a Macintosh

This exercise details the steps necessary to boot a Macintosh from a CD or DVD.

1. Power on the suspect Macintosh and immediately hold down the **Option key**.

2. If a Lock icon with an authentication dialog box is displayed, an Open Firmware Password has been applied. You need to consider Apple's technique for removing an Open Firmware Password versus losing the date and time information caused by the procedure.

3. If a list of bootable partitions and drives is presented, you have an open Macintosh. You can insert your bootable CD (or DVD) at this point.

4. If the CD does not automatically show in the list after a few seconds, click the **Refresh icon**. The icon looks like a curved arrow. If the CD still does not show, you may have a CD that this Mac does not recognize as a bootable disc. Consider a different disc.

End of Exercise

Once you have successfully booted from your Live CD of choice, you will also need an external hard drive to acquire to. Going into a situation, it is difficult to know how large your evidence collection drive should be. You be the judge of how much storage you can carry with you. In your laboratory, large amounts of storage will not be a problem. Some of the Live CDs will have the option of establishing a network connection to a storage medium in your laboratory so that you can acquire over gigabit Ethernet for optimal speed.

A last cautionary word about Live CDs before ending this section: Many more Linux distributions are available than Live CD Linux distributions. Moreover, many more Live CD distributions of Linux are available than forensically modified distributions of Live CDs. If you choose to boot from "any" Live CD, you may wind up doing the harm that computer forensic examiners always strive to prevent: system alterations. Most Live CD distributions are built with user convenience, not forensic examiners, in mind. These distributions will auto-mount all available media in a read/write state. That is a huge problem for computer forensic examiners. Choose your bootable media wisely and test it. Become familiar with its boot process, including all messages it typically displays, so that you are well aware of its functions during an evidence collection or preview.

Summary

Acquiring evidence can be considered the basis for everything else you do. Imaging a Macintosh can be challenging at times, when physical access to the hard drive is necessary. Fortunately, as you have learned, Apple has a unique technology known as Target Disk Mode that has made access to the digital data as easy as connecting a FireWire hard drive.

Also, because of the UNIX basis of the Mac operating system, you have the ability to conduct forensically sound acquisitions of Macs (or PCs) without having to purchase any other hardware or software. Taking control of a daemon known as DiskArbitration gives you complete control of media auto-mounting, and the Terminal has unique tools such as dd and MD5 for acquiring and verifying digital data.

Sometimes you cannot acquire data using two computers. In this chapter, you found that you can boot the Macintosh from a CD or DVD to a forensically sound distribution of Linux or the Mac operating system. Lastly, it is important to remember that there is not a single solution for imaging every Macintosh computer. As an examiner, you will need to be familiar with many imaging options so that you have each available when necessary.

Solutions Fast Track

Setting Up an Analysis Mac

☑ When you set up an analysis Mac you should conduct a secure erase of the internal hard disk and reinstall the operating system and all applications you intend to use. This methodology guarantees the contents of the system to be known to you.

☑ The installation DVD that comes with your Macintosh is extremely important. Many times, it is the only media that can reinstall the operating system to your specific hardware. Keep your media in a safe place.

☑ Disable insecure access methods to your analysis Mac. This includes services such as Bluetooth and Wireless networking.

Imaging a Mac with a Mac

☑ Target Disk Mode allows a Mac to act as an external FireWire hard drive. When you are in this mode and are using another Macintosh, you can make a physical image of the contents of the hard drive contained within.

☑ To use your analysis Mac for acquisitions, you need to control the DiskArbitration daemon. You need to disable DiskArbitration to stop connected physical media from being auto-mounted. Further, this prevents alterations to the content.

☑ Mac OS X has built-in utilities available to create and verify forensically sound images of devices. You can use the dd utility to acquire an entire physical image of a Macintosh and MD5 to mathematically compute verifications of the data acquired.

☑   Third-party utilities are available for imaging a Mac with a Mac. Some of these utilities are freely available, such as dcfldd and dc3dd, whereas others are purchasable products. Regardless of the product you choose, test and validate its use in your own controlled environment first before using it on evidence.

Imaging a Mac with a Live CD

☑   Macintoshes can boot from both CD and DVD available operating systems. There are many distributions of bootable operating systems on CD or DVD to choose from. For us as examiners, there are a subset of these that are considered forensically sound distributions. They can be found in distributions of the Linux operating system on CD and the Mac OS on DVD.

☑   Prior to booting from a Live CD, it is critical to check for the presence for an Open Firmware Password. If an Open Firmware Password has been applied, booting from a CD or DVD is not possible until the password has been removed.

☑   Using a Live CD as your imaging methodology requires that a storage medium be connected. If you are away from your laboratory, you will need to select storage that will "most likely" accommodate the Macs you will encounter. Inside your laboratory, where storage may be less of an issue, you will also have the option of acquiring over gigabit Ethernet with some Live CDs.

☑   There is not one single, perfect imaging solution for every Macintosh you will encounter. You should have several available to you, and be familiar with their operation.

Frequently Asked Questions

Q: Should I image a Mac using Target Disk Mode, remove the hard drive, or use a Live CD?

A: That answer will always depend on the circumstances of the day. Target Disk Mode alleviates the need of disassembling many of the more complicated Macs, but it is not available to every model. Using a Live CD offers the ability to carry a single CD and a storage solution only for a smaller on-scene toolkit when necessary.

Q: Is there a single Linux Live CD that seems to be better than any other?

A: Yes if you ask the developer of each of their respective distributions, and no when it comes to forensics. No single Live CD will boot every Macintosh. Each distribution offers similar features, yet differentiates itself with some unique feature that is not found in the others. You will be able to answer this question as you begin to familiarize yourself with the tools through usage.

Q: When imaging a Mac with a Mac, it seems highly inefficient to acquire the image without using some form of compression. Is there a way I can compress the data to save on space?

A: Yes, but there is a downfall to this. To conduct a full analysis of the acquired image, it will need to be uncompressed. Also, in compressed form, the image will not be recognized by other popular forensic applications, such as AccessData's Forensic Toolkit and Guidance Software's EnCase.

Q: Continuing with compression, Forensic Toolkit and EnCase can acquire using compression and can conduct an analysis of the acquired data. It seems highly inefficient to use uncompressed data for analysis.

A: On the contrary; uncompressed data offers the fastest of access times to the data at hand. Beyond that point, when Forensic Toolkit or EnCase indexes the data of an acquired image, each tool must create an external file, which is time-consuming. With Mac OS X, you can mount your acquired image and allow Spotlight to create a lightning-fast index of the data for easy searching. Spotlight searching is not the answer to a full analysis, though. A robust tool such as MacForensicsLab utilizes the efficiency of an uncompressed image to produce fast results as well when searching through unallocated space. There is not a single perfect tool for analysis, and the uncompressed image allows for the physical image to be examined by the widest range of forensic tools.

Chapter 8

Recovering Browser History

Solutions in this chapter:

- **Recovering Items from Web Cache**
- **Recovering Items from plist Files**

☑ **Summary**

☑ **Solutions Fast Track**

☑ **Frequently Asked Questions**

Introduction

When a user surfs the Internet, traces of the search are left behind on the user's system. These traces contain very valuable information to a computer forensic investigator. Items such as browser cache and cookies can indicate what Web sites the user visited. Cookies are traces with user specific settings that are left behind on users' systems. Pictures are stored on the local system cache to speed up Web browsing. As an investigator, it is imperative that you are able to find the traces left on a machine from a user's browsing sessions.

Mac users tend to migrate toward the built-in Safari browser. Safari does have limitations, such as running too slow and JavaScript problems, so users often will install additional browsers, such as Firefox and Opera. Firefox is a free browser created by the Mozilla project, and Opera is a cross-platform Web browser available from Opera Software.

It is important for computer forensic investigators to be able to recover artifacts from all Internet browsers, regardless of what browser is utilized. The information an investigator can recover from a browsing session can often help him or her prove what sites an individual visited, and thus can provide critical information in a computer forensic investigation.

Since most Mac users utilize the Safari browser, in this chapter we will focus on Safari. We will discuss how to recover items from a computer's Web cache, as well as how to recover items from property list (plist) files.

Recovering Items from Web Cache

Web cache can provide you as a computer forensic investigator with information regarding what Web sites a user has visited. Many investigations are tied to items within a user's Web cache. As an investigator, you will want to know where the items related to the user's Web cache are located, and how to view and analyze those items. In this section, we will concentrate on the artifacts left behind in the Safari cache.

~/Library/Caches/Safari

As noted earlier, Web browsers use a computer's cache file to speed up the user's Internet experience by holding information in the cache to re-create Web pages more quickly. Therefore, you can gather evidentiary information from the cache file. The location of the cache folder has not changed from Tiger to Leopard; the only difference is the way Leopard stores the cache file. Leopard's Safari cache is in the form of a database file, located in /[username]/library/Caches/com.apple.Safari.

Load the **ronaldcarter.dmg** image from the DVD that accompanies this book, and navigate to the /[username]/library/Caches/com.apple.Safari folder, as shown in Figure 8.1.

Figure 8.1 The Location of the Safari Cache

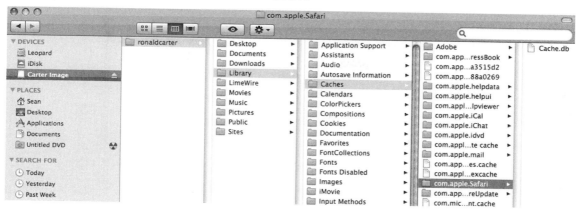

As you can see, the cache file is a cache.db file. The .db extension tells you that this is a database file. You can open this file with SQLite, but doing so will give you only a list of the images in the file. To actually view the images, you need to use File Juicer. Created by Echo One (www.echoone.com), the File Juicer software can parse out various file types.

Follow these steps to view the contents of the cache.db file:

1. Open the **ronaldcarter.dmg** image from the DVD that accompanies this book.

2. Download and install File Juicer (a trial version is available at www.echoone.com).

3. Start File Juicer. From the File Juicer toolbar, select **File | Open**, as shown in Figure 8.2.

Figure 8.2 Demonstrating the Use of File Juicer

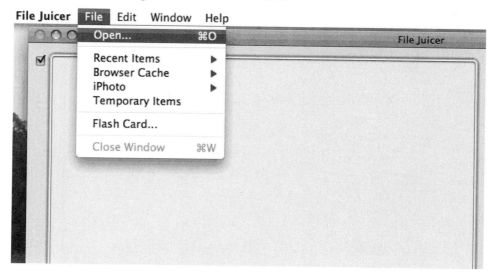

4.   Navigate to ronaldcarter/Library/Caches/com.apple.Safari/Cache.db, and click **Open**, as shown in Figure 8.3. File Juicer will parse through the cache.db file.

Figure 8.3 Opening the Cache.db File in File Juicer

After File Juicer has finished the parse, a window will present the results, as shown in Figure 8.4. The default location of these output files is the desktop.

Figure 8.4 Files Created by File Juicer

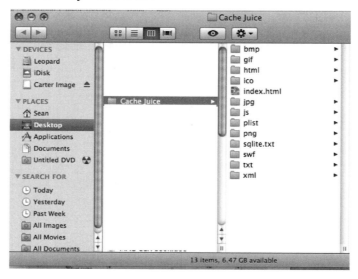

As you can see, many folders contain information that could be valuable in an investigation. In our example:

- The bmp or Bitmap folder and the .gif or Graphic Interchange Format folder both contain images that were parsed from the cache.db file.
- The html folder contains the Web pages that were visited.
- The ico folder contains icons parsed from the cache.db file. These icons are images that can be displayed in the Safari URL bar.
- The index.html file contains a complete Web page. This is not the user's home page.
- The jpg folder contains more images from the cache.db file.
- The plist folder contains numbered property lists that show the URLs the user visited.
- The png folder contains more images.
- The sqlite.txt folder contains a text file of all items parsed.
- The swf folder contains a Flash file of the Web sites visited.
- The txt folder contains numerous files of the HTML code from the Web pages visited, and more will be found in the XML folder as well.

So that you can associate a date and time with a possible piece of evidence, each file has the correct Modified, Accessed, and Created (MAC) times listed (see Figure 8.5).

Figure 8.5 Associating the Dates and Times with the Cache Files

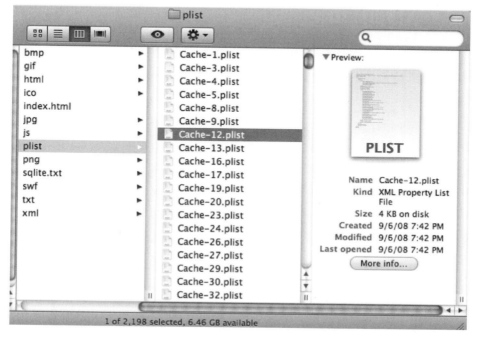

~Library/Safari

You can find more items of evidentiary value in the /[username]/Library/Safari folder. Bookmarks, Downloads, History, and cookie information are found in the ~/Library/Safari folder. This folder contains all the data that an investigator will need to ascertain the web related evidence as it pertains to Safari 3 and the Leopard operating system.

Recovering Items from plist Files

We will examine four essential plist files in this chapter. Each of these files can provide a wealth of information regarding a user's Internet activity:

- Bookmarks.plist
- Downloads.plist
- History.plist
- Cookies.plist

Bookmarks.plist

The Bookmarks.plist file tracks and maintains the bookmarks that the user created within Safari. Safari 3 users will get certain bookmarks by default. Figure 8.6 shows these default bookmarks you will encounter if you use Safari.

Figure 8.6 Default Bookmarks in Safari 3

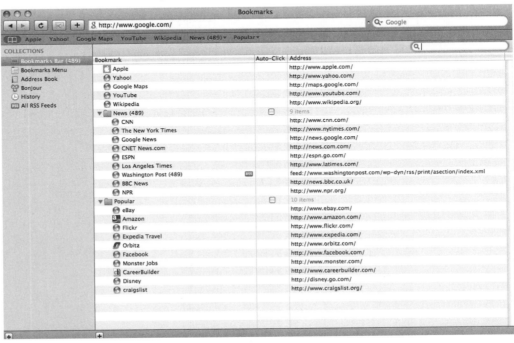

You can use Version Tracker's Safari Bookmark Exporter, which you can download from http://homepage.mac.com/simx/.Public/products/SBE1.1.dmg, to view the bookmarks of a user's image. This application will parse the Bookmarks.plist file and produce an HTML document that will list all the bookmarks. Follow along with Exercise 8.1 to see how this works.

Configuring & Implementing...

Exercise 8.1: Analyzing Safari Bookmarks

To view a user's bookmarks, follow these steps:

1. Download **Safari Bookmark Exporter** from Version Tracker (http://homepage.mac.com/simx/.Public/products/SBE1.1.dmg).

2. From your Mac forensic workstation, navigate to the **/[username]/Library/Safari/** folder.

3. Locate and delete the **Bookmarks.plist** file.

4. Open the **ronaldcarter.dmg** image from the DVD that accompanies this book, and navigate once again to the **/[username]/Library/Safari/** folder.

5. Copy the **Bookmarks.plist** file from the **ronaldcarter.dmg** image and paste it in the same location on your forensic machine.

6. Start **Safari Bookmark Explorer**. From the SBE Window, make sure the **Open Safari Bookmarks from Default Location** box is checked, as shown in Figure 8.7. Then select **Analyze Bookmarks**.

Continued

Figure 8.7 Opening Safari Bookmarks from the Default Location

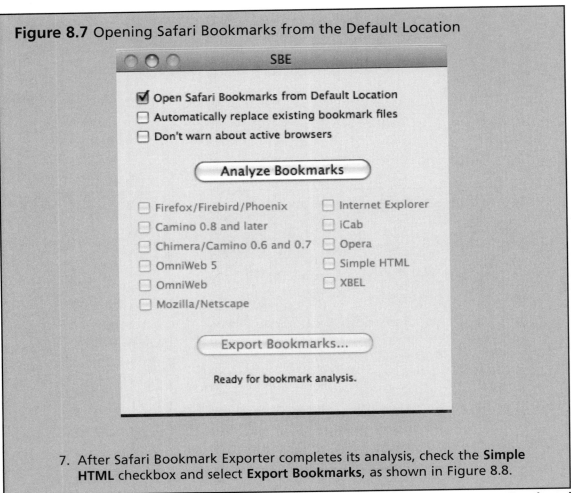

7. After Safari Bookmark Exporter completes its analysis, check the **Simple HTML** checkbox and select **Export Bookmarks**, as shown in Figure 8.8.

Continued

Figure 8.8 Configuration Settings for Safari Bookmark Exporter

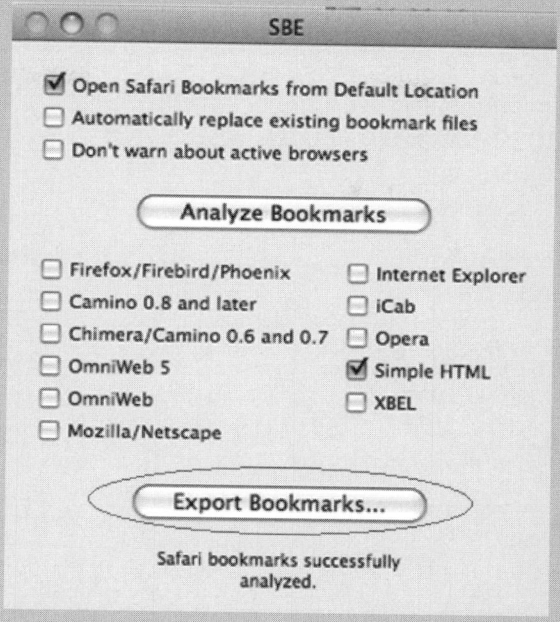

8. The application will ask where you want the output saved. Keep the default settings and select **Save**, as shown in Figure 8.9.

Figure 8.9 Exporting the Safari Bookmarks

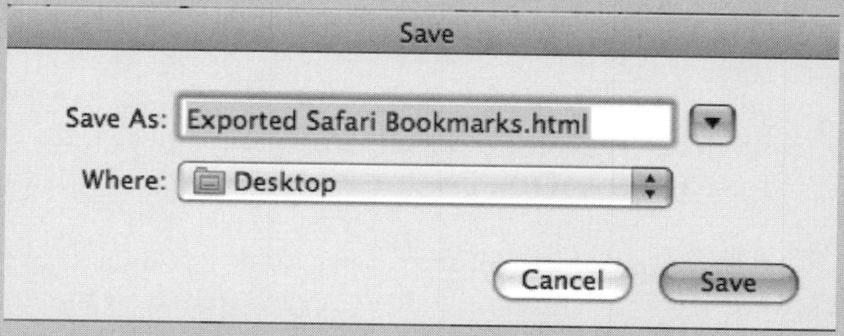

9. Review the results from the .html document that is created. Figure 8.10 is an example of the results generated by Safari Bookmark Exporter.

Continued

Figure 8.10 Viewing the Exported Safari Bookmarks

End of Exercise

Downloads.plist

Downloads.plist is an XML file that contains a history of all the items a particular user has downloaded. You can examine this file by opening the property list and viewing the information it contains.

To test-drive this technique, open the **ronaldcarter.dmg** image from the DVD that accompanies this book, navigate to **/ronaldcarter/Library/Safari/Downloads.plist**, control-click on the **Downloads.plist** file, and select **Open With**, and then select **Property List Editor** from the drop down menu.

Once the property list is opened, you will see information regarding each item the user downloaded, the URL from which the user downloaded each item, and the current location of each item (see Figure 8.11).

Figure 8.11 Downloads.plist File Results

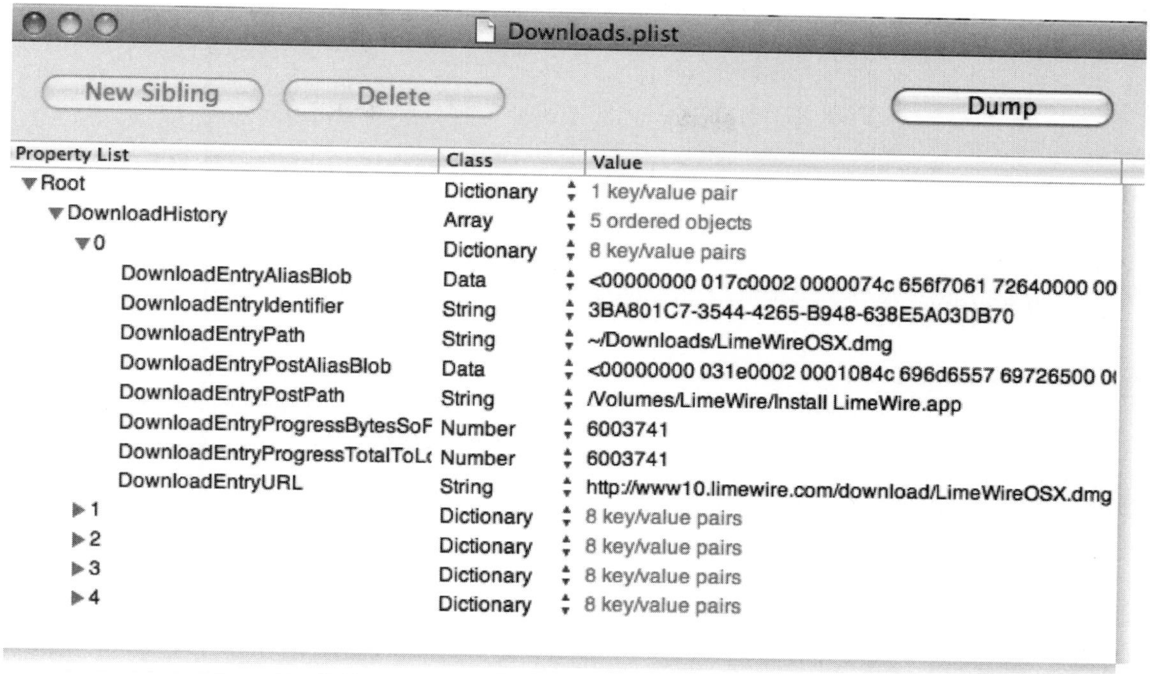

NOTE

The Form Values file, which is not humanly readable, is located at ~/Library/Safari/. It contains information from the auto fill function of Safari if the autofill has been enabled from the Safari | Preferences menu. The Form Values file is the location where items such as usernames, addresses, and phone numbers entered by the user are kept.

History.plist

The History.plist file provides information regarding the user's Internet history. Initially, the application that could parse the History.plist file in the Tiger operating system, called Retrospective, had to be downloaded from http://www.versiontracker.com/dyn/moreinfo/macosx/25612. However, Leopard does not support the Retrospective application, and at the time of this writing the developer, Joakim Nygard, does not have plans to update the application for Leopard. The native application Safari is also effective in manually reviewing the History.plist file, as shown in Exercise 8.2.

Configuring & Implementing...

Exercise 8.2: Examining the History.plist

In this exercise you will learn how to parse the History.plist file—first using Safari and then manually examining the property list.

1. Make sure Safari is not running, and then open the **ronaldcarter.dmg image** from the DVD that accompanies this book.

2. Navigate to the **/[username]/Library/Safari/Bookmarks.plist** file. Copy the **Bookmarks.plist** file.

3. From your forensic workstation paste the **Bookmarks.plist** file to the **/[username]/Library/Safari/** folder.

4. Start **Safari**. From the Safari menu bar, select **History** and then **Show All History**, as shown in Figure 8.12.

Figure 8.12 Showing All History in Safari

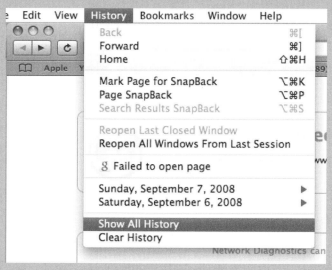

The browser history will be displayed. You will see the last Web site visited; the rest are separated by dates (see Figure 8.13).

Continued

Figure 8.13 Browser History

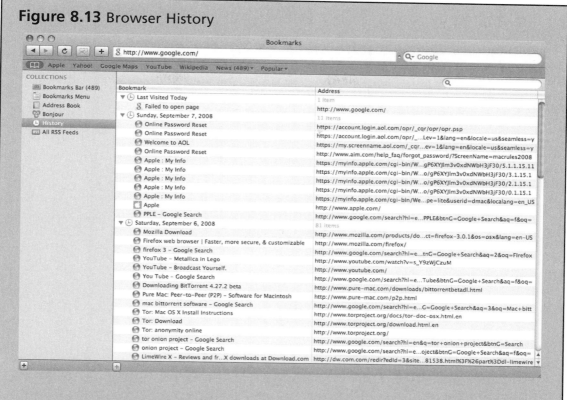

As noted earlier, you also can review the History.plist file manually. To do so, you need to utilize the Property List Editor, which is an application that is included in the Apple Developer Tools for editing plist files. The Property List Editor will open the XML-formatted property list in a readable fashion; then you can take a screen shot of the results and add it to your report.

5. Open the **ronaldcarter.dmg image** from the DVD that accompanies this book.

6. Navigate to **/Library/Safari/History.plist**, and use the **Property List Editor** to open the **History.plist** file. Figure 8.14 shows the opened History.plist file.

Continued

Figure 8.14 The History.plist File

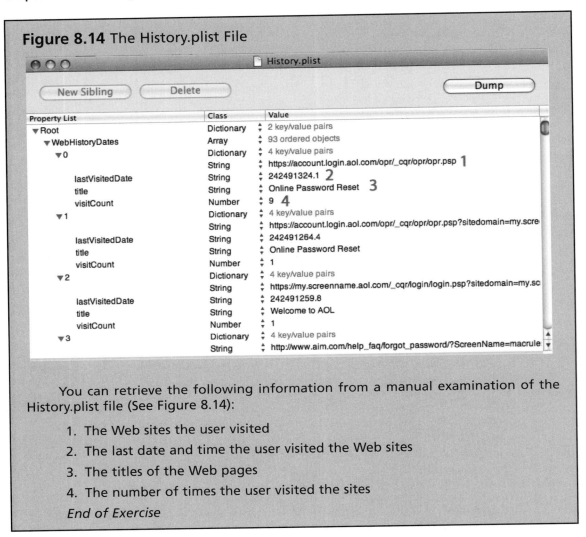

You can retrieve the following information from a manual examination of the History.plist file (See Figure 8.14):

1. The Web sites the user visited
2. The last date and time the user visited the Web sites
3. The titles of the Web pages
4. The number of times the user visited the sites

End of Exercise

All the information in the plist file is easy to read, except for the date, which is in absolute time. However, you can convert the absolute date and time to actual date and time using CFAbsoluteTimeConverter, an open source application that is included on the DVD that accompanies this book. Exercise 8.3 explains the steps to convert absolute date and time to actual date and time.

Configuring & Implementing...

Exercise 8.3: Converting Absolute Time

In this exercise you will learn how to convert the date and time from values within the **History.plist** file to actual date and time.

1. Open the **ronaldcarter.dmg image** from the DVD that accompanies this book, and navigate to the **/Library/Safari/History.plist** folder.

2. Open the **property list** with the **Property List Editor**. Expand the property list so that it shows all of the items in the list by holding down the **Alt** key and clicking the **triangle** at the top of the list.

3. Locate an item of interest. For this exercise, take note of the first item in the list, labeled "Online Password Reset," as shown in Figure 8.14.

4. Double Click the *lastVisitedDate* value.

5. Highlight the string.

6. Right click and select **Copy**.

7. Open the **CFAbsoluteTimeConverter** from the DVD that accompanies this book. Paste the value from the History.plist file into the **Enter the CFAbsoluteTime** window and select **Convert**. The results will be displayed under the Convert button, as shown in Figure 8.15.

Figure 8.15 History.plist Time Conversion

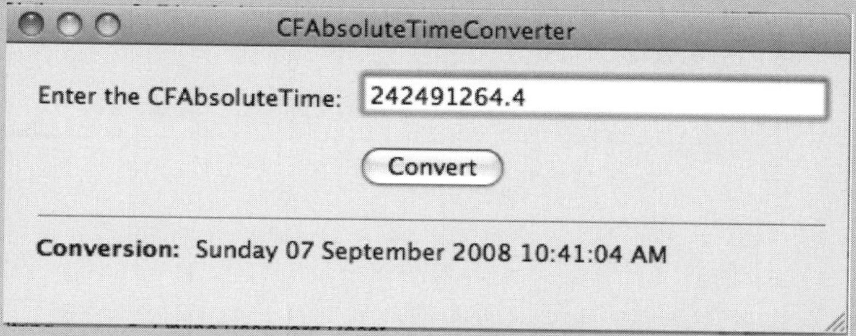

```
⊖ ○ ○            CFAbsoluteTimeConverter

Enter the CFAbsoluteTime:  242491264.4

                        ( Convert )

Conversion:  Sunday 07 September 2008 10:41:04 AM
```

End of Exercise

Also within the ~/Library/Safari folder, there are HistoryIndex.sk, LastSession.plist, and Webpageicons.db files. The HistoryIndex.sk file appears to have a lot of the same information as the History.plist file, along with a large list of words. This file can be opened and viewed with **TextEdit**.

LastSession.plist

The LastSession.plist file will contain URLs from the tabs of the last launch of Safari. You also can open and view this file with the Property List Editor (as shown in Figure 8.16).

WebpageIcons.db

The WebpageIcons.db file stores icons from Web pages that are displayed in the URL address bar of Safari. You can use File Juicer to open and view this .db file, as shown in Exercise 8.4.

Configuring & Implementing...

Exercise 8.4: Viewing Web Page Icons

In this exercise you will learn how to view URL address bar icons from Safari.

1. Open the **ronaldcarter.dmg** image from the DVD that accompanies this book.
2. Open File Juicer.
3. Select File, **Open**, from the File Juicer toolbar.
4. Navigate to the /Library/Safari/.
5. Select the Webpageicons.db, as shown in Figure 8.16.

Continued

Figure 8.16 Navigating to the /Library/Safari/WebpageIcons.db File

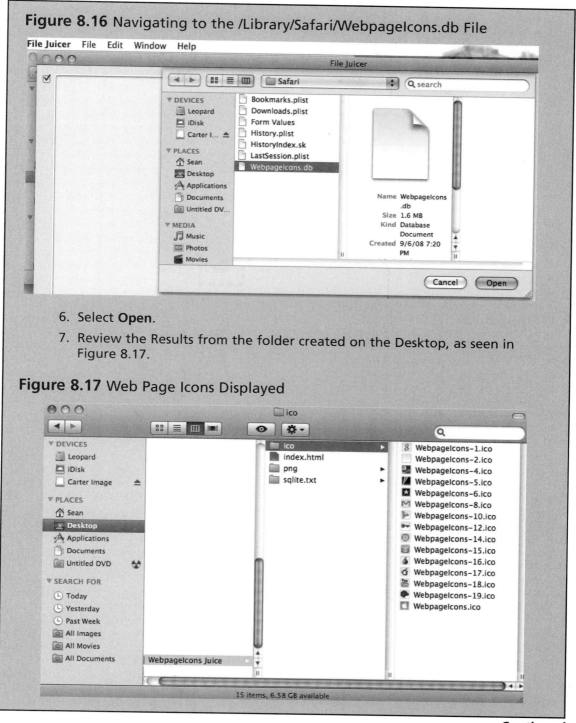

6. Select **Open**.
7. Review the Results from the folder created on the Desktop, as seen in Figure 8.17.

Figure 8.17 Web Page Icons Displayed

The items that File Juicer displayed (as shown in Figure 8.17) are as follows:

- **ico**

Displays Web page icons

- **index.html**

Provides nothing of evidentiary value

- **png**

Displays additional Web page icons

- **sqlite.txt**

A text file of all the values from the .db file

End of Exercise

Cookies.plist

Cookies are basically small pieces of data that Web servers use to identify Web users. Users tend to worry about cookies, but cookies typically don't damage file systems. As investigators, we can use cookies to track a user's Web browsing history.

The Safari Cookies.plist file is located in the /[username]/Library/Cookies/Cookies.plist folder. You can glean a mountain of information from this file. To view the contents of this file, Property List Editor can be used. Please follow the steps below to view the Cookies.plist folder.

1. Open the **ronaldcarter.dmg** Image from the DVD that accompanies this book.
2. Navigate to /Library/Cookies/Cookies.plist.
3. Right Click on the file and open the file with Property List Editor.
4. Review the Results, as shown in Figure 8.18.

Figure 8.18 The Cookies.plist File

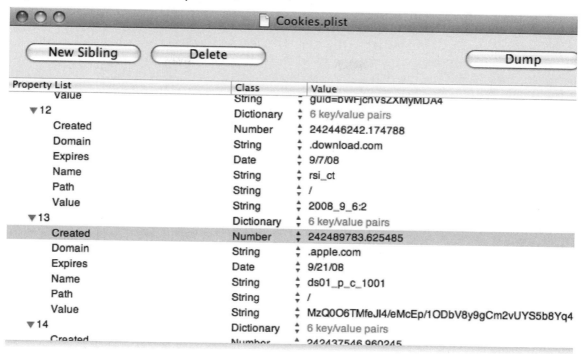

Let's review #13 from Figure 8.18. The plist will show:

- The date created in absolute time (**242489783.625485**) which can be converted using CFAbsoluteTimeConverter.

- The domain name where the cookie came from (**apple.com**).

- The expiration of the Cookie (**9/21/08**).

Summary

When users surf the Web they leave traces of data behind on their systems. Items such as browser cache and cookies can indicate what Web sites a user visited. Most Mac users use the built-in Safari browser, so as an investigator, it is important to be able to recover artifacts that are left behind by Safari. The information you can recover by browsing the History.plist, Cache.db, Bookmarks.plist, and Cookies.plist files can often help you to prove what sites an individual visited, the frequency of those visits, and a propensity for that individual to gravitate to particular Web sites. Lastly, recovering browsing history often plays a critical role in a computer forensics investigation.

Solutions Fast Track

Recovering Items from Web Cache

- ☑ You can use File Juicer to extract information from the Web cache database.
- ☑ You can recover such elements as images, HTML code, property lists, and date and time information.

Recovering Items from plist Files

- ☑ You can recover information from the Downloads.plist file by using the Property List Editor.
- ☑ Information regarding items a user has downloaded from the Internet via Safari can aid in an investigation, based on the type of case and the location of the items downloaded.
- ☑ The Downloads.plist file can tell you from which Web sites a user has downloaded information.
- ☑ You can recover a user's Web browsing history from the History.plist file.
- ☑ You can gather information from the History.plist file via File Juicer, Safari, and manual review methods.
- ☑ The Cookies.plist file can tell you which Web sites a user visited, as well as the date and time the user visited the sites.

Frequently Asked Questions

Q: What tool can I use to extract Web cache from the Safari browser?

A: You can use File Juicer to extract Web cache from the Safari browser.

Q: Is File Juicer an open source or proprietary tool?

A: File Juicer is a proprietary tool, but a free trial is available.

Q: What browser-related plist files should I examine?

A: It's important to examine the Bookmarks.plist, Downloads.plist, History.plist, Cookies.plist files.

Q: How can I recover information regarding the Web sites a user has visited, as well as when and how frequently the user visited the sites?

A: The History.plist file can tell you which Web sites a user visited, as well as when and how frequently the user visited those sites.

Q: How can I recover locations from which a user downloaded items?

A: You can recover such locations from the Downloads.plist file.

Q: How can I recover a user's Web browsing history?

A: The History.plist file will tell you a user's Web browsing history.

Q: How can I recover information from the Downloads.plist file?

A: The Property List Editor will enable you to recover information from the Downloads.plist file.

Chapter 9

Recovery of E-mail Artifacts, iChat, and Other Chat Logs

Solutions in this chapter:

- Popular E-mail Applications
- MobileMe (.Mac) and Web-Based E-mail
- Recovery of E-mail Data
- Address Book
- Popular Chat Applications
- Recovery of Chat Data

☑ Summary

☑ Solutions Fast Track

☑ Frequently Asked Questions

Introduction

E-mail and chat are the two most popular means of staying in touch with colleagues, friends, and family on the Windows platform. This is no different on the Mac. Watch your coworkers running to their desks and they will first check their e-mail before they check their voice mail. They may even have a chat window open at work to stay in instant communication with a friend or coworker. E-mail is used for business communications as well as personal conversations. E-mail might be gathered by a local application on the Macintosh, or it could be Web-based e-mail such as a Gmail account. Chats are used for the very same communications, except they will occur in real time. Chat has evolved from communicating via typed messages to including voice and video communication as well.

On the Macintosh, OS X Leopard includes some robust applications for handling e-mail and chat. Apple developed Mail to handle e-mail and iChat to handle instant messaging (IM). Of course, many other applications are available that boast features and nuances not available in the default Apple applications. In this chapter, we will explore some of these applications. We'll also look at the areas of interest for data recovery when performing forensics on a Macintosh. The Mac runs a well-organized operating system with OS X. This means you need to focus on specific areas of interest with every case before going "into the wild" and searching all over a suspect's hard drive for answers.

Popular E-mail Applications

E-mail is one of the most popular reasons a person uses his Macintosh. For this reason alone, you need to understand e-mail clients and data recovery. Apple includes with Mac OS X a robust e-mail application called Mail. Many times Apple's Mail will be referred to as Mail.app to distinguish it from mail a user receives in his Inbox or from Post Office mail! Apple's Mail supports both Post Office Protocol 3 (POP3) and Internet Message Access Protocol (IMAP) for configuration. By default, POP3 mail is downloaded to the user's system and removed from the server. IMAP mail resides on the server, much like Web mail. It has filtering for junk mail as well as customization for rules. Mail is the most popular e-mail application in use on the Mac, likely because it is included with the system and is configured on initial installation. Other popular e-mail applications include Microsoft's Entourage, Mozilla's Thunderbird, and Qualcomm's Eudora. Each application will attempt to suit a user's needs in a better way with better junk mail filtering, an easier user interface, and other features. What will be true of all of them are the historical remnants they leave behind; they all have forensic data!

In this chapter, we will explore Apple's Mail application. Techniques we demonstrate for this application will be easy to apply to other applications. And of course, we will also note data locations of interest for some third-party applications along the way.

NOTE

Even as we detail techniques for Apple's Mail application, Apple continues to enhance its security of both the operating system and Mail. This means that data locations can sometimes change, or that data formats can sometimes change. If you find that a technique described in this chapter does not seem to be directly applicable with your situation, check with Apple's Support Web site or Developer Web site to see whether something has changed.

MobileMe (.Mac) and Web-Based E-mail

Web-based e-mail is a popular way for people to receive their e-mail without worrying about being tied to a single computer to view it. Popular sources for Web-based e-mail include Yahoo!, Google, Microsoft MSN, and Hotmail. However, one e-mail service is unique in its presence on both the Web and the desktop. That service is MobileMe. MobileMe (formerly .Mac) is both Web-based and desktop-based e-mail. MobileMe is a service offered by Apple as an extension to the Mac OS X for a yearly fee. The fee varies depending on where a user shops, and typically ranges from $79 to $99 for one year of service for a single user account. You can expand the MobileMe service to five users through the family pack, which also expands the amount of online disk storage offered. Once a person subscribes to this service, he can obtain e-mail by configuring his local e-mail application to "fetch" his e-mail, or use Apple Mail, which supports the "push" feature of the MobileMe service.

NOTE

Fetching of e-mail can be defined as setting your client application to automatically check for e-mail at a set interval, such as every 15 minutes. *Pushing of e-mail* can be defined as a server-side update of your Inbox only when e-mail actually needs to be sent to you.

With MobileMe, users also can access their e-mail by visiting www.me.com and clicking the Apple Mail icon after authenticating. When a user has chosen to keep everything "in sync" through a MobileMe account, e-mail the user reads on the local machine will appear as having been read on the Web client at the MobileMe Web site.

Figures 9.1 and 9.2 show the interface of Apple Mail and MobileMe. In each figure, you can see that a single e-mail message is in the Inbox, shown with a blue dot. This means the message has been marked as unread. A properly configured MobileMe service will allow the user to read this message in Apple Mail or on the web at MobileMe, and the blue dot will disappear accordingly. In addition, if is the user deletes, forwards, replies to, or files this message in a MobileMe folder, that action will be reflected in Apple Mail. The MobileMe Web interface is supported fully through the Safari Web browser as well as Internet Explorer Version 6 and Firefox Versions 2 and 3. Does that mean you won't find MobileMe in other Web browsers? Of course not! Users will push the bounds and you should always be prepared to find data anywhere at any time. Internet Explorer 7 is the current browser on Windows XP and Vista releases and users will certainly attempt connections with this browser with regularity, just as an example.

Figure 9.1 Apple Mail Inbox

Figure 9.2 MobileMe Inbox

Other Web-based e-mail includes Yahoo!, Google, and Microsoft, with the "@yahoo.com", "@gmail.com", and "@hotmail.com" services, respectively. Each of these companies offers users free accounts and all of these services are extremely popular. Both Microsoft and Yahoo! force users to pay a fee to use their mail with a POP-based client, whereas Gmail does not charge for the service. When Web-based e-mail originated, a user would type in an e-mail address, such as mail.yahoo.com, and begin at the portal for authentication for Yahoo! Web-based e-mail. This was originally the only way to read your Web-based e-mail unless you chose to forward it to another account. This meant that Web-based e-mail would almost always be recovered as a part of browser history. Today, this isn't true. Not only can a user access his e-mail through the original portal, such as mail.yahoo.com, but also he can configure e-mail clients, such as Apple Mail, to access this e-mail as well. The service has developed on the Web side to support access from multiple methods. This means your examination of Apple Mail could include e-mail that is from what is now a Yahoo!-based e-mail account.

To further confuse (or better stated, blur) the technology lines, another Web-based e-mail method might be considered e-mail, might be considered chat, and might just fall into a class all its own. Web sites often have their own forums or communities. Within these forums, users can post to a forum topic which is a communitywide posting (and sometimes is public for the entire Internet). Even more interesting is the ability to send private messages within these communities. The message is sent through the Web site's messaging system to another user, and does not use a local e-mail application, nor does it use an e-mail account that receives e-mail outside that community. These can be some of the most difficult messages to track down until you can associate a username with a Web site. On the local machine, you'll find your best evidence in browser history, which we covered in Chapter 8.

Recovery of E-mail Data

Recovery of e-mail is always going to be based on the type of e-mail being recovered (locally stored versus Web-based e-mail) and on the application the suspect uses to access his e-mail. In this section, we will discuss Apple Mail for recovery, and then extrapolate on procedures that you can utilize for other e-mail applications, such as Microsoft Entourage.

We'll begin by defining the e-mail recovery scope. We'll be looking at a specific user account for the data that Apple Mail leaves with its use. We'll look at folders and files that exist on the Mac, within the Mac OS X file structure. We will not explore e-mail in the "deleted space" or unallocated clusters.

As you have seen so far with the Mac OS, the file structure is well defined. Apple Mail is no different and uses the user's Home directory efficiently. The Library folder for a user becomes a gold mine of data for e-mail recovery, whether it is Apple Mail or some other application. In Figure 9.3, you can see that the Library folder holds important folders for Apple Mail recovery.

Figure 9.3 The Library Folder Showing the Mail and Mail Downloads Folders

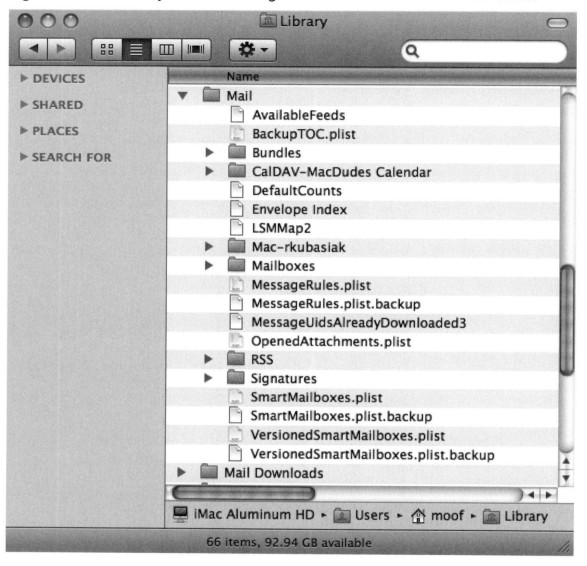

Figure 9.3 shows what are probably the two most important folders containing user data when dealing with Apple Mail as seen from the Finder. Specific to e-mail, you can see two folders: Mac-rkubasiak and Mailboxes. Let's deal with the Mac-rkubasiak folder first. This folder represents a MobileMe account with username "rkubasiak". Figure 9.4 shows the data contents of this folder.

Figure 9.4 MobileMe Stored in the User Library

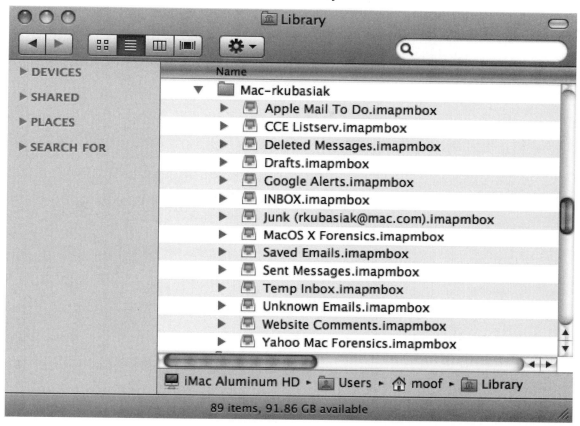

Figure 9.4 shows each mailbox used for this account. You can gather a lot of information by simply looking at this window. Let's begin to break it all down before we dig in even further. First, as stated before, you know this is a MobileMe (.Mac) account with a username of "rkubasiak". Immediately, you know you want to find out everything that has to do with the e-mail addresses rkubasiak@mac.com and rkubasiak@me.com. How can you come to that conclusion? MobileMe uses both of these domain names as a part of its service. The .Mac service users were all brought in with their .Mac addresses intact.

Next, you have the mailboxes that were created for this user named "moof"; default mailboxes created by MobileMe (such as the Inbox created by default) and custom mailboxes (such as MacOS X Forensics). Lastly, from this window view alone, you can see two usernames that we have discussed: "moof" and "rkubasiak". The username "moof" is the local account on this Macintosh and represents where you are gathering your current digital evidence. The username "rkubasiak" represents a username that is maintained by an Internet entity, in this case, Apple. You can always obtain more information through a subpoena to the provider, so consider preparing a subpoena in a criminal case for the accounts rkubasiak@mac.com and rkubasiak@me.com to be thorough.

Next, we'll look at the contents of an individual mailbox (see Figure 9.5).

Figure 9.5 Contents of the MobileMe Inbox

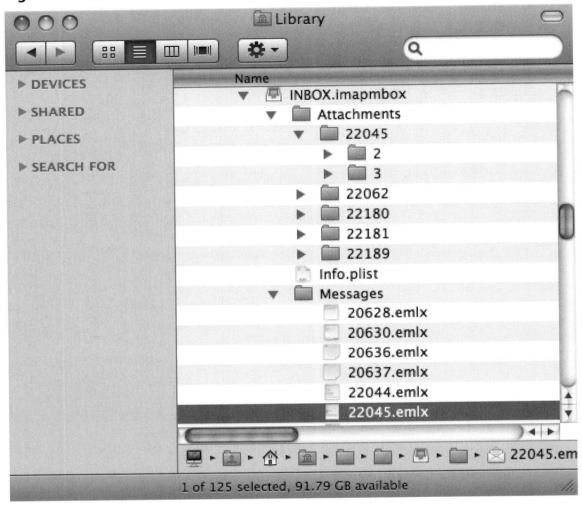

Figure 9.5 shows a portion of the MobileMe local contents for "rkubasiak" in the user's Home directory of "moof". You can see a folder for the "Messages" or the actual e-mail content and the "Attachments" or the items that were sent along with the messages. Each e-mail is numbered—specifically in this case, 20628, 20630, 20636, and so on. Each e-mail also ends with an extension of .emlx, which represents a specialized Extensible Markup Language or XML file. Corresponding to the e-mail is an Attachments folder containing like-numbered folders if any attachments were sent along within the e-mails. Note the file named "22045.emlx" that is highlighted in Figure 9.5. This e-mail message in the Inbox has a corresponding e-mail attachment folder: the folder named "22045" within the Attachments folder. That folder has been expanded to show the content of two additional folders, named "2" and "3". These two folders tell you that two attachments came along with this e-mail.

Locating a specific user's email information is the first step in a proper recovery of their communications. In Exercise 9.1 we will walk through the specific steps necessary in locating a user's Apple Mail data.

Configuring & Implementing...

Exercise 9.1: Locating Apple Mail for a Specific User

This exercise will familiarize you with the location of Apple Mail data.

1. Insert into your Macintosh the DVD Toolkit that accompanies this book.

2. Attach the sample disk image named "ronaldcarter." After mounting the image, double-click the **ronaldcarter** volume to open it and present its contents.

3. Navigate to the Library folder. Double-click the **Library** folder to open it and present its contents.

4. In the Library folder, locate the **Mail** folder and double-click it to open it and present its contents.

5. Browse the content of this folder and note its structure. Utilize Apple's Quick Look technology to view the contents of e-mails within this folder safely, without changing their contents.

6. Knowing that the user's Home directory is "ronaldcarter", are you able to obtain any other account information as you browse this folder? Did you note the folder named "POP-ronald.carter9@pop.gmail.com"? This folder means a POP3 account for the e-mail address ronald.carter9@pop.gmail.com is stored here.

End of Exercise

You've looked at the user's e-mail messages, but you haven't definitely shown what user or users are configured to send and receive e-mail using Apple Mail. Right now, you have the data. The next place you need to look is the user's Preferences folder. This folder, again located within the Library folder, is a huge gold mine of evidentiary value. As you can see in Figure 9.6, the Preferences folder contains several files.

Figure 9.6 The User's Preferences Folder

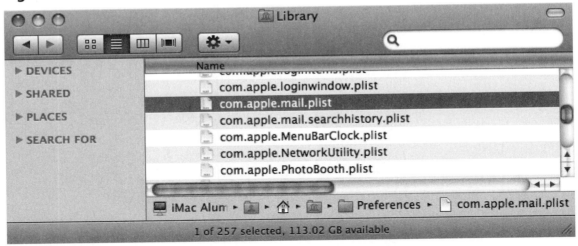

Figure 9.6 shows only a small portion of the multitude of files that you can find within the Preferences folder. A ".plist" is a Property List file that is an XML file containing information. The information can include configuration settings, serial numbers, the last 10 files opened in an application, and so on. Apple does not define what goes inside the .plist file; it only defines the format of the file itself. You can view Property List files in Leopard (Mac OS X 10.5) with Quick Look by clicking once on the **.plist** file and then tapping the **Spacebar** once. You'll see the contents of the file displayed on-screen and you can scroll through the files to view their contents.

> **NOTE**
>
> Apple provides a utility called Property List Editor as a part of its Developer Tools. Developer Tools are free; the latest version is available at http://developer.apple.com. You can install Developer Tools from your Leopard or Tiger Install DVD as well. Once you install Developer Tools, the Property List Editor will become available for your use. It is a graphical user interface (GUI)-based utility that we will use in this section as well.

Let's take a look at Apple Mail's associated .plist file is the Property List Editor application that is installed as part of the Developer Tools from Apple. Figure 9.7 shows the Property List Editor.

Figure 9.7 Property List Editor View of the plist File

Property List	Class	Value
▼ DeliveryAccounts	Array	2 ordered objects
▼ 0	Dictionary	9 key/value pairs
AccountType	String	SMTPAccount
Hostname	String	smtp.mac.com
MaxMessageBytes	Number	28311552
PortNumber	String	587
SecurityLayerType	Number	2
ShouldUseAuthentication	String	YES
SSLEnabled	String	YES
uniqueId	String	9e59ac4b-855b-4728-b3a5-217887bbe4d7
Username	String	rkubasiak

(Window title: com.apple.mail.plist; buttons: New Sibling, Delete, Dump)

TIP

Apple's naming guidelines for .plist files will clarify what you are looking at with the file named "com.apple.mail.plist". First, the extension is easiest; .plist you already know and understand to be a Property List file. That leaves you with "com.apple. mail". The name is in reverse URL notation, the opposite of a URL you would type into a Web browser. In addition, "apple.com" is the company and "mail" is the application the .plist file belongs to.

Figure 9.7 shows you a portion of the contents of the com.apple.mail.plist file for the local user "moof". As you can see from the size of the scroll bar in Figure 9.7, the com.apple.mail.plist file contains a huge amount of data. You are looking at the Simple Mail Transfer Protocol (SMTP) configuration for the user "rkubasiak". This is now "hard evidence" of the account being configured on this Macintosh versus just the folder name that you had before.

In Exercise 9.2 we will walk through the necessary steps to locate and examine a specific user's com.apple.mail.plist file. Having located this file, you will be able to examine the specific user's settings for Apple Mail.

Configuring & Implementing...

Exercise 9.2: Examining a User's com.apple.mail.plist File

This exercise will familiarize you with the location and data content of the Apple Mail .plist file.

1. Insert into your Mac the DVD Toolkit that accompanies this book.

2. Attach the sample disk image named "ronaldcarter." After mounting the image, double-click the ronaldcarter volume to open it and present its contents.

3. Navigate to the Library folder. Double-click the **Library** folder to open it and present its contents.

4. In the Library folder, locate the **Preferences** folder and double-click it to open it and present its contents.

5. Scroll through the contents of this folder until you find the file named "com.apple.mail.plist".

6. Click once on the file to select it.

7. Press the **Spacebar** to activate Quick Look and peer inside the file contents.

8. Scroll down through this file and locate the section labeled "<key>Delivery Accounts</key>". Do you see "ronald.carter9" listed?

9. Continue to scroll through this file and note the additional configuration information that this single XML file contains.

End of Exercise

Now, with an understanding of where e-mail data is contained and knowing where the configuration data is contained, you can re-create a user and view his Apple Mail, just as he would have viewed it!

Next, you're going to need to take the following steps:

■ Extract the Apple Mail data from the suspect user account.

■ Create a new, clean user account on your system.

■ Place the suspect's Apple Mail user account into your user account for examination.

■ Open your Apple Mail application and view all of the user's e-mail in its original form.

The first step is to extract the data from your suspect user account. We completed this step for you by providing the DVD Toolkit for you to use. In a real case, you would copy the same folders that we just examined to an external, HFS+ formatted drive. In other words, for local user "moof" you would copy his Mail folder in the Library to your external drive. You would also copy his com. apple.mail.plist preference file to your HFS+ external drive.

WARNING

For examination purposes on a Macintosh, you should always extract data to same the type of file system. In other words, if the suspect Macintosh was formatted with HFS+, as will be the case with any Mac OS X startup volume, the drive that you extract data to should always be HFS+ formatted as well. This is to preserve metadata attributes that come along with the files and folders, and to guarantee that nothing is changing in regard to contents. By doing this, you can now expect that the change made will be a date change only when you extract data and place it on your volume for manipulation.

With the data extracted to the HFS+ volume (the DVD Toolkit), you can now proceed to the next step. You need a clean user account, a task that's easy to accomplish by creating an account in System Preferences, which you'll do in Exercise 9.3.

Configuring & Implementing...

Exercise 9.3: Create a New User for Examination Purposes

In this exercise, you will create a clean user account for examining extracted suspect user data.

1. From the Apple menu, select **System Preferences**.
2. In System Preferences, select **Accounts**.
3. In the Accounts window, click the **Lock** icon to authenticate if necessary. If the Lock icon is already "open," no authentication is necessary.
4. In the Accounts window, click the + icon to add a new user.
5. In the New User window, create the account as an Administrator with a name of "ExaminationUser". Press the **Tab** key to automatically fill in the short name. Enter a **password** for this user to remain secure. Do not turn on FileVault. See Figure 9.8 for a properly completed New User dialog box.
6. Click the **Create Account** button and your new, clean examination account will be created.

End of Exercise

Figure 9.8 New User Creation Dialog Box

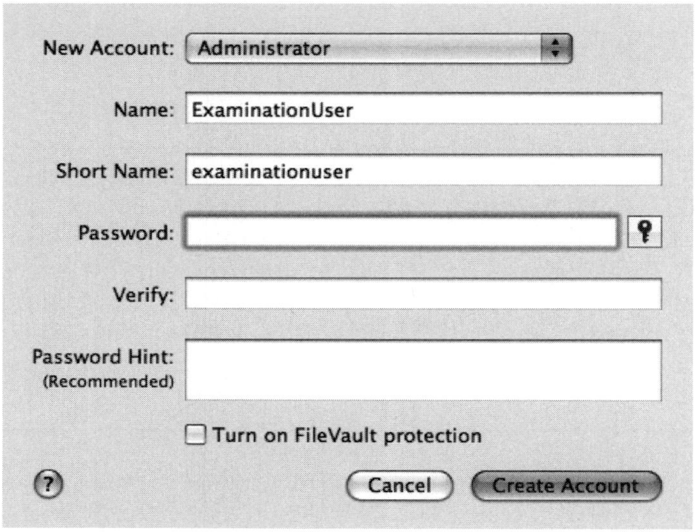

Figure 9.8 represents a new user that you will create every time you examine suspect user data. You create this account to guarantee no cross-contamination of data from past examinations.

The next step is to take the suspect Apple Mail data and place it into your new user account. You'll do this via the external HFS+ drive, in our case, the DVD Toolkit. To begin, log on to your newly created ExaminationUser account either by logging out of your current session or by using Fast User Switching. Once you are in the new user account, *do not access anything*! You want everything to remain pristine until you are ready to access an application. In this section, you want Apple Mail, so in Exercise 9.4 you'll begin by populating the correct locations with Apple Mail data from the suspect user.

Configuring & Implementing...

Exercise 9.4: Copy Suspect Apple Mail Data to New User Account

In this exercise, you will populate your new user account with the suspect user Apple Mail data to be examined.

1. Open the new user Library folder. From the Finder, click the **Go** menu and select **Home**. A new window will open and the new user Home folder will be presented, including the Library folder. Double-click the **Library** folder to open it and present its contents.

2. Insert the DVD Toolkit into your DVD drive. This represents your external HFS+ drive with suspect user data.

3. Double-click the **ronaldcarter.dmg** file to attach the volume. Double-click the ronaldcarter volume to open it and present its contents.

4. Double-click the **Library** folder to open it and present its contents.

5. Organize the two windows you now have open for easy viewing. You should be looking at the Library folder of your new user account and the Library folder of your suspect, "ronaldcarter".

6. Drag the **Mail** folder from the suspect Library folder to the new user Library folder to copy the contents. If the suspect had a Mail Downloads folder, you would also copy this folder as well.

7. In the suspect user window, double-click the **Preferences** folder to open it and present its contents.

8. Drag the **com.apple.mail.plist** file to the new user Preferences folder to copy the file.

9. Launch Apple Mail from the Dock to view the suspect user's e-mail as he would have seen it!

End of Exercise

By following the steps in Exercise 9.4, you will successfully recover Apple Mail in Mac OS X 10.5 every time! There is one note to make after you launch Apple Mail for the first time. Figure 9.9 shows you the details.

Figure 9.9 Password Request in Apple Mail

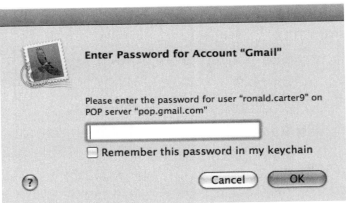

Figure 9.9 represents how Apple Mail is requesting the password for the account ronald. carter9@pop.gmail.com. The reason for the request is that the Keychain has never seen this account and has not stored a password for the account. As an examiner, you can safely click the **Cancel** button here. Apple Mail will go offline, and you can peruse the contents of your suspect user's mailboxes.

It is extremely important to note at this point, as you go through the user's e-mail, that you will be changing the status of each e-mail message from unread to read. You always have your original data to go back to, so you should not be concerned that you'll lose original evidence. However, you most likely will not be able to remember the status of every e-mail prior to reading it as you are in the process of viewing and reporting on their contents. This is where the Grab application becomes essential. It is part of the Mac OS X distribution and is located in the Applications folder. We highly recommend that you make use of this program, taking screen grabs to note e-mail status before actually reading e-mail. Figure 9.10 shows the first picture you should take when you enter Apple Mail after opening it for the first time.

Figure 9.10 Apple Mail Launched after Suspect Data Recovery

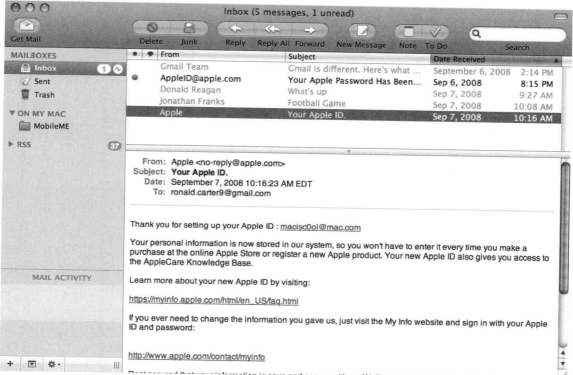

Figure 9.10 represents the initial status of Apple Mail before any actions have been taken. As an examiner, you can add this to your report, stating that this is the original status of the suspect's account. Note the lightning bolt icon next to the Inbox. This icon means the account is offline. At this point in the recovery process, you can open the suspect's e-mails and view them natively. You can also save any attachments, and print the e-mails to a PDF document for inclusion in your report.

How does all of this apply to other e-mail applications? It will truly depend on the application itself. Some e-mail applications you will find to be similar to Apple Mail, and you can follow these steps almost exactly if you simply change the name to the application you are dealing with. Other applications, such as Microsoft's Entourage, deal with e-mail differently, yet the concept of recovery can still be applied. Microsoft has chosen to save its user data in the Documents folder for each user. Within the Documents folder is a folder called "Microsoft User Data". Apply the same recovery concept of copying this folder from the suspect's Documents folder and into the same location in the new user account, gather the associated preference files, and try to launch Entourage. When you succeed and the Entourage mailboxes are populated, you can use the remaining reporting techniques of taking window screen grabs and printing e-mails to PDF files for your reports.

WARNING

When you're trying to analyze a new application, failures will occur until you find all of the correct data locations including the Library folder and Preferences folder. When you launch your new application in your ExaminationUser account and a failure occurs, start again by deleting this account and creating a new one. Each attempt should be done with a newly created ExaminationUser account, with the data to be examined "freshly" imported. Do not attempt to fix a failed launch of an application, as you will be altering your suspect's account with your fixes.

Address Book

Apple has built into the operating system a great application called Address Book. It is the basis for many of the other applications and technologies used in Mac OS X. Apple Mail integrates its iPhone with Address Book. In addition, other cell phones will synchronize with Address Book, as will MobileMe. Those are just a few examples of the many areas where the data contained in Address Book can be essential to any case. In this section, we will discuss where Address Book data resides as well as recover it so that you can add it to your reports.

You can find Address Book data in the user's Library folder. The first folder of interest to you is in the Application folder and it is called "Address Book". Figure 9.11 shows this folder.

Figure 9.11 Address Book Folder within the User's Library Application Support Folder

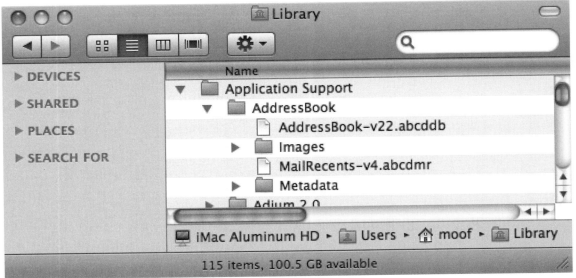

Figure 9.11 shows you where Address Book stores all of its data. The Images folder stores pictures that are associated with the entries in Address Book as assigned by the user. The Metadata folder contains vCard files for each person the user has entered into Address Book. As with Apple Mail, with Address Book you need to go to the Preferences folder and gather the associated .plist file for Address Book to be thorough. This means you need to gather the following three files:

- **AddressBookMe.plist** The actual entry for the suspect as gathered during the Apple registration of Leopard. This file is written only at the time of registration. It may not exist if the person chose to skip registration. It is not updated as the user updates his information in Address Book.

- **com.apple.AddressBook.abd.plist** A settings file. It is not of forensic value, but we wish to be complete.

- **com.apple.AddressBook.plist** The preference file for Address Book.

Figure 9.12 shows an expanded view of the Preferences folder for the user "moof".

Figure 9.12 Preferences Folder Showing Address Book Preference Files

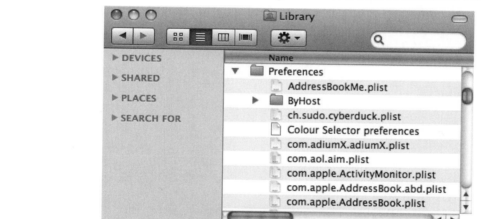

AddressBookMe.plist is useful for its contents. You can see whether the suspect entered information that may not exist in Address Book today, or that he may not have at all anywhere else. The file is not relevant to Address Book operation, though. When you recover data, you will need only the single preference file, com.apple.AddressBook.plist, for successful operation.

In the next exercise, we will look at the necessary steps for extracting the Address Book data from a suspect's account and placing it into our examination account. Exercise 9.5 will give us a complete view of the suspect's Address Book and allow us to develop a report using the Print to PDF function built into the operating system.

Configuring & Implementing...

Exercise 9.5: Copy Suspect Address Book Data to New User Account

In this exercise, you will populate your new user account with the suspect user Address Book data to be examined.

1. Open the new user Library folder. From the Finder, click the **Go** menu and select **Home**. A new window will open and the new user Home folder will be presented, including the Library folder. Double-click the **Library** folder to open it and present its contents.

2. Insert the DVD Toolkit into your DVD drive. This represents your external HFS+ drive with suspect user data.

3. Double-click the **ronaldcarter.dmg** file to attach to the image. Double-click the ronaldcarter volume to open it and present its contents.

4. Double-click the **Library** folder to open it and present its contents.

5. Organize the two windows you now have open for easy viewing. You should be looking at the Library folder of your new user account and the Library folder of your suspect, "ronaldcarter".

6. In the suspect Library window, double-click **Application Support** to open it and present its contents.

7. From the suspect account window, drag the **Address Book** folder to the new user account window and drop it onto the Application Support folder. This will copy the folder to the same location in your new user account. Note: You will receive a dialog to replace the folder that already exists. Click **Replace**.

8. In the suspect account window, click the **left arrow** in the window to navigate back to the Library folder.

9. In the suspect account window, double-click the **Preferences** folder to open it and present its contents.

10. From the suspect account window, drag the **com.apple.AddressBook.plist** file to the Preferences folder of the new user. This will copy the file to the new user account Preferences. Note: You will receive a dialog to replace the folder that already exists. Click **Replace**.

11. Launch Address Book to view contacts, as the suspect would have seen them!

End of Exercise

Once you have launched Address Book, you can peruse the contacts for the data that has been assigned to each contact. You can also use the Print to PDF feature of Mac OS X to print the contacts to a report file. Make certain to note in the Print dialog box the choices you will have for printing contacts. A standard print does not print all information about a contact. Figure 9.13 shows a suggested print to gather the most information for a report.

Figure 9.13 Address Book Print Dialog

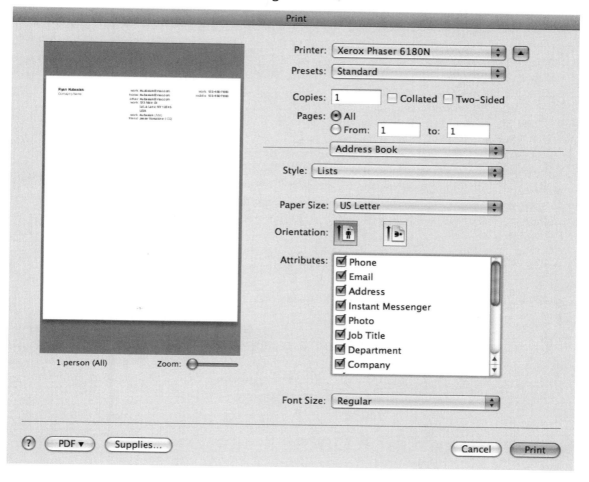

Figure 9.13 shows the Print dialog screen. Notice how the "Style" has been changed to "Lists". This will place all of the contacts you have selected into a neatly organized list for inclusion in your report. Also note the Attributes window and how each possible attribute has a checkmark next to it. This will allow for every attribute to be included in the PDF file if it exists.

Popular Chat Applications

Chat, or instant messaging (IM), is an easy and quick way for people to communicate with each other in real time. It is also available on cell phones with text messaging as well as on computers with IM applications. Recently, IM has crossed over to the cell phone world and now you will find notable applications such as Yahoo IM and Skype able to interact or even run on cell phones and smart phones. The iPhone has the AIM application available for free from the App Store as an example. Regardless of the source—cell phone, Windows computer, or Macintosh—IM will be another piece of data that you as an examiner will need to recover once it makes its way to the Macintosh. In this section, we will discuss some of the popular IM applications that you might find on a Mac. In the next section, we will look more deeply at the included application, iChat, and how it retains data on the system.

Included with every Mac is the IM application iChat. It has the traditional capabilities of sending text messages in real time to another user. It also has grown into a robust video conferencing application that can support high-quality video chat over the Internet, with up to four simultaneous users at one time. iChat users can be MobileMe (.Mac) accounts, AOL (AIM) accounts, or Jabber accounts. Jabber accounts allow for any service that is compliant to be added. Google Talk users can be added to the iChat buddy list. iChat is easy to set up, and because of this, it is popular on the Macintosh.

Skype is a cross-platform application that has IM capabilities. The client for the Macintosh interfaces well with all other clients and has been well received on the Mac. The application offers high-quality, one-to-one video chat as well as audio conferencing with multiple users. Skype also has capabilities to make calls to landline phones and cell phones as well as receive calls from these same phone services.

Yahoo! and Microsoft both offer IM applications for the Mac, but they have fallen behind in popularity. The client software for each has never kept parity with the Windows version; therefore, many Mac users have become disenchanted with the software. It is certainly in use, however, and is capable of text messaging. The Yahoo! and Microsoft services agreed to interact with each other in July of 2006, so clients can now send and receive messages natively. The Microsoft application still does not have video on the Macintosh side, however.

Adium is an all-in-one application that can interface with multiple services from a single application. It offers only IM capability, even when the service it is interacting with has video capabilities. Adium offers users the ability to sign into each service from one application and receive text messages in one location, rather than launching multiple applications for multiple services.

Recovery of Chat Data

Recovery of chat data is one of the more difficult tasks to accomplish. IM happens in real time, usually in the Macintosh memory, and IM data is not archived to the hard disk unless the user has chosen an archiving option. You certainly can find chat data in the unallocated space of a hard disk by using robust tools such as BlackBag's Macintosh Forensic Suite or Access Data's Forensic Toolkit, but that is beyond the scope of this book. Instead, we'll examine what is actually left in a user's Home folder from using iChat, and then extrapolate that into how you can examine other applications for chat data.

iChat data is saved in the user's Library folder. If you open the Library folder, you will find another folder named "Caches". Figure 9.14 shows a view of this folder.

Figure 9.14 User – Library – Caches Folder

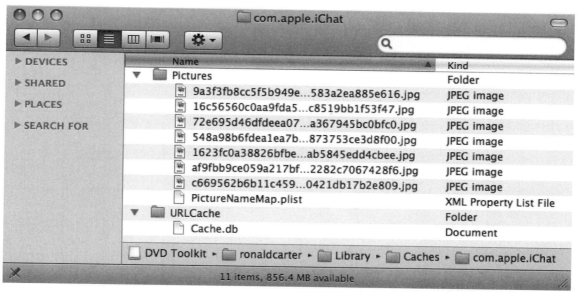

In Figure 9.14, you see the Library – Caches folder expanded and scrolled to a folder named "com.apple.iChat". This folder contains historical information for iChat. The Pictures folder contains JPEG files of the user icons in the buddy list for this person. The JPEG files do not indicate that a chat has taken place, but they do indicate the presence of this person in the buddy list. The PictureNameMap.plist file will help you associate whom each picture belongs to. Look at Figure 9.15 for more information.

Figure 9.15 Property List Editor View of the PictureNameMap.plist File

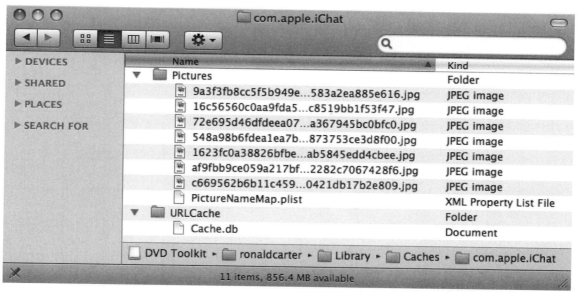

Figure 9.15 represents the information you can gather from the PictureNameMap.plist file for iChat. The important entry in this file is the "services" area on the left, under Property List. In Figure 9.15, AIM is the service that has two entries, with usernames of "macisc0ol" and "macrules2010". These two usernames have a UID that you can track back to an associated JPEG picture file in Figure 9.14. This is the buddy icon used for this person. The other files in the Cache folder may be outdated entries and may not be in the PictureNameMap.plist file anymore.

iChat buddy icons also come from the user's Address Book. If the user has set a picture for a person, we already reviewed in the preceding section how to recover Address Book data, including custom pictures. The PictureNameMap.plist file does not list any information about Address Book associations.

Archiving chat is not usually the default option for any of the available applications. It is not turned on by default in iChat either. In Figure 9.16, you can see iChat with transcripts set to the iChat folder.

Figure 9.16 iChat Transcripts Turned On

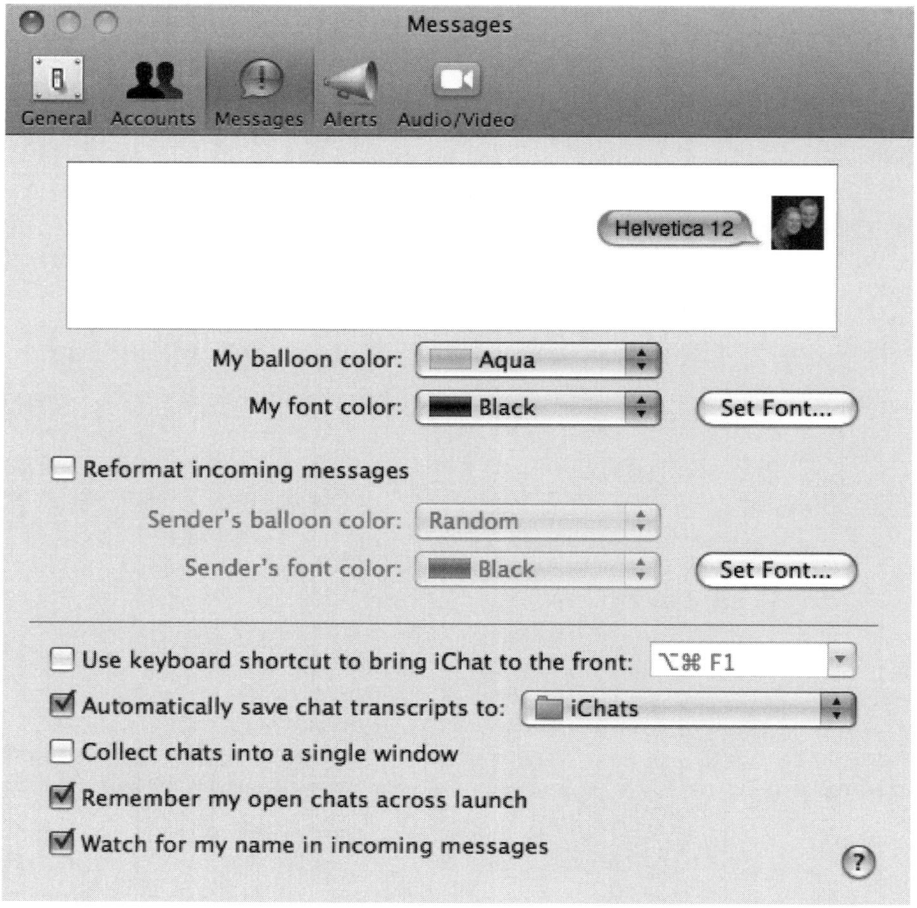

With transcripts turned on as shown in Figure 9.16, a folder named "iChats" will be collecting a history of the messages typed by each participant in the chats. As an examiner, you need to know how to view these archived chats when you come across them. iChat transcript files will be saved as .ichat files and the default application to view them is iChat. In fact, iChat is an excellent choice for viewing the transcripts. You will be able to view the chat dialog in the same manner as the suspect saw it.

You can recover other chat applications using techniques similar to those you learned in this chapter with e-mail, Address Book, and iChat.

Summary

The Macintosh provides for a robust platform for many means of communications. E-mail and IM are two forms of communication whose data you learned to successfully locate and recover from a suspect user. The best way to view data from a Macintosh environment is by using a Mac. We used this concept when we created a new user named "ExaminationUser" as our pristine account. With this account, it was possible to examine suspect data natively with the same application the data had come from.

Solutions Fast Track

Popular E-mail Applications

☑ Apple Mail is the most-used e-mail application on the Macintosh.

☑ Entourage, Eudora, and Thunderbird are other popular e-mail applications that add features not found in Apple Mail.

☑ A user can use two or more e-mail applications at one time, so always check for all installed applications.

MobileMe (.Mac) and Web-Based E-mail

☑ MobileMe (.Mac) is a service that offers both Web-based e-mail as well as e-mail that can be received through Apple Mail, the iPhone, and other compatible e-mail clients.

☑ Web-based e-mail traditionally was received by authenticating to a Web page such as mail. yahoo.com and viewing e-mail through a browser only.

☑ Today, Web-based e-mail can still be accessed through Web pages, but it also has grown to offer similar services such as POP3 and IMAP access.

Recovery of E-mail Data

☑ E-mail data is found in the user's Home folder in the Library.

☑ To perform a recovery for viewing of data, you need to copy all relevant data from the user's Library folder to an external HFS+ hard drive. You can then place the data into the same location in a pristine user account for viewing.

☑ Each e-mail application will store data, but it may not store it in the same manner as Apple Mail, as detailed in this section. As an examiner, you need to be able to adapt your techniques to locate the data stored by each specific e-mail application that is relevant to the case at hand.

Address Book

☑ Address Book is an application that is installed by Mac OS X. It is tightly integrated with the system and with many applications. Its function is to store contact information for people.

☑ When recovering Address Book data and creating reports, it's important to note all attributes selected for output; otherwise, you could miss important information.

☑ To recover Address Book data, copy the relevant folder and files to an external HFS+ hard drive. You can then place the data into the same location in a pristine user account for viewing.

Popular Chat Applications

☑ iChat is the IM application included with Mac OS X.

☑ Skype, Yahoo!, and Microsoft all offer IM clients for the Mac OS X as well. Adium is an all-in-one client that can interface with multiple services from one application.

☑ Chat applications offer more that just text messages. Expect video, landline telephone service, and voice mail as just some of the other competitive services that set each of them apart.

Recovery of Chat Data

☑ Chat application data will be found in the user's Library folder.

☑ Chat happens in real time, and because archiving is usually not turned on by default, recovery of conversations is usually quite difficult. You can find pieces of conversations in unallocated space.

☑ If a user has archived his chat to a history file, consider opening that history file with the application that created it for the best viewing experience. An iChat transcript is best viewed from within the iChat application.

Frequently Asked Questions

Q: How many e-mail applications do I need to worry about for the Macintosh?

A: A huge number of applications are available. We mentioned a few of the most popular in this chapter, but it would be impossible to list all of the custom-designed applications.

Q: Can I recover video chat from IM applications?

A: Typically, no. The video is "streamed" to the receiving client with no archiving to the local Macintosh. You will find indications of connection information in log files, however.

Q: Besides Address Book, can other applications store contact information on a Macintosh?

A: Yes! Many free and low-cost applications offer contact management. Always look for installed applications and research their functionality.

Q: Why do I need to create a new user account every time I export suspect data from e-mail, Address Book, or iChat?

A: You need to guarantee that you are always working with the data you expect. By creating a new user for each examination of suspect data, you guarantee that you are looking at only the data you have brought in and not at data that was left over from a previous examination.

Chapter 10

Locating and Recovering Photos

Solutions in this chapter:

- **Defining a Photo on a Macintosh**
- **iPhoto**
- **Recovering Images**
- **Spotlight and Shadow Files**

☑ **Summary**

☑ **Solutions Fast Track**

☑ **Frequently Asked Questions**

Introduction

The ease of use and functionality that have been a defining attribute of Apple are also characteristic of photography and imaging on the Mac. Today, every Macintosh computer sold comes with a powerful yet easy-to-use suite of software called iLife. Along with iLife, underlying technology seamlessly integrates the Mac OS with Mac hardware and peripherals, making the platform a robust source of data acquired from many external devices, including cameras, iPods, and iPhones. In fact, thanks to the technology in Mac OS X, users can plug almost any digital camera into the system and, upon answering just one simple question, link iPhoto, an application that's part of the iLife suite, to the computer and subsequently download all of their photos for easy manipulation. All Intel-based Macs also come equipped with a built-in iSight camera for capturing high-quality still and motion video.

When conducting a computer forensic investigation, being able to locate a user's photos and determine which ones are related to the case is critical. As a first responder, it is important that you know where the photos are typically saved and which user on the system owns those photos. It is also important to note that artifacts, such as thumbnails, can contain images even if the original photos have been deleted. Aside from cameras, devices such as iPods, iPhones, and other external drives can be sources of images.

In this chapter, we will explore how to locate evidence of images, even when the images no longer exist on the actual system. This will help to ensure that you as a forensic investigator are aware of where photos are located on a Mac and how to retrieve those photos.

Defining a Photo on a Macintosh

Photography has changed from the high-quality "roll of film" cameras that professionals used in the past. Today, anyone can take a high-quality picture using one of a vast array of digital cameras starting at less than $100. In addition to cameras, Webcams are also a source of imagery to every Mac, with their ability to capture still images as well as video. Therefore, as a forensic investigator, it is important that you are cognizant of Webcam features, because although people can use them with good intentions, they can also use them to commit crimes. In addition, almost every model of wireless phone comes with a digital camera as a feature today, adding to the source of images you might find on a Mac. To complicate the issue even further, users can create digital imagery using software such as Adobe Photoshop, or by importing a picture from a camera and then manipulating it with Photoshop.

What does this mean to us? First, it means we must understand the many different file formats in which digital imagery can be stored on a Mac. Here are some of the most popular formats:

- **RAW** Pronounced "raw," this is the highest-quality format available for a digital image.

- **JPG, JPEG** Pronounced "j-peg," this is one of the most popular formats for digital images because of its quality and compression.

- **GIF** Pronounced "gif," this is used mostly for small low-quality images such as Web banners.

- **BMP** Pronounced "bitmap," this is used for high-quality images but is considered too large for distribution with the quality of a JPG.

- **PSD** This is a proprietary Photoshop Document format.

- **TIFF** Pronounced "tiff," this is a high-quality image format with compression. It is the default image type for the Grab screen capture application that is included on the Mac.

- **PDF** This stands for Portable Document Format. It was developed by Adobe and is well integrated with Mac OS X.

- **PNG** Pronounced "ping," this is an advanced version of GIF.

We also need to be aware of the many different software applications used today to work with digital images. Three of the most popular are iPhoto, Adobe Photoshop, and Graphic Converter.

Personal photos taken with a digital camera likely will wind up being associated with iPhoto. Installed by default on every modern Macintosh and a part of the iLife software suite, iPhoto offers easy image download from almost any digital camera as well as well-crafted organization of images for later use. Most users will use this application to obtain their images from their digital camera, even if they intend to send their photos to another application for further editing. iPhoto is an extremely powerful application with advanced features, including the ability to categorize your photos by month.

Adobe Photoshop is the standard that almost every image editing application is compared to in software reviews. The latest versions of Photoshop are feature-equivalent on Mac and Windows platforms. Photoshop is a high-powered application offering image manipulation features beyond the basic editors offered in iPhoto. An image manipulated in Photoshop could indicate that the user has some knowledge of digital imaging.

Graphic Converter is a popular application available as shareware on the Internet. It has image manipulation capabilities as well as the ability to convert file types: With the Save As function, for example, users can save a JPG as a BMP with relative ease. The application has been available for years and has been updated frequently to stay current with the Mac OS.

As you can see from this brief discussion, an image you see on a Macintosh screen isn't just a picture taken with a camera. It isn't just a picture in iPhoto, or an image that was edited in Photoshop, either. In fact, most images go through a chain of events that can change the parameters of the image either slightly or enormously. For instance, a user can easily connect his digital camera to a Mac and then download all of the photos from the camera to iPhoto with the click of a button. The user can then send a single image to Photoshop for extensive editing—anything from manipulating the background to adding or deleting people from the photo. Finally, the user can use Graphic Converter to save the image in a format called PICT, which is an outdated format that was found in the Mac OS 8 and 9 days, for a friend who has an older Mac.

If nothing has been deleted from the Mac, you can reconstruct this path, showing the images that exist on the Mac, the HFS+ "created and modified" dates and times for each version of the image, and the metadata associated with each image to help complete the story of how the user manipulated the initial image into the final image.

In this chapter, we will discuss iPhoto and Graphic Converter in more detail so that you have a better understanding of Mac-based digital image manipulation. We'll start with a discussion of iPhoto, and learn where all of the associated data is stored. Once you've read this chapter, you'll better understand the chain of events that can occur during the image manipulation process and, as a result, how you must think as an examiner.

NOTE

Adobe Photoshop is one of the most recognized digital image applications on a Macintosh computer. Although it has attained such high recognition for its capabilities in digital artwork, it is not the most popular application for digital image intake such as iPhoto. However, the techniques that will be taught in this chapter for locating digital images will be directly applicable to locating images created or manipulated with Adobe Photoshop, or any other third party application.

iPhoto

Apple released iPhoto in 2002, and since then it has grown in capability and popularity. The application is included with every Macintosh sold, and you can purchase the current version, iPhoto '08, as a part of the iLife '08 software suite. iPhoto features an easy-to-use interface and simple connectivity to most digital cameras. Figure 10.1 offers a glimpse at the iPhoto '08 interface with a sample Event.

Figure 10.1 iPhoto 08 Interface

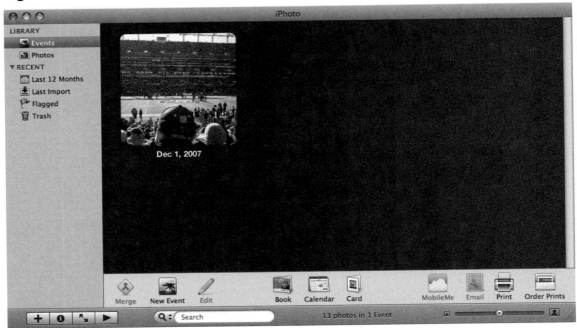

Figure 10.1 highlights the software's intuitive interface. Although I won't turn this section into an iPhoto How-To guide, as examiners there are a few key features we should be aware of because of the popularity of this application. At first launch of this application, the user is presented with the dialog box shown in Figure 10.2. This is the only time iPhoto will ask the user whether he wants to use iPhoto to connect his digital camera to the Mac.

Figure 10.2 iPhoto Default Camera Selection Dialog

As you can see from Figure 10.2, a simple click on the Yes button will allow iPhoto to interact will the user's digital camera at every connection from that point onward. Having answered "Yes" to this question causes iPhoto to automatically launch with each subsequent connection of this digital camera with an immediate presentation of an "Import" button. This makes it easy for the user to add the images from his or her digital camera to the iPhoto Library. Of course, clicking No means the user likely intends to install other camera software for use, and clicking Decide Later means this dialog box will appear again.

Referring back to Figure 10.1, across the bottom you can see the functions that are available to the user, which are of interest to us as examiners. iPhoto is tightly integrated with other applications, as well as with several services—namely, Book, Calendar, Card, and Order Prints, which are offered online for a fee after the user creates the associated media within iPhoto first. These services and easy-to-use features are one of the reasons the Mac is a popular computer choice for artists and graphic designers.

You can find what the user has created by looking at the left pane of the iPhoto interface. If the user has created something you'll see it listed under a custom name associated with whatever service the user used. Integrated applications include iTunes and iWeb; in addition, along the bottom of the interface you'll see a MobileMe button. Clicking MobileMe allows a user to publish photos using iWeb, or place slideshows and albums on the Web for others to view.

iPhoto also includes a built-in sharing feature for other users, as shown in Figure 10.3.

Figure 10.3 iPhoto Sharing Capabilities

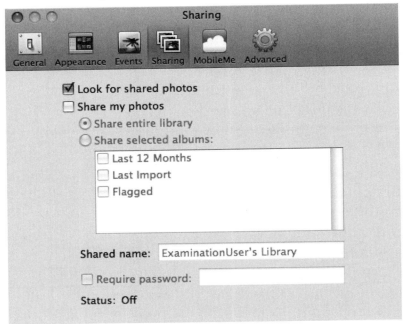

By clicking the "Share my photos" box in Figure 10.3, the user can share on the local network the items he selected in his iPhoto Library. By default, the "Look for shared photos" box is checked, and users on the local network will see all shared photos from other users.

Another powerful way users can share photos with iPhoto is through MobileMe and Galleries. The user can configure iPhoto with his MobileMe account, as shown in Figure 10.4, and have others not only see his photos, but also contribute to his collection.

Figure 10.4 iPhoto MobileMe Preferences

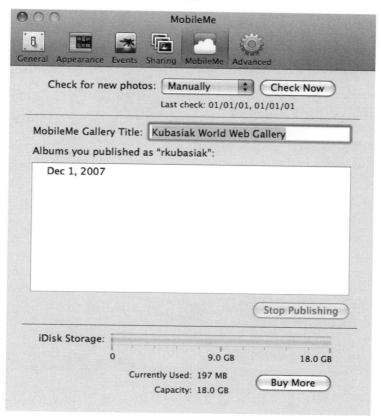

With the preferences shown in Figure 10.4 properly configured, iPhoto will publish a Gallery to the user's MobileMe account that can be viewed with any Web browser. Setting this apart from other applications is the fact that other users can also contribute their own photos to the Gallery by simply sending the photos to the linked (advertised) e-mail address that is displayed with the particular Gallery. Figure 10.5 shows how the iPhoto interface changes when a Gallery has been successfully published and how the addresses for access are displayed.

Figure 10.5 iPhoto Interface Displaying Gallery Information

Figure 10.5 is displaying a published Gallery. Notice the darkened bar across the upper portion of the iPhoto window; in that bar is the URL "http://gallery.me.com/rkubasiak/100039". This is the URL that anyone can type into his Web browser to access this Gallery on the Internet. On the right-hand side of that bar is the e-mail address "rkubasiak-9h35@post.me.com". This is the e-mail address anyone can send images to that will be automatically included in the Gallery.

Now that you understand the power of iPhoto, let's look at the data that it leaves on a user's hard drive. As we have stressed throughout this book, Mac OS X is an organized system that keeps user data in the user's Home folder. By default, iPhoto data is written to a folder which the Mac operating system creates, named Pictures. Figure 10.6 shows the default appearance of the iPhoto Library as seen from the Finder.

Figure 10.6 iPhoto Library As Seen from the Finder

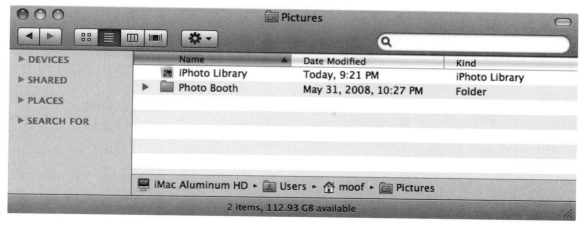

In Figure 10.6, you can see the iPhoto Library in the Pictures folder of user "moof". Notice that under "Kind" iPhoto Library is listed. The iPhoto Library is not a flat file, but rather a package file that we have referred to in Chapter 1. Recall that we can open a package file by **Control+clicking** the **iPhoto Library** icon and selecting **Show Package Contents**. Figure 10.7 shows the iPhoto Library layout upon clicking that icon.

Figure 10.7 iPhoto Library Package Contents

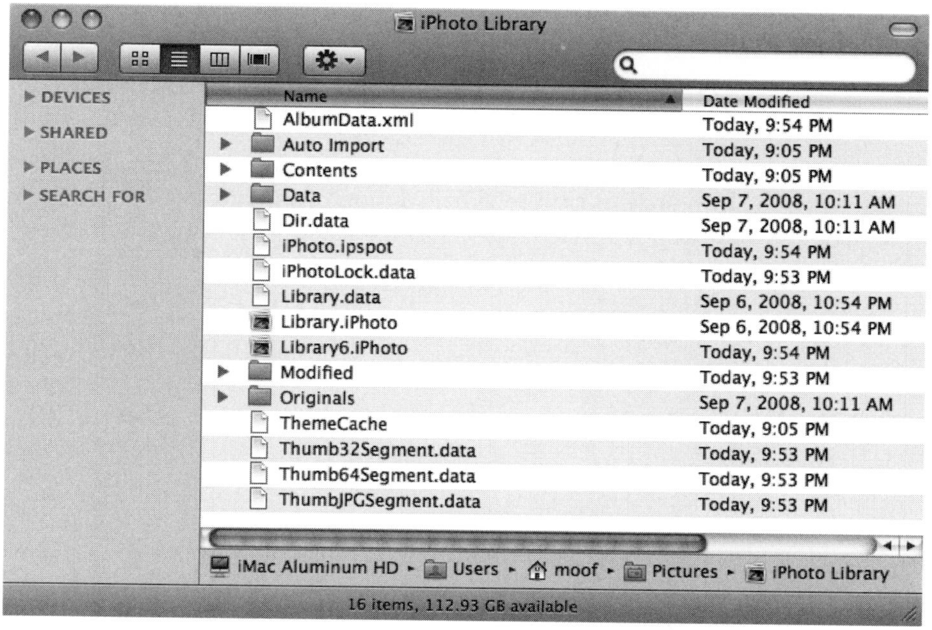

As you can see in Figure 10.7, the Data folder holds the images in the iPhoto collection, which is shown in Figure 10.8. The Modified and Originals folders contain copies of the images.

Figure 10.8 iPhoto Data Folder

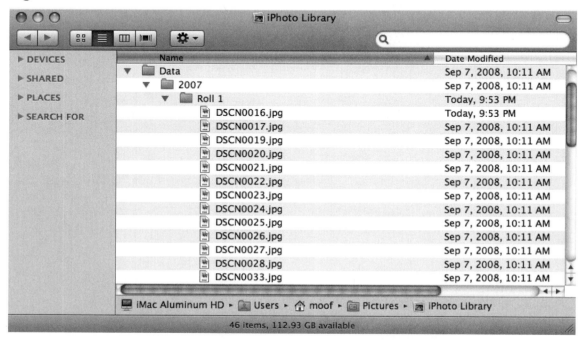

The Originals folder will always hold a copy of the original image as it first came into iPhoto. The Modified folder contains a copy of each modified version of a photo. Figure 10.9 shows the relationship of these two folders.

Figure 10.9 iPhoto Originals and Modified Folders

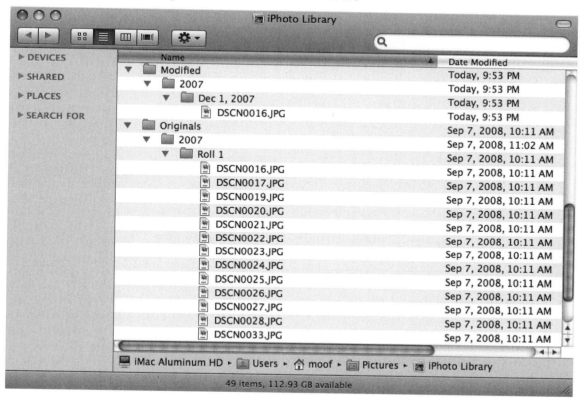

Notice in Figure 10.9 how the Modified folder contains only one image, labeled "DSCN0016. JPG". This is the only image the user manipulated within iPhoto so far. The "modified" version of an image is always the one being displayed in the iPhoto application unless there is no "modified" version. While in the application iPhoto, if the user selects an image and an "original" version exists, the user has the option to Revert to Original. If the user chooses at any time to "Revert to Original" the "modified" version is immediately deleted from the modified folder, and the "original" version becomes current in the library again.

The last important file to note appears at the top of Figure 10.7 and is named "AlbumData. xml". This is a standard XML file that you can read with a text editor, such as TextEdit. In this file you will find all of the iPhoto settings, including the Gallery URL and e-mail address mentioned earlier.

In a separate folder location from the iPhoto Library is the iPhoto Preference file. Located in the user's Library folder in Preferences, the file is named "com.apple.iPhoto.plist". In this file, you will find all of the settings for iPhoto, including where the iPhoto Library is being kept. If you can't find the iPhoto Library, or if the one you found in the default location is seemingly empty, the user might have changed the location for the iPhoto Library.

One last note regarding the iPhoto Library: A user can maintain multiple iPhoto Libraries by simply launching iPhoto while holding down the **Option** key. iPhoto will display a dialog box asking the user to choose a new Library or create a new one. It is possible to have an iPhoto Library on an external drive that is not connected to the Macintosh until the user wishes to utilize it.

Images in the iPhoto Library, although inside a package, are in fact indexed with an application called Spotlight. We will discuss this in more detail in the next section.

Recovering Images

In this section, we will not attempt to recover images from unallocated space or deleted files. On a Macintosh, just as on any other platform, once an image is deleted you need to perform your favorite file-carving techniques to bring the file back into existence. There is no "undelete" function on a Mac (unless the user is utilizing built-in Time Machine backup utility).

NOTE

Specialized applications such as AccessData's Forensic Toolkit and Guidance Software's EnCase enable you to file-carve in unallocated space based on a file's header and footer. However, if you decide to search for images that may have been created, altered, or manipulated with a program such as Graphic Converter, for example, first you should conduct a test on two of your own images. To do that, open the first image and save it with Graphic Converter. Open the second image, alter it, and save it with Graphic Converter as well. Be sure to save it in the form for which you intend to file-carve (e.g., JPG, GIF, PNG, etc.). Finally, open your sample files with a hexadecimal editor such as HexEdit from your favorite Mac download site (such as http://www.macupdate.com) and look at the header and footer of your sample data. This can give you a good starting point for file carving.

Recovering images on a Macintosh has been simplified with the addition of the most powerful indexing engine built into any operating system: Spotlight. With Spotlight, you can complete lightning-fast, complex queries for images across the entire system, or narrowly focus your query to a user's Home directory. In this section, we will see the power of Spotlight firsthand by conducting a search for some images.

Let's begin by looking at the Spotlight interface and how you can use it to search for images on connected media. You can access Spotlight in its basic form from the upper-right corner of the screen by clicking the **magnifying glass** icon. A dialog box will open where you can type criteria to search for, with immediate results appearing directly under where you type.

This is not the preferred method for us as examiners, though, as it doesn't allow us to access the full power and capability of Spotlight. Instead, from the Finder, open a new Finder window by clicking the **Finder** icon that is in the Dock. In this window, you are offered the same search capability but with many more configuration choices. Figure 10.10 shows the Spotlight interface from the Finder window, in which a search for "jpg" is being conducted.

Figure 10.10 Spotlight Search for "jpg"

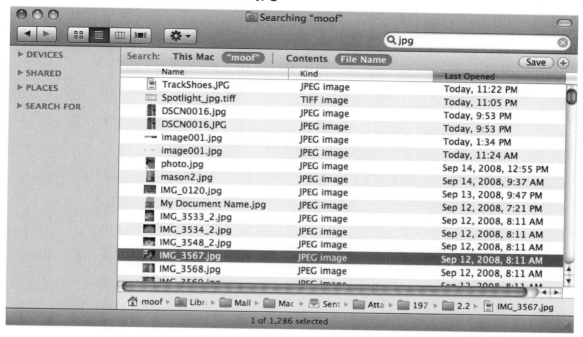

Notice in Figure 10.10 that two other descriptors have been clicked to narrow the focus of the search: "moof" and "File Name". This means this search will focus on files belonging to user "moof" and containing the letters "jpg" anywhere within the filename.

Although this is a neat feature, Spotlight is much more powerful than this. Let's begin by looking at the metadata of the first file that was returned in Figure 10.10, TrackShoes.JPG. Simply type the command *mdls* in the Terminal, as shown in Figure 10.11.

Figure 10.11 Terminal Window Showing the mdls Command

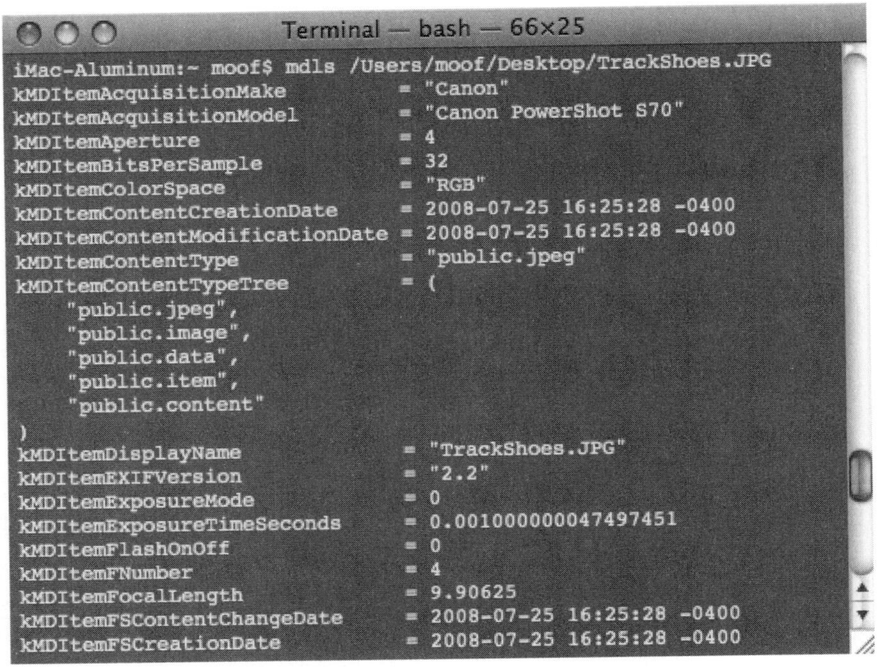

```
○ ○ ○            Terminal — bash — 66×25
iMac-Aluminum:~ moof$ mdls /Users/moof/Desktop/TrackShoes.JPG
kMDItemAcquisitionMake          = "Canon"
kMDItemAcquisitionModel         = "Canon PowerShot S70"
kMDItemAperture                 = 4
kMDItemBitsPerSample            = 32
kMDItemColorSpace               = "RGB"
kMDItemContentCreationDate      = 2008-07-25 16:25:28 -0400
kMDItemContentModificationDate  = 2008-07-25 16:25:28 -0400
kMDItemContentType              = "public.jpeg"
kMDItemContentTypeTree          = (
    "public.jpeg",
    "public.image",
    "public.data",
    "public.item",
    "public.content"
)
kMDItemDisplayName              = "TrackShoes.JPG"
kMDItemEXIFVersion              = "2.2"
kMDItemExposureMode             = 0
kMDItemExposureTimeSeconds      = 0.001000000047497451
kMDItemFlashOnOff               = 0
kMDItemFNumber                  = 4
kMDItemFocalLength              = 9.90625
kMDItemFSContentChangeDate      = 2008-07-25 16:25:28 -0400
kMDItemFSCreationDate           = 2008-07-25 16:25:28 -0400
```

Typing this command gives you all of the metadata associated with the file TrackShoes.JPG. The first two lines of metadata in Figure 10.11 contain the words "Canon" and "Canon PowerShot S70", which reveal the make and model of the camera used to take the photo. Hopefully, as an examiner working on this case, a Canon PowerShot S70 is among the equipment you seized during your search! If not, you have Spotlight to assist you.

That second line of metadata can help you refine your search to look for pictures on the hard drive that came from a "Canon PowerShot S70". Add additional criteria for the Spotlight search by clicking the + button on the top right of Figure 10.10, just above the scroll bar, and then selecting and entering the criteria for the search in the spaces to the left of the + button. In Figure 10.12, you can see that we want to return results that have been acquired by a "Device model" that "matches" "Canon PowerShot S70".

Figure 10.12 Spotlight Search Refined

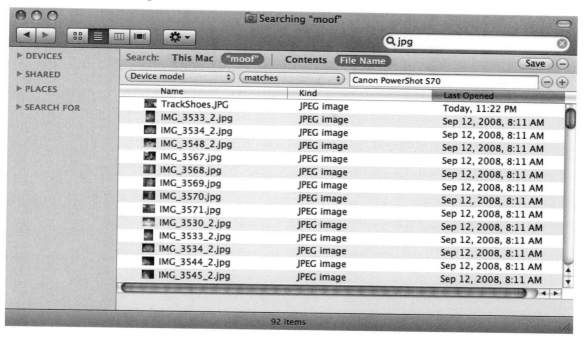

From the "Device model" pull-down menu you can choose any of the available metadata attributes that Spotlight indexes. Click this pull-down menu and one of the choices that appear is labeled "Other". Click that choice and a window similar to that shown in Figure 10.13 will provide you with the available attributes for the Spotlight metadata search.

In Figure 10.13, I scrolled the window down to the "Device model" description line. This is the description of the metadata we used when we performed the search in Figure 10.12. Notice all of the other criteria available for searching. You can refine a Spotlight search so that it is extremely granular and focused. This can be useful if your focus is on a certain date range. Spotlight allows for a range of dates as criteria for searches along with everything else that is being used.

In the search from Figure 10.12, if you needed to narrow the focus to a date range, clicking on the + icon above the scroll bar would add a third line of criteria. On this third line, using the pull-down menus you can search a date range, or an absolute date to narrow your focus even further. As you type your criteria, the results of your search begin to appear. Note that AccessData's Forensic Toolkit has an indexing engine that works similar to this, but can index unallocated space as well. Guidance Software's EnCase Version 6 also has an indexing engine, but it does not work in the same way and does not work as well as Spotlight or Forensic Toolkit.

Figure 10.13 Spotlight Metadata Attributes

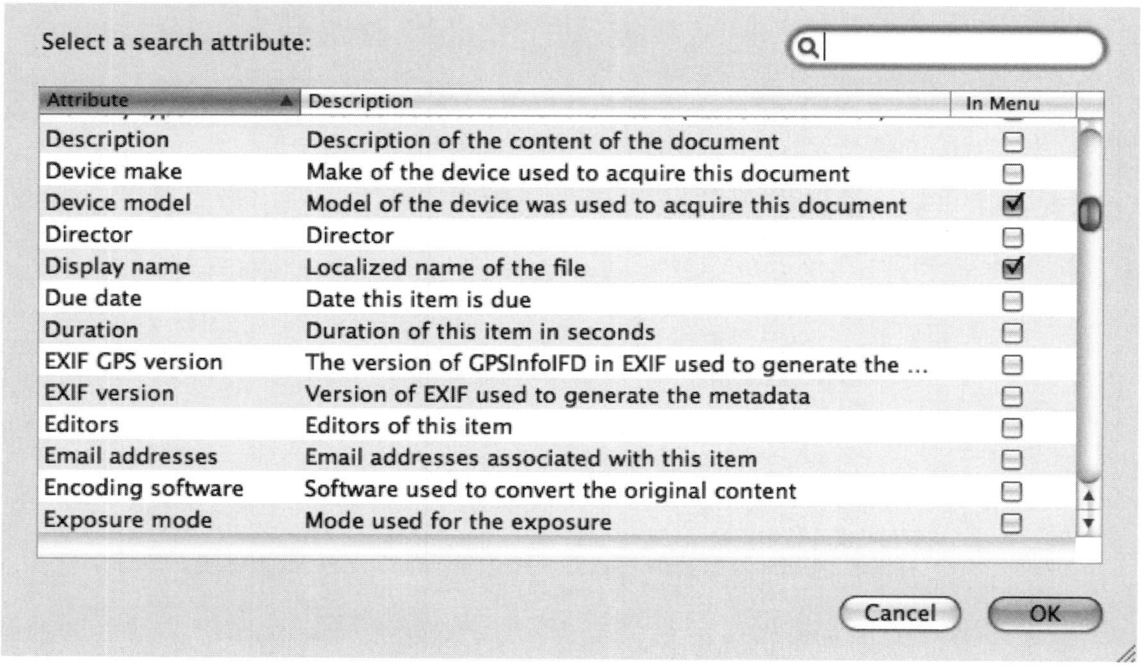

Select a search attribute: 🔍|

Attribute ▲	Description	In Menu
Description	Description of the content of the document	☐
Device make	Make of the device used to acquire this document	☐
Device model	Model of the device was used to acquire this document	☑
Director	Director	☐
Display name	Localized name of the file	☑
Due date	Date this item is due	☐
Duration	Duration of this item in seconds	☐
EXIF GPS version	The version of GPSInfoIFD in EXIF used to generate the ...	☐
EXIF version	Version of EXIF used to generate the metadata	☐
Editors	Editors of this item	☐
Email addresses	Email addresses associated with this item	☐
Encoding software	Software used to convert the original content	☐
Exposure mode	Mode used for the exposure	☐

(Cancel)   (OK)

Spotlight and Shadow Files

In this section, we are going to go one step further with the concept of recovering images. Let's look at the manner in which Spotlight functions. Spotlight will immediately index attached media to the Macintosh when it can write an index file to it. This is true of the internal hard drive during initial boot, any secondary hard drives, as well as any writeable media introduced during the normal operating of the Macintosh. When you use a DMG file such as the DVDToolkit.dmg included with this book, you use a best practice and "Lock" the file before using it. You do this to prevent changes to the file, such as Spotlight writing an index file to it when it gets mounted! The bad news is that you cannot use Spotlight to search a locked DMG, unless you mount the DMG using a "shadow file," which you will do in Exercise 10.1.

Configuring & Implementing...

Exercise 10.1: Locating Images on a Locked DMG File

This exercise will familiarize you with the location of Apple Mail data.

1. Insert into your Mac the DVD Toolkit that accompanies this book.

2. Copy the ronaldcarter.dmg file to your Desktop.

3. Lock the DMG file on your Desktop by **Control + Clicking** on the DMG file, selecting **Get Info**, and then clicking the **Locked** checkbox. You should now see a small "lock" icon in the lower left of the file's icon to indicate that the DMG file is properly locked.

4. Open the Terminal application on your Mac. It is located in the Utilities folder inside the Applications folder.

5. In the Terminal window, enter the command *hdiutil attach ~/Desktop/ ronaldcarter.dmg –shadow* to mount the DMG file of Ronald Carter's Home directory using a shadow file.

6. Also in the Terminal window, verify the status of Spotlight indexing by issuing the command *mdutil –sa*. Notice that "/Volumes/ronaldcarter" states "Indexing disabled".

7. Turn on indexing for DVDToolkit.dmg by issuing the command *mdutil –i on /Volumes/ronaldcarter/*.

8. Close the Terminal window by selecting **Quit** from the File menu. You have successfully indexed the Home folder for Ronald Carter.

9. Open a Finder window by clicking the **Finder** icon in the Dock.

10. In the left pane, click once on the **ronaldcarter** volume. You should now see the ronaldcarter home folder in the Finder window.

11. Click in the **Spotlight** search dialog box and type **jpg** into the dialog box. Notice the results that begin to populate the window immediately.

12. In the first line of search criteria, change "This Mac" to "ronaldcarter" by clicking on the words. On the same line, change "Contents" to "File Name" by clicking on the words. You will notice the results changing immediately again.

13. Click the + icon in the upper right just above the scroll bar, to add a second line of search criteria.

Continued

14. Click the **Kind** pull-down menu and change it to "Last opened is".

15. Click the **within last** pull-down menu and change it to "exactly".

16. Lastly, set the date criteria to **9/06/08**.

17. Did you just locate the image file named "gradient.jpg"? Double-click this file to safely open it and view its contents. You will not alter it because you mounted the ronaldcarter.dmg file using a shadow file.

End of Exercise

Using Spotlight to locate images through both filenames and file metadata is an extremely powerful capability on the Macintosh. In the introduction to this chapter, you learned how an image can move from a digital camera to iPhoto to Photoshop to Graphic Converter. Built in to the Macintosh operating system is the ability to find each version of the image, when we as examiners properly use metadata to our advantage.

Summary

Images on the Macintosh aren't just images. Besides the picture that you see on the screen, each image has associated metadata to go along with it. We as examiners can use this metadata to perform complex searches, thanks to the powerful Spotlight search engine built into Mac OS X. With Spotlight you can conduct lightning-fast, broad-sweeping or narrowly focused searches on the user's data, the entire Macintosh, or as you saw in this chapter, external data that you index on your own.

When recovering data from a Mac, it is important to stay aware of the metadata that images may contain by performing a controlled look at your own known images. A controlled look allows you to take your known image, view its metadata, and then formulate searches for suspect data based upon known criteria. Searching for images by looking for "files that end in JPG only" is an old-school way of performing file searches. That methodology occurred because search engines didn't support queries as powerful as Spotlight queries, and the size of the data repositories to be searched were much smaller. Utilize metadata to your advantage for searching as well as evidence.

Solutions Fast Track

Defining a Photo on a Macintosh

- ☑ Images come from many sources, including digital cameras, Webcams, and applications.

- ☑ Digital images can be saved in many formats for many reasons. Popular formats for pictures include JPG, PNG, GIF, PDF, BMP, and PSD. When encountering a file format, always look into the file format and the applications that can utilize it as a part of your case.

- ☑ Users can open, save, and convert images using several applications on the Macintosh. An image may start out as an image from a digital camera, but may go through many steps of editing. As examiners, we can use metadata to decipher when an image has been accessed by a particular application.

iPhoto

- ☑ iPhoto is the most popular photo application on the Mac because of its ease of use and its inclusion with every Mac sold.

- ☑ iPhoto includes functions that we as examiners need to be concerned about. iPhoto can share and publish images to the local network as well as the Internet with relative ease.

- ☑ iPhoto saves image data in the user's Home folder by default, but includes a hidden feature that allows the user to specify a different iPhoto Library at launch time by holding down the Option key. This makes it possible to have multiple Libraries in many locations, including external media that isn't necessarily connected to the Macintosh all of the time.

Recovering Images

☑ Recovering images is best done with Spotlight, a powerful, built-in indexing engine for Mac OS X. Spotl ight allows for basic file searching and file content searching along with powerful metadata searching.

☑ As examiners, we always lock our evidence disk image (DMG) files to remain forensically sound. When you mount a locked disk image, Spotlight will not index the contents of the disk image because it can't write the index file to it. You can use the built-in shadow files feature of Mac OS X to simulate read/write access to the disk image and then manually enable Spotlight indexing to regain this powerful tool on your evidence file.

☑ You can locate images by image type (JPG, GIF, etc.), but also can perform a much more granular search for the exact camera model that took the digital picture, or narrow your search to a specific date range.

Spotlight and Shadow Files

☑ Spotlight will index any writable media introduced to the Mac OS X computer.

☑ As examiners, we Lock our image files (DMG files) to prevent alterations. This, however, also prevents Spotlight from writing an index file to the DMG file, further preventing us from using Spotlight to perform searches. To overcome this, we use "shadow files" to simulate to ability to write to our Locked DMG file.

☑ A shadow file is a file that keeps all of the "writes" that would have occurred to the DMG file, and can safely be deleted after the DMG file is ejected.

Frequently Asked Questions

Q: Why are there so many file types on the Macintosh?

A: The file types mentioned are universally accepted file types that are standards across all operating systems, except for just a few. The select few, such as PICT, which started out as a Macintosh format, can be opened on multiple operating systems today. File types are created with different compression schemes. Some do better jobs at compression than others. File types are created to satisfy different quality and compression needs, as well as the age-old reason of money. There is money to be made in licensing a successful file format. Improvements upon file formats are constantly made as processing power and bandwidth gains are made.

Q: Photoshop is more popular than iPhoto. It is the defining application on the Macintosh. Why didn't you include a section for it?

A: In terms of popularity, iPhoto is definitively the winner. Although iPhoto is not in the same class as a high-powered application such as Photoshop, you should be able to apply the recovery techniques you learned in this chapter to any Photoshop image file, Quark image file, or any other image file you might come across. Recovery is a matter of finding the right combination of indexing and metadata.

Q: I just made a Spotlight query that is rather complex and works great! Can I save it or do I have to build a new query every time?

A: You can save Spotlight searches by clicking the **Save** button in the first search criteria line. The Finder allows you to save the Spotlight search for future use.

Q: You mention two files specific to iPhoto: AlbumData.xml and com.apple.iPhoto.plist. If I try to search for these files with Spotlight, I can't find them. Why?

A: By default, Spotlight indexes your entire hard drive, but returns results from areas that are not system areas of the hard drive. Areas of interest to us as examiners include system areas. You can change this in the same way you added other metadata. In the Metadata Attributes window, scroll down to "System files" and place a checkmark next to it. Then change "don't include" to "include" and you will get the results you were seeking.

Chapter 11

Finding and Recovering Quicktime Movies and other Video

Solutions in this chapter:

- Defining a Movie on a Macintosh
- iMovie
- Recovering Video

☑ Summary

☑ Solutions Fast Track

☑ Frequently Asked Questions

Introduction

Still images and photos are just the first aspect of power of desktop publishing done on a Macintosh. As we explored in Chapter 10, we found that every Macintosh computer sold comes with a powerful, yet easy-to-use suite of software called iLife. On a Macintosh it is very easy to connect a video camera because it connects so easily to download motion video to the hard drive for viewing, organizing and editing. The process is as simple as using a Macintosh with a digital camera to edit and view photos.

Macintosh computers are revered not only for their ease of use, but the high-powered applications available for digital video editing, high-speed digital processing, and the ability to publish the final product to many different types of media. A Macintosh that is purchased for home use and is used by a family for organizing home movies could very well be the same Macintosh purchased for studio use and used for high-end output of high-definition video. Macs are used by many of the television studios to edit digital video moments for example, of your favorite sporting event, because of the power and ease with which it can be accomplished.

This is not a sales pitch to buy a Mac, but a note to all examiners that digital video and Macs go hand-in-hand. Because digital video editing software is so prevalent on the Macintosh, examiners should remain especially aware of the existence of child pornography when performing analysis. A thorough analysis should always include a notation of the installed applications, their functions, the file types they, and then if applicable, whether the file types exist.

Defining a Movie on a Macintosh

Digital video on a Macintosh should be defined before we proceed. Let us begin by defining methods that digital video can be introduced to a Macintosh. First, all-Intel based Macintosh computers, except for the Mac Pro/Mac Mini, have an iSight camera built-in. The iSight camera allows for high-quality recording of digital video directly to the Mac. As with any other computer, an external Webcam could be attached as well, giving any Mac Pro/Mac Mini and the entire PowerPC-based line access to digital video. Figure 11.1 shows an iMac Aluminum with the popular iMovie application running.

Figure 11.1 Apple iMac Aluminum with iSight Camera

Courtesy of Apple

Until 2008, Apple included with every Macintosh an Apple Remote, which interfaced with the Front Row application. Apple Remote can still be purchased separately from the Apple Store.

Second, a DVD/CD drive on a Mac is referred to in one of two ways: SuperDrive or ComboDrive. The SuperDrive on Macs refers to a DVD drive that can burn both DVD and CD discs. The ComboDrive on a modern Macintosh refers to a DVD drive that is capable of reading DVD discs and burning CD discs. An examiner will always want to check the exact specifications to see exactly the type of discs that can be burned.

NOTE

As noted in Chapter 1, Macintosh specifications can be obtained from the **Apple Menu** by selecting **About This Mac**. In the window that opens, click on **More Info** to obtain the exact specifications about the Macintosh you are examining.

The number of available expansion ports on the Mac itself makes video possible. Connection ports such as USB 2.0 and FireWire allow for high-speed transfer of digital data such as digital video. FireWire has been the connection method of choice for high-end video cameras because of its speed. Mac Pro desktop models allow for additional expansion cards, which again add to the number of devices that an examiner might need to look if a case involves video. Some of the most difficult video expansion devices are wireless. These include home security monitoring system or simple wireless Webcams.

Once a video has actually been introduced to a Macintosh, we need to be concerned with file formats as with any other type of digital data. Digital video exists in many formats, sometimes even in proprietary formats, that can only be read with specialized software. Some of the most popular formats are listed here:

- *MOV* is pronounced *movie*, and is Apple's flagship video format, which is considered an industry standard for quality and compression.

- *MP4* is pronounced *em-peg 4*, and is a high quality, compressed digital video standard that is supported by many platforms and applications.

- *M4V* is a QuickTime movie format seen on iPhone, iPod and AppleTV. It is an Apple copy-protected version of MP4, although it can have no copy-protection applied as well. iTunes videos will download with the .m4v file extension.

- *FLV* is Flash video from Adobe Systems. Widely used on the Web for its ability to stream the video thru the browser. It is not a high-quality format. It is optimized for Web delivery.

- *DV* is pronounced *digital video*, and is streaming digital video typically used with digital video cameras. When transferred to a Macintosh it is converted to another format.

- *WMV* is Windows Media Player Video, the video format developed by Microsoft and a standard in the Windows world. QuickTime can interact with this format through the addition of free software from Flip4Mac (available at www.flip4mac.com)

- *DivX* is pronounced *div-ex*, is a proprietary form of the MPEG4 format that is a high quality and high compression standard for digital video files. DivX requires a player application to view the proprietary format. The players are easily obtained on the Web for multiple platforms.

As with digital image file formats, one could discuss digital video file formats for several more pages and multiple chapters could be dedicated to the debate of which one is the best. The point of the section is to note the number of possibilities when dealing with digital video, especially when it comes to a Macintosh.

Finally, in order to deal with the hardware and the file formats, we need applications. iMovie has been available since 1999 and has seen many improvements since version one. As with iPhoto, iMovie is meant to be an easy-to-use, beginner's movie editing software application. It integrates quite well with another bundled application called iDVD, which can make professional looking DVD discs with very little knowledge from the user. Other applications that are very prominent on the Macintosh will be Apple's Final Cut and Final Cut Express for high-end video editing. These applications, if they are in use, will indicate the user has a higher level of knowledge of digital video.

Applications for simply playing digital video on a Macintosh include Apple's QuickTime Player, Flip4Mac, VideoLAN's VLC Media Player, and MPlayer OS X. This short list of applications I have mentioned is the just the beginning of the long list available to any user. When examining for digital video content, it will be important as an examiner to determine what applications have been installed that support the file formats saved on the Macintosh.

Digital video files will have both a content and metadata component to every file. In recovering digital video, we will use this to begin our search, and then refine our search to drill down to the data we seek.

iMovie

iMovie is one of the applications included on every new Macintosh computers sold today. It is also a part of the iLife suite, just as iPhoto is. Many of the same integration qualities that we learned of in Chapter 10 regarding iPhoto will be true of iMovie as well. This application's functions are to import movies, allow for simple editing, and forward easily to others. Let's take a look at how this is accomplished by looking at the latest release of iMovie, called iMovie '08.

iMovie '08 is a part of the iLife '08 suite and is installed with all Macintosh computer sold since the iMovie '08 was released. Figure 11.2 shows us the interface of iMovie '08 and what a user would be presented with when the application is launched.

Figure 11.2 iMovie '08 Interface

In Figure 11.2, we see the editing interface of iMovie '08. There are five panes to work in, each having a specific function. Our key here is not to teach iMovie '08, so let us key in on just a few areas of interest. In the upper row, the left-most pane says *My First Project*. This is the default name by iMovie when the application first opens. The user will not need to change this name ever during the movie editing process, and it is very possible to find this name on the user's Macintosh as an iMovie project file. The middle pane is the current movie that is being created in sequence. When the user chooses to export or share their creation, this is the movie that will be produced. Lastly, the bottom row is the clips that are available to the user to add to the movie being made. The bottom row, left pane, is where additional imported movies would show after the import is complete. Lastly, notice in the available clips how iPhoto Videos and the picture from iPhoto are available. iMovie integrates with iPhoto directly.

When a movie is finally created in iMovie, it can be shared with the world in many different ways. As we can see in Figure 11.3, a user has several options to show the world their final product.

Figure 11.3 iMovie '08 Sharing Options

As seen with Figure 11.3 iMovie has the ability to create a final Movie product locally, or to publish to the Internet with other services. Looking at this menu, the choices of iTunes, Media Browser, Export Movie, Export using QuickTime, and Export Final Cut XML are all local publishing options. These options allow the user to export their movie creation into an appropriate format and publish directly to iTunes or to their Media Browser list for sharing with all iLife applications. A user can use these options to show their movie on their local AppleTV, to snyc with their iPod or iPhone, and to send to another iLife application, called iDVD, to create a playable DVD video disc.

More interesting to us are the next two options: YouTube and MobileMe Gallery. These options are a direct publishing pipeline from the user's iMovie creation to the Internet. In order for the user to accomplish this, a YouTube or MobileMe account must exist first. Let's look at the YouTube dialog window first, as shown in Figure 11.4.

Figure 11.4 iMovie '08 YouTube Publishing

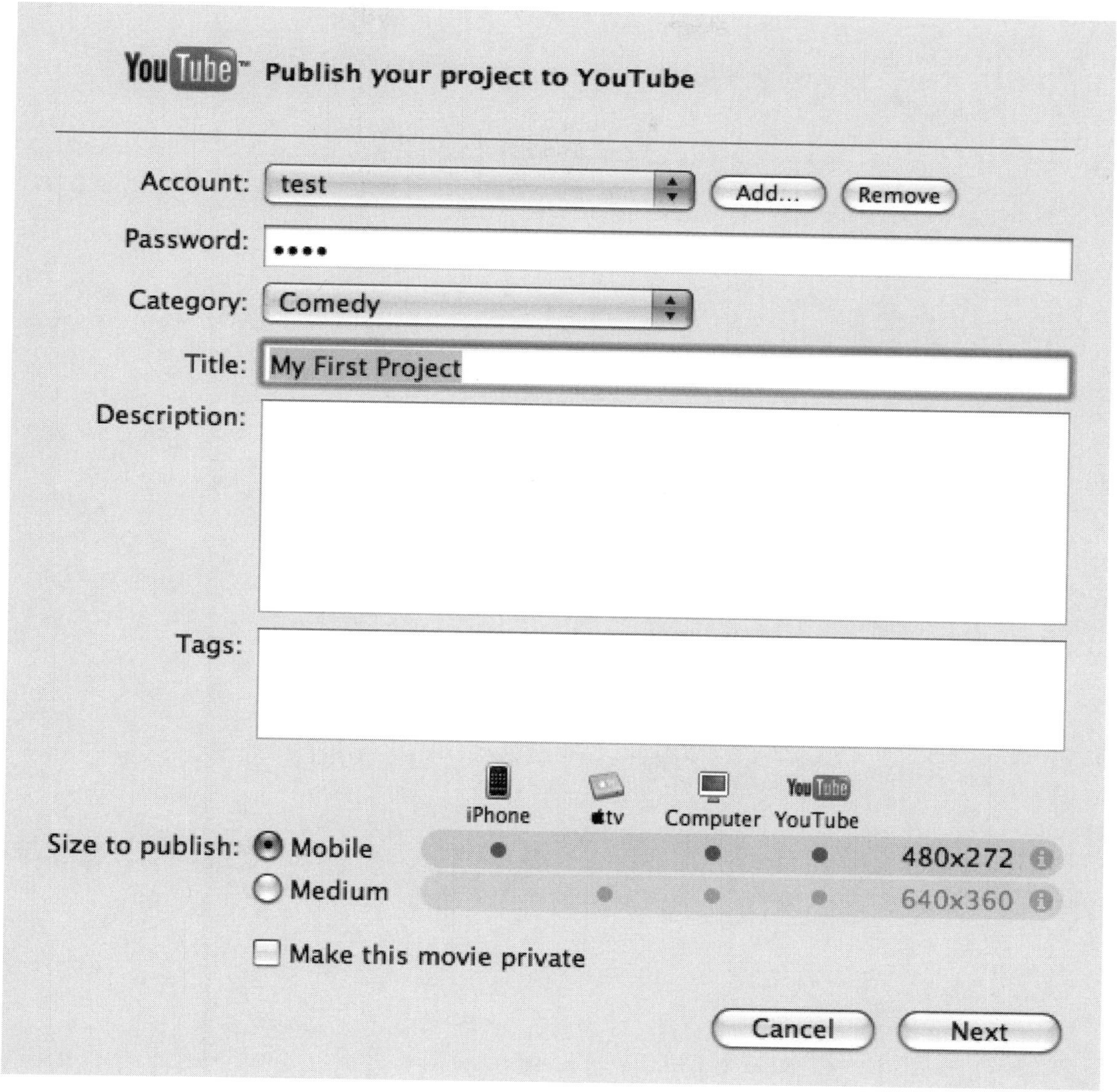

Figure 11.4 shows the easy integration between iMovie '08 and YouTube. In this example, the account used is named *test*. This is the account that must exist on the YouTube site in order for this process to be completed. When a user publishes to YouTube, iMovie records the user account information in the iMovie .plist file. We will look at this file later in the section.

Also available to users is the MobileMe Gallery. Looking at Figure 11.5, we see the similarities in publishing content to MobileMe.

Figure 11.5 iMovie '08 MobileMe Gallery Publishing

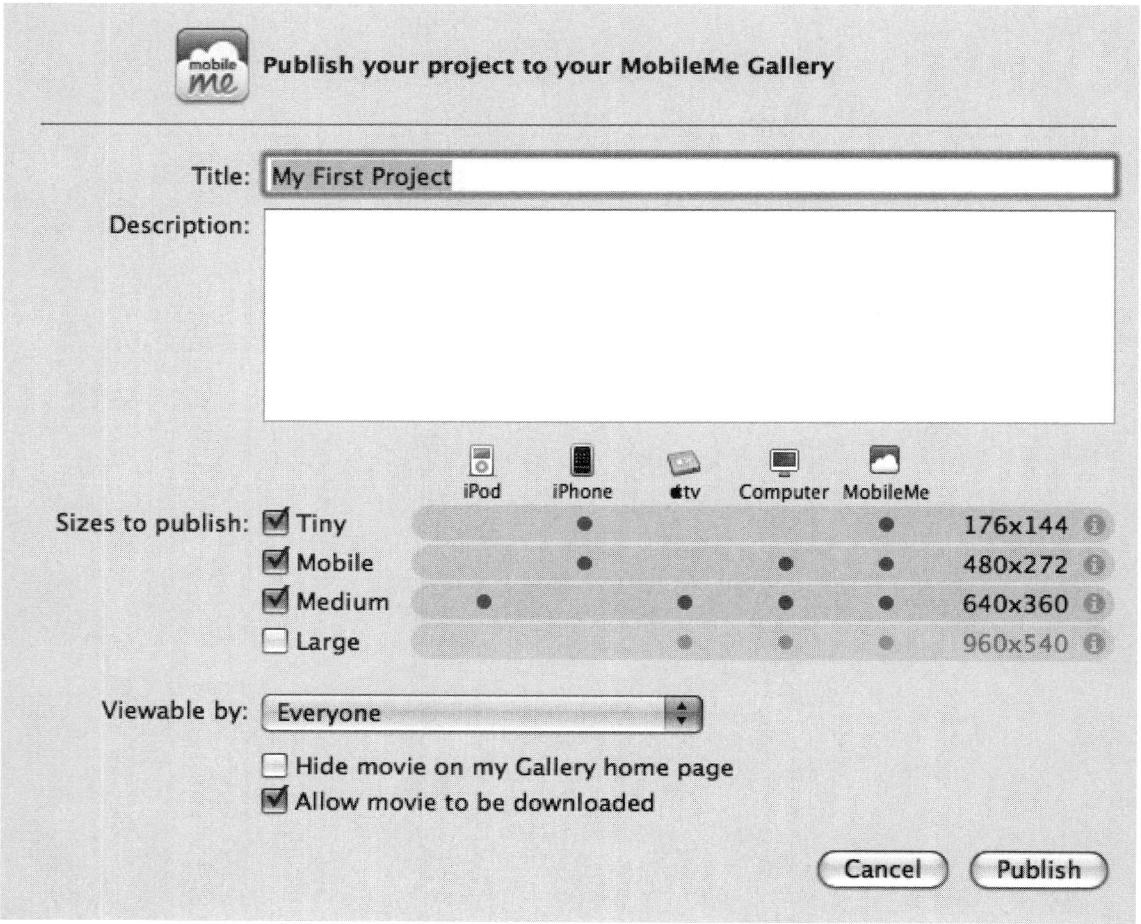

Just like with YouTube publishing, Figure 11.5 shows us how the user names and describes a project. There is a notable difference in this window; no username and password authentication. MobileMe is a service that is configured as a part of the Macintosh system. iMovie has recognized that MobileMe is already configured for this user and allows for publishing immediately. The publishing page is interesting to note for us as examiners. When examining a QuickTime video, the quality is notable because of the media it can be played on. For instance, the chart in Figure 11.5 shows us that a 640x360 QuickTime movie cannot be played on an iPhone. Because of this fact, look for different versions of the same video.

After the user clicks on the **Publish** button, the selected QuickTime video file types will be published to the user's MobileMe Gallery. As soon as the upload is complete, iMovie will display that the movie is now being published as seen in Figure 11.6.

Figure 11.6 iMovie '08 Mobile Published Movie

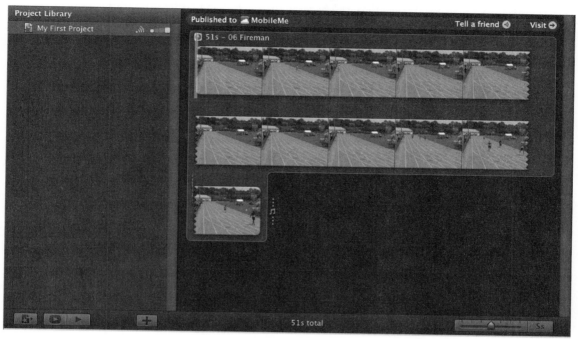

Figure 11.6 is a focused picture of the two upper left panes of iMovie '08. Notice how My First Project is now displaying the publishing icon similar to how iPhoto displayed a publishing icon? Also, note the "Published to MobileMe" title across the top. iMovie does not display the actual link to the Web page like iPhoto did in the browser window. From this window, a user would need to click on the **Visit** link arrow in order to access the MobileMe Gallery.

Now let's look at the data associated with iMovie '08 and how we can reconstruct a user's actions within this application. iMovie '08 saves its settings into a preference file called *com.apple.iMovie7.plist*, which is saved in the user's Preferences folder. Figure 11.7 shows this file for the user *moof*.

Figure 11.7 User 'moof' iMovie Preference File

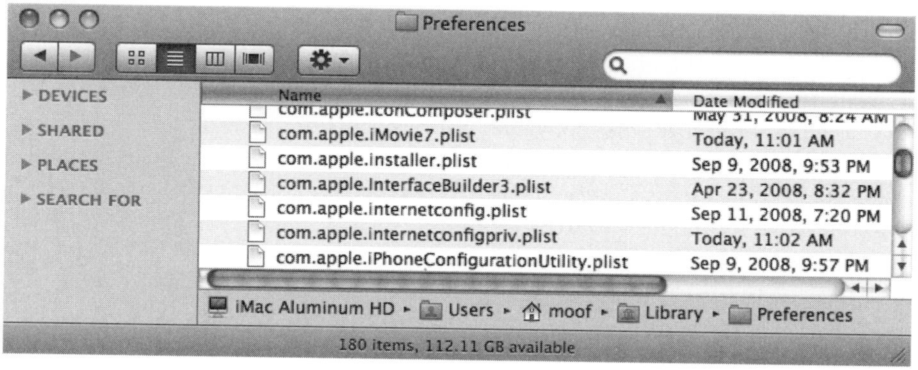

The very first question you might ask yourself after viewing Figure 11.7 is, Why iMovie7? While I can't answer questions for Apple's developers, the best reason I can come up with is this: iMovie '08 is considered the seventh version of iMovie to be released and it seems that the Apple Developers continued to use the version number in the .plist file naming convention instead of the application name itself. The file's contents can be viewed by clicking once on the **com.apple.iMovie7.plist** file and pressing the **Space Bar**. This activates Quick Look, allowing you to scroll thru the XML code of the file. An even better choice for viewing this file is to use Property List Editor, the application available for free as a part of the Developer Tools from Apple. Let's examine the settings file by using Property List Editor, as seen in Figure 11.8.

Figure 11.8 iMovie '08 com.apple.iMovie7.plist File

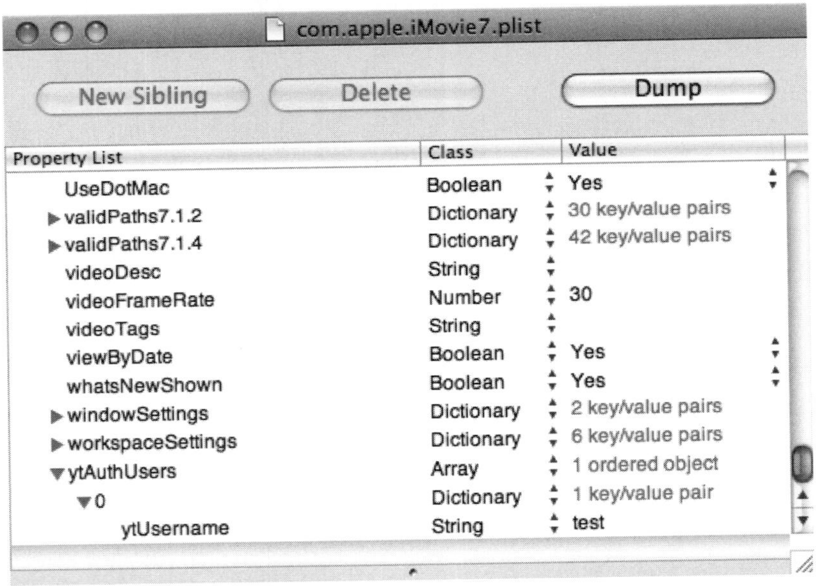

Figure 11.8 is a view of just some of the information stored in the com.apple.iMovie7.plist file. This selected section is notable because it contains the publishing information regarding YouTube and MobileMe. Notice the top of Figure 11.8, where the key reads *UseDotMac*. If you recall, .Mac (phonetically read *dot mac*) is the previous name for MobileMe. This key has a value of *Yes*, meaning that MobileMe is configured for use. Note at the bottom of Figure 11.8 there is a key named *ytUsername* with a value of *test*. This is the username that was entered in the dialog box for publishing. It does not indicate a valid YouTube account! It merely reflects an attempted YouTube account name for publishing. You, as an examiner, will need to look into the YouTube account names listed for validity and successful publication.

Next, let's look at the iMovie project file itself and the data it holds for us when examining a Macintosh case. By default, iMovie will save its projects to the Movies folder located in the user's Home folder. A user always can change this location when saving a project. If a user keeps the default name for My First Project, then an iMovie project file will look much like the one seen in Figure 11.9.

Figure 11.9 iMovie '08 Project File Seen in Finder Window

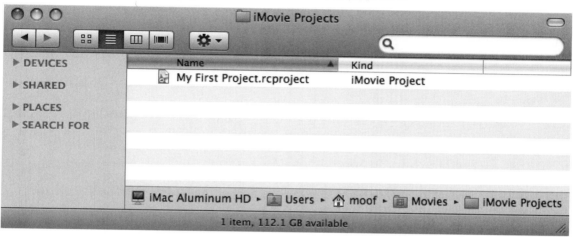

In Figure 11.9, we see a "package" file just as we saw with iPhoto in Chapter 9. What we are seeing here is a specialized folder with the extension ".rcproject". In order to view the contents of this project, Control-click on the file, and choose **Show Package Contents** from the pop-up menu. This will bring up a new Finder window similar to the one in Figure 11.10.

Figure 11.10 iMovie '08 Project File Contents

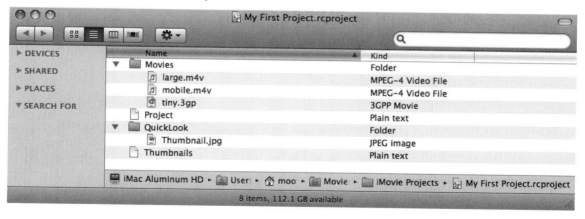

The contents of this project are important to note and will be the most important data regarding the project itself. Recall that during the publication to MobileMe (Figure 11.5) we were able to choose, based on quality, three different movie formats for publication. Notice in the Movie folder

that we have three movie files that are named similarly to the choices we made in the publication to MobileMe (Figure 11.5). The file named *Project* and noted as a *plain text* file is really a .plist file and can be opened with Property List Editor! Open this file and you will find all of the specific settings having to do with this project file, including the Web site address for publishing to the MobileMe Gallery.

TIP

When we looked at the iPhoto Library, we found that Spotlight would locate photos inside of the *package* file. With an iMovie project file, however, Spotlight does not look inside the package file. If you use Spotlight to search for tiny.3gp, there will be no hits (unless this exists elsewhere on the hard drive, of course). What we can search for in Spotlight is iMovie project files, and then examine the contents of those packages. To locate iMovie project files, search for the .rcproject extension or the "Kind is Other" metadata and enter **"iMovie Project" into the Spotlight dialog box.**

As you have seen, iMovie '08 includes some very easy-to-use features for the import, editing and sharing of digital video. We have begun to explore where to look for the data that shows a user has taken advantage of these features in the application. Now in the next section, let's tie it all together with specifics on how to recover video.

Recovering Video

As with recovering images, recovering video can elicit many thoughts from a digital examiner when those words are read. Let's define the scope of our recovery for this section. Here, we are not going to attempt to recover any video from unallocated space or deleted files. On a Macintosh, just like on any other platform, once a video is deleted, you will need to perform your favorite file carving techniques to bring the file back into existence. There is no "undelete" function on a Macintosh (unless the user is utilizing Time Machine). File carving for video is a much more difficult task than with other files. Video is inherently larger in size and uses more space on the hard drive. When the video file is deleted and the space is marked "unallocated," it becomes highly probable that another, new file will quickly overwrite a portion of the deleted video. When this happens, the deleted video file becomes *corrupt* for recovery purposes, and the chances are lessened greatly that we will be able to see anything of value. In this section, we will work with files that have not been deleted from the file system, and are actively being stored by the user for access.

Again, searching for video on the Macintosh has been made easy and fast with the built-in search engine Spotlight. We will use Spotlight to search for video files based on filename criteria, metadata criteria, and refined search locations such as a user's Home folder. Let's begin with a simple exercise (see Exercise 11.1) in locating a video file using Spotlight.

Configuring & Implementing...

Exercise 11.1: Locating Video on a Locked DMG File

This exercise will familiarize you with basic Spotlight searching.

1. Insert into your Mac the DVD toolkit that accompanies this book.

2. Copy the **ronaldcarter.dmg** file to your Desktop.

3. Lock the DMG file on your Desktop by **Control-clicking** it, selecting **Get Info**, and then clicking the **Locked** checkbox. You should now see a small lock icon in the lower left corner of the file's icon, indicating that the DMG file has been properly locked.

4. Open **Terminal** on your Mac. It is located in the Utilities folder inside the Applications folder.

5. In the Terminal window, enter the command **hdiutil attach ~/Desktop/ronaldcarter.dmg –shadow**, to mount the DMG file of Ronald Carter's Home folder using a shadow file.

6. Also in the Terminal window, verify the status of Spotlight indexing by issuing the command **mdutil –sa**. Notice that /Volumes/ronaldcarter states "Indexing disabled".

7. Turn on indexing for DVDToolkit.dmg by issuing the command **mdutil –i on /Volumes/ronaldcarter/**.

8. Close **Terminal** by selecting **Quit** from the **File** menu. You have successfully indexed the Home folder for Ronald Carter.

9. Open a Finder window by clicking the **Finder** icon in the Dock.

10. In the left pane, click once on the **ronaldcarter** volume. You should now see the ronaldcarter home folder in the Finder window.

11. Click in the **Spotlight** search dialog box and type **m4v** into the dialog box. Notice the results that begin to populate the window immediately.

12. In the first line of search criteria, click **ronaldcarter**. On the same line, click **File Name**. You will notice the search results changing immediately again.

13. Click the + icon in the upper right just above the scroll bar, to add another line of search criteria.

14. Click the **Kind** pull-down menu and change it to **Last opened date**.

Continued

15. Click the **Any Date** pull-down menu and change it to **exactly**.
16. Set the Date Criteria field to **9/07/08**.

Did you just locate three files matching the results window of Figure 11.11? Double-click any of these files to safely open and view the contents. You will not alter it because you mounted the ronaldcarter.dmg file using a shadow file.

End of Exercise

Figure 11.11 Results Window for Exercise 11.1 Spotlight Search

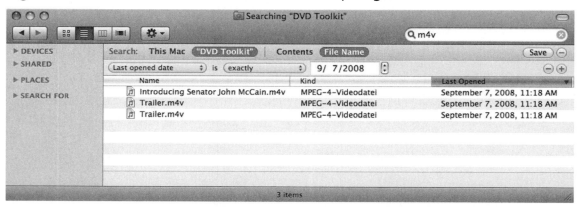

Of course, that is a very easy search to perform, and certainly does not show off the abilities of Spotlight as a forensic tool.

In order to have Spotlight start working for us, we need to see some of its power. We used metadata criteria in Chapter 9. Here, we are going to used "Saved Searches" to easily locate video of different types quickly. In Exercise 11.2 let's create a Spotlight search that locates all videos from all locations that Spotlight is currently indexing.

Configuring & Implementing...

Exercise 11.2: Using Spotlight Saved Searches for Quick Video Searches

This exercise will show you how to perform quick searches for various video formats using Spotlight.

1. Open a Finder window by clicking the **Finder** icon in the Dock.
2. Click in the **Spotlight** search dialog box and type **mov** into the dialog box. Notice the results that begin to populate the window immediately.
3. Verify that "This Mac" is the selected search source in the first line search criteria.
4. Click the + icon in the upper right just above the scroll bar to add a second line of search criteria.
5. Click the **Any** pull-down menu and change it to **Movies**.
6. Lastly, click on the **Save** button to save this search for future use. A dialog box will appear similar to the one in Figure 11.12. Name your search with something informative for future use. Always be certain to check the box **Add to Sidebar**.

End of Exercise

Figure 11.12 Spotlight Save Search Dialog Box

Specify a name and location for your Smart Folder

Save As: "This Mac" Movies

Where: Saved Searches

☑ Add To Sidebar

Cancel   Save

Figure 11.12 shows us how to properly save a Spotlight search with an informative name. This name indicates where the results will be obtained from (This Mac) and what the results will be (Movies). Figure 11.13 is an example of how we can now use this saved search to our benefit.

Figure 11.13 Saved Spotlight Search Results

Notice in Figure 11.13 how the Finder sidebar is showing the name of our Spotlight saved search, and the right pane is showing the results? The results of the search are immediately available by simply clicking on the Smart Folder and watching the right pane populate with results. If we mount the supplied DVD Toolkit.dmg utilizing the shadow file feature, any videos on that DMG will also show up in this window! You are probably beginning to feel the power of a saved search and how this can be useful for video searching.

The difficultly with our current saved search, however, is how broad the scope is when it comes to the media. Recall, when we made this particular search, I guided you to select "This Mac" as the first line search criteria. By selecting this, our Saved Search is looking at all media connected to "This Mac". Do you see the problem when looking for suspect files? This search returns results from our Macintosh and all of its connected devices. How could we use Spotlight to narrow the focus of a search? This is easily answered by looking at the steps we have taken with each exercise. The first line of criteria in each Spotlight search is where the location gets narrowed. To Spotlight search for the DVD Toolkit.dmg file after it has been properly mounted with the shadow file option, we can click on it in the Devices section of the left pane in the Finder window. Our broad search was created and saved for demonstration purposes. Such a broad Spotlight search being performed would create more work during a forensic examination than was intended.

As we saw in Chapter 9, Spotlight allows you search for a vast array of metadata. Video files have the possibility of containing almost no metadata or a huge amount of metadata, depending on the hardware and software that was used. When using Spotlight to locate a video, always start with a broad search and allow the results window to populate. If you wind up with too many resulting files, consider which files in the initial search are useful. Then refine the search by adding a second line of search criteria. If the second line of search criteria has not narrowed the focus sufficiently, add a third line. Spotlight criteria can be narrowed continuously until the results are useful. Always be certain that your search includes the media you intended to search as well! It is quite easy to get started and accidentally click on the user's name when you intended to click on the "This Mac" for the first line search criteria. You would have unintentionally narrowed your search to the user's Home folder with a single click, potentially missing evidence outside of the Home folder.

Summary

Digital video shares many traits with the digital images that were discussed in Chapter 9, including the manner in which we search for the files. Spotlight indexes digital video and all associated metadata just as it does with every other file on the Macintosh. As we saw with iMovie '08, digital video can be found inside of package files, which cannot be initially seen through a Spotlight search. As examiners, we need to be cognizant of what Spotlight indexes when it comes to digital video, as well as how to locate the data that will be contained within files that are not initially noted as video files. iMovie project files are not considered video files when it comes to a Spotlight search. However, in this chapter we used Spotlight to locate three movie files that were published on the Internet inside a project file itself! Always look at the installed applications on the Macintosh to best understand the possible file types you may be looking for during your examination.

Solutions Fast Track

Defining a Movie on a Macintosh

- ☑ Every Intel-based Macintosh except the Mac Pro/Mac Mini comes with a built-in iSight camera. This means digitized video is readily available by simply launching the correct application.

- ☑ Macs are compatible with almost all of the digital formats available today. Apple uses the QuickTime video format most often with their software. File extensions for the QuickTime format include .mov and .m4v.

- ☑ Included applications on the Macintosh for digital video are iMovie and iDVD. Both applications are a part of the iLife suite and integrate with the MobileMe service. We need to be aware of these applications for both their movie editing functions and their Internet publishing abilities.

iMovie

- ☑ iMovie is an easy-to-use, bundled application, which allows for importing, editing, and publishing of digital video.

- ☑ With iMovie, a user can easily share digital video with others by publishing to YouTube or to MobileMe. Fortunately for digital forensic examiners, iMovie retains evidence of this publication to the Internet in .plist files.

- ☑ iMovie '08 saves its data into an iMovie project file. This is a fancy name for a package file that we can look inside to see the contents. Inside of this package, we will find the actual digital videos associated with the project, as well as the .plist file showing exact locations for any Internet publications that have been made.

☑ Spotlight does not index the contents of an iMovie project file. This means we must first locate iMovie project files using Spotlight, and then examine the contents of the project files manually. Without taking the manual step of looking inside of the package, we would miss crucial evidence having to do with iMovie and its usage.

Recovering Video

☑ Spotlight has the ability to locate video quickly and easily. A broad search for a file extension will yield an initial window of results that can be overwhelming. Use Spotlight second and third line search criteria to narrow the focus when performing searches.

☑ When you have found a Spotlight search that attains useful results, use the Save feature and add that Spotlight Search to your Finder Sidebar for easy future searches.

☑ Use the metadata of digital video to assist in creating focused Spotlight searches. In this section, we focused on iMovie. It is possible to find a Macintosh that has several digital video applications installed. In this case, digital videos that have been manipulated by other applications may have varying metadata. Use this to your advantage when searching and narrowing your focus.

☑ Lastly, Spotlight searches do not always need to be narrowed when recovering video. They should always be focused on the media you intend to search, but you as the examiner will determine how narrow you need to make the criteria. If a results window that contains 1000 digital videos is acceptable, then you have performed a perfect Spotlight search!

Frequently Asked Questions

Q: How do I recognize a Macintosh that has the built-in iSight camera?

A: Visually, although the iSight camera can be difficult to find on some Macs. The camera is always a small hole just above the screen, and it is always centered. If the camera is active (ON), a green light will also be on right next to the iSight camera hole.

Q: Is iMovie a popular method for publishing child pornography?

A: I have never seen a single statistic published on iMovie's usage for this. This chapter has shown you how easy iMovie makes it to publish any digital video to both YouTube and MobileMe. YouTube is monitored for content quite well and is not common source of child pornography. However, it is certainly possible that the user publishes a movie to their MobileMe account. This is not actively monitored for content (Apple actively takes down any source known to contain contraband) and could further be published with a password for only a select group of people to view.

Q: Does iDVD create DVDs that work with all computers?

A: When a user sends their digital video to iDVD, iDVD creates a professional looking DVD that meets the standards for the disc to be played in all DVD players. This includes stand-alone players as well as software-based players on Macs, Windows, Linux, Solaris, so on.

Q: Using Spotlight to locate digital video seems trivial. Am I missing something?

A: No, you are not. Spotlight has indexed everything for you already. What is non-trivial is knowing where Spotlight won't look by default (system locations) and knowing that your locked evidence files need to be mounted with the shadow file option. Of course, when a digital video format comes along that isn't being found by the broad search of Kind is Video, you may have to do more research. Always remember that Spotlight won't look inside of an iMovie project file, and this could be the answer to missed results to a new type of digital video file as well.

Chapter 12

Recovering PDFs, Word Files, and Other Documents

Solutions in this chapter:

- **Microsoft Office**
- **Recovering Office Files, PDFs, and Other Documents**

☑ **Summary**

☑ **Solutions Fast Track**

☑ **Frequently Asked Questions**

Introduction

Often, a suspect's computer documents can contain a treasure-trove of valuable information related to the case you're working on. Such information can include names, dates, times, organizations, and much more.

However, suspects can store their documents in a variety of different formats. For instance, they can store them as PDFs, text files, or Microsoft Office files. Therefore, as a computer forensic investigator, it is important that you know how to recover documents, regardless of format, and determine whom they belong to.

In this chapter, we will discuss metadata and the preferences of Microsoft Office as it pertains to the Macintosh platform. Next, we will discuss different document types of Office 2008, and then we'll end the chapter with a discussion of evidence retrieval, especially Entourage, which contains similar information as that found in its counterpart, Microsoft Outlook.

Microsoft Office

Microsoft Office is available in three versions, all of them in use on many Macintosh systems worldwide: Office X, Office 2004, and Office 2008. Just as with many other applications, however, different versions provide different features. In this Section, we will discuss Office 2004 and 2008.

Office 2004

The Microsoft Office 2004 suite for the Mac includes most of the applications available in the standard versions of the Windows Office 2003 suite, including Word, Excel, and PowerPoint. Office 2004 for the Mac also includes Entourage, which is an application similar in nature to Outlook for Windows in that it provides e-mail support, calendar management, contact management, and task lists. The Office 2004 package stores data in the traditional Office compound document format and is completely independent of the file system. The Mac version of Office is identical in structure to the Windows versions of Office. Given the similarity of these files, they are easy to locate, carve, and extract the metadata that may provide additional investigative information.

With both versions of Office, you can gather certain information from the metadata associated with files. Commonly defined as "data about data," *metadata* is the data that describes the context, content, and structure of files and their management through time. High-profile cases have been solved by finding metadata in files and tying that information to a particular user. For example, the "BTK Killer" was caught because metadata from a church computer he had used was saved as part of the file on the floppy disk the killer sent to law enforcement.

When you save an Office 2004 Word document, you are prompted to enter a filename and a format in which to save the document. A feature in Word which lots of users tend to ignore is the Preferences and Properties menus. With these menus, a user can adjust global preferences in Word (for instance, auto-recover, printing preferences, user information, auto-correct, and much more). It is these settings that can be found later in metadata. To set a document's preferences, select **Word** from the menu bar and then select **Preferences**, as shown in Figure 12.1.

Figure 12.1 Setting Microsoft Word Preferences

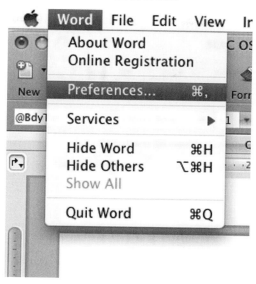

You will see the following subcategories:

- General
- View
- Edit
- Spelling and Grammar
- Auto Correct
- Save
- Print
- Compatibility
- Track Changes
- Audio Notes
- User Information
- Security
- Feedback
- File Locations

Any change in any setting will affect the metadata information of all documents. One of the ways you can add metadata to Word documents is by adding information related to the user/creator of those documents. Click **User Information** and a screen similar to that shown in Figure 12.2 will appear.

Figure 12.2 User Information Preferences for a Microsoft Word Document

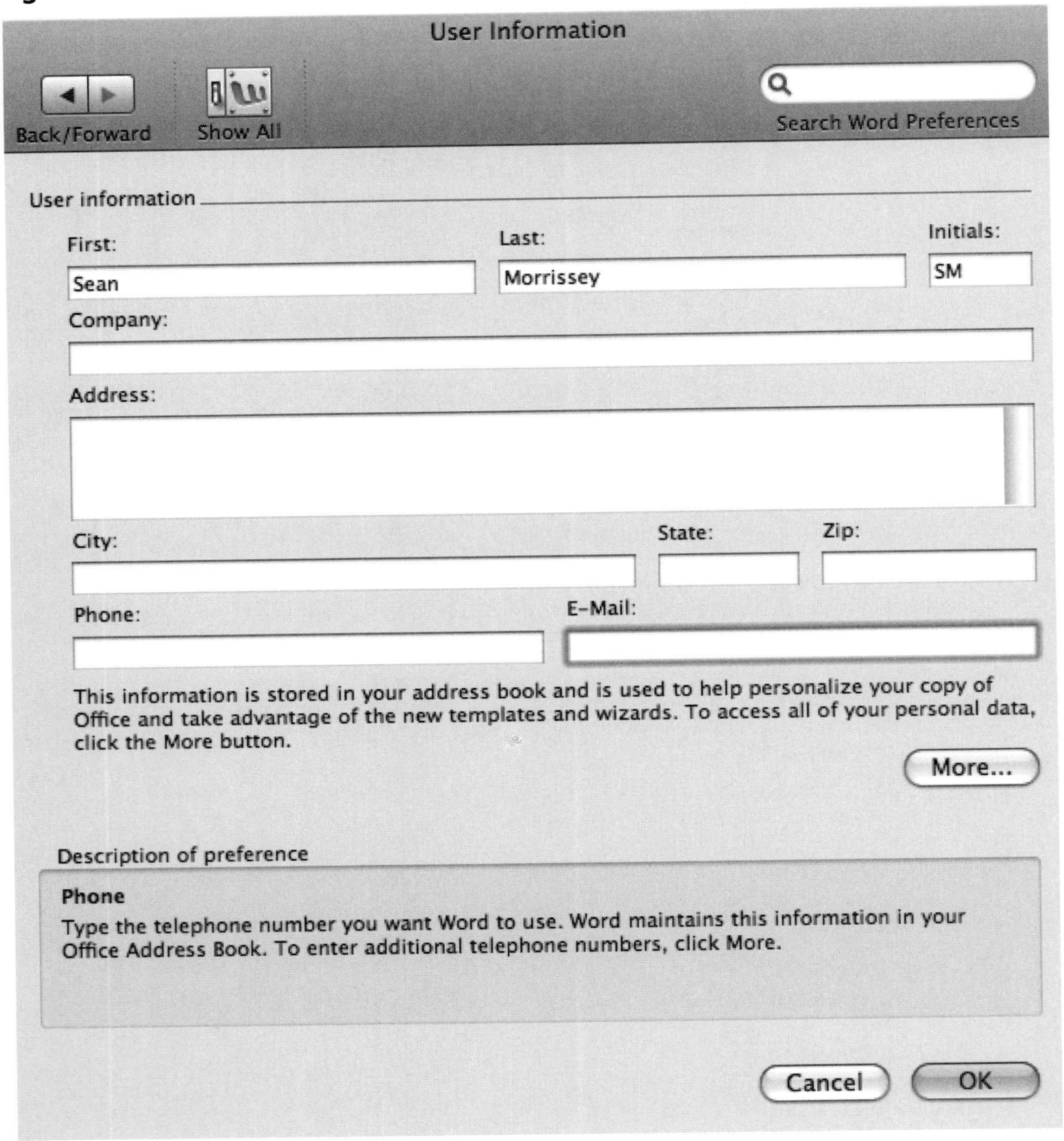

Here you can provide a plethora of metadata information to be associated with your documents, including your name, initials, company name, address, phone number, and e-mail address.

By clicking the **More** button, you can add even more metadata. The information you can provide, shown in Figure 12.3, is divided into seven categories:

- Summary
- Name & E-mail
- Home
- Work
- Personal
- Other
- Certificates

Figure 12.3 More Preferences for a Microsoft Word Document

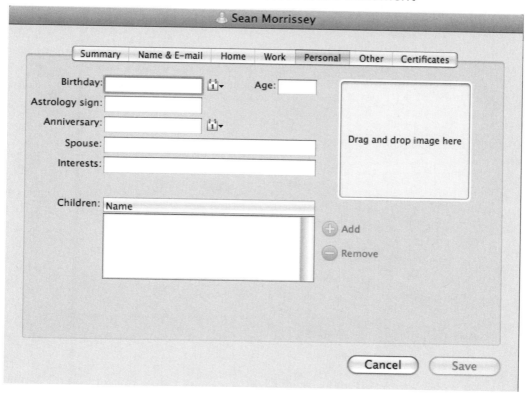

The information you provide in these fields will be added to your files as metadata. For example, the information you provide in the First and Last name fields in Figure 12.2 will be added to the Author field of the document properties, as shown in Figure 12.4. To view a document's Author field, open the document in Word and select **File | Properties** from the menu bar.

Figure 12.4 Document Properties

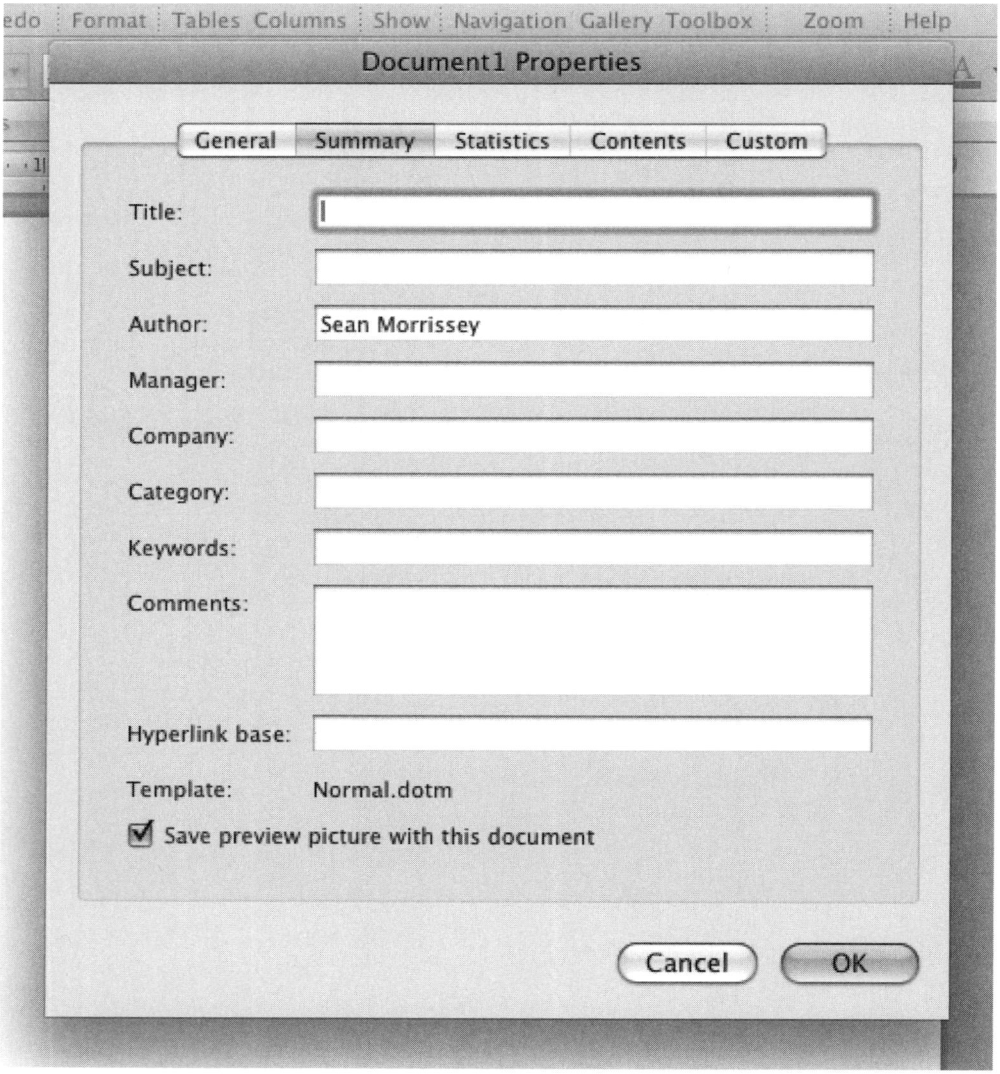

At the top of the window shown in Figure 12.4 is a series of tabs. If you click on the Summary tab or the Custom tab, you can edit the contents of the page that appears (clicking on the General, Statistics, or Contents tab will not bring you to a user-editable page). Figure 12.4 shows the contents of the Summary page. From here, it would be easy for someone to remove some of the metadata associated with the document, such as the document title, the author, or the company name. It would also be easy for someone to enter other information of his or her choice into these fields. Note that by default, the Summary page is not displayed as a part of the document-saving process; so many users do not even know that the information is being recorded in the file.

Office 2008

Office 2008 for the Mac is similar to previous versions of Office for the Mac. Office 2008 does require Tiger, Mac OS X Version 10.4.9 or later, at a minimum. The interface of Office 2008 resembles the interface of Office 2007 for Windows. The most notable change for computer forensic investigators is the new Object-Oriented XML (OOXML)-type format (discussed next). However, the Office 2008 version still maintains the traditional File menu bar, unlike its Microsoft Office 2007 counterpart.

Object–Oriented XML Format

Microsoft Office uses the new Object-Oriented XML (OOXML) format to store the content of files as well as metadata. With the introduction of this new file format and storage methodology, Microsoft decided to include the ability to compress documents to save space and increase document portability. Microsoft Office documents that are saved in this XML format are nothing more than Zip archives which contain a series of XML documents.

With the change in Office 2008, it is important to know that the standard way to locate Word, Excel, and PowerPoint metadata has changed. Table 12.1 lists the new file extensions for Word 2008.

Table 12.1 Office 2004 versus Office 2008 File Extensions

Program	Office 2004 Extension	Office 2008 Extension
Microsoft Word	.doc	.docx
Microsoft Excel	.xls	.xlsx
Microsoft PowerPoint	.ppt	.pptx

To view the metadata in a Word 2008 document (XML document), you must change the file extension from .docx to .zip, and open it through Dash Code, a utility within the Mac. Here's what to do:

1. Right-click the document and select **Get Info**.
2. Delete the **.docx** in the filename and replace it with **.zip**.
3. Select **Open With | Archive Utility**.
4. Return to the Finder and double-click the **Word document**. Another folder will have been created with the same name as the Word file, but with a .zip extension.

When you unzip the file, you'll see that it contains three folders and one file, as shown in Figure 12.5.

Figure 12.5 Uncompressed Folders and Files

Within the docProps folder is a file called core.xml. The core.xml file, as shown in Figure 12.6, contains a subset of information regarding the document itself. Using Figure 12.5 as a guide, navigate to the core.xml file and open it in Notepad or Internet Explorer. When the file is open, it may look something like Figure 12.6. Keep in mind that the information displayed here may be more extensive in some documents than in others.

Figure 12.6 The core.xml File from an Office 2008 Document

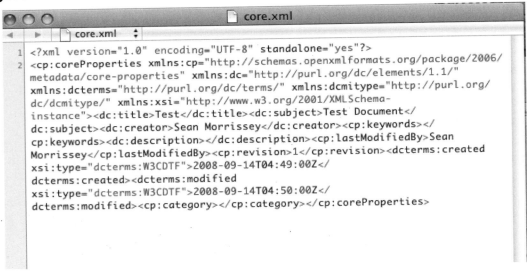

You can locate the following information and possible XML tags in this file:

- **<dc:title>** The document title as defined by the user.

- **<dc:subject>** The document subject as defined by the user.

- **<dc:creator>** The user's name as the user entered it the first time Word was launched. The user can edit this data through the Office Options dialog box. Typically, this information is set once and is never changed.

- **<cp:keywords>** The document keywords as defined by the user.

- **<dc:description>** T he document description as defined by the user.

- **<cp:lastModifiedBy>** The user's name presented in the same way it was added for the creator tag. The distinction within this tag is that it shows the name of the person who last edited the document, not the original creator of the document.

- **<cp:revision>** The revision number of the document. Office maintains this information and the only way to edit it is by accessing and modifying the XML data that is contained within the file.

- **<dcterms:created>** The date/timestamp for the creation of the document. This information is based on the date/time of the system clock and is as reliable as normal modification, access, and creation dates. It is important to note that the data stored in this field is converted to UTC time without daylight saving time bias. Therefore, the calculation of UTC time is directly dependent on daylight saving time bias based on the time zone settings employed by the user.

- **<dcterms:modified>** The date/timestamp for the last modification of the document. This **information** is stored in the same manner as the creation timestamp and should be afforded the same level of trust as the creation timestamp.

The app.xml file also contains a standard set of tags that provide information about the document. Here is a list of the XML tags that you would find in a Word 2007 file and a description of the information that is contained in each:

- **<Template>** The default template that was used to create the file. On most new documents, the template will be Normal.dot.

- **<TotalTime>** The total amount of time the document was opened for editing. This does not change when a document is opened for several hours and no changes were saved to the file. If a document has a *TotalTime* value of *16*, and a user opens it and makes changes for another nine minutes and then saves the file, the *TotalTime* value would change to *25*. If the user waits another 15 minutes, makes no changes, and then saves the file again, the *TotalTime* value would change to *40* since a save is an implied edit to the document.

- **<Pages>** The number of pages in the document.

- **<Words>** The number of words in the document.

- **<Characters>** The number of characters in the document. This value does not include spaces or linefeeds (carriage returns).

- **<Application>** The application name used for the last edit.

- **<DocSecurity>** Provides a numeric value that indicates a security level being applied to the document. Microsoft does not publish the different values of document security. Additional testing will be required to determine all of the different values of document security that are available in Word 2007. By default, this value is *0*, which indicates that there is no security on the document.

- **<Lines>** The number of lines in the document.

- **<Paragraphs>** The number of paragraphs in the document.

- **<ScaleCrop>** A boolean value (*TRUE* or *FALSE*) which indicates whether any images within the document are scaled or cropped.

- **<Company>** The user-entered company name. This value is set in the properties for each Microsoft application.

- **<LinksUpToDate>** A boolean value indicating whether linked data has been refreshed.

- **<CharactersWithSpaces>** The character count, as noted earlier, except this value includes spaces. Linefeeds are not counted.

- **<SharedDoc>** A boolean value indicating whether this document is marked for collaboration through Microsoft SharePoint. The default value for this tag is *FALSE*.

- **<HyperlinksChanged>** A boolean value indicating whether the linked data within a file has changed. The default value for this tag is *FALSE*.

- **<AppVersion>** The numeric version number for the version of Office that was used in the last save of the **document**. Documents created using Office 2008 will show a version of 12.000.

If the document contains graphics, there will be a /word/media folder which will contain copies of the images used in the Word document. This folder may include images that were used in this document in a previous revision and were subsequently removed. For instance, if a person uses a template to create a document and removes a graphics file that is included in the template and then saves the file, the original image will likely be in the /word/media folder. This can be applied for all types of Office documents.

OpenOffice for Mac

OpenOffice for Mac is software produced by Sun Microsystems and is free to the general public for use. OpenOffice for Mac can open documents produced in the traditional Office format as well as the new XML document format. In addition to opening these two Microsoft document standards, OpenOffice works with an array of formats including plaintext documents and Rich Text Format (RTF) documents. Generally speaking, OpenOffice is an alternative to the native Office package that you may run into, but keep in mind that if you are working with documents that are saved in the Office or XML format, they will conform to the specific requirements of that particular format regardless of what software was used to create them. Because the documents produced by OpenOffice must adhere to specific document standards, we will discuss document recovery in a manner that is independent of the actual word processor that created the document.

Portable Document Format (PDF)

The Portable Document Format, or PDF, was created by Adobe as an open document standard intended to easily traverse the various operating platforms, such as Windows, Macintosh, Linux, and Unix. Though PDF documents can be used on different platforms, they are not always forensics-friendly in that the various versions of PDF can have different file signatures. Having different file signatures can make these documents difficult to carve out of unallocated space if they were deleted, and can also create problems if a file signature analysis is performed.

The Mac no longer needs to have Adobe Acrobat Reader to view PDFs. The "Preview" Application has the ability to open and view PDF documents. Within the print utility, you can easily create a PDF using the Mac, as shown in Figure 12.7.

Figure 12.7 Using Print Utility to Create a PDF

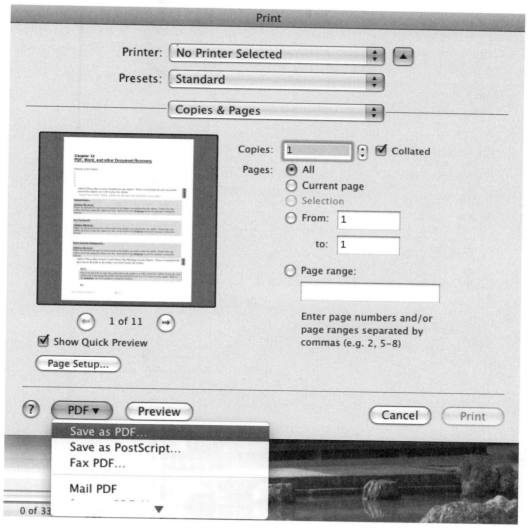

Text Documents

Text documents can be created with Text Edit or most other word processing engines. Files created with Text Edit will have the extension .txt.

Recovering Office Files, PDFs, and Other Documents

Now that we have looked at the various tools and format changes that have occurred recently, we're ready to examine a hard drive to find the files that were saved and exist naturally within the file system, as well as some that were deleted and will be carved from unallocated space. We'll look at both commercial and open source tools that can assist us in the recovery of documents.

The Mac is the best tool for finding and locating documents. Of course, the Mac has the advantage of requiring no additional software. The disadvantage of using the Mac, however, is that you will not find deleted files, or folders or items within unallocated space. To recover those files you will need a forensic tool, such as EnCase or FTK.

You can locate files within a Mac by using the Finder. Here's how.

1. Make sure your image is locked, and then open the **Finder**.
2. From the top menu bar select **File**.
3. Navigate to **Find**.
4. Highlight the volume you wish to search.
5. In the two drop-down menus, select **Name** and **matches**.
6. To the right of the drop-down menus, you will see a window in which you can place variables. Type **.doc** in that window. Finder will automatically search for .doc files and produce hits, as shown in Figure 12.8.

Figure 12.8 Searching for .doc Documents

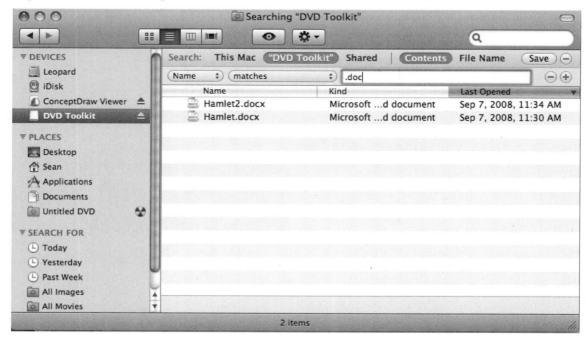

You can follow these steps to locate PDFs and any text document. Just change the variable to the file extension you are searching for.

Default Locations of Office Artifacts

By default, all Office documents are saved in /Users/[username]/Documents. Office 2008 Word documents are saved with the extension .docx, Excel documents with the extension .xlsx, and PowerPoint documents with the extension .pptx.

Property lists of interest include the following:

- **com.microsoft.Excel.prefs.plist** Here you can find recently opened files.

- **com.microsoft.Word.plist** This will show the location of saved files and a list of recently opened files.

- **com.microsoft.Excel.plist** This also will show the location of saved files and recently opened files.

Entourage

You can obtain a plethora of items of forensic interest from users utilizing Entourage, the Macintosh version of Microsoft Outlook. Some of the artifacts of interest include the following:

- Mail:
    - E-mail account information
    - E-mails and associated metadata
- Address Book:
    - Local user information including name and other contact information
    - Contact information for all associated individuals that were placed in the address book
- Notes:
    - Notes the user may have made through Entourage
    - Dates and times such notes were created
- Tasks:
    - Scheduled tasks, and dates and times such items were created
- Calendar:
    - Calendar appointments
    - Possible names and addresses included in appointments
    - Meetings and associated information

Most of the forensic tools on the market today can't really extract information from Entourage and present it to an investigator. The best way to examine Entourage data on a system is once again to use the Mac. First it is important to find where the evidence files are located.

Entourage files are located at /[username]/Documents/Microsoft User Data, as shown in Figure 12.9.

Figure 12.9 Microsoft User Data

The first two folders in Figure 12.9, Entourage Script Menu Items and Excel Script Menu Items, don't contain items of evidentiary value. The Office 2008 AutoRecovery folder will hold copies of files if the option is set from the **Word | Preferences**, as discussed earlier in this section. The next folder, Office 2008 Identities, contains numerous files that could contain evidence. For instance, some of the files within the Identities folder include files pertaining to the Newsgroup Cache, Database, Mailing Lists, Rules, and Signatures, as shown in Figure 12.10.

Figure 12.10 Main Identity Folder

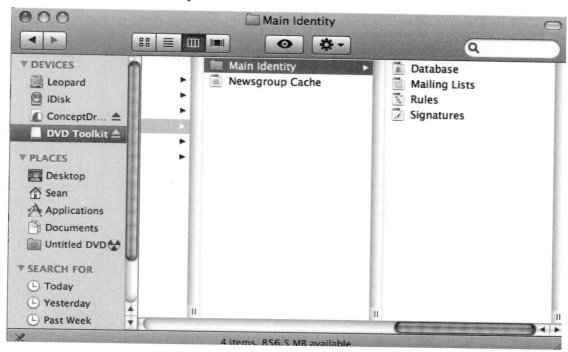

The Newsgroup Cache file may contain evidence if the suspect subscribes to newsgroups. The main file to consider is the Database file. This is the database of all items within Entourage. Since these are rather large files, you can open them with Text Edit and see e-mails, calendar items, and so forth. The best way to view the Entourage database is to use Entourage. First, if your forensic workstation contains a Microsoft User Data folder, delete that folder. Next, ensure that no Microsoft programs are running.

Once you've done this, follow the steps in Exercise 12.1 to examine a user's Entourage data.

Configuring & Implementing…

Exercise 12.1: Examining a User's Entourage Data

In this exercise, you will recover sample Entourage evidence with the DVD Toolkit included with this book. You will also examine the Entourage menu bar, as well as process Entourage e-mail, address book, calendar, notes, tasks and projects

1. Make sure that all wired and wireless connections are closed.

2. Locate and open the provided DVD. Double click on the "Locked" ronaldcarter.dmg

3. Navigate to ronaldcarter/Documents/Microsoft User Data/.

4. Using a "copy over technique," right-click the **Microsoft User Data folder** and select **Copy Microsoft User Data Folder**.

5. Paste the copied Microsoft User Data folder to the same location on your forensic workstation.

6. Open Entourage. You should see something similar to Figure 12.11.

Figure 12.11 Entourage Interface

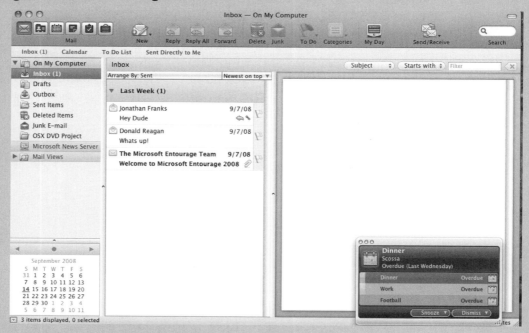

Continued

7. Select the top left icon that represents an envelope. Mail is the default e-mail application shown in Entourage (see Figure 12.12). Notice that the word *Mail* is displayed in the pane below the icon.

Figure 12.12 The Mail Icon

8. Select the **Address Book** icon, which is the second icon from the left in the Entourage menu bar. Determine whether there are any items of evidentiary value by clicking on this icon, as shown in Figure 12.13. Notice that the words *Address Book* are displayed in the pane below the icon.

Figure 12.13 The Address Book Icon

9. Select the **Calendar** icon, which is the third icon from the left in the Entourage menu bar. Determine whether there are any items of evidentiary value by clicking on this icon, as shown in Figure 12.14. Notice that the word *Calendar* is displayed in the pane below the icon.

Figure 12.14 The Calendar Icon

Continued

10. Select the **Notes** icon, which is the fourth icon from the left in the Entourage menu bar. Determine whether there are any items of evidentiary value by clicking on this icon, as shown in Figure 12.15. Notice that the word *Notes* is displayed in the pane below the icon.

Figure 12.15 The Notes Icon

11. Select the **Tasks** icon, which is the fifth icon from the left in the Entourage menu bar. Determine whether there are any items of evidentiary value by clicking on this icon, as shown in Figure 12.16. Notice that the word *Tasks* is displayed in the pane below the icon.

Figure 12.16 The Tasks Icon

12. Select the **Project Center** icon, which is the last icon on the right in the Entourage menu bar. Determine whether there are any items of evidentiary value by clicking on this icon, as shown in Figure 12.17. Notice that the words *Project Center* are displayed in the pane below the icon.

Figure 12.17 The Project Center Icon

Continued

13. To the left of "Send/Receive," there is an icon labeled "My Day." This is a new feature in Office 2008 and it is visible by a box that can be shown on the Desktop or within Entourage (see Figure 12.18). Click on the "My Day" icon. My Day will also show up on the desktop upon start up and will list the events for that day.

Figure 12.18 My Day

End of Exercise

In the following exercises, we will examine the Mail, Address Book, Calendar, and Notes features in more detail (See Exercises 12.2–12.5). We'll start with Exercise 12.2, with a look at Entourage e-mail messages.

Configuring & Implementing…

Exercise 12.2: Examining Entourage E-mail Messages

The following exercise will explain how to process e-mail messages in Entourage.

1. From the E-mail view, click an item of interest to view the e-mail, as shown in Figure 12.19.

Continued

Figure 12.19 The E-mail View

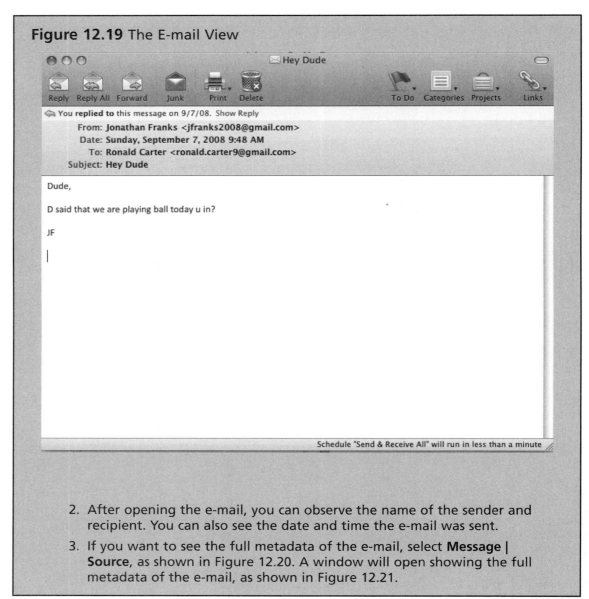

2. After opening the e-mail, you can observe the name of the sender and recipient. You can also see the date and time the e-mail was sent.

3. If you want to see the full metadata of the e-mail, select **Message | Source**, as shown in Figure 12.20. A window will open showing the full metadata of the e-mail, as shown in Figure 12.21.

Continued

Figure 12.20 Selecting Message | Source to View E-mail Metadata

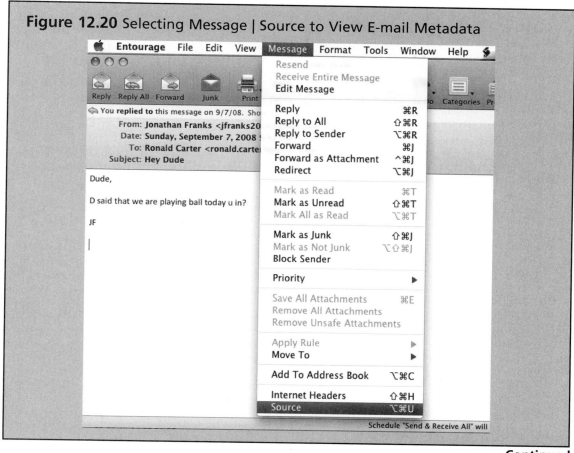

Continued

Figure 12.21 E-mail Metadata

```
                          Source: Hey Dude

Delivered-To: ronald.carter9@gmail.com
Received: by 10.180.246.12 with SMTP id t12cs168912bkh;
        Sun, 7 Sep 2008 06:48:32 -0700 (PDT)
Received: by 10.187.252.8 with SMTP id e8mr2780346fas.92.1220795312028;
        Sun, 07 Sep 2008 06:48:32 -0700 (PDT)
Received: by 10.187.228.5 with HTTP; Sun, 7 Sep 2008 06:48:31 -0700 (PDT)
Message-ID: <73ec860208090070648y7cf9eb27m1998f2f7f708c6be@mail.gmail.com>
Date: Sun, 7 Sep 2008 09:48:31 -0400
From: "Jonathan Franks" <jfranks2008@gmail.com>
To: ronald.carter9@gmail.com
Subject: Hey Dude
MIME-Version: 1.0
Content-Type: multipart/alternative;
 boundary="----=_Part_66408_19902955.1220795312025"

------=_Part_66408_19902955.1220795312025
Content-Type: text/plain; charset=ISO-8859-1
Content-Transfer-Encoding: 7bit
Content-Disposition: inline

Dude,

D said that we are playing ball today u in?

JF

------=_Part_66408_19902955.1220795312025
Content-Type: text/html; charset=ISO-8859-1
Content-Transfer-Encoding: 7bit
Content-Disposition: inline

<div dir="ltr">Dude,<br><br>D said that we are playing ball today u in?
<br><br>JF<br></div>

------=_Part_66408_19902955.1220795312025--
```

4. Look through all of the e-mail folders: Inbox, Drafts, Outbox, and so on, as shown in Figure 12.22.

Continued

Figure 12.22 E-mail Folders

5. Take screen shots of their contents, create a PDF of their contents, or just print the e-mails and add them to your report.

End of Exercise

Configuring & Implementing...

Exercise 12.3: Examining the Entourage Address Book

In this exercise, you will take a more in-depth look at the Entourage Address Book and Processing Contacts.

1. Select **Address Book** from the top menu bar.

2. In the **View** pane select a contact of interest.

3. **Double**-click the **contact** and view the associated metadata information, as shown in Figure 12.23.

Continued

Figure 12.23 Address Book Contact

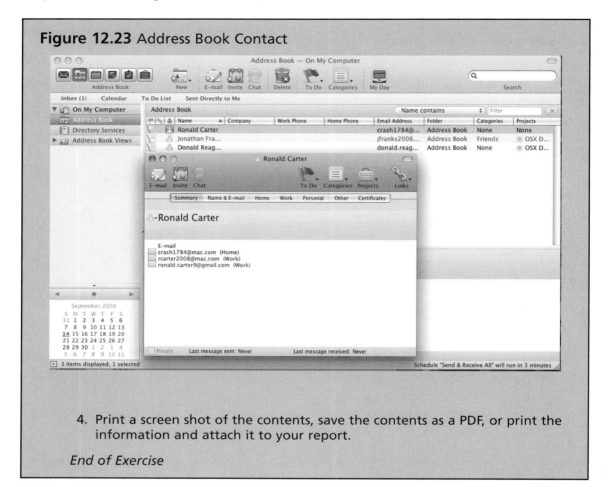

4. Print a screen shot of the contents, save the contents as a PDF, or print the information and attach it to your report.

End of Exercise

Configuring & Implementing…

Exercise 12.4 Examining the Entourage Calendar

Follow these steps to process Calendar items in Entourage.

1. View the different calendars in Entourage by looking at the left sidebar, as shown in Figure 12.24.

Continued

Figure 12.24 Calendar Sidebar

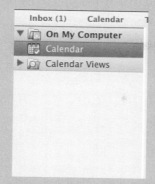

2. Look for items of interest. When you find one, double-click it and view the appointment. You can take a screen shot of the contents of the calendar, or print it out. However, you cannot see when this calendar item was created. To accomplish that, follow these steps:

3. Navigate to /ronaldcarter/Library/Caches/Metadata/Microsoft/ Entourage/2008/Main Identity/Messages.

4. Continue to navigate to /0T/0B/0M/0K/. You will see several .Rvge08Event files, as shown in Figure 12.25.

Figure 12.25 Event Preview

5. Double-click the events until you locate the item you want. When you have located it look to the right in the Preview and note the date and time this appointment was created.

6. Add the information regarding the appointment, as well as the date and time information, to your report.

End of Exercise

Configuring & Implementing…

Exercise 12.5: Examining the Entourage Notes and Tasks

Follow these steps to process Note items and Tasks in Entourage.

1. Select **Notes** from the top sidebar.
2. Peruse the folders within this item, as shown in Figure 12.26.

Figure 12.26 Notes Folders

3. Select the note(s) that are of value, as shown in Figure 12.27, and double-click them. Take a screen shot or print the contents of these notes and add them to your report.

Continued

Figure 12.27 Searching for Notes of Value

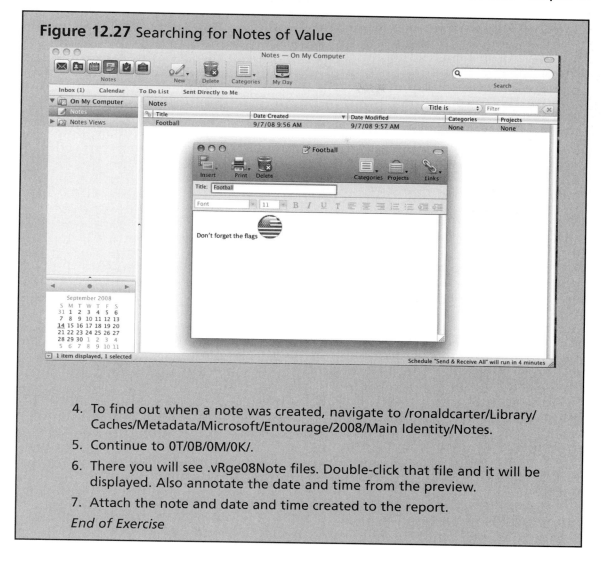

4. To find out when a note was created, navigate to /ronaldcarter/Library/Caches/Metadata/Microsoft/Entourage/2008/Main Identity/Notes.

5. Continue to 0T/0B/0M/0K/.

6. There you will see .vRge08Note files. Double-click that file and it will be displayed. Also annotate the date and time from the preview.

7. Attach the note and date and time created to the report.

End of Exercise

The steps for examining Tasks in Entourage are the same as the steps for examining e-mail and notes, with the exception that actual notes that contain date and time information are located within the Library/Caches/Metadata/Microsoft/ folder. Projects are a combination of items from within Entourage. A Project can associate e-mail, calendars, contacts, and notes. Projects can also attach files like Word Docs, Excel Spreadsheets, and associate them to the Project, as shown in Figure 12.28.

Figure 12.28 Projects

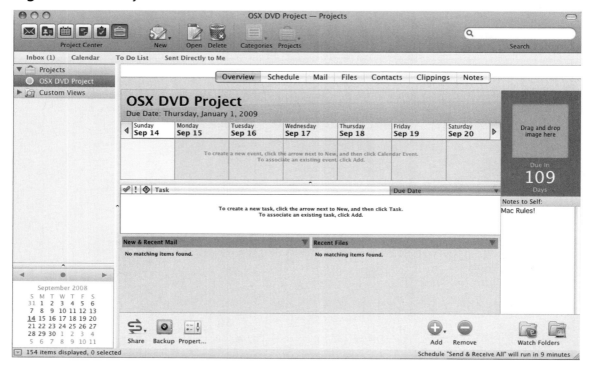

The last folder that an investigator should manually review is /[username]/Documents/Microsoft User Data/Saved Attachments. You can find saved attachments from his or her e-mails, as shown in Figure 12.29. By default Entourage will save email attachments to this location. However, the user sometimes does not realize this, and will save the attachment again to a known location. A copy can be found here in addition to anywhere the user saved that attachment.

Figure 12.29 Saved Attachments

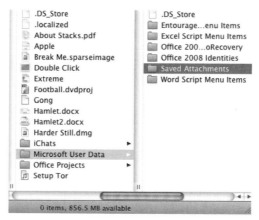

Summary

Office 2008 poses a new challenge for forensic investigators in terms of finding Office documents. However, you can use the power of the Mac to find those files. Evidence can be lurking in e-mails, tasks, calendar, notes, and projects. The best tools for viewing these items are the Mac and Office 2008. You can view metadata without the use of expensive forensic tools. Using a "copy over technique" to take items from the suspect's locked DMG and paste that data into the same location on the forensic machine, you can now see those items just as the suspect saw them. In addition, you can locate dates and times for all data in Entourage and add them to your reports.

Solutions Fast Track

Microsoft Office

- ☑ Office metadata can contain information about users.
- ☑ Office metadata can be cleared in an attempt to thwart detection.
- ☑ New Office 2008 documents can be saved in an XML format.

Recovering Office Files, PDFs, and Other Documents

- ☑ Microsoft Entourage is a program similar to Microsoft Outlook.
- ☑ The Mac is a good forensic platform for locating Microsoft Office files.
- ☑ Without a forensic tool, you will not be able to locate deleted items, or items in slack space.

Frequently Asked Questions

Q: Can I use a Mac as a forensic platform to recover Office files, PDFs, and other documents?

A: Yes

Q: Using the all the steps described in this chapter, what kind of information cannot be retrieved?

A: You will not be able to locate deleted items, or items in slack space.

Q: What is the Mac version of Microsoft Outlook?

A: Entourage.

Q: What is a .docx file?

A: A Microsoft Office 2008 Word file.

Q: What is the definition of metadata?

A: Data attached to a file about the file.

Q: How can I view the metadata of a .docx file while using the Mac as a forensic Platform?

A: Rename the file to .zip and analyze the recovered folders.

Q: What metadata information can we garner from a Word Document?

A: Names, addresses, e-mail addresses, company information, and personal information.

Chapter 13

Forensic Acquisition of an iPod

Solutions in this chapter:

- Documenting the Seizure of an iPod
- Using Open Source Acquisition Tools
- Using Proprietary Acquisition Tools

☑ Summary

☑ Solutions Fast Track

☑ Frequently Asked Questions

Introduction

The iPod has been on the market since 2001, and has become one of the most popular MP3 devices. Also, many people find them convenient places to store all types of media. If you are performing a search and seizure in the field, you may want to consider seizing a suspect's iPod if it is within the scope of your warrant. With up to 160 GB of storage, there is a good chance that information related to your case may exist on an individual's iPod.

iPod forensics is a new and exciting field; there have already been cases where individuals have been convicted of crimes because of the artifacts that were stored on their iPods. It is your job as an investigator to use sound forensic principals to obtain an image of the iPod and find these artifacts.

A variety of open source and commercial forensic tools can be used when imaging an iPod. The procedures for seizing an iPod and analyzing its data are very similar to the forensic acquisition of a computer. For that reason, you may want to consider using a write-blocker, such as FastBloc, when conducting an iPod acquisition. Always test your write-blockers, because sometimes they don't work with a Mac. Therefore, alternative solutions may be used, for example, performing a procedure using *disk arbitration*, which is similar to a software write-blocker.

In summary, as the numbers of iPods continue to proliferate, people will use them to store various digital media. Artifacts from these devices can be extracted, if necessary.

Documenting the Seizure of an iPod

It is important to an investigator or crime scene technician to know how to document the seizure of the iPod. The examiner needs to know what kind of iPod was seized, for example. This information will determine the method used to capture an image of the device. The host operating system can often provide details about what devices were connected to the Mac.

The following should be included in your documentation:

- Establishing a chain of custody
- Photography
- Case information
- Good local time and time zone
- Any other information deemed pertinent by your organization

The chain of custody is always a paramount procedure in any court proceeding; that is, establishing where the iPod has gone from seizure to court. Your organization will most likely have standard operating procedures on how to document the chain of custody.

When seizing any piece of evidence, it is important to photograph the iPod before removing it, using good crime scene procedures, for example, always using gloves. All iPods have smooth surfaces that may contain fingerprints. Therefore, only touch the sides of an iPod when seizing it.

As with any case, remember to annotate the case number and any evidence control number that your organization uses. Also, depending on the standard operating procedures of your organization, include the type of case investigated and the statute associated with the investigation.

Apple iPods

Depending on the type of iPod you have, there are two ways that imaging can be accomplished. First, it is important to know what type of iPod is being imaged. An iPod either has an internal hard drive or flash memory. If the iPod seized has an internal hard drive, the best way to image this device is to disassemble it and remove the drive. Using a zif adapter, the drive can be imaged with a variety of tools. Any iPod that contains flash memory can presently be imaged via its USB cable with a write-block device and forensic tools. Since there are so many varieties of iPods that have been released since 2001, it is important to know what type of hardware is present in the device you are seizing. Once you know what type of device you have, you can determine what procedure to use to image the device.

It is important to know some of the multimedia file types that are supported on an iPod. They are as follows:

- aac
- mp3
- mp3 vbr
- Apple Lossless
- wav
- aiff
- m4v

Here is a timeline that details the release dates and features of the different generations of iPods:

- The first-generation iPod was introduced in October, 2001. The first model had a 5 GB hard drive, FireWire 400 connector, and one 3.5 mm stereo headphone jack.

- The second-generation iPod was released in July, 2002. It had 10 or 20 GB hard drives. Due to consumer need it became available for the Windows operating system. These also came with a 4 to 6 pin FireWire connector.

- The third-generation iPod was released in October, 2004. It had 10,15,20,30, and 40 GB hard drives. This generation was redesigned. It was thinner, and the interface was different.

- The fourth-generation iPod was released in July, 2004. Again Apple redesigned the interface used on all future iPods. This was the first model with a click wheel. The fourth-generation iPod was the first model to have a USB or FireWire connection. This was invaluable for Windows consumers that did not have a FireWire port. The fourth-generation iPod had 20, 40, and 60 GB hard drives. A second fourth-generation iPod was released in October, 2004. This was known as the iPod Photo. This model had a color LCD screen and 30, 40, or 60 GB hard drives. A third version was released in June, 2005. This combined the capabilities of the previous fourth-generation models into one iPod. The iPod Color had a 20 GB drive.

- Before the fifth-generation iPod was released, Apple released the U2 Special Edition iPod. The U2 iPod only had a 20 GB drive. Apple dropped the U2 in October, 2005.

■ The fifth-generation iPod was released in October, 2005. This generation gave the user the ability to view video files. This made the iPod a total multimedia device. The fifth-generation iPods were thinner than previous models and were released with 30, 60, and 80 GB hard drives. Apple also released another U2 fifth-generation iPod for one year in 2006. This iPod only had a 30 GB hard drive.

■ The sixth-generation iPod, as shown in Figure 13.1, which was given the "Classic" moniker, was released in September 2007. It was given a thinner, slightly redesigned exterior. It incorporated the cover flow mode graphics seen in iTunes, and later used in the Finder in OS X 10.5 Leopard.

Figure 13.1 The iPod Classic

Courtesy of Apple

■ When imaging any of the "Classic-Generation " iPods it is best to extract the hard drive from the device and image it using a zif connector and forensic-grade command line or GUI tools. If imaging on a Mac remember to turn off Disk Arbitration.

The second type of iPod released was the iPod Mini, as shown in Figure 13.2. This was the first iPod that Apple released that catered to consumers that wanted smaller media devices. The iPod Mini was only able to play audio media.

Figure 13.2 The iPod Mini

- The Mini had a 4GB Micro-Drive and a USB connection.
- This model uses a Compact Flash card which can be removed and imaged using a hardware write-blocker and Forensic tools. When imaging on a Mac remember to turn off Disk Arbitration.

After the iPod Mini, Apple introduced the iPod Shuffle in January, 2005. The colorful iPod Shuffle is shown in Figure 13.3.

Figure 13.3 The iPod Shuffle

Courtesy of Apple

- The first-generation Shuffle had 512 MB or 1.0 GB of flash media available. The Shuffle can only support audio files. It only had a USB connector and did not have an LCD screen.

- The second-generation Shuffle was introduced in September, 2006. It contained 1.0 or 2.0 GB of flash media. This generation came in five different colors. It had a 3.5 mm stereo jack and Shuffle USB Dock. It was much smaller than the first-generation Shuffle, and also didn't have an LCD screen.

- You can only image the Shuffle via its USB connector while utilizing a hardware write-blocker.

WARNING

If the write-blocker does not recognize the device, a software write-blocker needs to be utilized (disable diskarbitrationd). You should only use forensic tools to image the Shuffle.

Replacing the iPod Mini was the iPod Nano, as shown in Figure 13.4. The Nano was introduced in September, 2005.

Figure 13.4 The iPod Nano

Courtesy of Apple

- The first-generation Nano was introduced in September, 2005 and discontinued in September, 2006. It only came in two colors: White and black. It had flash capacities of 1, 2, and 4 GB. It had a USB connection, a small color LCD screen, and supported audio and photo file formats.

- The second-generation Nano was introduced in September, 2006. It had flash memory drives of 2, 4, and 8 GB. This generation was the first Nano offered in six colors. It had a USB connector and supported audio and photo formats. As with the first-generation, the second-generation Nano also had a small color LCD Screen.

- The third-generation Nano was introduced in September, 2007. It came in five colors and had two flash media sizes: 4 and 8 GB. This generation iPod changed to a square shape, which gave it the nick name "fat Nano."

- The fourth-generation iPod was introduced in September, 2008. It came in five colors and two drive sizes: 4 and 8 GB. It could support audio, photo, and video formats. It had a USB connection and supported the color flow mode graphic format seen in the sixth-generation iPod Classic.

- You would use exactly the same procedure to image a Nano as you would a Shuffle. If imaging on a Mac remember to turn off Disk Arbitration.

The newest device released in September 2007 was the iPod Touch, as shown in Figure 13.5.

Figure 13.5 The iPod Touch

Courtesy of Apple

The iPod Touch was radically different than the classic iPod. The interface of the iPod Touch changed to a multi-touch screen. The iPod Touch has a USB connector as a port and it is wireless via 802.11b.g. The iPod Touch has a capacity of 8, 16, and 32 GB of flash memory. The iPod Touch also supports various audio, photo, and video formats. The iPod Touch has the capacity to surf the Internet, and email. With the advent of the 2.0 software upgrade, numerous applications can now be found on this device.

Using Open Source Acquisition Tools

There are many tools that can be used to image an iPod. One method to image an iPod is to use a Mac as the forensic platform. To do this the examiner may need to compile and install on the Mac either *dcfldd* or *dc3dd*, which are variations of the UNIX *dd* command. These command line tools are available for download from SourceForge:

- *dcfldd*

  http://sourceforge.net/project/showfiles.php?group_id=115587

- *dc3dd*

  http://sourceforge.net/project/showfiles.php?group_id=212454

Because an iPod's operating system is a live system that does not shut down, to forensically acquire an image of its file system, you need to use hardware write-blockers and / or disable the Disk Arbitration (*diskarbitrationd*) daemon, which auto-mounts volumes on a Mac. Disabling *diskarbitrationd* is done differently in Tiger than in Leopard.

Disabling the Disk Arbitration Daemon (Tiger)

To disable *diskarbitrationd* on a Mac running Tiger, please use the following steps:

1. Open the **Terminal.app**, located in the **Applications/Utilities/**.
2. Create a folder on the desktop where you will move the *diskarbitrationd.plist*.
3. From the Terminal window, type **sudo mv /etc/mach_init.d/diskarbitrationd.plist ~/Desktop/[*created folder name*]**. This command moves the *diskarbitrationd.plist* from its present location to the folder you created on the desktop, as shown in Figure 13.6.

Figure 13.6 Moving the *diskarbitrationd.plist* File

```
Last login: Sat Sep 27 19:20:45 on ttys000
sean-morrisseys-macbook:~ Sean$ sudo mv /etc/mach_init.d/diskarbitrationd.plist ~/Desktop/Moved
```

4. Press **Enter**.
5. Enter a password, if required.
6. After the property list has been moved, type **sudo reboot.**
7. Press **Enter**.

Reenabling the Disk Arbitration Daemon (Tiger)

After you finish forensically acquiring an image of an iPod, you will want to re-enable Disk Arbitration using the following steps:

1. Open the **Terminal.app**, located in the **Applications/Utilities/**.
2. From the Terminal window, type **sudo mv ~/Desktop/[*created folder name*] /diskarbitrationd.plist /etc/mach_init.d/**, as shown in Figure 13.7.

Figure 13.7 Returning the *diskarbitrationd.plist* File to Its Original Location

```
Terminal — bash — 118×22
Last login: Sat Sep 27 19:22:08 on ttys000
sean-morrisseys-macbook:~ Sean$ mv ~/Desktop/Moved/diskarbitrationd.plist /etc/mach_init.d/
```

3. Press **Enter**.
4. Type **sudo reboot**.
5. Enter a password, if required.
6. Press **Enter**.

Disabling the Disk Arbitration Daemon (Leopard)

The process in disabling disk arbitration in Leopard is basically the same as in Tiger, except that in Leopard the location of the daemon has been moved to the **/System/Library/LaunchDaemons/** folder. To disable Disk Arbitration on a Mac running Leopard, use the following steps:

1. Open the **Terminal.app**, located in the **Applications/Utilities/**.
2. Create a folder on the desktop where you will move the *diskarbitrationd.plist*.
3. From the Terminal window, type **sudo mv /System/Library/LaunchDaemons/ com.apple.diskarbitrationd.plist ~/Desktop/[*folder_name*]**. This command moves the *diskarbitrationd.plist* from its present location to the folder you created on the desktop, as shown in Figure 13.8.
4. Press **Enter**.
5. Enter a password, if required.

Figure 13.8 Moving the *diskarbitrationd.plist* File

```
Terminal — bash — 118×22
Last login: Sat Sep 27 19:32:48 on ttys000
sean-morrisseys-macbook:~ Sean$ sudo mv /System/Library/LaunchDaemons/com.apple.diskarbitrationd.plist ~/Desktop/Moved
```

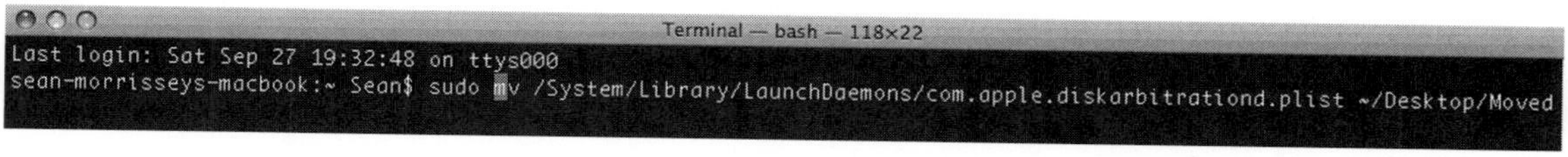

6. Type **sudo reboot**.
7. Press **Enter**.

Reenabling the Disk Arbitration Daemon (Leopard)

After you finish forensically acquiring an image of an iPod, you will want to re-enable Disk Arbitration on the Macintosh using the following steps:

1.   Open the **Terminal.app**, located in the **Applications/Utilities/**.
2.   From the Terminal window, type **sudo mv ~/Desktop/[Name of Folder created]/ diskarbitrationd.plist /System/Library/LaunchDaemons/**, as seen in Figure 13.9.

Figure 13.9 Moving the *diskarbitrationd.plist* File

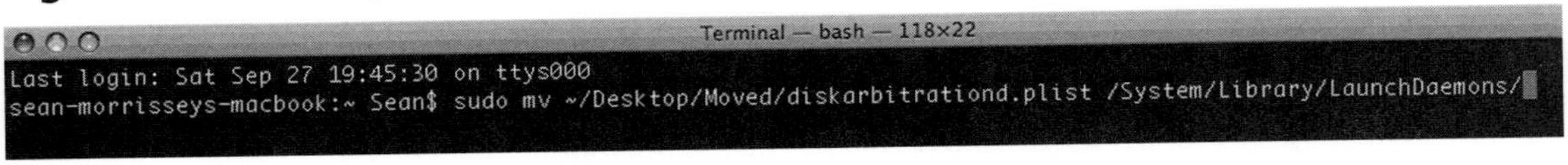

3.   Type **sudo reboot**.
4.   Enter a password, if required.
5.   Press **Enter**.

Creating an Image

Now that Disk Arbitration has been disabled, you can image the iPod. Using either the *dcfldd* or *dc3dd* command line utilities, you can create a raw data image. When imaging an HFS-formatted iPod and using a Mac as the forensic platform, you won't have to split the image. However, if you intend to view the image on a PC using either EnCase or FTK, you will need to split it. Windows has a 2GB limitation and cannot use an image file greater than this. Most of today's iPods have storage capacities from 1 to 160 GB.

Before you can image the iPod, make sure that your target media has been wiped. Also, always use a hardware write-blocker.

Live CDs

Any Live CD that includes Helix, SPADA, Backtrack 3, or any version of Linux can image an iPod. Helix, SPADA, and Backtrack have forensic tools like *dcfldd, dc3dd*, linen, FTK Imager and can be accessed either through the command line or using a graphical user interface (GUI).

Verifying the Integrity of the Raw Data

First, as with all command line tools, the proper procedure for imaging is to hash your media, then image and hash again. MD5Deep is one tool you can use to hash media. This is a compiled command line tool. The following is a procedure for hashing your media (iPod):

1.   Disable Disk Arbitration.
2.   Open a Terminal window.

3. Before you attach the iPod to the computer being used as the forensic platform, type **ls /dev/rdisk***. You should see output similar to that shown in Figure 13.10.

Figure 13.10 The ls /dev/rdisk* Command

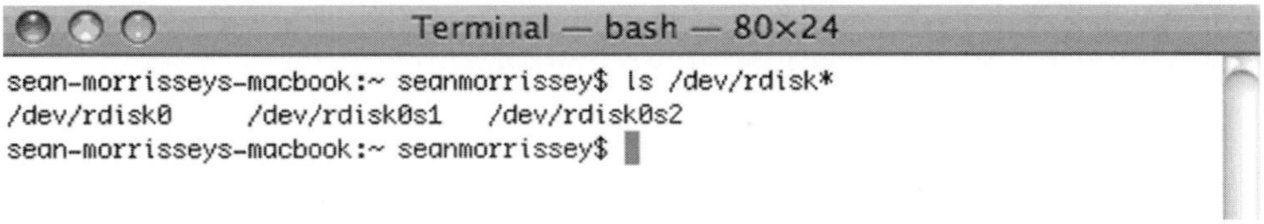

```
● ○ ○              Terminal — bash — 80×24
sean-morrisseys-macbook:~ seanmorrissey$ ls /dev/rdisk*
/dev/rdisk0     /dev/rdisk0s1    /dev/rdisk0s2
sean-morrisseys-macbook:~ seanmorrissey$ ▊
```

Please note that in Figure 13.10, **/dev/rdisk0** is the forensic Mac's hard drive.

4. Connect the iPod to the forensic Mac.

5. Retype **ls dev/rdisk***. You should then see output similar to that shown in Figure 13.11.

Figure 13.11 The ls /dev/rdisk* Command after You Connect the iPod

```
● ○ ○              Terminal — bash — 80×24
sean-morrisseys-macbook:~ seanmorrissey$ ls /dev/rdisk*
/dev/rdisk0     /dev/rdisk0s2    /dev/rdisk1s1
/dev/rdisk0s1   /dev/rdisk1      /dev/rdisk1s2
sean-morrisseys-macbook:~ seanmorrissey$ ▊
```

Please note that in Figure 13.11, **/dev/rdisk1** refers to the iPod that was just connected to the computer.

6. Type **sudo md5deep −e /dev/rdisk1 | tee −a /[*full path including a filename where you want the output to go*]**. The −e parameter gives you a progress indicator. The */dev /rdisk1* hashes the raw or whole disk.

7. Redo these steps after you have imaged the iPod, as demonstrated in the next section.

Imaging the iPod Device with *dc3dd*

dc3dd is the updated version of *dcfldd*. After you have hashed your iPod, complete the following steps:

1. Open the **Terminal.app**, located in the **Applications/Utilities/**.

2. Type the following to image the iPod: **sudo dc3dd conv=sync,noerror if=/dev/rdisk1 of=/[full path and filename of where you want the image to go] hashwindow= 1000000 hash=md5,sha1 hashlog=/[*full path and filename where you want the logfile to go*] bs=4k progress=on.**

3. Press **Return**.

If you are imaging the iPod for use on a Windows-based system, use the following steps:

1. Open a Terminal window.
2. Type the following to image the iPod: **sudo dc3dd conv=sync,noerror split=650MB if=/dev/rdisk1 of=/[full path and filename of where you want the image to go] hashwindow=1000000 hash=md5,sha1 hashlog=/[full path and filename where you want the logfile to go] bs=4k progress=on**.

The following bullets describe the *dc3dd* command in more detail:

- *dc3dd* is the command.
- *conv* converts the file.
- *sync* is used to pad every input block with nulls.
- *split* is used to split the image into smaller files, due to Windows' 2GB limitation. Normal file sizes are 650MB and 1GB.
- *noerror* states to continue after read errors.
- *if* is the input file (that is the full path of the device being imaged).
- *of* is the output file of where the *dd* image will be saved. It's best to have a filename such as "image.dd."
- *hashwindow* is the variable for the number of bytes for piecewise hashing.
- *hash* is what kind of hash values you want.
- *dc3dd* can generate *md5* and *sha1* values
- *hashlog* is where you want the hashlog to go.
- *bs* is the block size that is copied at one time.

Using Proprietary Acquisition Tools

While open source tools can be used to acquire forensic images, some of them require you to use the command line. Unfortunately, some of the commands that have to be typed are quite long. Even worse, if the wrong commands are accidentally entered because the user does not understand drive lettering and numbering conventions, the investigator may accidentally delete the evidence drive. The proprietary acquisition tools, such as FTK, EnCase, X-Ways, and BlackBag, often offer GUI alternatives. While the analysis tools are not free, these companies often offer their acquisition software at no cost. Regardless of the tools you use, you should always follow sound forensic principals.

Imaging the iPod Device within FTK Imager

FTK Imager, as shown in Figure 13.12, is a free utility that is offered by Access Data. It can be downloaded from http://www.accessdata.com/downloads.html.

FTK Imager is a tool that is also incorporated into Helix. To image an iPod using FTK Imager, perform the following steps:

1. Open FTK Imager.
2. Connect the iPod to a hardware write-blocker.
3. From the top menu bar, select **File**.
4. From the file menu, select **Create Disk Image**, as shown in Figure 13.12.

Figure 13.12 Creating a Disk Image in FTK Imager

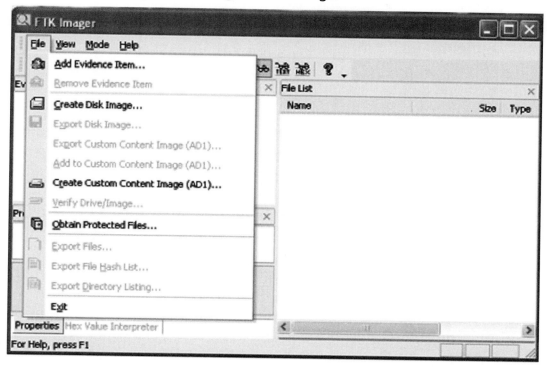

5. From the **Select Source** window, select **Physical Drive**; then select **Next**, as shown in Figure 13.13.

Figure 13.13 Selecting the Physical Drive in FTK Imager

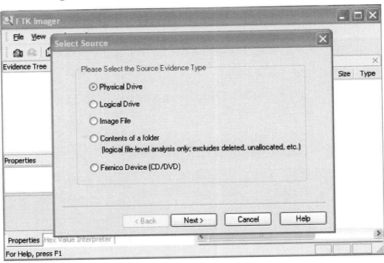

6. From the **Select Drive** window, locate the drop-down menu and select the **Apple iPod USB Device** as shown in Figure 13.14.

7. Click **Finish**.

Figure 13.14 Confirming the Apple iPod as the Physical Device in FTK Imager

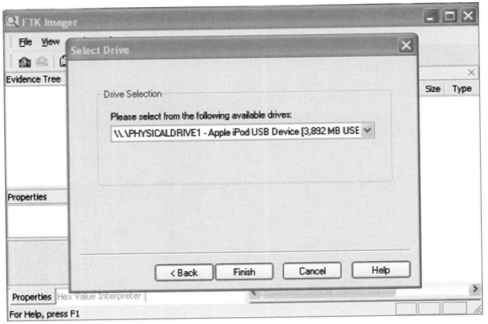

8. From the **Create Image** window, select **Add**, as shown in Figure 13.15.

Figure 13.15 The Create Image Screen in FTK Imager

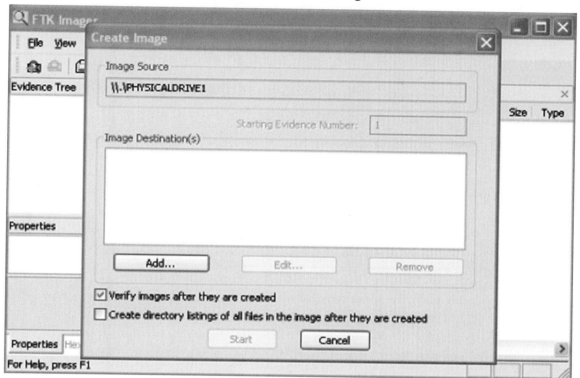

9. There are three selections in the **Select Image Type** window: (1) *Raw (dd)*, (2) *Smart*, and (3) *E01*. The most commonly used image types are the *Raw (dd)*, which are raw images or bit-for-bit copies of the iPod. *E01* images are compressed and contain useful information like device hash values, case information and creation information. Select the type of image that you would like to create and click **Next**, as shown in Figure 13.16.

Figure 13.16 Selecting the Image Type in FTK Imager

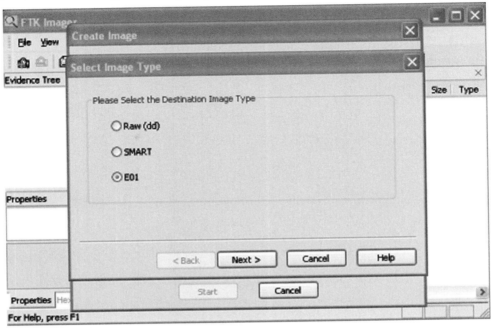

10. In the **Evidence Item Identification** window enter the required case information, as shown in Figure 13.17.

Figure 13.17 Evidence Item Information Window in FTK Imager

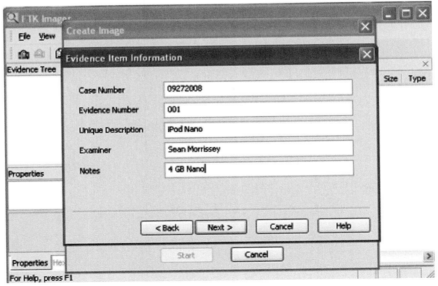

11. In the **Select Image Destination** window, browse to a folder where you would like to place the image, preferably a drive that is separate from your forensic machine. Enter a filename, and then click **Finish,** as shown in Figure 13.18.

12. This will bring you back to the **Create Image** window. Select **Start**.

Figure 13.18 FTK Imager Destination Folder Selection

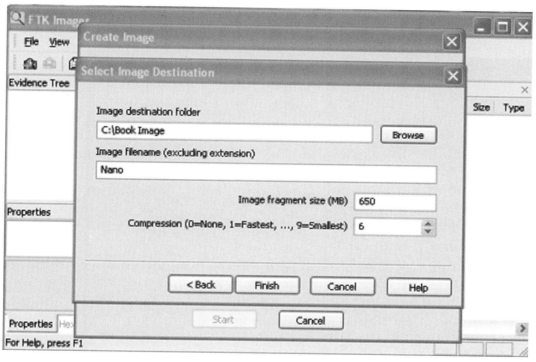

FTK Imager will then create the image. After the image has been created, Imager adds a text document that contains all the information about the imaging process: Case information, device hashes, verification hashes, and acquisition date and time.

13. Examine the Image with a forensic application.

Image the iPod Device using EnCase

Guidance Software's EnCase allows you to image devices without the need for a dongle. EnCase is normally used to create an .e01 image file. As with any other device, you will need to use a hardware or software write-blocker. Take the following to image an iPod with EnCase:

1. Start the EnCase Application.

2. From the top menu bar, select **New**.

3. In the case options, enter a name for the case and the examiner. Click **Finish**.

4. From the top menu bar, select **Add Device**.

5. In the **Choose Devices** window, select a local drive, and click **Next**.

6. In the **Choose Devices** window, locate the selection that corresponds to the iPod. In the label column you should see "Apple," which indicates the iPod. Select this item and click **Next**.

7. From the **Preview Devices** window, click **Next**.

8. In the **Table Pane** you will see a "1" icon, as shown in Figure 13.19.

Figure 13.19 EnCase Entry

9. Right click on the icon and select **Acquire** from the menu.

10. In the **After Acquisition** window, select **Replace Source Device**.

11. Click **Next**.

12. In the **Options** window, give your image a name and the case number, add any notes, keep the compression default setting, and give the destination of the image file in the output field.

13. Select **Finish**. EnCase will then acquire the image.

Imaging the iPod Device Using BlackBag's BBTImagerLite

BlackBag Technology has developed an application for the Mac, called BBTImagerLite (see Figure 13.20). This application is an easy-to-use GUI tool to image an iPod.

Figure 13.20 BlackBag's BBTImagerLite

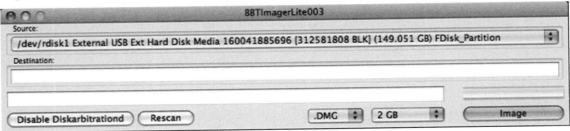

Take the following steps to create an image using this tool:

1. Click the **Disable Diskarbitrationd** button to turn off Disk Arbitration.
2. Connect the iPod to the Mac.
3. Select the iPod from the **Source** drop-down menu.
4. Select the type of image file, either **Raw (*dd*)** or **.DMG** files. You can create full-size *dd* or *.dmg* files, or split them (from 10MB up to 2GB sized files).
5. Click the **Image** button; then select the **Destination** folder for the image.
6. BBTImagerLite will then create the image and notify you when it is completed.

Summary

The introduction of the iPod in 2001 changed the way people store portable media. For the forensic examiner, it is important to know the different models of iPods, and that the iPod is a live operating system that does not shut down. There are various command line and GUI tools that are available to image an iPod.

Solutions Fast Track

Documenting the Seizure of an iPod

- ☑ Document the chain of custody.
- ☑ Document the information deemed pertinent by your organization.
- ☑ Take photographs of the scene.

Using Open Source Acquisition Tools

- ☑ Live CDs often have Open Source Acquisition Tools.
- ☑ Be comfortable with disk naming and numbering conventions.
- ☑ Be comfortable with using the command line.

Using Proprietary Acquisition Tools

- ☑ FTK Imager is a free tool for Microsoft Windows from Access Data.
- ☑ Use a write-blocker to image an iPod on the Microsoft Windows platform.
- ☑ Create two types of image files on the Macintosh with BBTImagerLite, Raw (*dd*) and .DMG files.

Frequently Asked Questions

Q: What are some proprietary acquisition tools?

A: EnCase, FTK, BlackBag, and X-Ways.

Q: What are some open source acquisition tools?

A: The utilities *dc3dd* and *dcfldd*.

Q: Is FTK Imager a free product?

A: Yes.

Q: What establishes who is in possesion of the evidence at a given point in time?

A: The chain of custody.

Q: What is the name of the write-blocker that Guidance Software sells?

A: FastBloc.

Chapter 14

iPod Forensics

Solutions in this chapter:

- **Analyzing iPod Partitioning**

- **Analyzing the iPod Image File on a Mac**

- **Viewing iPod Artifacts
  from a Corresponding Mac**

☑ **Summary**

☑ **Solutions Fast Track**

☑ **Frequently Asked Questions**

Introduction

Like many electronic devices, the iPod contains an operating system and a file system. As a computer forensic investigator, it is important to understand how and where data is stored on the device. To do this, you will need to know how to analyze iPod partitioning. You will also need to know how to mount an iPod image file from a Mac, and how to access its hidden files and folders. This Section will assist the investigator in viewing possible evidence that can be found on an iPod, such as multimedia files and images. When an iPod is configured as an external device you can locate any type of file. Though it was not discussed in this chapter, you should be aware of an application called slurp.exe which can configure an iPod to "slurp," or retrieve information from any system that the iPod is connected to.

Analyzing iPod Partitioning

The iPod uses the Apple partition map as its partitioning scheme. When used on a Mac, the *hdiutil* is a native command line for working with disk images. The switches *pmap* and *imageinfo* allow you to see how the Apple partition map is configured. To view a partition map of an iPod image from your Mac, perform the following steps:

1. Choose **Go > Utilities** from the **Finder** menu bar.
2. Select **Terminal.app** from the **Utilities** window.
3. From the command line, type a command such as: **hdiutil pmap /[drag and drop the .dmg image file]**.
4. Hit Return.

Figure 14.1 shows the partition map for the image file of an iPod.

Figure 14.1 Results of the *hdiutil pmap* Command on an iPod DMG Image File

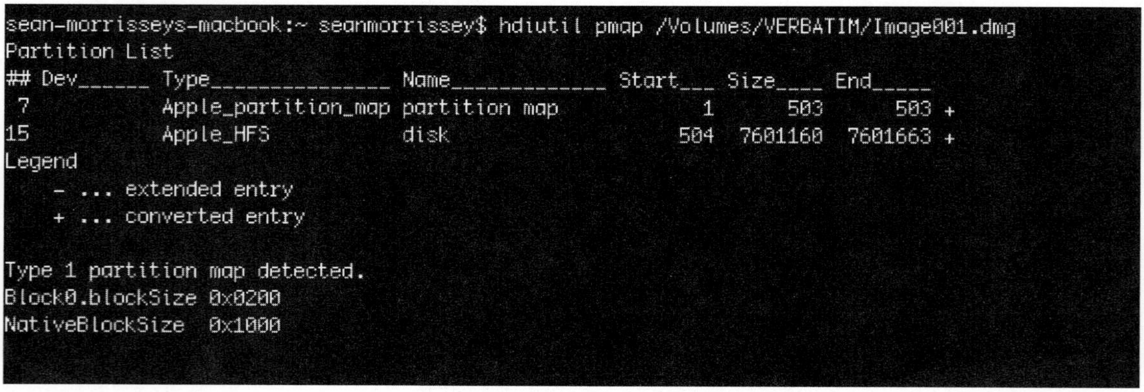

```
sean-morrisseys-macbook:~ seanmorrissey$ hdiutil pmap /Volumes/VERBATIM/Image001.dmg
Partition List
## Dev_____  Type_____  Name_____  Start___ Size____ End_____
7             Apple_partition_map partition map            1      503      503 +
15            Apple_HFS           disk                   504  7601160  7601663 +
Legend
   - ... extended entry
   + ... converted entry

Type 1 partition map detected.
Block0.blockSize 0x0200
NativeBlockSize  0x1000
```

The *hdiutil imageinfo* command will provide you with even more information. After typing *hdiutil imageinfo* from the command line, you can drag and drop a .dmg image file onto the terminal window to bypass entering the full pathname to the file:

hdiutil imageinfo [*drag and drop dmg image file here*]

Figures 14.2 and 14.3 show the output from the *hdiutil imageinfo* command.

Figure 14.2 Results of *hdiutil imageinfo* Command on an iPod DMG
Image File

```
sean-morrisseys-macbook:~ seanmorrissey$ hdiutil imageinfo /Volumes/VERBATIM/Image001.dmg
Format: UDRW
Backing Store Information:
        Name: Image001.dmg
        URL: file://localhost/Volumes/VERBATIM/Image001.dmg
        Class Name: CBSDBackingStore
Format Description: raw read/write
Checksum Type: none
partitions:
        appendable: true
        partition-scheme: Apple
        block-size: 16
        burnable: true
        partitions:
                0:
                        partition-length: 1
                        partition-synthesized: true
                        partition-hint: DDM
                        partition-name: Driver Descriptor Map
                        partition-data: 0x45521000000E7FC000000000000000000000000000000000
0000000000000000000000000000000000000000000000000000000000000000000000000000000000
0000000000000000000000000000000000000000000000000000000000000000000000000000000000
0000000000000000000000000000000000000000000000000000000000000000000000000000000000
0000000000000000000000000000000000000000000000000000000000000000000000000000000000
0000000000000000000000000000000000000000000000000000000000000000000000000000000000
0000000000000000000000000000000000000000000000000000000000000000000000000000000000
0000000000000000000000000000000000000000000000000000000000000000000000000000000000
0000000000000000000000000000000000000000000000000000000000000000000000000000000000
0000000000000000000000000000000000000000000000000000000000000000000000000000000000
0000000000000000000000000000000000000000000000000000000000000000000000000000000000
0000000000000000000000000000000000000000000000000000000000000000000000000000000000
0000000000000000000000000000000000
                        partition-start: 0
                1:
                        partition-length: 7
                        partition-synthesized: true
                        partition-hint: Apple_Free
                        partition-name:
                        partition-start: 1
                2:
                        partition-length: 496
                        partition-hint: Apple_partition_map
                        partition-number: 1
                        partition-name: partition map
                        partition-start: 8
                3:
                        partition-length: 7601160
                        partition-hint: Apple_HFS
                        partition-number: 2
                        partition-name: disk
```

Figure 14.3 Results of *hdiutil imageinfo* Command on an iPod DMG Image File, **Continued**

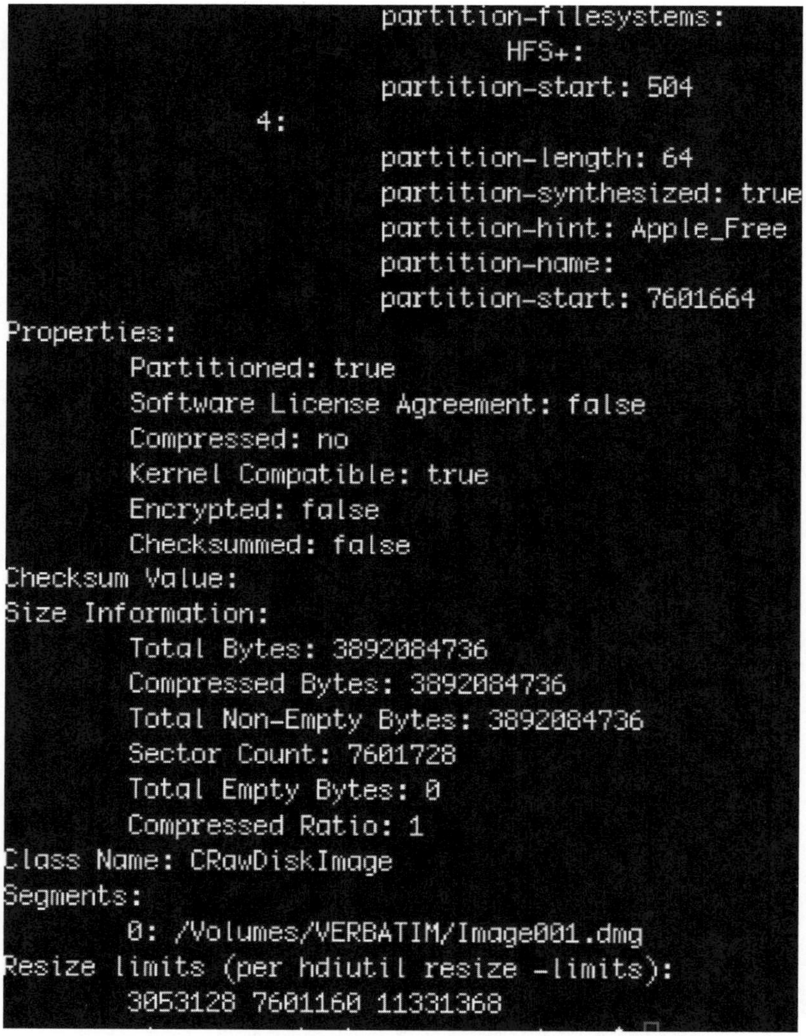

```
                                  partition-filesystems:
                                         HFS+:
                                  partition-start: 504
                     4:

                                  partition-length: 64
                                  partition-synthesized: true
                                  partition-hint: Apple_Free
                                  partition-name:
                                  partition-start: 7601664
Properties:
        Partitioned: true
        Software License Agreement: false
        Compressed: no
        Kernel Compatible: true
        Encrypted: false
        Checksummed: false
Checksum Value:
Size Information:
        Total Bytes: 3892084736
        Compressed Bytes: 3892084736
        Total Non-Empty Bytes: 3892084736
        Sector Count: 7601728
        Total Empty Bytes: 0
        Compressed Ratio: 1
Class Name: CRawDiskImage
Segments:
        0: /Volumes/VERBATIM/Image001.dmg
Resize limits (per hdiutil resize -limits):
        3053128 7601160 11331368
```

NOTE

In Figures 14.2 and 14.3, the first partition in the Apple partition Map scheme is the DDM (Driver Descriptor Map). It is always one sector in length and provides information about system drivers. The drivers themselves normally reside on a separate partition. The second partition is labeled Apple_Free. Apple_Free is actually a few sectors in length and is free space. Next is the Apple partition map, which is usually 63 sectors in length and responsible for keeping track of all the partitions on the iPod. Each partition is described by an entry in the partition map. The partition map is described as an entry in and of itself. After the Apple partition map is a partition labeled Apple_HFS. This is where the file system resides, and where all the data such as songs, pictures, and videos are stored. Most of the significant data related to your cases will be located on Apple_HFS partitions.

Analyzing the iPod Image File on a Mac

It is the opinion of many people that it is best to use a Mac as the forensic platform to analyze an image of an iPod. One of the benefits of doing this is that you will not need to purchase any additional forensic software tools. One of the disadvantages is that you will not be able to recover deleted files or folders or items within slack space.

Mounting an iPod Image File on a Mac

To view an iPod Image File on a Mac you will first need to lock and mount the file.

1. First, select either the .dmg or .dd iPod image file, then select **File > Get Info**.

2. If your image file is a .dd file, click the down arrow in front of the **Name and Extension** category and rename the file extension from **.dd** to **.dmg**.

3. Lock the file by clicking on the Locked button, as seen in Figure 14.4. For more about file locking and its forensic implications, see Chapter 3: "Mac Disks and Partitioning."

Figure 14.4 Locking the iPod Image File on a Mac

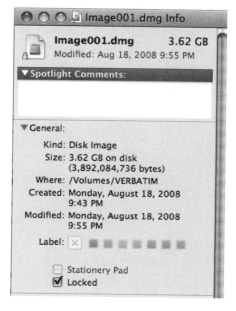

After the DMG is locked, just double click on the image file to mount it. This will mount the image and with the image locked, nothing can be written to the image, thus preserving the integrity of the image file. There should be five visible folders: **Calendars, Contacts, Notes, Photos**, and **Recordings**, as shown in Figure 14.5.

Figure 14.5 The Five Folders from a Mounted iPod Image File

Viewing Hidden Folders and Files

You will also want to see the hidden files and folders in the image file. To see all hidden files on a Mac, follow these steps:

1.   First you need to open a Terminal window by selecting **Go**, then **Utilities**, as shown in Figure14.6.

Figure 14.6 Showing the Navigation to the Finder Utility

2.   Select **Terminal.app** from the **Utilities** window, as shown in Figure 14.7.

Figure 14.7 Show All Finders Navigating to Terminal Application

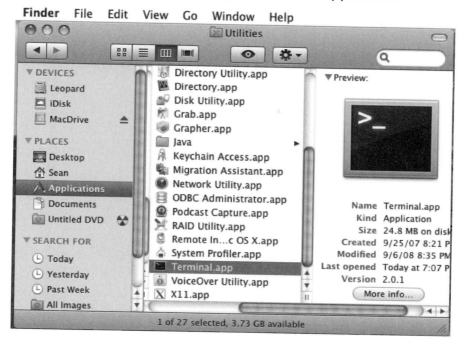

3. At the command prompt type: **defaults write com.apple.Finder AppleShowAllFiles Yes**, as seen in Figure 14.8.

4. Press **Enter**.

5. Relaunch the **Finder** to view hidden files by typing the command line **KillAll Finder** as shown in Figure 14.8.

Figure 14.8 Kill All Command

```
Last login: Wed Sep 24 19:23:57 on ttys000
sean-morrisseys-macbook:~ Sean$ defaults write com.apple.Finder AppleShowAllFiles Yes
sean-morrisseys-macbook:~ Sean$ KillAll Finder
```

6. From the **Finder**, select **Show All** to display all the hidden files and folders in the image file, as seen in Figure 14.9.

Figure 14.9 Results of Finder > Show All Command

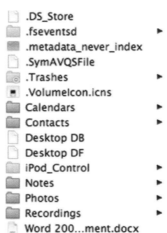

To reverse the process so that hidden files and folders are no longer visible, run the following two commands from the terminal, as seen in Figure 14.10.

1. From the command line, type **defaults write com.apple.Finder AppleShowAllFiles No**.
2. Then relaunch the finder by typing **KillAll Finder**.

Figure 14.10 Configuring the Mac to Hide Hidden Files and Folders

```
sean-morrisseys-macbook:~ Sean$ defaults write com.apple.Finder AppleShowAllFiles NO
sean-morrisseys-macbook:~ Sean$ KillAll Finder
```

The second method of relaunching the finder is through the Mac's graphical user interface (GUI) (see Exercise 14.1).

Configuring & Implementing...

Exercise 14.1: Relaunching the Finder from Mac OS X Graphical User Interface

Use the following steps to relaunch the finder through the Mac's graphical user interface:

1. To relaunch the finder. Go to the apple icon, as shown in Figure 14.11.

Continued

Figure 14.11 Showing Relaunch Finder from the GUI

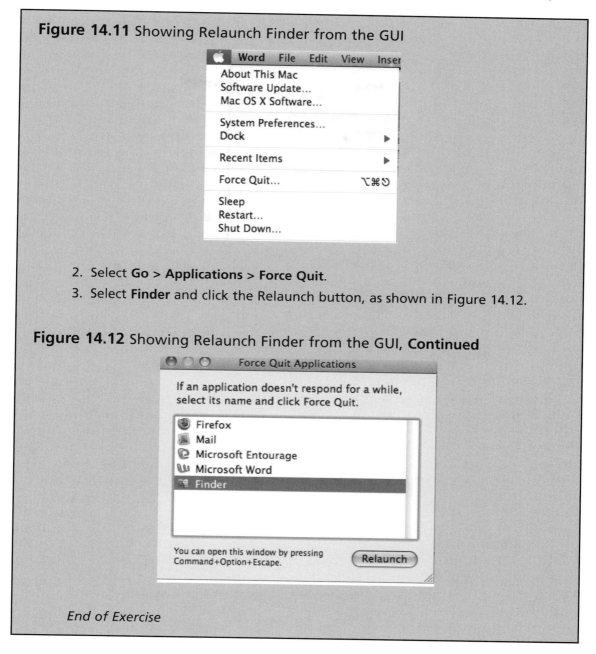

2. Select **Go > Applications > Force Quit**.
3. Select **Finder** and click the Relaunch button, as shown in Figure 14.12.

Figure 14.12 Showing Relaunch Finder from the GUI, **Continued**

End of Exercise

Examining iPod Files and Folders

Once the Finder relaunches with the hidden files and folders displayed, you will see a layout similar to that shown in Figure 14.13.

Figure 14.13 Displaying Hidden Files and Folders on the iPod Image

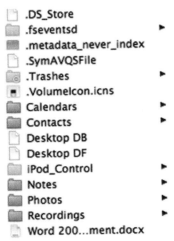

The following is a brief description of some of the files and folders shown in Figure 14.13.

- *.DS_Store* is a file that OS X creates in every folder it touches.

- *.fseventsd* writes event logs for every volume.

- *.metadata_never_index* allows indexing on the specified volume.

- *.SymAVQSFile* is a Norton AntiVirus file.

- *.Trashes* stores deleted items.

- *.Volumeicon.icns* is the icon that OS X uses to symbolize the iPod when it is mounted on a Mac.

- *Calendars* displays items that were synced if the subject syncs calendars from iTunes to the iPod. You can view calendar items in this folder with the iCal application.

Calendars

The procedure for viewing the iPod calendar file with the **iCal** application is described in the following steps. You can use the iPod image provided with the DVD that accompanies this book to complete this exercise.

1. Make sure that **iCal** is not running on the Mac.

2. Mount the iPod image.

3. Make sure that the following folders and files have been deleted from the Mac:

   - ~/Library/Calendar folder

   - ~/Library/SyncServices folder

- ~/Library/Caches/com.apple.iCal folder

- ~/Library/Preferences/com.apple.iCal.plist file

4. Locate the **/Calendars/ iSync-OSX Forensics.ics** file (where *OSX Forensics* is the name of the calendar).

5. Copy the **OSX Forensics.ics** file to a folder on the Mac.

6. Drag and drop the **OSX Forensics.ics** file to the **iCal** icon. The image file's calendar items appear on the screen, as shown in Figure 14.14.

Figure 14.14 Displaying the Calendar Items from an iPod Image

To see the information in any calendar entry, click on any item in the calendar, as shown in Figure 14.15.

Figure 14.15 Calendar Item Details from the iPod Image

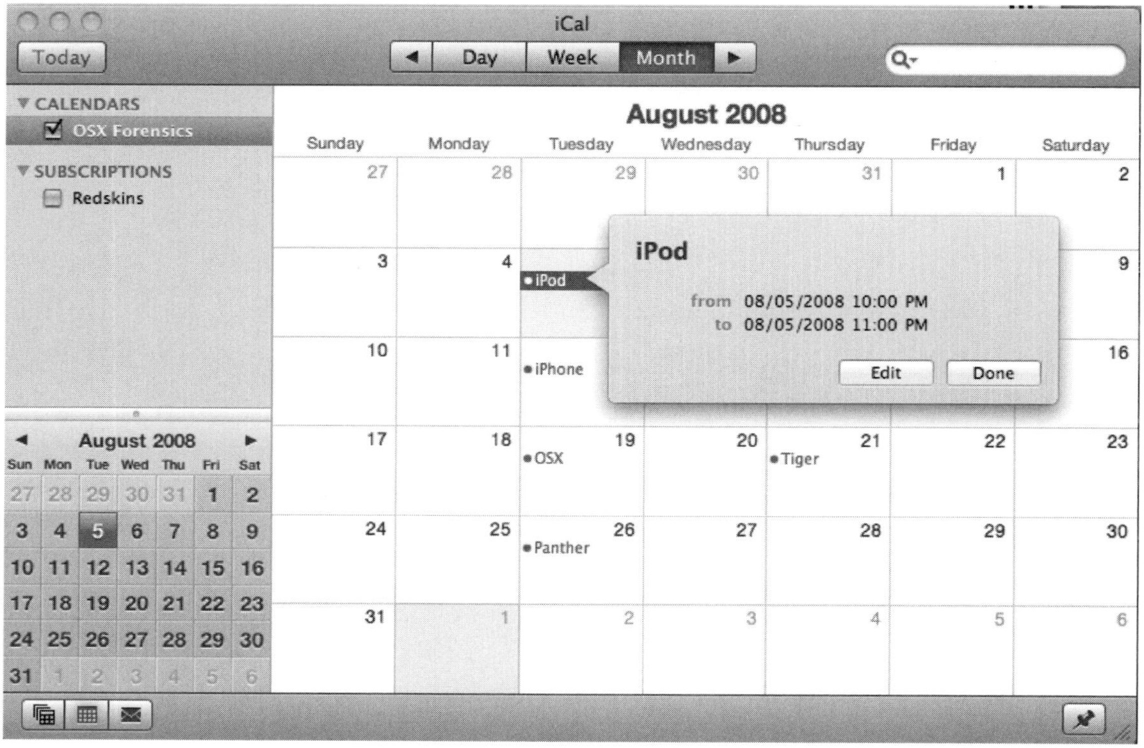

Contacts

As with the Calendar folder, the Contact folder files can be seen with a native Mac application, called **Address Book**. You can identify address book files with the .vcf extension.

For examining address book items from an iPod, follow these steps:

1. Make sure that Address Book is not running.

2. Make sure that there is no contact information on the Mac you are using as the forensic workstation. Delete the ~/Library/ApplicationSupport/AddressBook folder.

3. Copy the **Contacts** folder from the iPod to a forensic Mac workstation.

4. Double click on any contact file to open it with **Address Book**.

Desktop Files

The files Desktop DB and Desktop DF have nothing of evidentiary value.

iPod Control

The iPod_Control folder is where an iPod's multimedia files are located. Within this folder there are several sub folders. The first folder is called **Artwork**. This folder contains album artwork that can be seen through the iPod in cover flow mode or during music playback. There can be numerous files located in this folder. The first is the ArtworkDB file. This keeps track of the synced album artwork that is shown on modern iPods. In the artwork folder are files that have an .ithmb extension. These are basically thumbnails similar to those found in Microsoft Windows. The thumbnail files are compressed image files that are synced from the Mac to the iPod. To view these files, you can use a free application called Keith's iPod Photo Reader 2.0, which can be downloaded from www.cs.unm.edu/~kwiley /Downloads/KeithsIPodPhotoReader.zip.

The following are the procedures for using Keith's iPod Photo Reader to view .ithmb files on an iPod.

1. Copy the **.ithmb** files into a folder on the Mac.
2. Open Keith's iPod Photo Reader from the DVD that accompanies this book.
3. Click the **Load .ithmb** file button…
4. Select an **.ithmb** file, then select the correct settings from Keith's reader to view the images contained in the .ithmb file. Table 14.1 shows the settings from a text file that comes with the reader.

Table 14.1 Keith's Resolution and Encoding Settings for iPod Photos

Generation	Resolution	Encoding
1st Generation iPod Nano	176x132	16-bit RBG, 6-bit green
2nd Generation iPod Nano	176x132	16-bit RBG, 6 bit green
3rd Generation iPod Nano	640x480 or 720x480	16-bit RGB, 6-bit green, or 12-bit YCbCr 4:2:2, Blue first, half image padded
4th Generation iPod	720x480	16-bit YCbCr 4:2:2, Interlaced Shared Chrominance
5th Generation iPod	Same as the 4th Generation	Same as the 4th Generation
6th Generation iPod	720x480	12-bit YCbCr 4:2:0, Blue first, half image padded
iPod Touch	640x480	16-bit RBG
1st Generation iPhone	Same settings as the Touch	Same settings as the Touch
2nd Generation iPhone	Same Settings as Touch	Same Settings as the Touch

If no images exist, your display will be similar to that shown in Figure 14.16.

Figure 14.16 View of an Unreadable Image

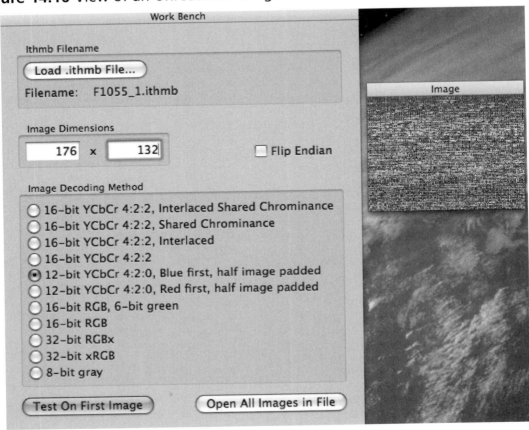

5.   When you have loaded a file that has images, Keith's reader will show the first image in that file. Select **Open All Images in File** to view all images in an .ithmb file.

Note that these images were modified when they were synced through iTunes; therefore, hashes of the .ithmb photos on an iPod will be different.

6.   To export these images from Keith's reader and add them to your report, go **to File > Save all images**, choose a location for the images, and select **Choose**. The images will be saved as .pct files.

iTunes

The iTunes folder has a file called iTunesDB. This can be opened with the **Text Edit** application and contains information about Podcasts and video that were downloaded to the iPod.

iTunes Prefs can also contain the name of the syncing computer. This is important if the investigator is trying to link an iPod to a certain computer (see Figure 14.17).

Figure 14.17 iTunes Prefs Showing the Computer Name of the Syncing Mac

New to the iPod is a *Rentals.plist*. This property list will display the filename of a movie that was rented through iTunes.

The **Music** folder contains audio and video files. The actual filenames from the synced Mac change when placed on an iPod. The filenames always start with the letter "F" and then two numbers used in sequential order. The naming convention of the files themselves uses a four-character filename and the file type extension. The hashes of these files will match to music files found in the iTunes Library of the syncing Mac (See Figure 14.18).

Figure 14.18 Music Folder Media Files

Notes

Normally you will only be able to see text files in this folder if the user has enabled disk usage.

Photos

The **Photos** folder uses .ithmb files. To access these files, use the same procedure described for the iPod Control folder.

Within the **Photo** folder, the examiner may encounter full resolution photos. There is a subfolder within the **Photos** folder, called **Full Resolution**. The hashes of these photo files will match the files with a syncing Mac; that is they will still contain metadata, including MAC times, camera type, and model. There is also a subfolder called **Thumbs** which also may contain several .ithmb files. These files can also be viewed with Keith's iPod Photo Reader.

To view photos from the **Photo** folder, complete the following steps:

1. Locate an image from the iPod image file.
2. Click on the image and open it with the **iPhoto** application.

3. Click on the image while holding down the **ctrl** key, then select **Show Info** to view the metadata for that image, as shown in Figure 14.19.

Figure 14.19 Photo Metadata

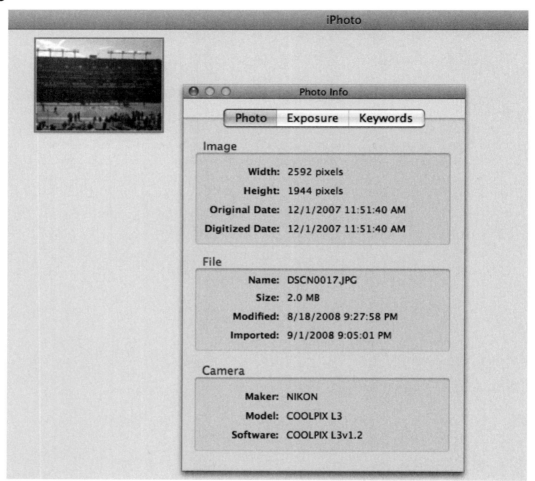

Recordings

Recordings is a folder seen in newer generation iPods. With the new in-ear headphones available from Apple, users will be able to make voice recordings on the iPod. Recordings files will have an .amr file extension.

iPods as External Storage Devices

If a user has decided to use the iPod as an external storage device, the investigator can find a variety of items stored on the device, as shown in Figure 14.20. Therefore, a manual examination of all the folders and files may be necessary. Be aware that extensions may be changed to obfuscate evidence on the device.

Figure 14.20 iTunes Showing Disk Usage Options

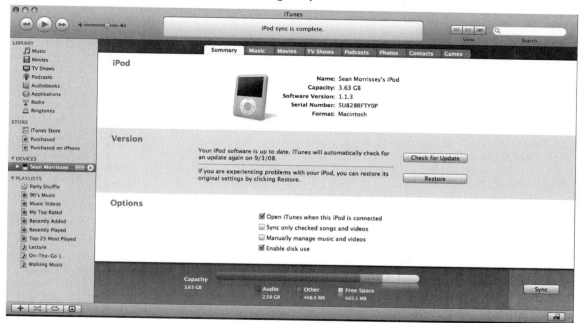

Viewing iPod Artifacts from a Corresponding Mac

When you sync an iPod with a Mac, data from the following applications are synced: **iCal, Address Book, Mail, iPhoto, and iTunes**. It is important to know that all data is user-specific and can be found in each user's domain. Each user has an iPod property list at /[*username*]/Library/Preferences /com.apple.iPod.plist. The property list will show you all the iPods and iPhones that have been connected to the Mac by each Mac user. There is a second property list in the local domain:

/Library/Preferences/com.apple.iPod.plist. This local domain property list will contain a list of all iPods and iPhones connected to the Mac. Both property lists also give the following information and are further illustrated in Figure 14.21.

- Firmware version
- iPod serial number
- Last date connected
- The number of times connected

Figure 14.21 Viewing the com.apple.iPod.plist File

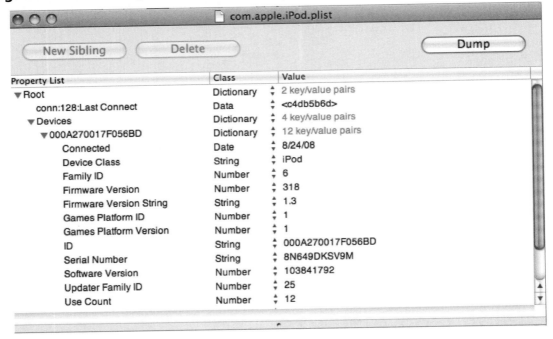

Summary

This chapter focuses on how to use a Mac to analyze the iPod Apple Partition Map and view hidden folders and files acquired with an iPod image file. This chapter also discusses the artifacts that can be located on an iPod. It also briefly discusses artifacts that can be located on a Mac.

Solutions Fast Track

Analyzing iPod Partitioning

☑ Use *hdiutil pmap* to view iPod Apple Partition Map information.

☑ Use *hdiutil imageinfo* to get extended information about the iPod image.

☑ Most of the significant data related to your cases will be located on these HFS+ partitions.

Analyzing the iPod Image File on a Mac

☑ To show hidden files, use the command line **defaults write com.apple.Finder AppleShowAllFiles Yes**.

☑ Contact, Calendar, and other iPod information can be viewed using Macintosh applications.

Viewing iPod Artifacts from a Corresponding Mac

☑ When the iPod is synced with a Mac, the Mac retrieves all the iPod data.

☑ View the *com.apple.iPod.plist* file for detailed information about an iPod

☑ The iPod *plist* files located in user's and local libraries at /[*username*]/Library/Preferences /com.apple.iPod.plist and /Library/Preferences/com.apple.iPod.plist

Frequently Asked Questions

Q: How can I view the Apple partition map from an iPod image file?

A: Use the *hdiutil pmap* command to view iPod partition map information.

Q: How can I view the extended disk information from iPod image file?

A: Use *hdiutil imageinfo* to get more disk information from an iPod image file.

Q: What file system does an Apple iPod normally use?

A: An Apple iPod normally uses the HFS+ File system.

Q: Where is the iPod *plist* file located?

A: The iPod *plist* file is located in each user's library at /[*username*]/Library/Preferences/com.apple.iPod.plist

Q: Where on the disk will be the data with evidentiary value?

A: Most of the significant data related to your cases will be located on HFS+ partitions.

Q: When will a Mac have information about an attached iPod?

A: The Mac will have a *plist* after the iPod has been synced with it.

Q: Can you view the suspect's calendar information from the iPod image?

A: Yes, the iPod's calendar information can be viewed using the iCal application.

Q: How can I show hidden files on a Mac?

A: At a terminal window command line, type **defaults write com.apple.Finder AppleShowAllFiles Yes**.

Chapter 15

Forensic Acquisition of an iPhone

Solutions in this chapter:

- iPhone & iPod Touch Forensic Concerns
- iPhone & iPod Touch Logical Acquisitions
- Acquiring a Physical Image of an iPhone
- Analysis of the iPhone Image
- iPhone Firmware 2.1
- Terminology

- ☑ Summary
- ☑ Solutions Fast Track
- ☑ Frequently Asked Questions

Introduction

The iPhone is among the most popular phones on the market and was released with much fanfare in July 2007. The iPhone is the among the most affordable large storage phone devices on the market at this time. Phones have been able to do what the iPhone does for a long time; but the addition of a touch screen and virtual keyboard leaves more room for a larger screen allowing viewing of movies, and Web surfing on the go. The first generation of iPhones was released in 4GB and 8GB flash memory models. The 4GB model was taken off the market two months after it was released. Current iPhones come with 8GB or 16GB of storage, and there are plans in the works to release iPhones with even greater storage capacities.

The iPod Touch is similar to an iPhone in looks and functionality, but lacks the GPS and calling capabilities. The iPod Touch was released in September 2007, and was available in 8GB and 16GB versions. This is a lot of data to be carrying in such a small device, and there is plenty of room to store photos, video, or other data on them. The techniques used to image and analyze the iPod Touch will be the same as those techniques used to image and analyze the iPhone.

The iPhone 3G, or 3rd Generation Cellular Communication Device, was released in July 2008, and has GPS services, as seen in Figure 15.1, and faster downloading of internet services. The download speeds of the iPhone 3G are comparable to that of WiFi speeds. The speeds of the device, GPS functionality, and the addition of Apple's App Store mean that this device will be playing a larger role in enterprise communications. This enhanced role of the iPhone will present special forensic concerns for the investigator.

As speeds continue to increase and prices continue to drop, the iPhone will likely enjoy an even larger percentage of the smart phone market share. For this reason, there is a good chance that you will come across an iPhone when performing a search and seizure. Seizing iPhones will involve procedures similar to that of seizing a computer, such as providing documentation and establishing a chain of custody.

Figure 15.1 The GPS Capability of the New iPhone 3G

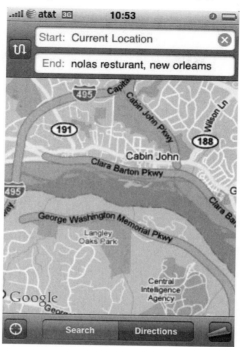

Unlike computer forensics, though, iPhone forensics is a relatively new field and agreed upon procedures and standards have not been finalized. The forensics of these devices are considered gray areas whose legality and admissibility still has to be worked out in the courts, and will likely vary from jurisdiction to jurisdiction. You may want to use a Faraday Shield when you seize the iPhone to prevent all outside communications from altering data once it is in your possession. An example is the possibility that someone will attempt to connect to the phone remotely and delete its data. Later in this chapter, we will discuss how you can connect to your iPhone remotely via the SSH protocol. The Faraday Shield, as seen in Figure 15.2, is useful because it can help prevent someone from deleting data on the iPhone remotely. If you do not have one of these bags at your disposal, some people claim that a potato chip bag will accomplish the same goal. In summary, while the field of iPhone forensics is still in development, good sound computer forensics should be utilized when conducting a search and seizure.

Figure 15.2 Faraday Shield (Made by Paraben, a Cell Phone Forensics Company)

Courtesy Paraben Corporation.

iPhone & iPod Touch Forensic Concerns

In January 2008, I spoke with a representative from Apple off the record at a conference I attended. The representative from Apple was exclusively hired to work with law enforcement to create an imaging solution. Conversations with this individual and written communications with Apple foretold of the coming of a developer's kit that would allow an imaging solution to be created. While I was anxiously waiting for the release of these tools and excited by the prospect of how such a tool set might help law enforcement, nothing has been released by Apple as of this writing. I have talked to other colleagues in the forensic community and some of these individuals have gotten the impression that Apple is not ready to release a tool that will allow the iPod-Touch/iPhone to be imaged in a forensically sound matter. In my opinion, this is somewhat problematic as Apple seems to be one of the few cellular phone vendors that do not want to assist law enforcement in the area of imaging and incident response, let alone the necessity of creating base images for an enterprise rollout solution.

Methods to Acquire Data from an iPhone

The Apple Support knowledge base document, http://support.apple.com/kb/HT1766, describes the procedures and limitations of the backup process for an iPhone and iPod Touch. Apple Computer has made it clear, with the implementation of Digital Rights Management, that you can only backup certain items like pictures, contacts, and voice messages. There are also some configuration settings that can be backed up. Music and videos and other binary data have to be imported through iTunes. Apple uses the AFS (Apple File Sharing) protocol to exchange encrypted data between the iPhone and the host computer. With the logical copy method offered by Apple, you won't recover certain files like deleted or recovered files. The best way to get a full raw image of the iPhone data partition is by using innovative unorthodox "hacking" methods. Keep in mind, however, that these unorthodox methods of acquiring evidence may or may not be allowed in a courtroom. Consult your legal point of contact before proceeding with any *jailbreak-type* of operation on an iPhone or iPod touch.

One old school method to get the data off the iPhone (or iPod Touch) is to ask a suspect for permission to examine their media. However, I do not recommend examining an iPhone if you have never used one before. Try to get your hands on one and become familiar with the navigation and location of critical artifacts. Keep in mind that it is always preferable to get an image instead of doing an actual examination of the phone. If you do get permission to examine the device, I suggest that you document your actions every step of the way. Besides looking at the phone and recording the data that is visible, there are at present three ways to get data off an iPhone:

1. Viewing the iTunes Sync on a host computer
2. Hacking into the iPhone
3. Disassembling the iPhone

Each of the methods is discussed in this chapter, along with the pros and cons associated with each method.

iTunes Sync

You can use the iTunes Sync program to make a logical copy of iPhones data. Keep in mind, however, that you will not retrieve any deleted files or folders using the iTunes Sync method. In order to make a logical copy utilizing the iTunes Sync program, locate the host system, image it using forensically sound methods, and then perform an iTunes Sync. After completing the sync operation, back up the iTunes Sync folder.

Another issue with the iTunes Sync method is if you cannot locate the host system, you will not get all the data off of the iPhone. For example, if a suspect has put in binary data like movies or music on their system, you will not get these artifacts due to the Digital Rights Management (DRM) features. If you sync the iPhone to another computer besides the suspect's host computer, data is lost due to DRM. The only way to get these artifacts is to sync the iPhone through the suspect's host system or to transfer the purchases they have made though the iTunes store. Items the suspect places on the system, like ripped music and video, will be lost unless you can acquire the host system.

Hacking the iPhone

A jailbreak technique can be used to hack into the iPhone, and common UNIX tools can be installed to extract a bit-for-bit-copy logical image of the data partition across a WiFi connection. With this method, you must sync the suspect's contacts and photos or they will be lost when you upgrade the firmware. Another problem with this technique is that all applications installed through the iTunes application will have to be reinstalled. After reinstallation, some original configuration data may be missing. This technique also involves altering firmware, and defense attorneys may attack this approach to acquiring an image.

Disassembly

In order to disassemble the iPhone, you will need to be a bit mechanically inclined. You will actually have to unsolder the flash Read-Only-Memory (ROM) chips from the iPhone and extract the data with a NAND dump. This is beyond the scope of this book, and you should contact an electrical engineer who could be of assistance. Keep in mind that this method may also damage or destroy the iPhone. Some agencies try to avoid these techniques because, if equipment is damaged, there may not be a possibility of recovering any data, and they will have to pay the suspect for a replacement phone.

iPhone & iPod Touch Logical Acquisitions

If at any time the suspect has performed a sync operation with a computer that you have seized during your investigation, this could be good news from a forensic standpoint. Backup copies of information from the iPhone or iPod Touch will exist if the suspect performed an automatic sync, a software update, or if they chose to restore their device to its original factory settings. Any of these three actions will create a backup. Keep in mind, however, that the backup only stores certain items like pictures, contacts, voice messages, and confirmation information. Unfortunately, items like visited Web pages, deleted files (pictures and emails) are not available unless they are still in the Trash folder or in the Recycle Bin on the host computer's image.

Use any of the approved forensic methods your agency has in place to make a forensic image of the suspect's host computer. These methods can include acquiring the system through the use of open source tools like dc3dd, proprietary tools like LinEN, or any other types of forensic acquisition software. Using a physical write blocker is never a bad idea, and be sure to do so if your agency dictates the use of one. For more information on performing an acquisition, see Chapter 7: "Acquiring Forensic Images." Keep in mind that Chapter 7 only describes how to acquire images on an iMac even though a suspect can use a Microsoft Windows operating system to sync their iPhone or iPod Touch device. Syngress offers many other books that describe how to obtain an image from a computer running the Microsoft Windows operating system.

Backup a Logical Copy of the iTunes Sync Folder

On the Mac OS X system, the iTunes Sync folder is located in the user's /Music/iTunes/ folder. It is my recommendation that you back up this entire folder to an external source such as a USB mass storage device or FireWire drive. It is always a good practice to have a forensic copy of the host computer if at all possible.

Configuring & Implementing...

Exercise 15.1: Creating a Logical Image of an iPhone or iPod Touch

Please document the steps you take during this procedure in your notes.

1. Hook your iPhone or iPod Touch to the host computer. If you receive messages about upgrading to newer firmware, syncing libraries, or registration, please avoid this step! Notice that information pertinent to your case, such as phone name, capacity, software version, serial number, and phone number are displayed, as seen in Figure 15.3.

Figure 15.3 The Name and Other Pertinent iPhone Information Is Displayed

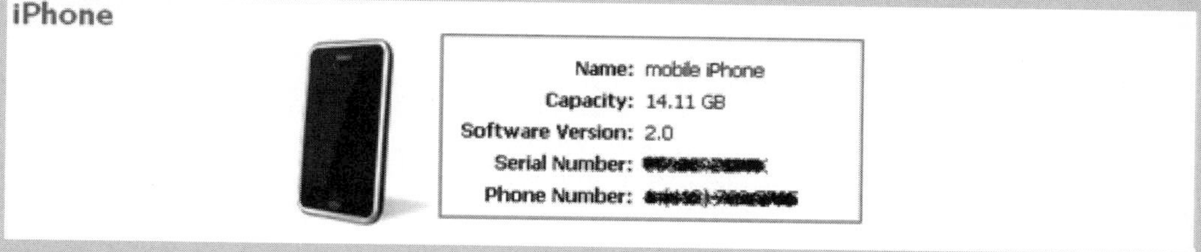

iPhone

Name:	mobile iPhone
Capacity:	14.11 GB
Software Version:	2.0
Serial Number:	██████████
Phone Number:	██████████

2. From the devices menu, choose **Back-Up**, as seen in Figure 15.4.

Continued

Figure 15.4 The Backup Process Used to Create a Logical Copy of the iPhone

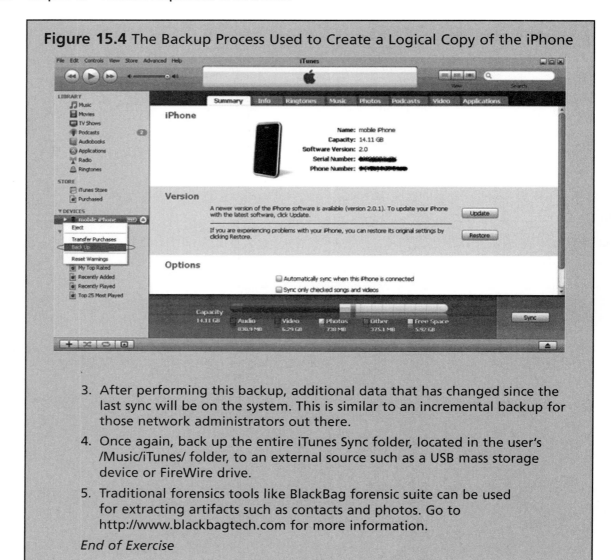

3. After performing this backup, additional data that has changed since the last sync will be on the system. This is similar to an incremental backup for those network administrators out there.

4. Once again, back up the entire iTunes Sync folder, located in the user's /Music/iTunes/ folder, to an external source such as a USB mass storage device or FireWire drive.

5. Traditional forensics tools like BlackBag forensic suite can be used for extracting artifacts such as contacts and photos. Go to http://www.blackbagtech.com for more information.

End of Exercise

In summary, a logical backup of the iTunes Sync folder can be performed easily in six steps. The steps below are written for the OS X system, but can be easily modified for a Windows system.

1. Open the **iTunes** application.
2. Choose **Preferences** from the iTunes menu.
3. Choose **Syncing**.
4. Click **Remove Backup**.
5. Press **OK** to exit **Preferences**.
6. Sync your iPhone

It is advisable to back up the iTunes folder prior to syncing in case any pertinent data has been deleted from the phone. The sync step will ensure that the backup of the iPhone is current. If you are hunting for artifacts such as contacts and bookmarks, they are stored in the /Users/<user name>/Library/Application Support/MobileSync/Backup/ folder.

Acquiring a Physical Image of an iPhone

Obtaining a physical image of an iPhone is not a difficult process, but it is a rather tedious task. A physical image of the *slice* may recover deleted items, as well as items from slack space. Obtaining the iPhone image will require basic networking knowledge as well as some UNIX knowledge. A step-by-step procedure will be provided; so do not feel anxious if you lack some understanding of networking or UNIX concepts. Just make sure you document everything you do during this process, so you will be able to explain these steps in case you are called upon to testify about what you did and why you did it. If you need to gain a more in-depth understanding on a particular step that was taken, you can contact any of this book's authors for further clarification.

If you capture a physical image of an iPhone, understand that the image you obtain may not be allowed in a court of law. However, with that being said, it is still valuable for discovery purposes (did the suspect do what he/she is accused of) and evidence seized might give us the location of systems where we can acquire court acceptable images containing the same data. It might also be useful in obtaining a confession.

WARNING

An investigator who acquires a physical image of Slice 2 needs to be aware that it may not be acceptable evidence in a court of law and is for discovery purposes. On the other hand, obtaining a logical copy, as described in Exercise 15.1, is more likely to be accepted because the device is not being altered in any way. Unfortunately, however, a logical copy of the iPhone or iPod Touch will lack items such as deleted files and folders. Please consult with your legal contact for clarifications on these issues.

As of this writing, Apple has not yet provided an acceptable imaging tool for the iPhone. To obtain a physical image of Slice 2, you can use the *dd* utility, which is included in about every distribution of Linux, UNIX, and BSD. The *dd* utility is similar to the *dc3dd* utility, but doesn't have some additional features, such as a status bar and the ability to perform an on the fly hash. Where the *dd* command originates from is a subject of debate. There is a general consensus, however, that the *dd* command traces it origins to CC, or carbon copy. The good news about the *dd* command, from a forensic perspective, is it will create a block-for-block image of the suspect's iPhone second slice, allowing the investigator to get deleted files and slack space.

There are two separate partitions on the iPhone. These partitions, as seen in Figure 15.5, are listed as /dev/rdisk0s1 and /dev/rdisk0s2. These partitions are referred as Slice 1 and Slice 2. The *ls /dev/rdisk** command, as seen in Figure 15.5, displays the disk /dev/rdisk0 as well as the two partitions. These partitions can be imaged when you gain access to the iPhone through a hack or jailbreak.

Figure 15.5 The Two iPhone Partitions

The layout of an iPhone or iPod Touch disk is explained below. This should be helpful if you are unfamiliar with Macintosh disk naming conventions.

/dev/rdisk0 (Disk)

The disk /dev/rdisk0 is the entire disk of the iPhone, including all the slices. Taking an image of the entire disk will present problems because currently there are not any forensic tools that can break this up into useful sectors. If you are so inclined, you can try to view the disk image, look for the Mac Unique offsets, calculate the partition size, and run *dd* against this image to get slices that will import into the MacForensicsLab iMac forensic suite. However, this is not an easy task, and you can use the separate partitions to accomplish the same task with a lot less work.

/dev/rdisk0s1 (Slice 1)

Slice 1 or /dev/rdisk0s1 is the firmware partition of the iPhone or iPod Touch. Slice1 holds the basic applications or links to these applications and the basic operating system. The basic OS used to operate the iPod Touch is Mac OS X Leopard in a slimmed down form. In my opinion, this partition contains little evidentiary value. When you perform a jailbreak operation, you alter this partition.

/dev/rdisk0s2 (Slice 2)

Slice 2 or /dev/rdisk0s2 is the partition where the user's data is stored. This includes any applications, iTunes store preferences, downloads, and any other stored data. Once you image this partition, you can just rename it with the DMG extension and view it on an iMac. However, you will need a forensic tool to view deleted files, slack space, and unallocated space from these partitions.

> **NOTE**
>
> All of the 10 steps needed to perform a logical image of Slice 2 of an iPhone or iPod Touch will be detailed in the rest of this chapter.

In order to obtain an image of an iPhone or iPod Touch, each of the following 10 steps will be needed. This is a summary of the steps that will be detailed in the remaining part of this chapter.

1. Jail break an iPhone or iPod; that is, replace the Apple firmware (first partition or slice) with a hacked firmware. This is accomplished with an installer package that allows us to install our tools.
2. Disable the power and screen lock feature.
3. Install UNIX utilities on an iPhone.
4. Install the SSH daemon on an iPhone.
5. Install netcat on an iPhone.
6. Set up a peer-to-peer wireless network between an iPhone and iMac.
7. Establish a secure shell or SSH connection to an iPod.
8. **Ping** your listener system.
9. Set up the listener.
10. Start the imaging process.

> **NOTE**
>
> The iPhone with Firmware version 1.1.1 could be altered by going to the Web site Jailbreakme.com. The alteration takes place when a buffer overflow crashes the system due to a flaw in the unpatched Safari browser. Once Safari crashed, you could obtain the same permission level as the program that crashed. In this case, the access is root level. Once you get root privileges, you can install an installer application and get all your tools off the Internet. This has changed since iPhone Firmware version 1.1.1.

Step 1 – Jailbreak the iPhone

The term "Jailbreak the iPhone" means that existing Apple firmware (first partition or Slice 1) is replaced with an alternate or hacked firmware. The hacked firmware contains an installer package that allows you to install your tools. These types of modifications, while possible, are not considered part of an appropriate forensic acquisition technique. Please see Exercise 15.2 to learn how to perform a jailbreak operation on the iPhone.

Configuring & Implementing...

Exercise 15.2: Jailbreaking the iPhone

In this exercise we will use a software tool to perform a jailbreak operation on the iPhone.

1. Download the latest iPhone firmware to your local computer. At the time of this writing, the latest firmware can be downloaded at the following link from Apple:
   http://appldnld.apple.com.edgesuite.net/content.info.apple.com/iPhone/061-5134.20080729.Q2W3E/iPhone1,2_2.0.1_5B108_Restore.ipsw

2. Place this firmware in a location on your local computer where you can easily find it.

3. There are a variety of tools available to alter the firmware of the iPhone, iPod Touch, and the iPhone 3G. In this example, I use the Pwnage Tool, as seen in Figure. 15.6. This tool is available from the following link: http://www.modmyifone.com/forums/downloads.php?do=file&id=16871. There are other tools available for both Mac OS and Windows platforms that perform the same firmware alteration.

Figure 15.6 The Pwnage Tool Is Displayed

Continued

4. After you have downloaded the firmware, start the program. You will see a screen is similar to the one in Figure 15.7. Choose the iPhone or iPod Touch you have (Generation 1 or 3G).

Figure 15.7 Installing the Pwnage Tool Is for the iPhone 3G

The Pwnage Tool can be installed on the iPhone, iPod Touch, and iPhone 3G.

5. Choose the Cydia packages, as seen in Figure 15.8. The rest of the tools that are needed can be downloaded from the Internet to the Apple device through a wireless access point. The Cydia package is critical because some of the applications have dependencies. If Cydia is installed, these dependencies will still work if connecting to the Internet is not an option.

Continued

Figure 15.8 Choose the Cydia Packages

6. Save the iPhone/iPod Firmware Update, or IPSW file to a location you can easily find, as seen in Figure 15.9.

Figure 15.9 Saving Custom iPhone or iPod Touch Firmware File

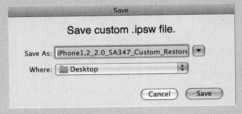

7. Next, select the option to perform a custom build, as seen in Figure 15.10.

Continued

Figure 15.10 Building a Custom iPhone or iPod Touch

8. After a few minutes you will be prompted for your iMac password. When you enter it, the firmware takes a few more minutes until the successful build pop-up appears.

9. Now put the iPhone in Device Firmware Upgrade, or DFU mode (serial mode), as seen in Figure 15.11, to "re-flash" the firmware you want on it. Before you do this, make sure that you have quit the iTunes application!

Figure 15.11 Putting the iPhone in DFU Mode (Serial Mode)

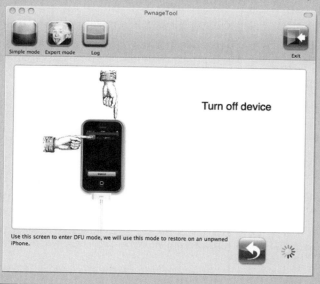

Continued

10. Press on the Apple icon at the top of the screen, navigate to Force Quit, and kill the iTunes application.

You will eventually get a window that comically states the phrase "I HAZ SUCCESS".

11. Continue following the on-screen instructions from the Pwnage Tool. The square button at the bottom is called the Home button, and the top one is called the Power button.

12. When the device completes the power down and recycle after the countdown, press the **Power** and **Home** button at the same time, as seen in Figure 15.12.

Figure 15.12 Pressing Power and Home Buttons at the Same Time

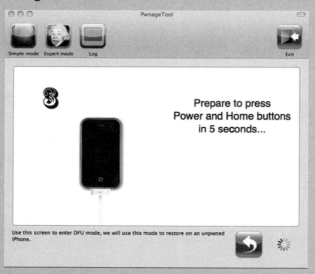

13. Now start the iTunes application to get the following message, "iTunes has detected a phone in recovery mode." See Figure 15.13.

Figure 15.13 Using iTunes to Detect an iPhone in Recovery Mode

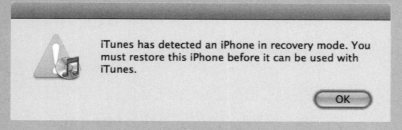

Continued

14. Hold down the **Option** key and click the **Restore** key, as seen in Figure 15.14. Note: If you do not hold down the option key, the default un-hacked firmware will be restored.

Figure 15.14 Holding Down the Option Key and Clicking the Restore Key

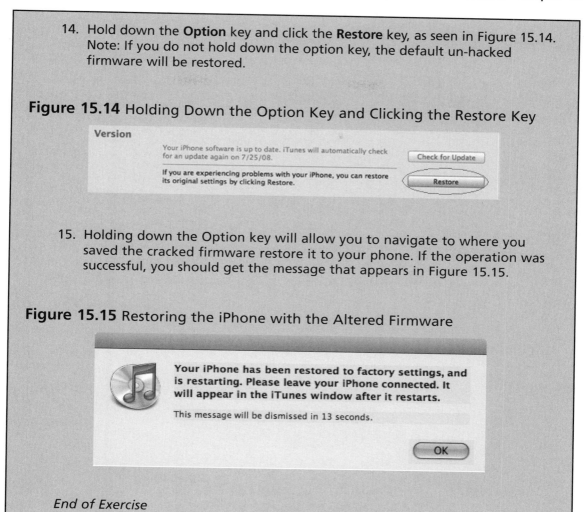

15. Holding down the Option key will allow you to navigate to where you saved the cracked firmware restore it to your phone. If the operation was successful, you should get the message that appears in Figure 15.15.

Figure 15.15 Restoring the iPhone with the Altered Firmware

End of Exercise

Let your iPhone restart. When the iPhone has restarted and reconnected to iTunes, you will get the Earth screen and the settings will be overwritten. It's important to do this on a fresh install; otherwise, you would be syncing foreign data to this phone if you did not.

WARNING

Leave the defaults when you use Altered iPhone Firmware. Don't add any other applications or custom bootload pictures. The reason to avoid doing this is that you might have to return this phone to its owner, and you probably don't want to have to explain why his bootload picture has changed.

Step 2 – Disabling the Power and Screen Lock Feature

When the iPhone is ready, log in, go to the settings under General Settings, and set the Auto Lock to **Never** and the Passcode Lock to **Off**, as seen in Figure 15.16. Ensure that the phone is connected to a power source since the imaging procedure could take more time than the battery capacity will allow.

Figure 15.16 Setting the Auto Lock to Never and Passcode Lock to Off

Step 3 – Install UNIX Utilities on the iPhone (Choose the Cydia Installer)

The Mac OS X runs BSD, which is a variant of the UNIX operating system. There are many valuable forensics tools that come with some versions of UNIX, including *dd* and *ssh*. Also, the netcat tool is used by people within the forensic and hacker community. To install UNIX utilities on the iPhone, choose the Cydia Installer, as seen in Figure 15.17.

Figure 15.17 Choosing the Cydia Installer

Step 4 – Install the SSH Daemon on the iPhone

SSH stands for secure shell. It is a way to remotely connect to a system from a command line. SSH uses port 22 and is commonly used in Linux and UNIX to administer machines remotely. An SSH client is not included in any version of Windows, but it can be added easily by downloading an application such as Putty. Putty will allow a Windows-based machine to remotely connect to an iMac running an SSH server. Figure 15.18 shows the SSH service running on the iPhone.

Figure 15.18 Installing the SSH Daemon on the iPhone

Step 5 – Install netcat on the iPhone

Netcat is known as the "Swiss Army Knife of networking tools." It can be used to do a number of things, including scan systems for open ports. Within the forensics community, it is often used to send an image to a remote system. The netcat service is seen running on the iPhone in Figure 15.19.

Figure 15.19 Installing netcat on the iPhone

The easiest way to gain access to a wireless access point is through the Settings of the iPhone or iPod Touch. Go to Settings – WiFi and connect to the desired network, as seen in Figure 15.20 All iPhones have the ability to connect to 802.11B/G wireless networks.

Figure 15.20 Using the iPhone's Built-in WiFi Capability

Installing the Boss Prefs, as seen in Figure 15.21, makes imaging the phone easier because you do not need to stop and start applications from the command line. Follow the instructions to install these applications. After they are installed, you will be ready to get an image of this iPhone. Keep in mind that the iPhone is broken up into two partitions, as pointed out earlier, and you are trying to obtain an image the second partition or slice.

Figure 15.21 Using the Boss Prefs

Step 6 – Set Up a Peer-To-Peer Wireless Network between an iPhone and iMac

Now we are ready so set up basic networking. A peer-to-peer network from the iPhone to the system receiving the data stream can be set up easily. The benefit of a peer-to-peer or ad-hoc network is that no additional equipment, such as a Wireless Access Point, is required. When you set up an ad-hoc network, both clients, in this case the iPhone and iMac, will receive IP Addresses in the range of 169.254.X.X. These addresses are also known as APIPA, which stands for Automatic Private IP Addressing. These addresses are used by many operating systems, including Mac OS and Windows, when a DHCP server is unavailable and no static IP address has been set.

You can also use your wireless access point to connect your iPhone to the same wireless network as your iMac. This will accomplish the same task, and will not require you to set up the ad-hoc network.

For the sake of ease, you can use an open network. Not only will adding encryption make the whole acquisition process more difficult, it will slow down the acquisition time. If you want to securely transfer the image, it is advisable to use some type of encryption. WEP (Wired Equivalent Privacy) encryption is easily defeated; therefore WPA or WPA2 is recommended if you want to use encryption. With a strong passphrase, WiFi Protected Access, or WPA cannot be easily hacked. Finally, if you need to be compliant with Federal Information Processing Standard (FIPS) 140-2, use WPA2 with Advanced Encryption Standard (AES) encryption and a very strong passphrase.

In the following example, WEP encryption will be used for the ad-hoc network. Although it is not very secure, it is adequate for this demonstration.

WARNING

It is best to be in a room or box that does not get any cell phone reception at all since incoming calls might stop the imaging procedure and force you to start all over again.

To set up networking on a Macintosh system:

1. Click the AirPort icon on the Finder menu bar, as seen in Figure 15.22, and choose **Create Network.**

Figure 15.22 Creating an Ad-Hoc Network

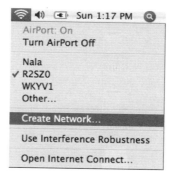

2. Click **Show Options**. Give the network an SSID (Service Set Identifier). In Figure 15.23, the SSID is "IMAGE." The SSID is also known as the name of the wireless network. For the password, you can use 10 letter *A*'s. Make sure the required password filed is checked and click **OK**. You are now finished creating the ad-hoc wireless network via your iMac.

Figure 15.23 Creating an Ad-Hoc Network Using an iMac

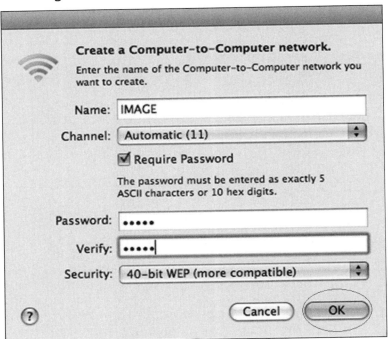

TIP

You can also use the Microsoft Windows operating systems, including Vista and Windows 2008, to set up the network and receive the image. You will need to download the netcat program from http://netcat.sourceforge.net/. It works best on Windows if the *nc.exe* program is placed in your Windows\System32 folder. When you first try to use the netcat program on your Windows System, you may receive a firewall warning, as seen in Figure 15.24. Click **Unblock** to disable the firewall.

Figure 15.24 Enabling netcat through the Windows System Firewall

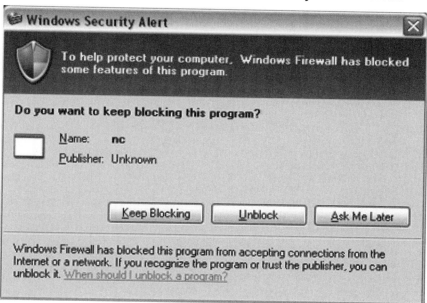

3. From the iPhone, go to Settings – WiFi, and connect to it an SSID, for example IMAGE, as seen in Figure 15.25. Remember that all iPhones have the ability to connect to 802.11B/G wireless networks. Also, don't forget the passphrase of 10 A's, or whatever you used, for the WEP key.

Figure 15.25 Joining a WiFi Network from the iPhone

at&t 3G
9:55
100
Settings
Wi-Fi Networks
Wi-Fi
ON
Choose a Network...
IMAGE
Other...
Ask to Join Networks
OFF
Known networks will be joined automatically.
If no known networks are available, you
will have to manually select a network.

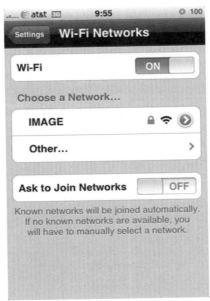

Step 7 – Establish a Secure Shell or SSH Connection to an iPod

Now go on the iPod, find the Boss Prefs application you installed through the Cydia application, and ensure that *ssh* is enabled. Now open a window on your Macintosh system and type the following command within the terminal window, as seen in Figure 15.26: **ssh <ipaddress of the iPod> -l root**

Figure 15.26 Piping the *dd* through netcat

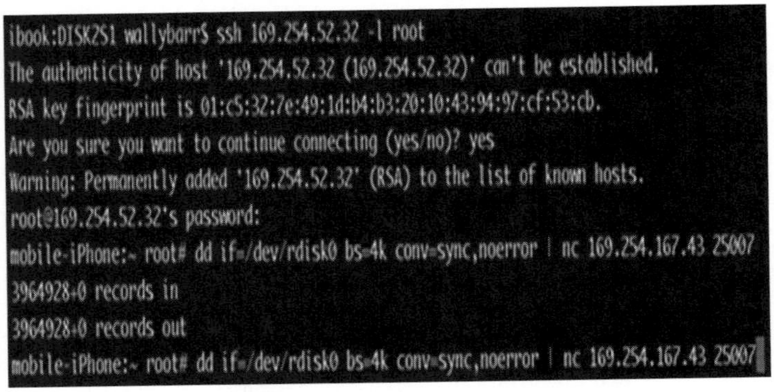

ibook:DISK2S1 wallybarr$ ssh 169.254.52.32 -l root
The authenticity of host '169.254.52.32 (169.254.52.32)' can't be established.
RSA key fingerprint is 01:c5:32:7e:49:1d:b4:b3:20:10:43:94:97:cf:53:cb.
Are you sure you want to continue connecting (yes/no)? yes
Warning: Permanently added '169.254.52.32' (RSA) to the list of known hosts.
root@169.254.52.32's password:
mobile-iPhone:~ root# dd if=/dev/rdisk0 bs=4k conv=sync,noerror | nc 169.254.167.43 25007
3964928+0 records in
3964928+0 records out
mobile-iPhone:~ root# dd if=/dev/rdisk0 bs=4k conv=sync,noerror | nc 169.254.167.43 25007

Type the following command within the terminal window:

ssh <ip address of the iPod> -l root

The –l parameter means log me in as the root user. You should get an option for a key exchange the first time you log in as root. Answer "yes" and then when prompted for a password, enter alpine. If that doesn't work, try entering **dottie**. So far Apple has used only these two passwords; so they should work. The firmware build also gives you the option to set a password.

NOTE

If you get a connection refused error, ensure that the *ssh* service is running on the iPod and your firewall is allowing outbound *ssh* connections.

Step 8 – Ping Your Listener System

Open up a terminal window on your Macintosh system and run the **ifconfig** command. Note the IP address of the wireless adapter. Figure 15.27 shows the network setting of an iMac.

Figure 15.27 Finding Your IP Address on Your iMac

```
whiteyComputer-3:~ wallybarr$ ifconfig
lo0: flags=8049<UP,LOOPBACK,RUNNING,MULTICAST> mtu 16384
        inet 127.0.0.1 netmask 0xff000000
        inet6 ::1 prefixlen 128
        inet6 fe80::1%lo0 prefixlen 64 scopeid 0x1
gif0: flags=8010<POINTOPOINT,MULTICAST> mtu 1280
stf0: flags=0<> mtu 1280
en0: flags=8863<UP,BROADCAST,SMART,RUNNING,SIMPLEX,MULTICAST> mtu 1500
        ether 00:0a:95:84:81:fa
        media: autoselect (none) status: inactive
        supported media: none autoselect 10baseT/UTP <half-duplex> 10baseT/UTP <full-duplex> 10baseT
w-loopback> 100baseTX <half-duplex> 100baseTX <full-duplex> 100baseTX <full-duplex,hw-loopback>
en1: flags=8863<UP,BROADCAST,SMART,RUNNING,SIMPLEX,MULTICAST> mtu 1500
        inet6 fe80::203:93ff:feef:11f1%en1 prefixlen 64 scopeid 0x5
        inet 192.168.1.36 netmask 0xffffff00 broadcast 192.168.1.255
        ether 00:03:93:ef:11:f1
        media: autoselect status: active
        supported media: autoselect
fw0: flags=8863<UP,BROADCAST,SMART,RUNNING,SIMPLEX,MULTICAST> mtu 2030
        lladdr 00:0a:95:ff:fe:84:81:fa
        media: autoselect <full-duplex> status: inactive
        supported media: autoselect <full-duplex>
whiteyComputer-3:~ wallybarr$ ping 192.168.1.1
PING 192.168.1.1 (192.168.1.1): 56 data bytes
64 bytes from 192.168.1.1: icmp_seq=0 ttl=64 time=1.732 ms
64 bytes from 192.168.1.1: icmp_seq=1 ttl=64 time=2.738 ms
64 bytes from 192.168.1.1: icmp_seq=2 ttl=64 time=2.667 ms
```

Your IP address should be a 169.254.xxx.xxx address. This is the address of the listener we will be piping our image to. Type the following command within the terminal window: **ping −t 4 169.254.xxx.xxx.** You should get a **reply from** response. If you do not get a reply, check your network settings and the firewall settings on your iMac.

Step 9 – Set Up the Listener

Type the following commands within the terminal window to verify that netcat and *dd* have been installed:

1. Type **nc −h** to get a help menu.
2. Then type **dd** and press **Enter**. Press **Control C** if you want to stop the process.

Now set up the listener on the iMac. To do this, navigate to the folder where you want to save the forensic image. Open up a terminal window, type: **nc −l 26000 > slice2.dd**, and press **Return.** This command means "listen on port 26000 and send what you get to a file called *slice2.dd.*"

Step 10 – Start the Imaging Process

In the window where you have a remote connection using *ssh,* type the following:

> **dd if=/dev/disk0s2 conv=sync,noerror bs=4k | nc −w1 <ip address of mac> 26000**
> See Figure 15.28.

Figure 15.28 Just *dd* It!

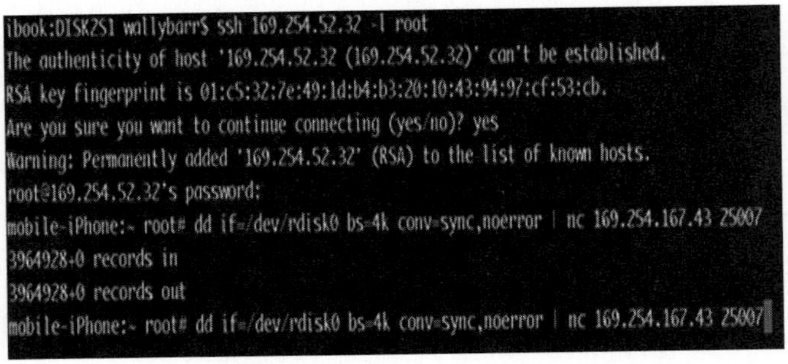

The following describes what occurred in the remote terminal window in more detail:

■ *dd* is the name of the imaging program that is being run.

■ *if=* is the input file, in this case the second partition.

■ bs= block size

■ conv=sync,noerror -> Pad with zeros if there is an error.

■ Pipe (|) the out put it to netcat.

- Wait one second until the end of the data transfer and terminate the socket.

- Use port 26000. Note that you can use any port you want as long as it isn't being used by another service.

Open up a third terminal window on the iMac and navigate to the folder where your image is being saved and run a directory listing, **ls –la,** to check your progress, as seen in Figure 15.29. The number should be increasing every time you run the program. Imaging a 16GB iPhone across a WiFi network could take five to six hours if you don't have to restart the process. It is recommended, as stated earlier, that you stay in a room that does not get any signal reception and you have the iPod attached to an external power supply. Be careful if you work in a government or corporate environment that has air sensors installed because they discourage WiFi signals in enterprise environments. They do not jam them, because that would be illegal; so they just disrupt WiFi communications.

Figure 15.29 Would You Care to Have a Slice?

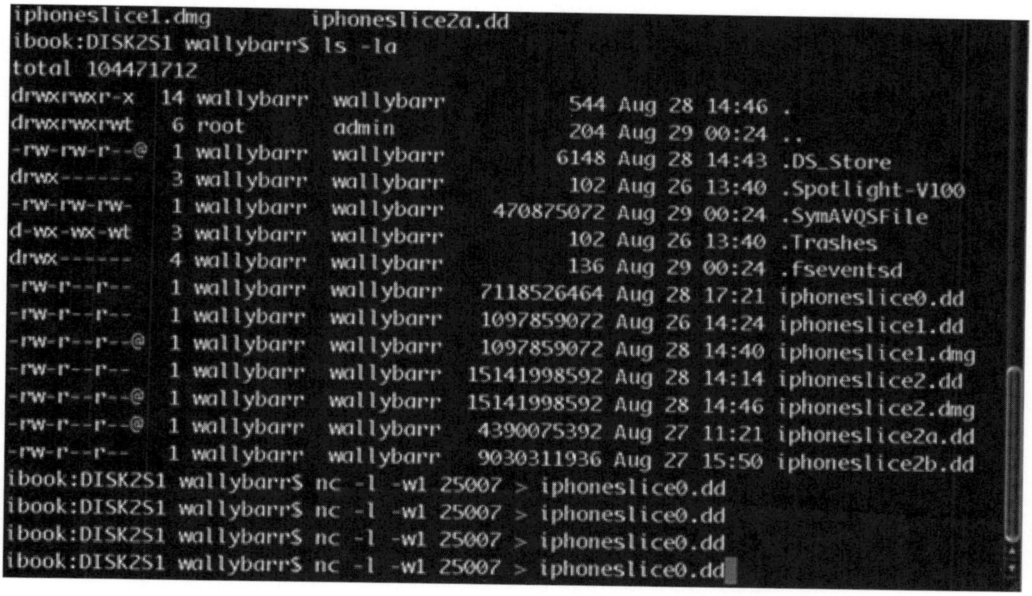

```
iphoneslice1.dmg            iphoneslice2a.dd
ibook:DISK2S1 wallybarr$ ls -la
total 104471712
drwxrwxr-x  14 wallybarr   wallybarr         544 Aug 28 14:46 .
drwxrwxrwt   6 root        admin             204 Aug 29 00:24 ..
-rw-rw-r--@  1 wallybarr   wallybarr        6148 Aug 28 14:43 .DS_Store
drwx------   3 wallybarr   wallybarr         102 Aug 26 13:40 .Spotlight-V100
-rw-rw-rw-   1 wallybarr   wallybarr   470875072 Aug 29 00:24 .SymAVQSFile
d-wx-wx-wt   3 wallybarr   wallybarr         102 Aug 26 13:40 .Trashes
drwx------   4 wallybarr   wallybarr         136 Aug 29 00:24 .fseventsd
-rw-r--r--   1 wallybarr   wallybarr  7118526464 Aug 28 17:21 iphoneslice0.dd
-rw-r--r--   1 wallybarr   wallybarr  1097859072 Aug 26 14:24 iphoneslice1.dd
-rw-r--r--@  1 wallybarr   wallybarr  1097859072 Aug 28 14:40 iphoneslice1.dmg
-rw-r--r--   1 wallybarr   wallybarr 15141998592 Aug 28 14:14 iphoneslice2.dd
-rw-r--r--@  1 wallybarr   wallybarr 15141998592 Aug 28 14:46 iphoneslice2.dmg
-rw-r--r--@  1 wallybarr   wallybarr  4390075392 Aug 27 11:21 iphoneslice2a.dd
-rw-r--r--   1 wallybarr   wallybarr  9030311936 Aug 27 15:50 iphoneslice2b.dd
ibook:DISK2S1 wallybarr$ nc -l -w1 25007 > iphoneslice0.dd
ibook:DISK2S1 wallybarr$ nc -l -w1 25007 > iphoneslice0.dd
ibook:DISK2S1 wallybarr$ nc -l -w1 25007 > iphoneslice0.dd
ibook:DISK2S1 wallybarr$ nc -l -w1 25007 > iphoneslice0.dd
```

After four or five hours, your image should be complete. You can also image the whole disk, but everything of evidentiary value will be in the second slice. But most forensic software, as of this writing, cannot break the blob into the original partition schemes.

Analysis of the iPhone Image

Once you have Slice 2 of the iPhone on your system, you can actually use an iMac without any forensic tools to view the files and folders. Keep in mind that you can only view the non-deleted items on the Mac. If you want to try to recover deleted files or items from slack space, you will need a forensic tool such as Encase, X-Ways, or Blackbag. Locate the *dd* file on the Mac system. It may be quite large, as seen in Figure 15.30.

Figure 15.30 Viewing the Acquired Image

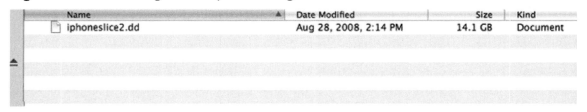

To read the created image file, rename the *dd* extension to *DMG*. To rename a file, just hold down the **Control** key and select **Get Info** from the pop-up menu. In the Info window, find the Name & Extension field. Click the down arrow in front of the Name & Extension, as seen in Figure 15.31, and rename the file extension from *dd* to *DMG*.

Figure 15.31 Renaming the File Extension from *dd* to *DMG*

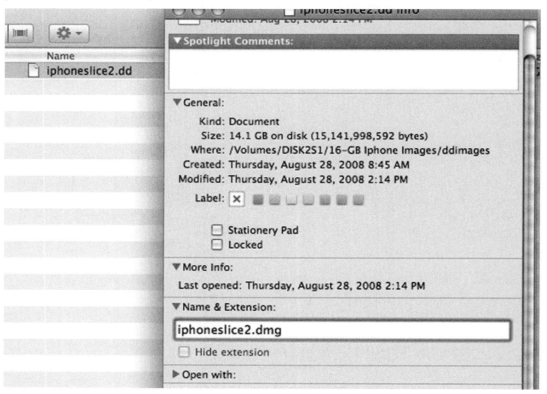

Once the file extension has been renamed, you may look at the files and folders from the second slice, as seen in Figure 15.32. While you will not see any deleted files or folders by viewing the image with an iMac, you may find deleted artifacts if you view the *dd* using a forensic software tool such as BlackBag or X-Ways.

Figure 15.32 Viewing Artifacts from Slice 2

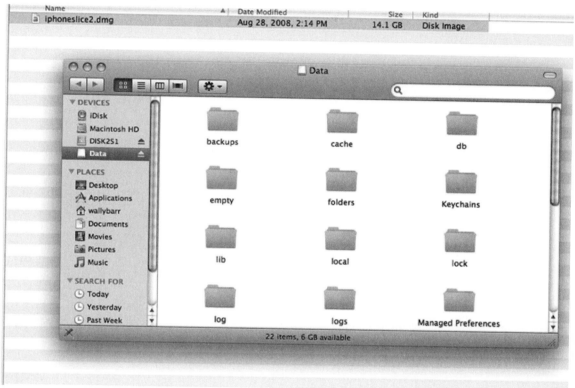

iPhone Firmware 2.1

Your iPhone may soon ask you to upgrade to the new 2.1 firmware, as seen in Figure 15.33. As discussed in the introduction to this chapter, Apple has created certain problems that investigators and first responders will need to face. In Firmware 2.0 the passcode lock could be circumvented. More than likely, owners of 1G and 2G phones will update to 2.1 to take advantage of the fixes than came with that update. In Firmware 2.1 Apple has fixed that security problem and added a wipe function if the passcode is entered incorrectly 10 times. The question is: What should you do if you have a case that involves an iPhone? The only equipment you will need in this instance is a Faraday Bag and a portable charger. Be sure to document all of the steps you take during this process. Please see Exercise 15.3 to learn how to deal with an iPhone with Firmware 2.1.

Figure 15.33 Downloading the iPhone Firmware 2.1 Update

Configuring & Implementing…

Exercise 15.3: Dealing with an iPhone with Firmware Version 2.1

These steps will describe the process used to avoid having the suspect's phone lock during a seizure.

1. Click the **Home** button, and check if there a passcode has been activated, as seen in Figure 15.34.

Continued

Figure 15.34 Activated Passcode on an iPhone

2. If you encounter an iPhone with an activated passcode, attempt to ascertain that code from the suspect. So far there is no known vulnerability to this new passcode. Without getting a passcode, an investigator will only be able to get images of the iPhone by syncing it to a computer. However, syncing to a computer is not a forensic method of retrieving those images.

3. If you encounter no passcode or you were able to retrieve the passcode, first go to the Settings button, as seen in Figure 15.35.

Figure 15.35 Settings Button

4. At the top of the Settings menu turn on Airplane mode. This will help prevent the device from receiving communication.

5. Click the General button, as seen in Figure 15.36.

Continued

Figure 15.36 Turning on Airplane Mode

6. From the General Settings, go to Auto Lock Settings, as seen in Figure 15.37, where you can both activate the passcode and determine if a passcode lock has been turned on.

Figure 15.37 Adjusting the Auto-Lock Setting from the General Settings

Continued

7. From the Auto-Lock menu, select **Never**, as seen in Figure 15.38.

Figure 15.38   Adjusting the Auto-Lock Setting to Never

8. Now that you have the ability to stop the iPhone from rolling over to the passcode, you need to then supply power to the phone. If you do not supply power to the phone, you will need the passcode once again when it is powered back on. A company called Voxred International LLC has developed a portable charger for iPods and iPhones. Attach such a portable charger and, if you want to be extra secure, place both items into a Faraday Bag and transport them to the lab a soon as possible.

9. Once at the lab, consult your legal point of contact and determine whether you are allowed to go through the procedures for jailbreaking the device to get an image of Slice 2.

End of Exercise

Terminology

These are common terms you come across when trying to hack the iPhone. They sound the same but mean different things in the forensic community.

Baseband

This is the part of the cell phone that handles telephone communications. It is located in flash ROM and is protected because of the FCC regulations that make providers secure this. Cell phone manufacturers do not want users tweaking the settings that could endanger the reliability of the cell phone network. For example, users may change or alter these frequency settings or attempt to increase call priority (implemented after 9/11 for emergency responders), or increase cell phone power. To obtain items of interest like contacts stored on the SIM card use conventional cell phone recovery tools like Paraben's device seizure.

Unlocking

This refers to opening up the cell phone in order to use other providers, for example, T-Mobil, other carriers that work on the 3G network, or bypassing ATT's data plan for iPhone and using a pay-as-you-go plan or the normal (cheaper) plan without the extra charges (which go into Apple's pockets).

Jailbreaking

Jailbreaking means to open the cell phone so it can be accessed via a secure shell terminal (SSH). This allows a user to copy and moves files off and on to the iPhone like any other remote computer system. This method was used in this chapter to capture an image of the iPhone data and recover it.

SIM Card

The Subscriber Identity Module card (SIM card) stores the service key (MSI) and allows for the unique identification of a phone on the cell phone network. Subscribers can remove the SIM card. iPhone users can just insert a paper clip near the top of the device to remove the SIM card. The article at http://www.maclife.com/article/how_to_remove_the_iphone_sim_card describes the procedure to remove the SIM card.

Summary

The acquisition of an iPhone can be performed by completing a logical copy or a physical copy. A logical image can be acquired by performing a backup using the iTunes Sync application. This method will not provide you with items in slack space or deleted items. In order to perform a physical image of Slice 2, a jailbreak needs to be performed. When you get a physical image of Slice 2, you can obtain items in slack space or deleted items. Consult with your legal consul before determining which method to use to perform your image acquisition.

Solutions Fast Track

iPhone and iPod Touch Forensic Concerns

☑ Apple cannot release an acquisition tool.

☑ A jailbreak may need to be used.

☑ An iPhone that has been hacked into might not be allowed as evidence in a court of law.

iPhone and iPod Touch Logical Acquisitions

☑ Logical acquisitions do not get deleted files of folders.

☑ Logical acquisitions do not get items from slack space.

☑ Logical acquisitions may involve an iTunes Sync.

Acquiring a Physical Image of an iPhone

☑ Slice 1 is replaced by a jailbreak.

☑ Slice 1 has little of evidentiary value.

☑ Slice 2 has the user's data.

Analysis of the iPhone Image

☑ Rename the *dd* file extension to *DMG*.

☑ You can view the image on an iMac, but will not see deleted files.

☑ Use a software forensic tool to view deleted files and slack space.

iPhone Firmware 2.1

☑   Do not let the iPhone turn off.

☑   Keep the iPhone powered in a Faraday Bag.

☑   Do not allow an iPhone that you have access to go into a passcode protected phase.

Terminology

☑   *Unlocking* opens a cell phone to the use of other providers.

☑   *Jailbreaking* changes Slice 1.

☑   A *SIM* card uniquely identifies the iPhone.

Frequently Asked Questions

Q: Surely there is a forensic tool that can do a physical acquisition of the iPhone?

A: Nope, sorry there is not. Tools costing hundreds of dollars claim to perform digital forensics on the iPhone, but in reality just back up the contacts and photo area. Other data sites are not captured.

Q: What forensic tools are good tools for recovering lost data from a damaged disk?

A: Data Carving in EnCase is a good too. You can also just rename the *dd* extension to *DMG*, allowing Mac OS X to repair the data and recover as many usable files as possible.

Q: My image stopped being acquired after three hours.

A: This may happen because the phone part of the iPhone has priority over data. So at any time processes can be stopped to ensure call stability. That is why you should put the phone in a Faraday Bag when acquiring an image.

Q: Why do I need to use WiFi that's unsecure?

A: Apple does not provide, as they did with the first firmware, a way to extract an image using tethered cable. My suggestion, if this is a concern, is to use a Faraday Bag.

Q: Dude, this is so forensically unclean you will never get this entered into court as evidence?

A: This may be correct. But until Apple releases a forensic tool or allows a forensically clean way of getting an image off with a write blocker, you are stuck to using this unconventional hack method. I can imagine an organization's standard operating procedure could allow for an iPhone jailbreak so that it could be accepted in a court of law as evidence. Law enforcement seizes evidence on live server systems and has formulated ways that are clear and understandable that could pass evidentiary requirements. Even if the hack method isn't allowed, knowing what the potential data is on the iPhone can be useful in getting a confession or going to the other side of the communication (email, Web site) to find useful forensic evidence that will be admissible in a court of law.

Q: Why do I need to work with these hacker types to image an iPhone or iPod?

A: As data becomes more secure through the installation of encryption and other methods, law enforcement will have to start hacking these systems in order to acquire evidence. This is not new to law enforcement since for the past 30 years they have had to adapt and adjust to acquire forensic evidence. The hacker types are resources that provide a bridge to help you get this evidence.

Chapter 16

iPhone Forensics

Solutions in this chapter:

- iPhone Functions
- Carving
- Non-Jail Breaking Method of iPhone Analysis

☑ Summary
☑ Solutions Fast Track
☑ Frequently Asked Questions

Introduction

The field of iPhone forensics is still currently under development. There are currently nonforensic methods that can be used in order to get an image off an iPhone. Some of these tools and methods involve altering the iPhone in some manner, which may cause any evidence retrieved in this manner to be considered inadmissible in a court of law. At any rate, a defense lawyer would be able to plant enough doubt in the minds of a jury to have the evidence dismissed.

New tools being released in the market allow you to gather the same information when iPhone data is backed up to a Mac or PC. Using proven forensic methods, artifacts from the iPhone can be retrieved.

Both nonforensic and forensic methods of acquiring artifacts from an iPhone will be discussed in this chapter.

iPhone Functions

With the release of the iPhone, Apple has changed the cell phone marketplace in which manufacturers like HTC, and services like "Google" are releasing phones to compete with the iPhone. The main functions of the first iPhone were cell communications, Web access, e-mail, and personal data assistant (PDA) applications such as Calendar, Address Book, and Notes. The first iPhones could also connect to iTunes and You Tube.

The Second-generation iPhones have more functions such as GPS services, which can be paired with Google Maps to tell the user their exact location. The iPhone can act just like any GPS device, with routes and locate services through the Google Map function. When the 3G iPhone was introduced, it had problems with the GPS function. However, with the 2.1 update, these problems seem to have been fixed. With the arrival of the 3G iPhone and the 2.0 software, this enabled First-generation and Second-generation iPhones to access the "App Store." This is a marketplace for free and paid applications that can run on the iPhone. There are 19 different categories and hundreds of applications for the iPhone to download either straight from the "App Store" or via iTunes. These applications can utilize some of the features of the iPhone, like the accelerometer, GPS, video, audio, productivity tools, and games. See Figure 16.1 for an image of the Second-generation iPhone.

Figure 16.1 The Second-Generation iPhone

Courtesy of Apple

iPhone Partitioning

The partition scheme of an iPhone resembles an Apple TV. The first partition on the iPhone is the Master Boot Record (MBR). The Master Boot Record is one sector in length and is responsible for loading the operating system on the iPhone. Following the Master Boot Record, there is an Apple_Free area. Immediately following the Apple_Free area is the first HFSX partition, which primarily stores the iPhone's operating system. Then, there is another Apple_Free area, and then the second HFSX partition. The second HFSX partition holds all individual user data, including evidentiary data such as movies, pictures, and contact information.

The partitioning scheme for the First-generation (1G) and Second-generation (2G) iPhones that have the new 2.0 firmware is shown in Figure 16.2.

Figure 16.2 iPhone Partition Scheme as Seen by hdiutil pmap

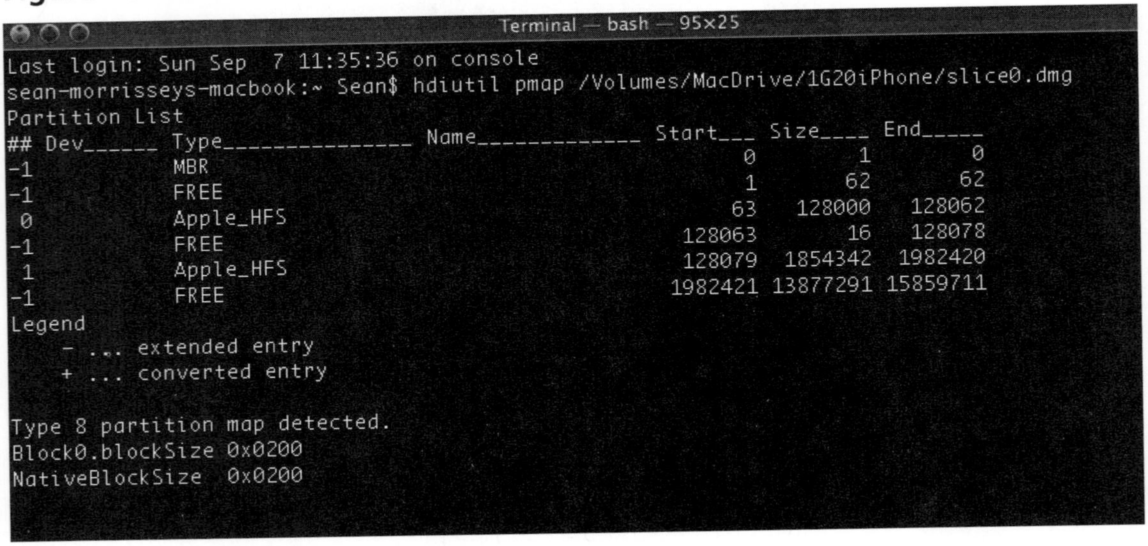

First Partition

The size of the first partition of the iPhone is generally 500 MB and uses the HFSX file system. The iPhone appears to have its origins from both the iPod and AppleTV. As shown in Figure 16.3, you will notice that the iPhone and AppleTV look very similar. Both are lean and mean operating systems with little overhead. Both have two partitions, one for operating and one for storage. Although the partition schemes are different, the file systems are also similar in structure.

Figure 16.3 iPhone and AppleTV Partitions

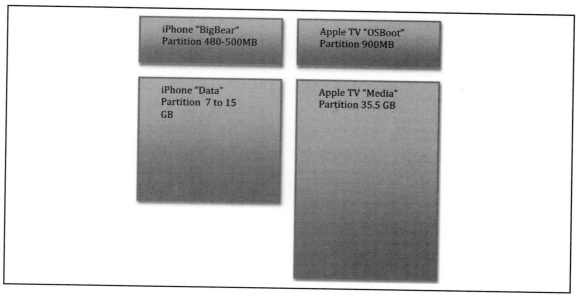

The BigBear partition of the iPhone is the HFS Plus partition, where the operating system is stored. The layout of the file and folder structure is shown in Figure 16.4.

Figure 16.4 BigBear File Structure

The OSBoot File partition of AppleTV is the HFS Plus partition where the phone's operating system is stored. The layout of the file and folder structure is shown in Figure 16.5.

Figure 16.5 OSBoot File Structure

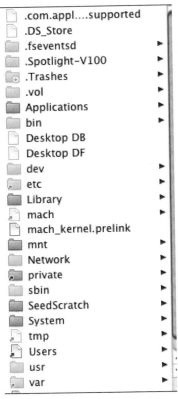

First Partition Folder Structure

Let's examine the folder structure of the first partition of the iPhone in a bit more detail. A detailed view of the BigBear partition file structure is shown in Figure 16.6.

Figure 16.6 Detailed View of BigBear Partition File Structure

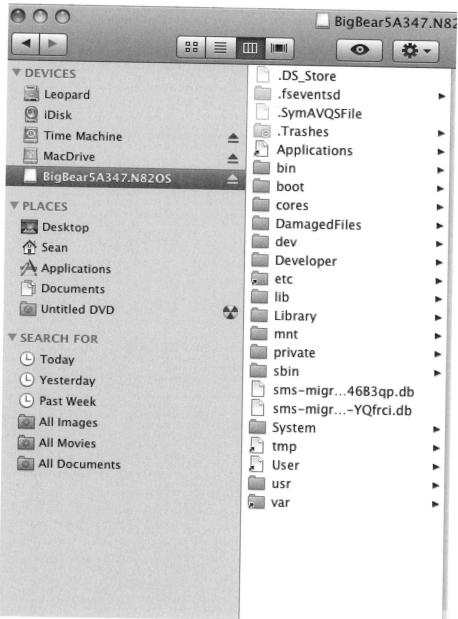

First you will see that the first partition is labeled BigBear (see Figure 16.6). BigBear comes from the 2.1 Firmware update. The numbers *5A347.N82OS* denotes the firmware version. The size of the first partition of an 8 GB and 16 GB iPhone is about 484 MB. The Jail Break of the phone can manipulate the size of this partition.

The First Folder **Applications** is a symbolic or alias link. This folder is empty and points to **/var/stash/**. The **stash** folder actually resides on the second partition.

The second folder is the **bin** folder. **bin** normally contains command line binaries. This folder should be devoid of such binaries. All the binaries located in this folder have been placed here from the jailbreak. Until Apple releases the ability to image the device, jailbreaking the iPhone is the only way at this point to create images of it. It can't be stated enough, however, that this is not a sound forensic imaging method.

The third folder is a *boot folder*, which is empty. The *cores, dev, and developer* folders are also empty.

Below the cores folder is a folder called *Damaged Files*. Within this folder are symbolic links to a *.plist* file and a file that is a remnant from the jailbreak.

The *etc* folder is really an alias to the location of the actual folder, which is */private/etc*. The most important file within the /private/etc folder is the *passwd* file.

NOTE

The examination of a decrypted Firmware .dmg file will also show the same password hash values as seen upon examination of the iPhone's /private/etc/passwd file. It seems that Apple keeps using the same password over and over again.

As indicated in Figure 16.7, other than root, there is only one other user on the iPhone, called "Mobile." The Mobile user has a user identification number (UID) of "501"and a group id of "501". After the user name, you will see a small hash value of "smx7MYTQIi2M". This value is the same value associated with root. Using John the Ripper against this file, the password for both root and mobile is "alpine". There have been reports that another password is "dottie." After examining three different iPhones, all of them had the alpine password.

Figure 16.7 iPhone *passwd* File Showing Passwords for Root and Mobile

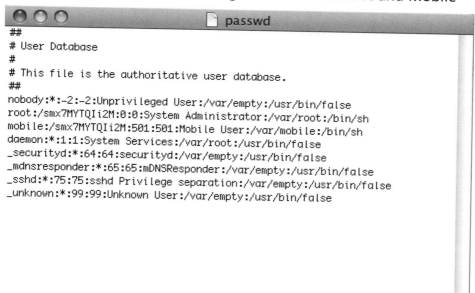

```
##
# User Database
#
# This file is the authoritative user database.
##
nobody:*:-2:-2:Unprivileged User:/var/empty:/usr/bin/false
root:/smx7MYTQIi2M:0:0:System Administrator:/var/root:/bin/sh
mobile:/smx7MYTQIi2M:501:501:Mobile User:/var/mobile:/bin/sh
daemon:*:1:1:System Services:/var/root:/usr/bin/false
_securityd:*:64:64:securityd:/var/empty:/usr/bin/false
_mdnsresponder:*:65:65:mDNSResponder:/var/empty:/usr/bin/false
_sshd:*:75:75:sshd Privilege separation:/var/empty:/usr/bin/false
_unknown:*:99:99:Unknown User:/var/empty:/usr/bin/false
```

Note that the *passwd* file shown in Figure16.7 was taken from a Firmware 2.0. .dmg file. The root and mobile users are the same in both files.

Also in the /private/etc folder, there is a *master passwd* file. This is a duplicate of the *passwd* file.

Just as in normal OS X forensics, there is a group folder that shows and validates that the 501 UID and the mobile user group, as seen in Figure 16.8. According to this file, mobile is a limited user, which will explain why forensic companies cannot access all data except the data Mobile has access to, for example, Contacts, Call Logs, and SMS. Also note that the mobile user syncs the iPhone with iTunes and creates backups.

Figure 16.8 Group Folder Showing Mobile User Group

```
                                  group
_cvs:*:72:
_svn:*:73:
_mysql:*:74:
_sshd:*:75:
_qtss:*:76:
_mailman:*:78:
_appserverusr:*:79:
admin:*:80:root
_appserveradm:*:81:
_clamav:*:82:
_amavisd:*:83:
_jabber:*:84:
_xgridcontroller:*:85:
_xgridagent:*:86:
_appowner:*:87:
_windowserver:*:88:
_spotlight:*:89:
accessibility:*:90:
_tokend:*:91:
_securityagent:*:92:
_calendar:*:93:_teamsserver
_teamsserver:*:94:
_update_sharing:*:95:
_installer:*:96:
_atsserver:*:97:
_lpadmin:*:98:
_unknown:*:99:
mobile:*:501:mobile
_securityd:*:64:_securityd
```

To better illustrate this point, you can see the active mobile user from a jailbroken iPhone that has a terminal application, as depicted in Figure 16.9.

Figure 16.9 Seeing an Active Mobile User from iPhone Terminal

Now that we have extensively discussed password and group files related to the /private/etc folder, let's return to our discussion of the folder structure of the first partition. The *Lib* directory, which stands for *library*, is also empty. The Library is also known as the local Library normally within either Tiger or Leopard. However, this Library contains mostly system settings, and nothing of evidentiary value.

When you examine an iPhone that has been jailbroken, there is a profile that you can see from a Mac, which shows the PATH and a *path daemon*. Because of the jailbreak method to access data, there is no assurance that the PATH you see is the original PATH and that the shells you see in *pathd* are accurate.

The *sbin* folder contains command line binaries that are normal in an OS X system. The examination of a decrypted 2.0 .dmg indicates that there are a few command line binaries, as depicted in Figure 16.10.

Figure 16.10 Showing the File Structure of the *sbin* Folder

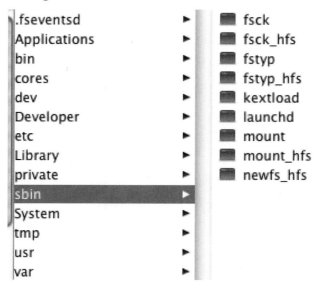

Other artifacts in this folder come from the jailbreak. Underneath the *sbin* folder are two *sms migration* folders, which are also empty.

The folder located directly below *sbin* is the **System** folder. First look in the **/System/Library**. Here there is a *USBDeviceConfiguration.plist* file. This appears to be the device configuration of the Apple Mobile Device and Picture Transfer Protocol (PTP).

In the **/System/Library/CoreServices** folder, there is a *SystemVersion.plist* file, as shown in Figure 16.11. This *.plist* file gives the investigator the build version of the iPhone.

Figure 16.11 iPhone *SystemVersion.plist* File

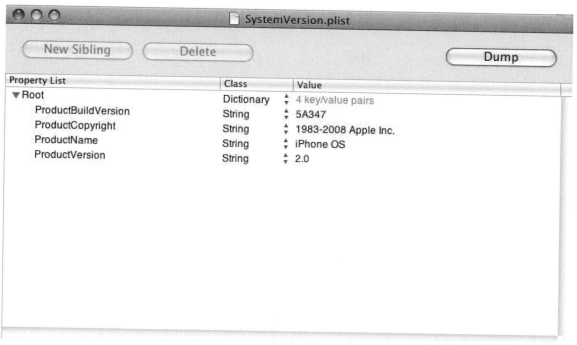

The **System/Library/DataClassMigrator** folder contains executables for the Address Book and for Calendar migration. These appear to reference other frameworks and libraries that are associated with Address Book and Calendar sync functions.

The next folder of interest within **System** is **/System/Library/LaunchDeamons**. Here are items that get started automatically. The first is the *AddressBook.plist*, as shown in Figure 16.12.

Figure 16.12 iPhone *com.apple.AddressBook.plist,*
Showing the Username Mobile

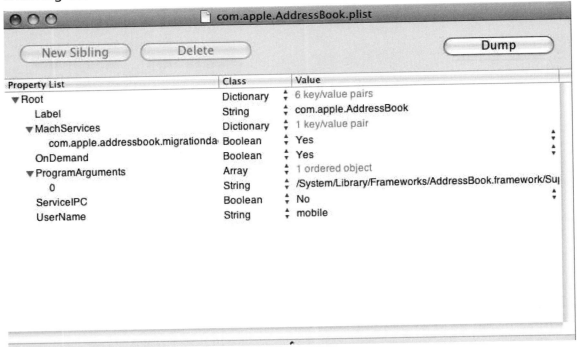

In Figure 16.12 you see the related User "Mobile" that the migration services have marked for startup and the frameworks associated with this *.plist.*

There is little of evidentiary value in the first partition. There are numerous other *.plist* files and frameworks that deal with all aspects of the operating system of the iPhone. The data, or the fruits of the examination, will be located in the second partition.

The Second Partition or Data Partition

On a 16 GB iPhone, the second partition is 14.1 GB. On an 8 GB iPhone the second partition is 7.07 GB. In Figure 16.13, the second partition is shown in a Terminal by using the command *hdiutil imageinfo.* The figure shows that the second partition has the HFSX File System and a volume name of "Data."

Figure 16.13 Data Partition as Seen with *hdiutil imageinfo*

```
Format: UDRW
Backing Store Information:
        Name: iphoneslice2.dmg
        URL: file://localhost/Volumes/MacDrive/16-GB%20Iphone%20Images/iphoneslice
        Class Name: CBSDBackingStore
Format Description: raw read/write
Checksum Type: none
partitions:
        appendable: true
        partition-scheme: none
        block-size: 512
        burnable: true
        partitions:
                0:
                        partition-length: 29574216
                        partition-synthesized: true
                        partition-hint: Apple_HFSX
                        partition-name: whole disk
                        partition-filesystems:
                                HFSX:
                        partition-start: 0
Properties:
        Partitioned: false
        Software License Agreement: false
        Compressed: no
        Kernel Compatible: true
        Encrypted: false
        Checksummed: false
Checksum Value:
Size Information:
        Total Bytes: 15141998592
        Compressed Bytes: 15141998592
        Total Non-Empty Bytes: 15141998592
        Sector Count: 29574216
        Total Empty Bytes: 0
        Compressed Ratio: 1
Class Name: CRawDiskImage
Segments:
        0: /Volumes/MacDrive/16-GB Iphone Images/iphoneslice2.dmg
Resize limits (per hdiutil resize -limits):
        17977080        29574216        95390728
```

This partition is where the majority of the valuable information that investigators may find useful is located. Let's look at the second partition and where all the data lives. The folder structure is depicted in Figure 16.14.

Figure 16.14 Second Partition Data Folder Structure

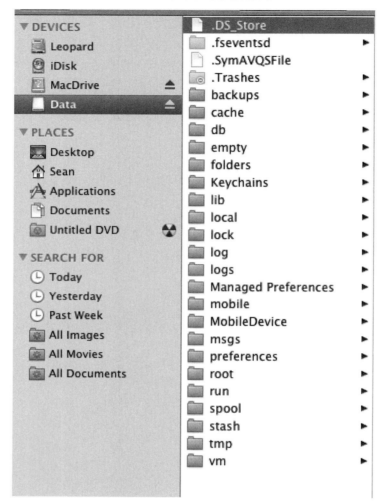

First is the .**Trashes** folder. Normally no evidence is located there. However, you may want to consider analyzing its contents during your examination process.

The next folder is the **cache** folder. Here again there isn't anything of evidentiary value; however, there was evidence that a jailbreak occurred on this partition.

The **db** folder is located directly below the **cache** Folder. Within the **db** folder are three subfolders:

- *dhcpclient*
- *PanicReporter*
- *timezone*

In the *dhcpclient* folder is a file that contains the network settings, as shown in Figure 16.15. In the figure you can also observe the IP and router addresses.

Figure 16.15 Wireless Settings from *dhcpclient*

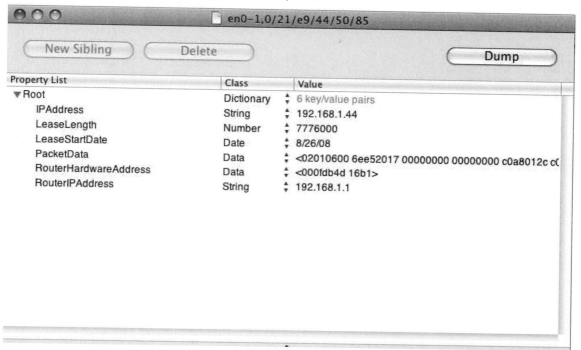

The next folder to examine is the *timezone* folder. As the name implies, this is where you will find typical time zone settings for this device. However, the *Localtime* file is really an alias to the /usr/share/zoneinfo/US/ Eastern file. Remember that /usr/share/ in the first partition is another alias to the /var/stash, which is really a pointer to the /stash folder on the root of the second partition. Figure 16.16 shows the path to where the time zone settings reside.

NOTE

Depending on the time zone from which the iPhone was seized, your actual path may be different. However, the common path will be **/stash/share.spOSjO/zoneinfo**.

Figure 16.16 Path to Where Time Zone Settings Reside (EST)

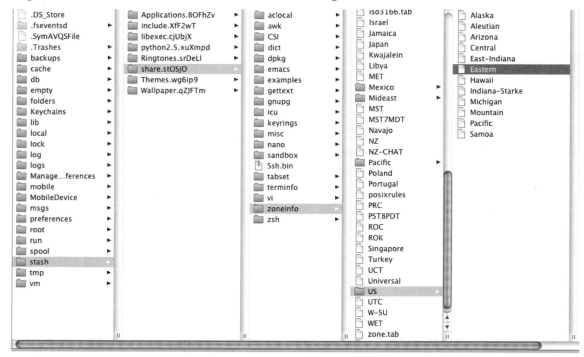

The files themselves are not all readable. However, you can follow the steps below to get readable text from files.

1. Open **Terminal**.
2. Type **strings**.
3. Drag and drop the Eastern time zone file onto the command line.
4. Press **Enter**.

Figure 16.17 shows what the completed exercise would look like if it had been configured for EST.

Figure 16.17 Eastern File Output from Strings Command

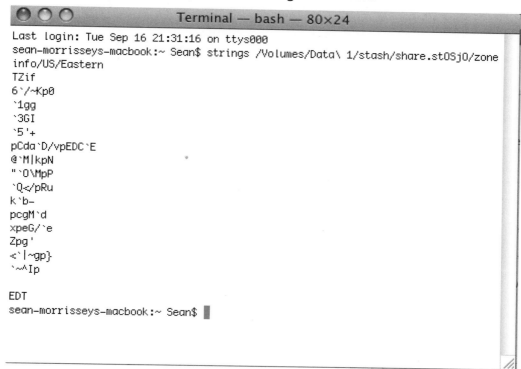

The results in Figure 16.17 show TZ (time zone) and EDT (Eastern Daylight Time). This is the only information that will be found in reference to time zone.

The **Empty** folder appears after the **cache** folder. Below the **Empty** folder is the **folders** folder, which is also empty.

Within the **Keychain** folder are two SQL databases. **Keychain-2.db** can be opened with SQLite Database Browser (see Exercise 16.1). SQLite Database Browser is a public domain application, which is available from Sourceforge or from Apple's developer tools for Leopard. This application, developed by T.P. Tabuleiro, is an excellent tool to view all database files on a Mac, and of course, the iPhone.

Configuring & Implementing...

Exercise 16.1: Opening Keychain-2db

1. Open the SQLite Database Browser.
2. Go to the open database icon and click once.
3. Navigate to the **Keychain-2.db** file, as shown in Figure 16.18.

Figure 16.18 SQLite Showing How to Open a File into the Application

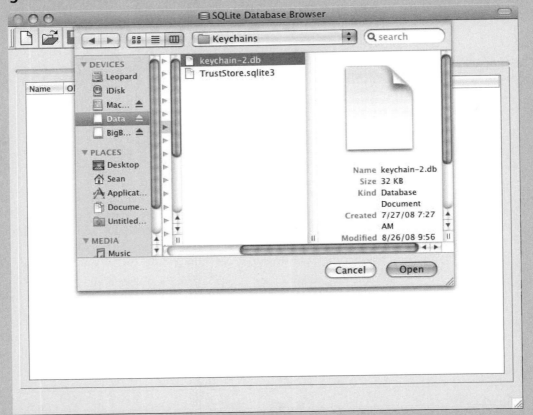

Continued

4. Once you open this folder, select the **Browse Data** tab, and then select **gnep** from the **Table** field, as shown in Figure 16.19.

Figure 16.19 Keychain Results

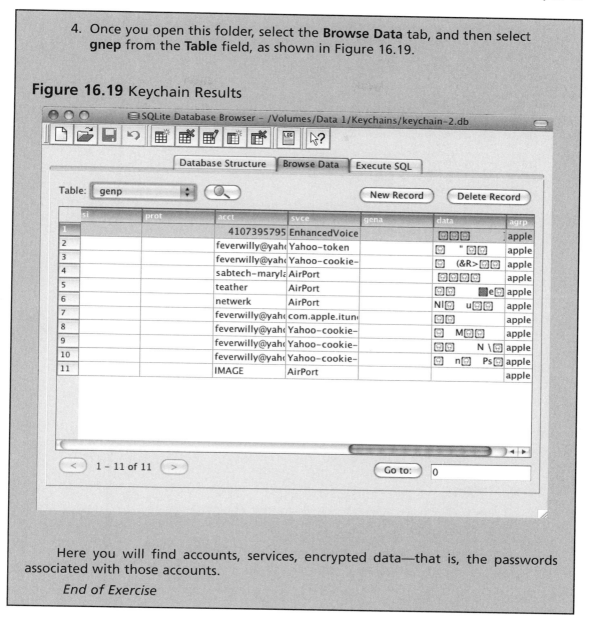

Here you will find accounts, services, encrypted data—that is, the passwords associated with those accounts.

End of Exercise

Returning to our discussion of the folder structure on the second partition of the iPhone, the **lib** folder does not contain any evidentiary matter. This is also true for the **local**, **lock** and **log** folders.

The **logs** folder below the log folder does have data. The first subfolder in the **logs** folder is the **Apple Support** folder. This folder has one **general.log** file. As shown in Figure 16.20, this log file gives us the OS version, iPhone model and serial number. It also lists dates, time, and service names.

Figure 16.20 General Log Excerpt

```
●  ●  ●                                          general.log
Device Software Diagnostic Log
Version: 2
OS-Version: iPhone OS 2.0 (5A347)
Model: iPhone1,2
Serial Number: 88828PZGY7K
Created: 7/27/2008 4:26:34 -0700

2008-07-27 10:59:20 -0400,115,DC90FE33-F0C8-4220-B1CC-F4D5AB019E66,1
2008-07-27 10:59:54 -0400,109,DFC03C16-D292-414D-BE9E-61894A88BBDA,1,http,KERN_PROTECTION_FAILURE at 0x00000010
2008-07-27 10:59:54 -0400,109,123D0020-6F0A-4747-A374-D87459240329,1,http,KERN_PROTECTION_FAILURE at 0x00000010
2008-07-27 10:59:54 -0400,109,AE7FB076-E9DF-451C-9F91-7B79C8907E0A,1,http,KERN_PROTECTION_FAILURE at 0x00000010
2008-07-27 10:59:54 -0400,109,F38F6759-EDC5-40E6-AD3E-3D4AF225F18E,1,http,KERN_PROTECTION_FAILURE at 0x00000010
2008-07-27 10:59:54 -0400,109,BFDA8067-FBC5-4EEA-B575-76DA18AB22A3,1,http,KERN_PROTECTION_FAILURE at 0x00000010
2008-07-27 13:38:12 -0400,198,1C0AE54D-9416-4F84-9395-1BB0FC077558,Bible,SpringBoard,32550912
2008-07-27 13:40:20 -0400,198,AAC8A3FF-1537-4554-A2FE-2281BDBB9A0D,Bible,SpringBoard,36954112
2008-07-27 13:43:02 -0400,198,581BE759-AF37-4FE3-BA01-18FB64AC2593,Where,SpringBoard,29523968
2008-07-27 13:44:51 -0400,198,164F319E-22F7-4E8D-B2E0-8771FCA6C929,Where,SpringBoard,29470720
2008-07-27 17:03:24 -0400,198,2CDBCB36-AFF5-4594-8D0A-8E55B6EC161F,MobileSafari,MobileSafari,35274752
2008-07-27 17:06:15 -0400,198,326ADB97-4B15-49AB-85EC-5A01FF9A5945,MobileSafari,MobileSafari,35160064
```

The next subfolder in the **logs** folder is labeled **baseband**. Even though baseband deals with the communication partition, which deals directly with the cellular and GPS functions of the iPhone, this folder is empty.

The last subfolder in the **logs** folder is **CrashReporter**. Here are numerous log files. These logs deal with services such as mediaserverd, MobileSafari, and reset counter. In general, these log files contain little or no evidentiary value.

The **Managed Preferences** folder has a subfolder called **mobile**. Examination of this revealed nothing of evidentiary value.

The **Library** and **Media** folders are the holy grail of the iPhone. They store the bulk of the data on the iPhone. The **Applications** subfolder contains all the preloaded applications on the iPhone and those that have been downloaded either as paid or free from the "App Store." All the application subfolders have files that appear to be GUID numbered filenames and represent applications. The applications are bundled and structured as follows:

- **Documents** – Here there can be items located that are of evidentiary value.

- **Library** – Here you can locate the *.plist* for that application.

- **Tmp** – Normally nothing is located here.

- **iTunesMetadata.plist** – You will find the application name, purchase information, username, e-mail addresses, etc., as shown in Figure 16.21.

Figure 16.21 *iTunesMetadata.plist*

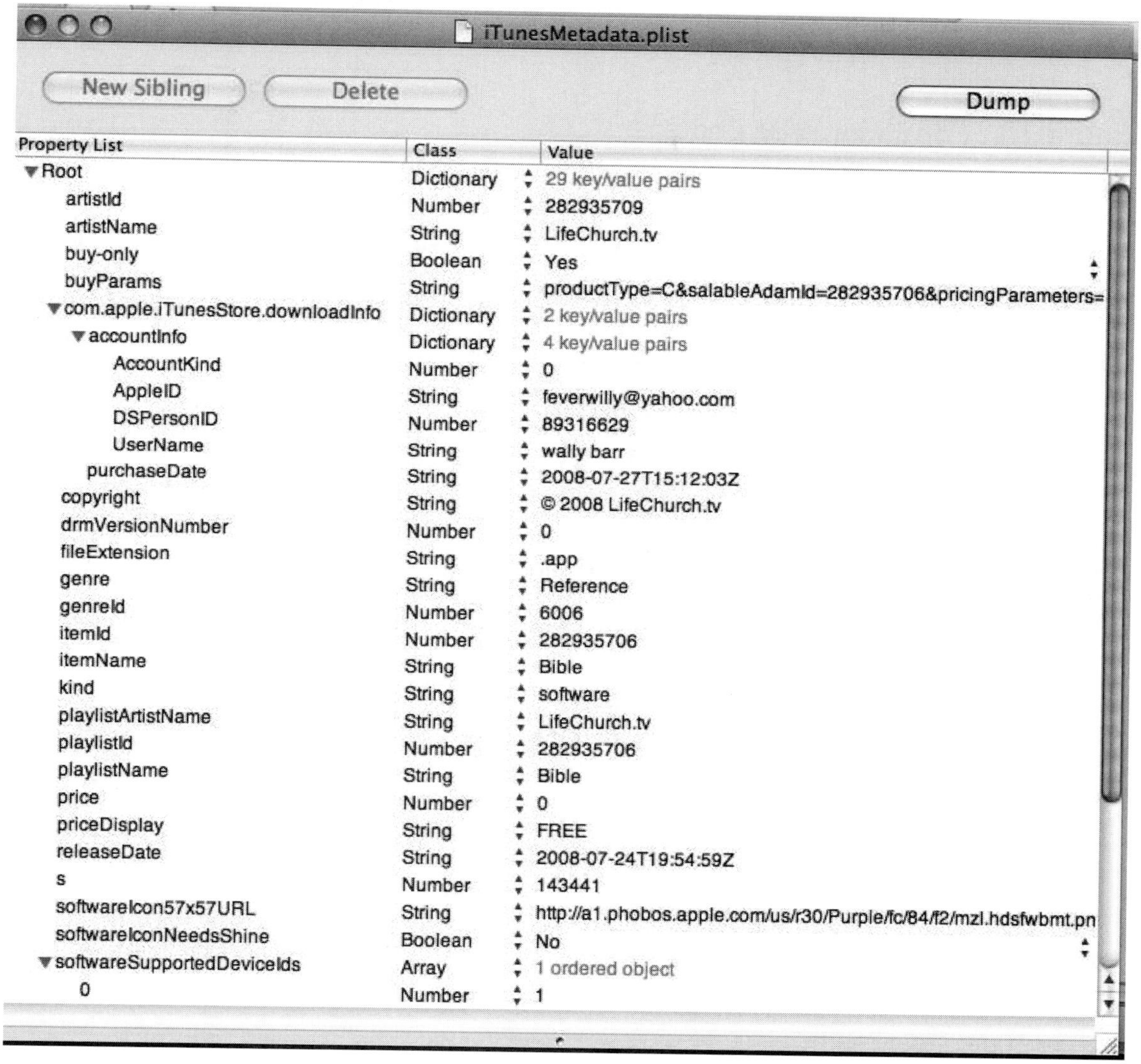

Property List	Class	Value
▼ Root	Dictionary	29 key/value pairs
artistId	Number	282935709
artistName	String	LifeChurch.tv
buy-only	Boolean	Yes
buyParams	String	productType=C&salableAdamId=282935706&pricingParameters=
▼ com.apple.iTunesStore.downloadInfo	Dictionary	2 key/value pairs
▼ accountInfo	Dictionary	4 key/value pairs
AccountKind	Number	0
AppleID	String	feverwilly@yahoo.com
DSPersonID	Number	89316629
UserName	String	wally barr
purchaseDate	String	2008-07-27T15:12:03Z
copyright	String	© 2008 LifeChurch.tv
drmVersionNumber	Number	0
fileExtension	String	.app
genre	String	Reference
genreId	Number	6006
itemId	Number	282935706
itemName	String	Bible
kind	String	software
playlistArtistName	String	LifeChurch.tv
playlistId	Number	282935706
playlistName	String	Bible
price	Number	0
priceDisplay	String	FREE
releaseDate	String	2008-07-24T19:54:59Z
s	Number	143441
softwareIcon57x57URL	String	http://a1.phobos.apple.com/us/r30/Purple/fc/84/f2/mzl.hdsfwbmt.pn
softwareIconNeedsShine	Boolean	No
▼ softwareSupportedDeviceIds	Array	1 ordered object
0	Number	1

To view the contents of a bundled application you should ctrl-click on the application name, for example AOL Radio, and select **Show Package Contents**, as shown in Figure 16.22.

Figure 16.22 Show Package Contents

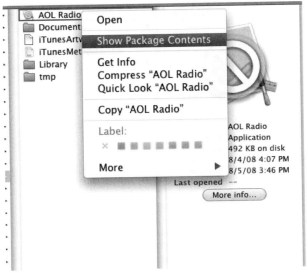

Once you show the contents of a package, you will see a breakdown of all items in the package, as shown in Figure 16.23. This is a good sample of the types of items needed for the application to run on the iPhone.

Figure 16.23 Application Contents

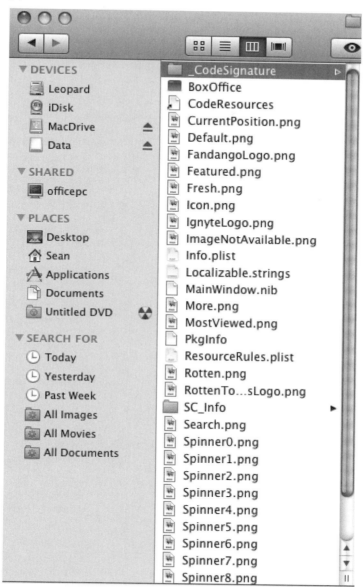

The applications that have been downloaded will determine what kind of artifacts you can locate on an iPhone. For example, there is an application that presents a slide show of images that could be downloaded and saved in the same location where pictures are saved.

For example, you could also find a folder called **GRiS**. This is an application for the Google Reader iPhone Sync. **GRiS** is another application that was installed along with the jailbreak.

Library

The following folder is the **Library** folder, which contains a lot of significant data. The directory structure of the **Library** folder is displayed in Figure 16.24.

Figure 16.24 Library Folder Structure for the Mobile User

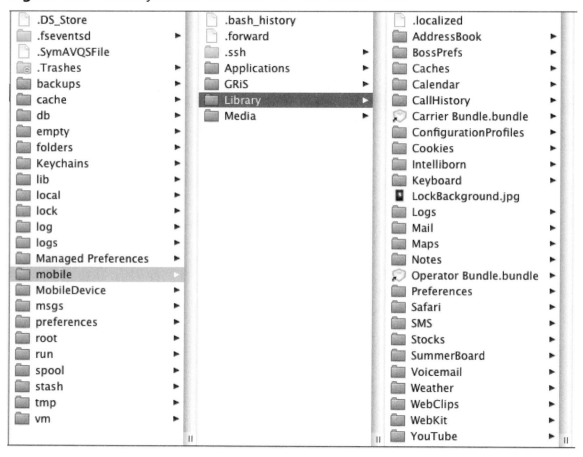

Address Book

Let's first examine the **Address Book** subfolder within the **Library** folder. There are two files, **AddressBookimages.SQLitedb** and **AddressBook.SQLitedb**. The **AddressBook.SQLitedb** is a database of contacts that sync with a Mac. To examine this file, you will have to use the application SQLite Database Browser, as shown in Figure 16.25. See Exercise 16.2 to learn how to export data from SQLite Database Browser to another file. Then in the **Table** drop-down menu, select **ABPerson**. This will give you contact information that includes creation and modification dates.

Figure 16.25 SQLite Database Browser Address Results

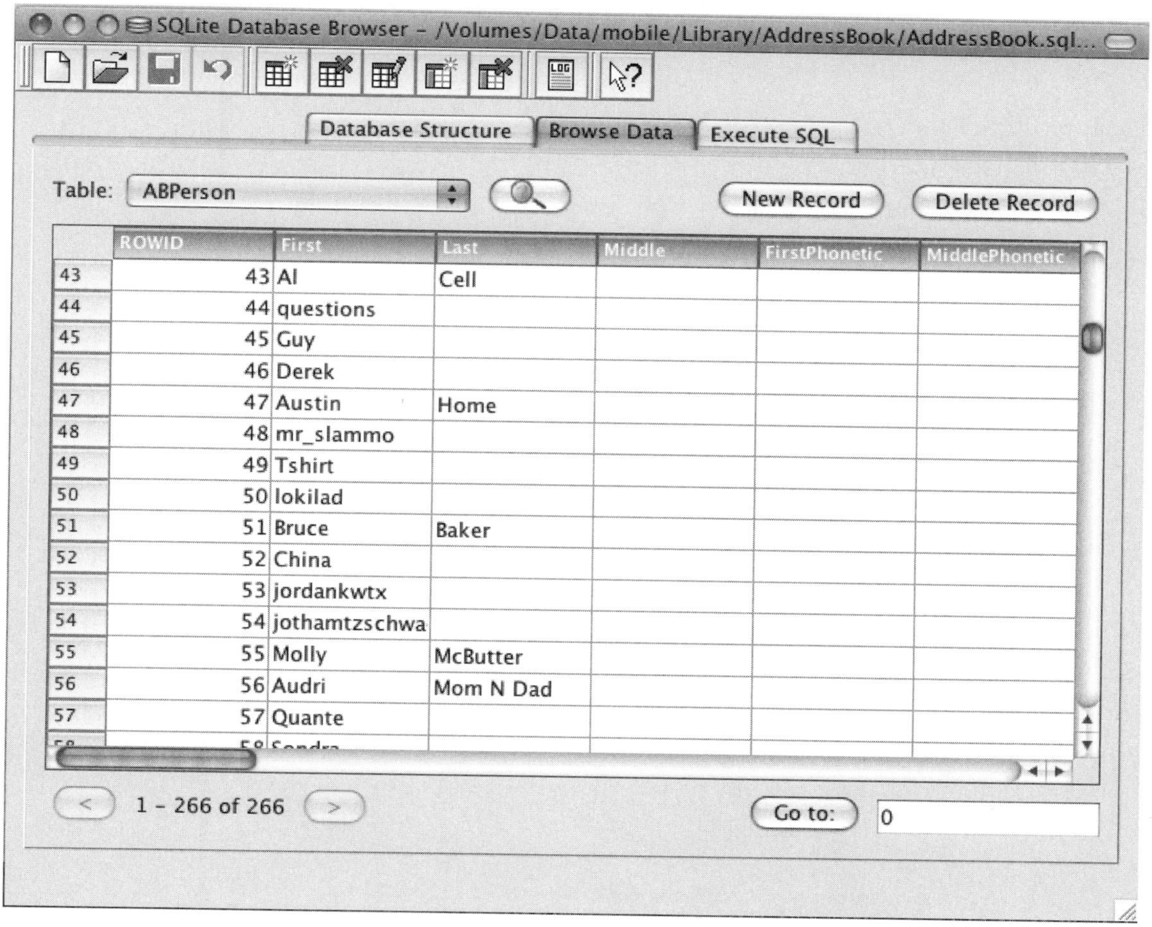

Configuring & Implementing…

Exercise 16.2: Exporting Data from SQLite Database Browser to Another File

To export data from SQLite Database Browser to another file, for example, a .csv file, take the following steps:

1. From the SQLite Database Browser menu bar, select **File > Export, >Table as CSV file** as shown in Figure 16.26.

Figure 16.26 Using SQLite to Export Data

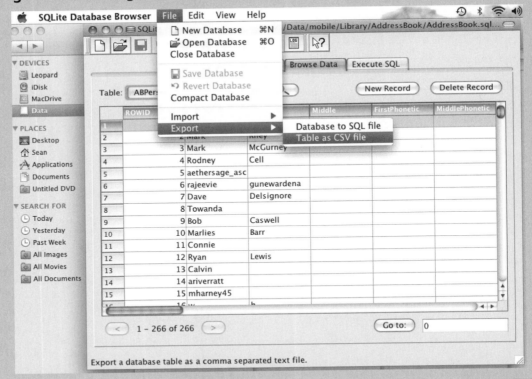

Continued

2. In the **Choose Table to export as CSV text** window, go to the **Table** field and select **ABPerson**, as shown in Figure 16.27.

Figure 16.27 Choose table to export as CSV text Window

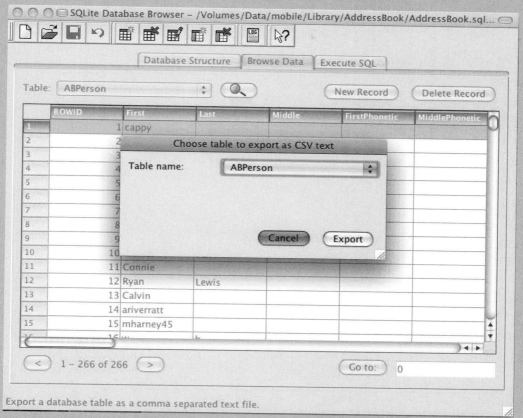

3. A finder window will appear and ask for a filename and location to save the file. Name the file as "AddressBook," then select **Save**, as shown in Figure 16.28.

Continued

Figure 16.28 SQLite Database Browser's Export Save As Window

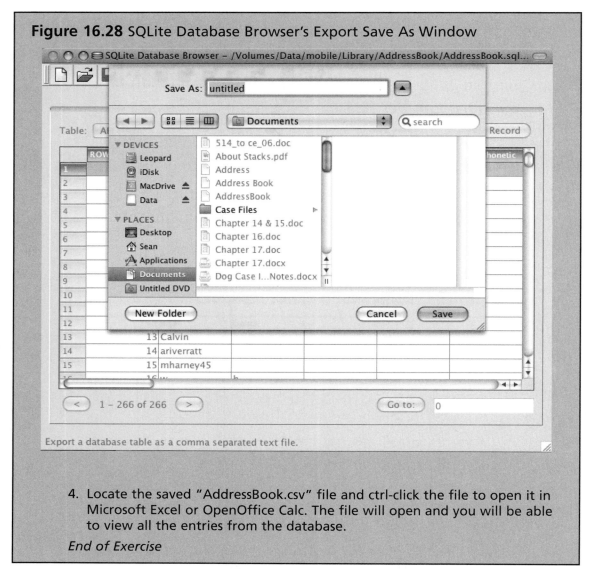

4. Locate the saved "AddressBook.csv" file and ctrl-click the file to open it in Microsoft Excel or OpenOffice Calc. The file will open and you will be able to view all the entries from the database.

End of Exercise

Boss Prefs

The **Boss Prefs** folder is a file from the jailbreak. Within this folder is an interesting file, **df.txt**. The **df.txt** file, as shown in Figure 16.29, shows the partitions and mount points of the iPhone.

Figure 16.29 The *df.txt* File Showing Partitions and Mount Points

```
                    df.txt
Filesystem        Size  Used  Avail  Use%  Mounted on
/dev/disk0s1      1.1G  439M  598M    43%  /
devfs              25K   25K     0   100%  /dev
/dev/disk0s2       15G  8.1G   6.1G   57%  /private/var
```

Caches

In the **/mobile/Library/Caches** folder are several *.plist* files that track all the applications on the iPhone. The *com.apple.installation.plist* file lists all the native and downloaded applications on the iPhone. Also, in the **Cache** folder you may find several other folders such as **MapTiles** and **Safari**. The **Safari** folder maintains thumbnails of Web pages that were visited in Safari so the user can return to those pages faster, as shown in Figure 16.30.

Figure 16.30 Saved Web Page as Seen from the iPhone

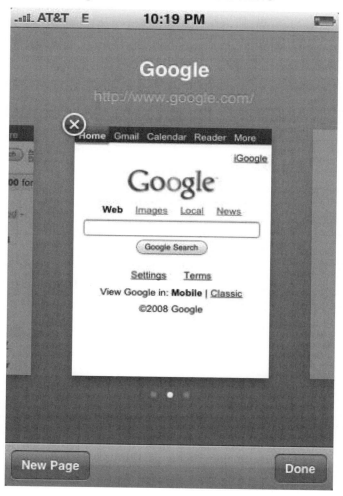

Mobile Calendar

The **Calendar** folder will also contain another database file that you will have to open with SQLite Database Browser. Follow the directions as stated in the Address Book.

Figure 16.31 shows a view of the Calendar Event table using SQLite Database Browser. There you will see the summary of the event, start and end dates, and time zone information.

Figure 16.31 SQLite Database Browser Showing iPhone Calendar Information

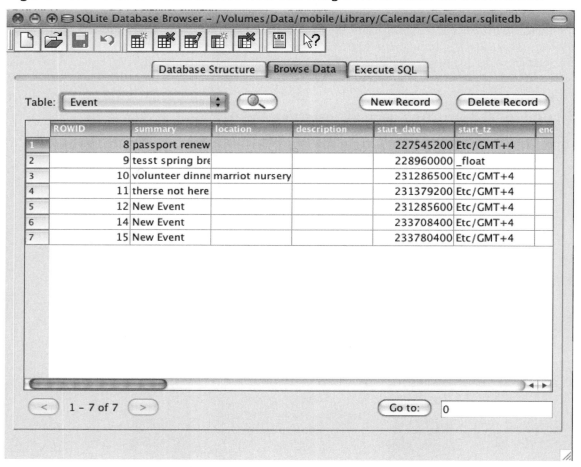

ROWID		summary	location	description	start_date	start_tz	end
1	8	passport renew			227545200	Etc/GMT+4	
2	9	tesst spring bre			228960000	_float	
3	10	volunteer dinne	marriot nursery		231286500	Etc/GMT+4	
4	11	therse not here			231379200	Etc/GMT+4	
5	12	New Event			231285600	Etc/GMT+4	
6	14	New Event			233708400	Etc/GMT+4	
7	15	New Event			233780400	Etc/GMT+4	

Call History

In **/mobile/Library/** folder, there is a file called *call_history.db*. Open this file with SQLite Database Browser. Select **Call** from the Table drop down. The database can also be exported to a .csv file, as previously discussed. When the values appear, as shown in Figure 16.32, the address values column refers to phone numbers. There is also date and duration of calls. The logs do not differentiate between incoming and outgoing calls, just a straight log of all calls received or missed. From this log it is difficult to tell which calls were missed. As with other types of phones, it may be necessary to retrieve further information from the carrier. The values in the **Date** field can be converted using the CFAbsoluteTimeConverter.

Figure 16.32 iPhone Call Log

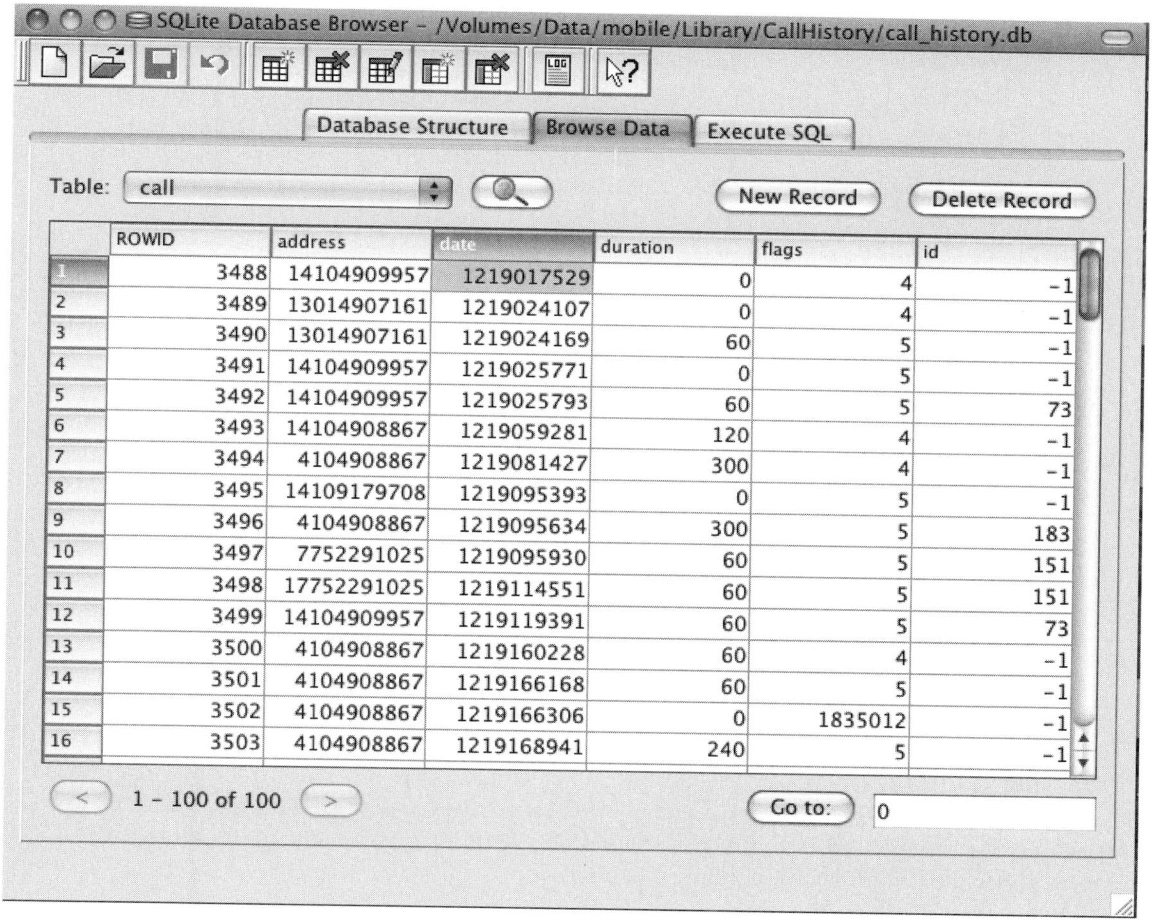

	ROWID	address	date	duration	flags	id
1	3488	14104909957	1219017529	0	4	-1
2	3489	13014907161	1219024107	0	4	-1
3	3490	13014907161	1219024169	60	5	-1
4	3491	14104909957	1219025771	0	5	-1
5	3492	14104909957	1219025793	60	5	73
6	3493	14104908867	1219059281	120	4	-1
7	3494	4104908867	1219081427	300	4	-1
8	3495	14109179708	1219095393	0	5	-1
9	3496	4104908867	1219095634	300	5	183
10	3497	7752291025	1219095930	60	5	151
11	3498	17752291025	1219114551	60	5	151
12	3499	14104909957	1219119391	60	5	73
13	3500	4104908867	1219160228	60	4	-1
14	3501	4104908867	1219166168	60	5	-1
15	3502	4104908867	1219166306	0	1835012	-1
16	3503	4104908867	1219168941	240	5	-1

Cookies

The next folder within the **Library** subfolder of note is the **Cookies** folder. There is the *Cookies.plist* file, as shown in Figure 16.33, within that subfolder. The *.plist* file contains much of the same information as discussed in Chapter 8. The *.plist* file gives domain names and cookie expirations.

Figure 16.33 *iPhone Cookies.plist* File

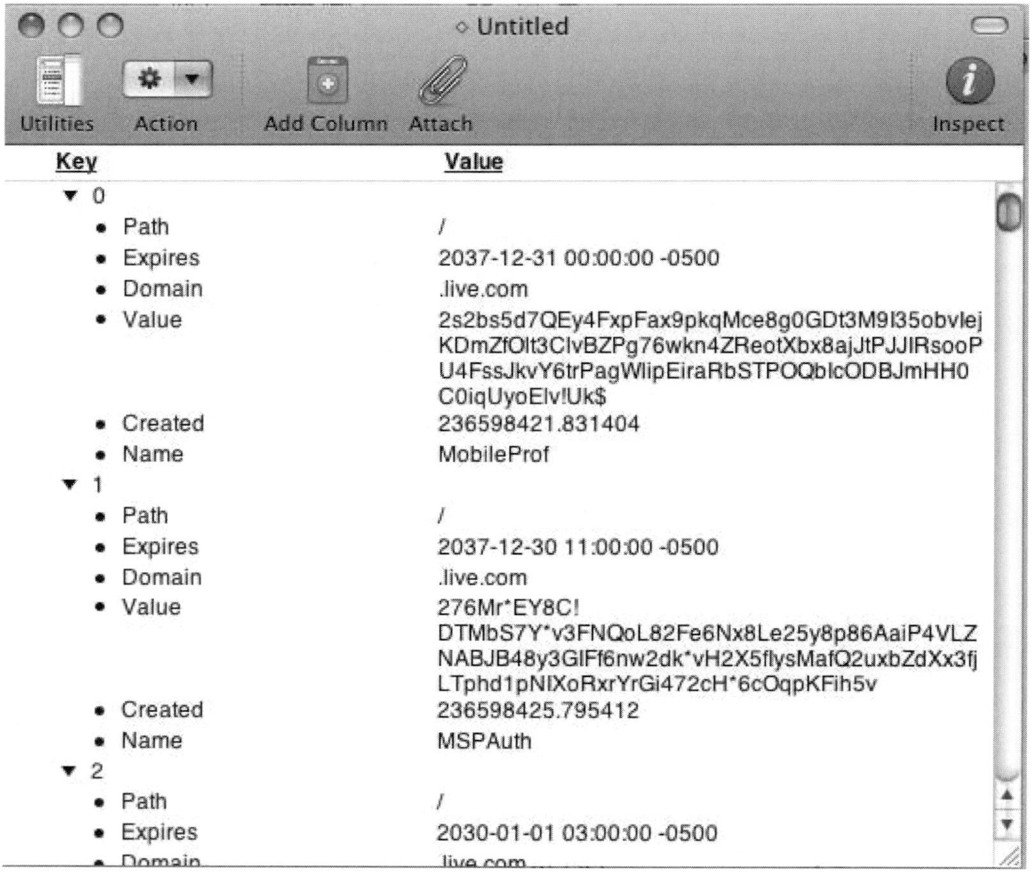

Keyboard

The **Keyboard** subfolder of **Library** contains a file called *dynamic-text.dat.* This file is a list of words that is used when the autocorrect function is used on the iPhone. This file could possibly have significant evidentiary value, depending on the user.

Background/Wallpaper Image

Between the **Keyboard** and **Logs** folders there is a .jpg file in the root of the **Library** folder. In this case, the picture labeled LockBackground.jpg, is the wallpaper image that is seen when the iPhone reverts to the screen lock, as shown in Figure 16.34.

Figure 16.34 The Background Wallpaper for Screen Lock

Logs

The log files in the **Logs** folder duplicate those files that were found in the first partition. The **Logs** folder is located directly below the LockBackground.jpg, as shown in Figure 16.34.

Mobile Mail

The next subfolder of the **Library** folder to discuss is the **Mail** folder. This is where you will find e-mail account information.

In the **Mail** folder is the *Accounst.plist* file, which shows all e-mail account information from the iPhone, as shown in Figure 16.35.

Figure 16.35 iPhone E-mail *Accounts.plist*

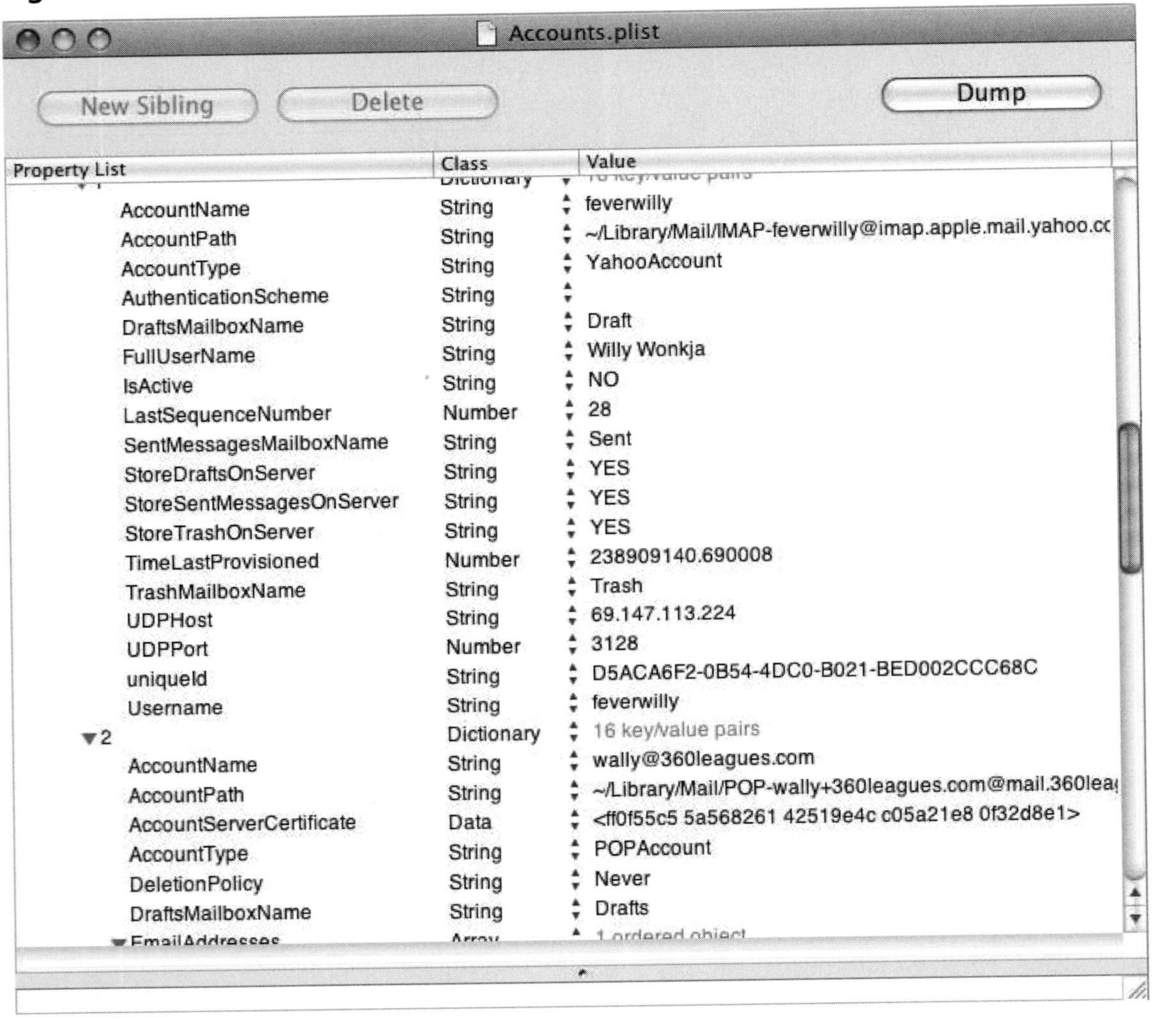

After the *Accounts.plist* file there could be several folders that contain e-mail messages based on the number of accounts found in the *.plist* file. It is possible to find POP and IMAP accounts on the phone as well as mail from Exchange, Gmail, Yahoo, MobileMe, AOL, and so on. Based on the user's settings, you may be able to locate items in the Inbox, Outbox, Sent, and Trash folders.

One of the better tools to extract iPhone e-mail is Emailchemy (see Exercise 16.3). This application will extract the e-mails from the **Mail** folder and convert them so that you can view them through **Mail** on your Mac. Emailchemy is available at www.weirdkid.com/products/emailchemy. Remember that it is not a free product, however. They also have a forensic edition on their Web site. The following is an exercise on how to extract e-mails from the iPhone and view them with the Mac **Mail** application.

Configuring & Implementing...

Exercise 16.3: Using Third-Party Software to Extract iPhone E-mail

The following is the procedure to examine e-mails from an iPhone using Emailchemy.

1. Open the **Emailchemy** application from the DVD that accompanies this book.

2. From **Step 1** of the Email Conversion Wizard, select **OS X Mail**, as shown in Figure 16.36.

Figure 16.36 Emailchemy Step 1

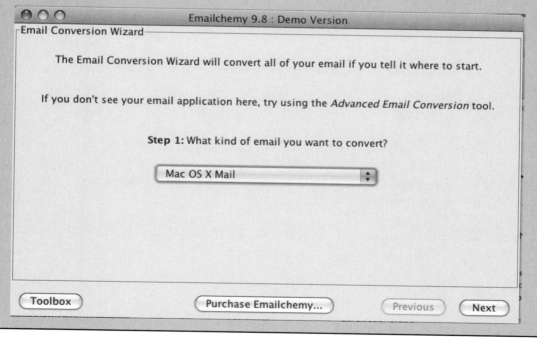

Continued

3. Click the **Next** button.

4. In **Step 2** select **Browse** and navigate to the **/Data/Library/Mail/** folder. Emailchemy will add additional path information after selecting your folder, as shown in Figure 16.37.

Figure 16.37 Emailchemy Step 2 and Step 3

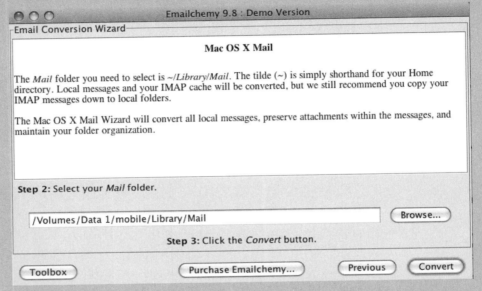

5. To perform **Step 3**, click the **Convert** button.

6. Click the **New Folder** button, located in the lower left corner of the **Save Converted Mail As** dialog box.

7. Create a folder to gather the results, as shown in Figure 16.38.

Continued

Figure 16.38 Saving the Converted File

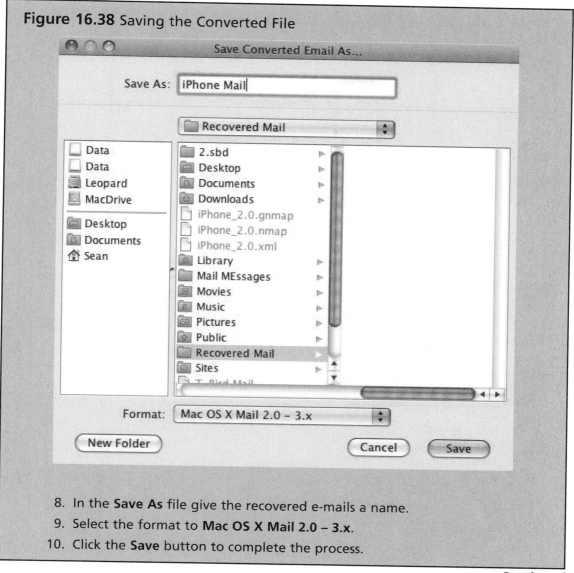

8. In the **Save As** file give the recovered e-mails a name.

9. Select the format to **Mac OS X Mail 2.0 – 3.x**.

10. Click the **Save** button to complete the process.

Continued

Emailchemy will convert and place the e-mails into the folder you created. Navigate to that folder and double-click on any file and they should open with **Mail**. If they don't, ctrl-click the file and open it with the Mac **Mail** application. View e-mails, as shown in Figure 16.39.

Figure 16.39 E-mail from iPhone

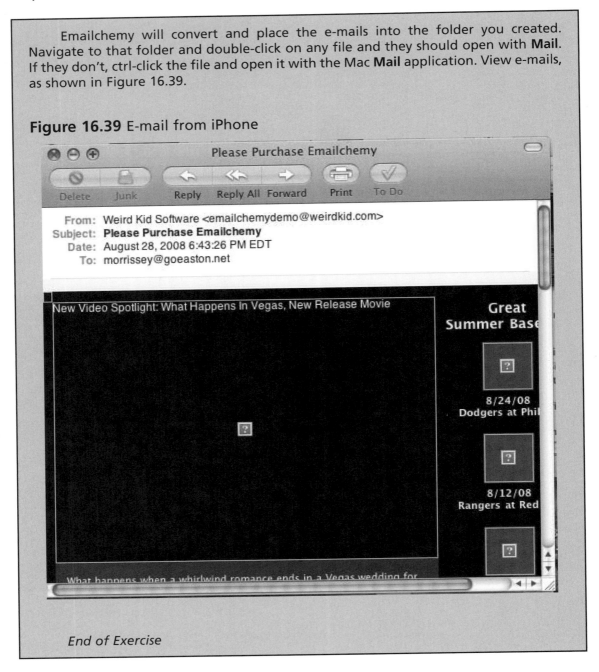

End of Exercise

You may not be successful opening IMAP e-mail messages with Emailchemy. There is, however, another application that can assist you with IMAP mail.

File Juicer is a proprietary program that can parse multiple file types. It can take the IMAP folders and parse the mail and embedded attachments. File Juicer is available from http://echoone.com.

To view IMAP e-mail using File Juicer, complete the following steps:

1. Start the File Juicer application
2. Select **File > Open** and point File Juicer to one of the folders you wish to examine, as shown in Figure 16.40.

Figure 16.40 File Juicer

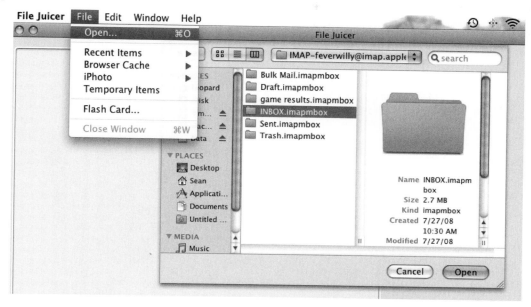

File Juicer will begin to parse the files, and by default places the results on the desktop. The results folder has a naming convention of [*BOX Name* juice], for example, INBOX juice. The data is separated by file type in a separate folder. You can go through each folder, as shown in Figure 16.41, and see if there is anything of evidentiary value and attach it to your report.

Figure 16.41 File Juicer Folders

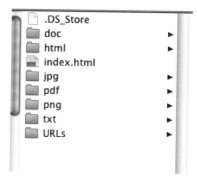

Mobile Maps

The **Maps** folder is the next subfolder of interest within the **Library** folder. The **Maps** folder is located directly underneath the **Mail** folder. Inside this folder are two property lists, *History.plist* and *Route.plist*.

When a user accesses the Google Maps function, as shown in Figure 16.42, and creates a route to follow, that route will be entered in the *History.plist* file.

Figure 16.42 Google Maps on iPhone

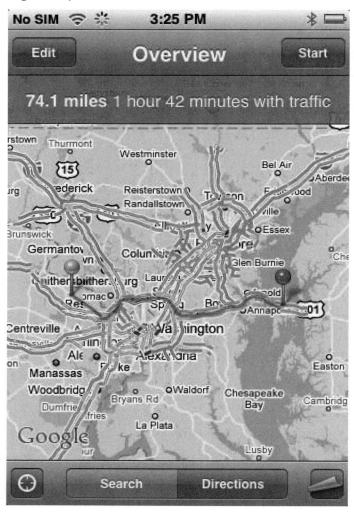

The *History.plist* file, as shown in Figure 16.43, can be very valuable because it can have starting and ending locations, and GPS tags.

Figure 16.43 *History.plist* File Showing GPS Tags

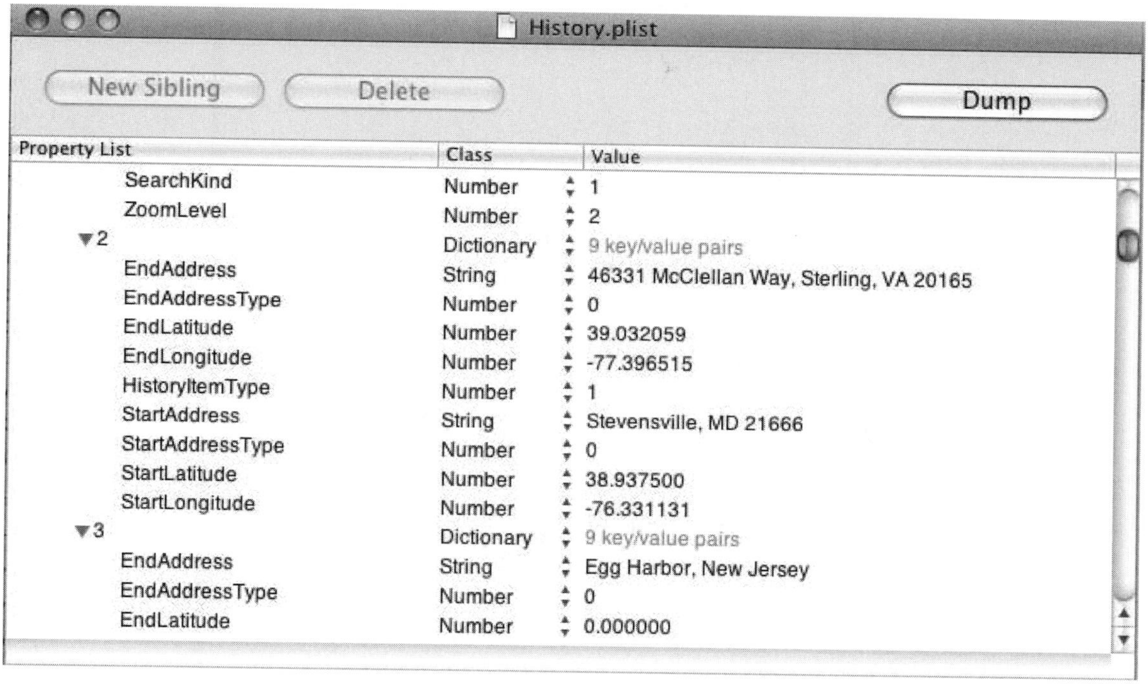

The second property list is *Routes.plist*. The *Routes.plist* file only contains a number that is the same as the zip code. The zip code used in the *Route.plist* file is the end route zip code, from the last route used on the iPhone.

Notes

The **Notes** subfolder within the **Library** folder is related to the **Notes** application on the iPhone. The Notes application allows users to type just about anything they want and keep these notes, as shown in Figure 16.44.

Figure 16.44 iPhone Notes Application

The **Notes** folder contains another database file. Again, this can be opened and viewed with SQLite Database Browser. The *notes.db* file, as seen in Figure 16.45, shows the dates, titles, and the body of the note. These can be exported, as discussed previously in this chapter. The creation date can be converted into actual date and time using CFAbsoluteTimeConverter.

Figure 16.45 iPhone *notes.db*

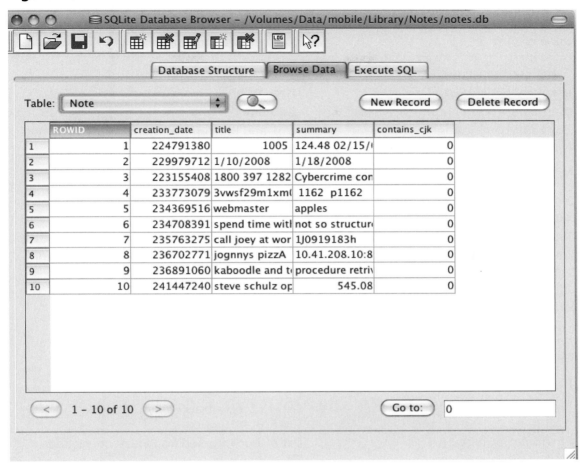

Preferences

The **Preferences** subfolder of the **Library** has a large amount of property lists. Table 16.1 is not a complete list, but contains the more significant property lists.

Table 16.1 Significant Property Lists from
the Preferences Subfolder of the iPhone Library

Name of plist	Type of Data Provided
.GlobalPreference.plist	Phone Number
[username]_AIM.plist	Username
[username]@hotmail.com_MSN.plist	Username
com.apple.commcenter.plist	ICCIS and IMSI information
com.apple.locationd.plist	Shows if Location services was enabled
com.apple.Maps.plist	Latitude and Longitude and if a Pin was dropped when a search was conducted in Maps
com.apple.mobilecal.plist	Time Zone information
com.apple.mobilemail.plist	E-mail fetching Dates
com.apple.mobilephone.speeddial.plist	Favorites Phone Numbers, Names and Phone Numbers
com.apple.mobilesafari.plist	Recent searches
com.apple.preferences.network.plist	Airplane Mode, Bluetooth and WiFi. "No" not activated, "Yes" Activated.
com.apple.Preferences.plist	Keyboard Language settings
com.apple.springboard.plist	Springboard is the GUI and the settings of the application icons that are displayed on the iPhone when operating.
com.apple.stocks.plist	Lists of Stocks tracked by the Stocks Application
com.apple.youtube.plist	List of bookmarked You Tube videos and viewed videos.
Mobile RSS	Database of RSS Feeds

There is one other property list in Preferences, called *com.apple.carrier.plist*. This file is an alias that points back to a file in the first partition called **/System/Library/CarrierBundles/310410/ carrier.plist**. The numbers 310410 are area codes for Maryland. The **/System/Library/ CarrierBundles/310410/carrier.plist** is an alias that points to a file in the same folder called **ATT_US.bundle**. ctrl-click on this file and select **Show Package Contents**. From here there are numerous files that deal with carrier information, as shown in Figure 16.46.

NOTE

The area codes will mirror those from where the iPhone was seized.

Figure 16.46 *Carrier.plist* File

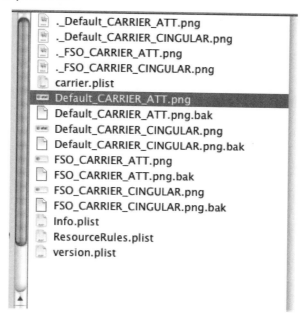

Mobile Safari

The **Safari** subfolder within the **Library** folder is related to the **Safari** application. Apple uses Mobile Safari as the default Internet browser on the iPhone. Within this folder there are two *.plist* files:

- History.plist
- Bookmarks.plist

The *Bookmarks.plist* file, as shown in Figure 16.47, will contain a list of the URLs of the bookmarked Web sites.

Figure 16.47 *Bookmarks.plist* File

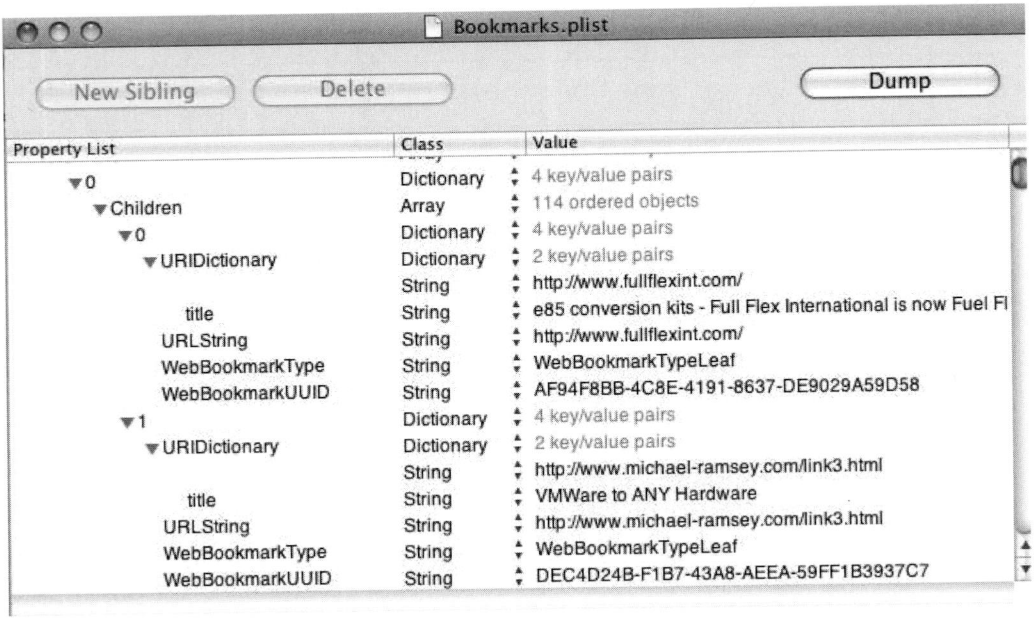

The *History.plist* file, as shown in Figure 16.48, is a similar list to the one that is found on the Mac OS X Leopard operating system. This property list shows URLs, dates, and names of the visited sites. The dates can be converted into actual dates and times with CFAbsoluteTimeConverter.

Figure 16.48 Safari *History.plist* File

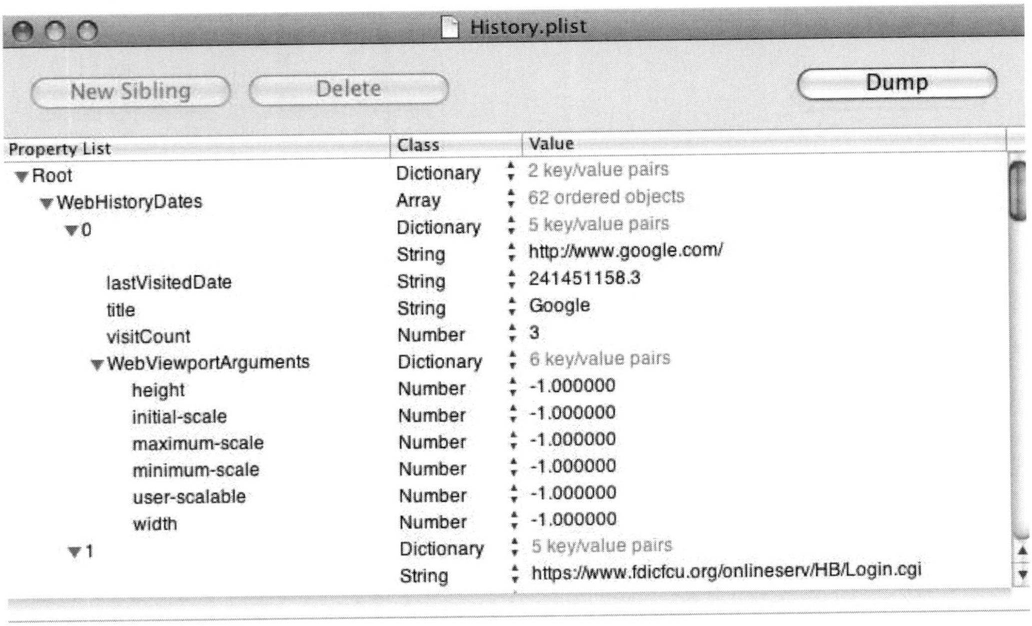

SMS (Short Message Service)

The **SMS** folder in the **Library** folder also contains a database that can be opened with SQLite Database Browser. Open this database with SQLite, as shown in Figure 16.49, then select **Message** in the **Table** field. Here you will find phone numbers, dates and times when they were sent or received, and complete messages. The dates and times can be converted into actual dates and times with CFAbsoluteTimeConverter and exported, as previously discussed.

Figure 16.49 SMS Database

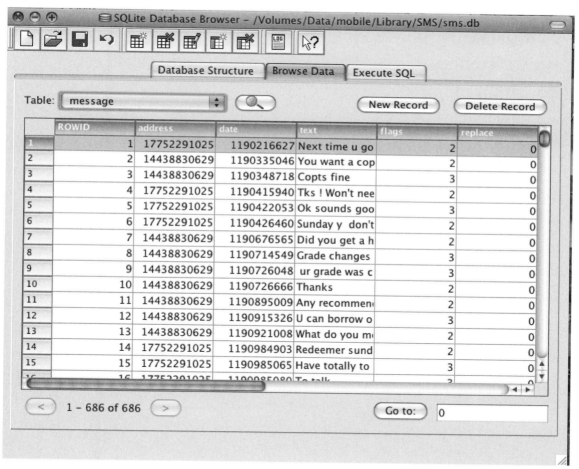

Voicemail

One reason to look at the **Voicemail** subfolder of the **Library** folder is that the voicemails on an iPhone are stored locally. Not all phones work this way. The messages that are stored in **/mobile/ Library/Voicemail** are stored with the .amr format, as shown in Figure 16.50. The .amr files are a speech encoding format that can be played with applications like QuickTime or Real Player.

Figure 16.50 iPhone Voicemail Folder

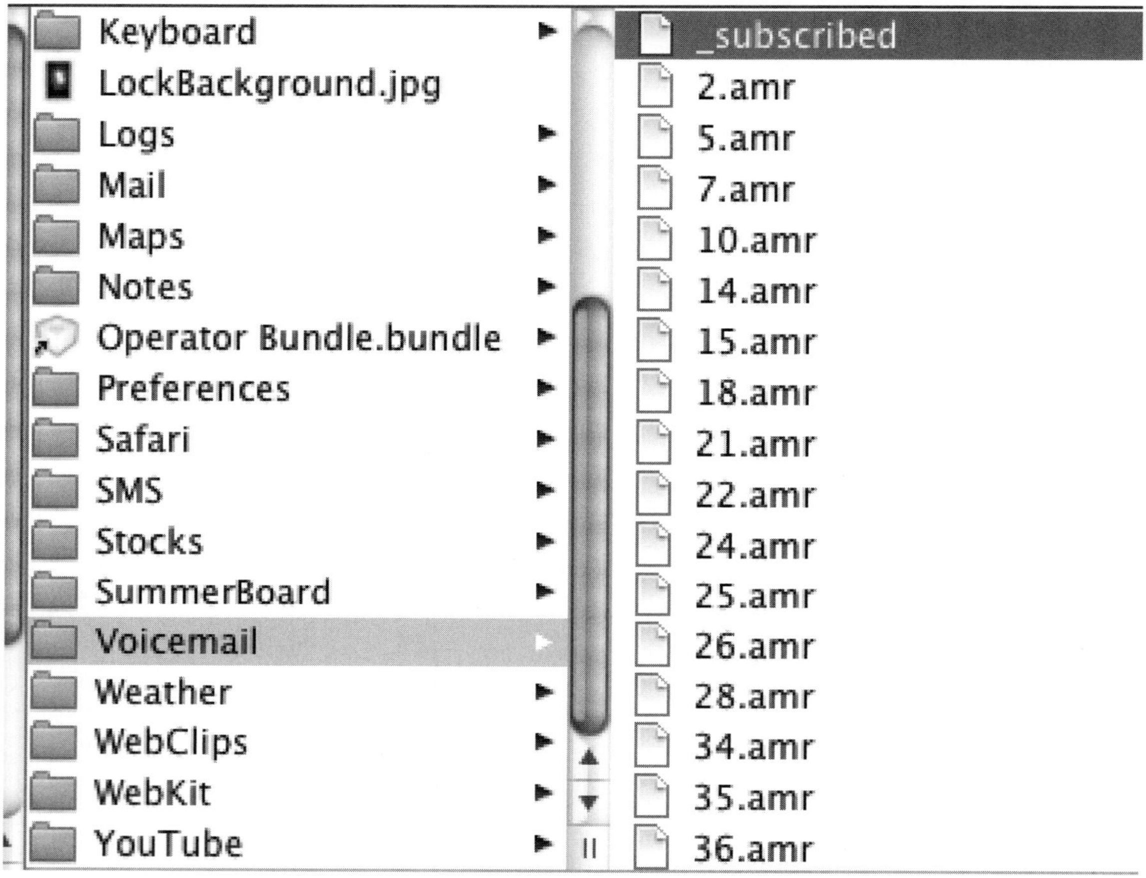

Within the **Voicemail** subfolder is a database file. This is opened with SQLite Database Browser, as shown in Figure 16.51. As with other .db files, go to the **Browse Data** tab and select **voicemail** from the **Table** field. The database file will store voice mail dates and times, phone number from the sender, and the date and time that the message was deleted.

Figure 16.51 *voicemail.db* Database File

ROWID	remote_uid	date	token	sender	callback_num	duration	expiration	trashed_date	fl
10	65	1218513595	Complete	4103370345	4103370345	25	1220907393		0
14	67	1218464827	Complete	4104908867	4104908867	10	1221056827		0
15	68	1218469423	Complete	4104908867	4104908867	29	1221061423		0
18	71	1218625321	Complete	4104908867	4104908867	56	1221217321		0
21	74	1218810236	Complete	4437397839	4437397839	13	1221402236		0
22	75	1218916754	Complete	4104908867	4104908867	77	1221508754		0
24	77	1219024142	Complete	3014907161	3014907161	18	1221616142		0
25	78	1219166393	Complete	4104908867	4104908867	70	1221758393		0
26	79	1219201168	Complete	4104908867	4104908867	48	1221793168		0
28	81	1219494824	Complete	4104908867	4104908867	16	1222086824		0
34	87	1219682499	Complete	4439951306	4439951306	4	1222274499		0
35	88	1219698183	Complete	4107141413	4107141413	13	1222290183		0
36	89	1219700522	Complete	4104908867	4104908867	56	1222292522		0
37	90	1219759800	Complete	7708588888	7708588888	112	1222351800		0
38	91	1219849283	Complete	4105960630	4105960630	12	1222441283		0
39	92	1219852683	Complete	4104908867	4104908867	56	1222444683	241547334	
40	93	1219930052	Complete	7752291025	7752291025	48	1222522052	241623597	

1 – 20 of 20

YouTube

The last subfolder of the **Library** folder that will be discussed is the **YouTube** sub folder. In the **YouTube** sub folder is a *bookmark.plist* file. This *.plist* file holds a list of bookmarked YouTube sites. The next file is Video Cache, as shown in Figure 16.52. This file is a database of YouTube videos, and shows URLs, titles, authors, dates, times, and descriptions. These files can be of evidentiary value based on the type of investigation.

Figure 16.52 Video Cache

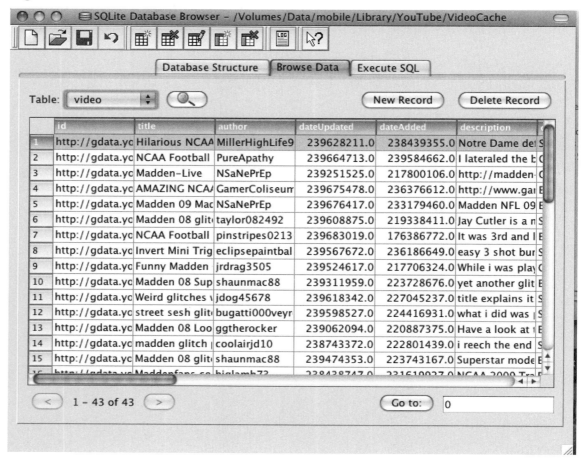

Media Folder

The **Media** folder is another subfolder of the **mobile** folder and is located directly below the **Library** folder. Within the **Media** folder is a **DCIM** subfolder, located at **/mobile/Media/DCIM**. The **DCIM** folder contains all the images on the iPhone. Within the **DCIM** folder, there can be two subfolders named **100APPLE** and **999APPLE**, as shown in Figure 16.53. The images within the **100APPLE** folder are taken with the internal iPhone camera. The images within the **999APPLE** folder contain screenshots that can be taken from the iPhone by holding down the **HOME** button and pressing the **POWER** button at the same time.

Figure 16.53 100APPLE and 999APPLE Folders

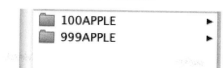

To view these 100APPLE and 999APPLE images, perform the following steps:

1. From your Mac forensic workstation, open the Finder.
2. Navigate to **/Users/[*username*]/Pictures/iPhoto Library**.
3. Delete all items contained in this folder.
4. Start the **iPhoto** application.
5. Select **File > Import to Library**, as shown in Figure 16.54.

Figure 16.54 Import Photos

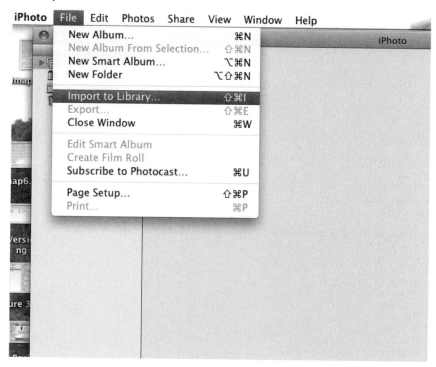

6. Navigate to the **100APPLE** folder and click **Import**, as shown in Figure 16.55.

Figure 16.55 Importing Images to iPhoto

7. Repeat steps 1 through 6 with the **999APPLE** folder.

8. Open **iPhoto** and review the photos.

iPhoto can display image Exif data. To see the Exif data:

9. Select an image.

10. ctrl-click and select **Show Info**, as shown in Figure 16.56.

Figure 16.56 iPhoto Show Info

11.   View the Photo data, as shown in Figure 16.57.

Figure 16.57 Exif Data

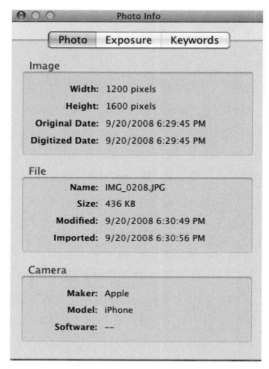

If you click on the **Exposure** tab in the **Photo Info** window, you will see fields for GPS tags. The location services must be turned on in order for data to be present. There have been some reported problems with the GPS tags even with the location services turned on. One of these problems is that the images did not have GPS tags. This has been fixed with Firmware 2.1, so be aware that you can find GPS tags on photos. Figure 16.58 shows the fields where you will find GPS data. The Exif data shown in Figure 16.58 came from a 3G iPhone with location services turned on. Even on First-generation iPhones it is possible to locate GPS tags on images. However, these tags aren't from a GPS service, but are from the triangulation of cell towers.

Figure 16.58 GPS Tag Fields for iPhones

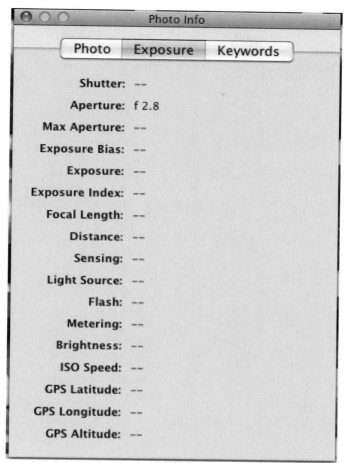

iTunes_Control

The **iTunes_Control** folder is another important folder within the **Media** Folder. The **iTunes_Control** folder, located at **/mobile/Media/iTunes_Control**, holds media synced from iTunes. Within the **iTunes_Control** folder there can be multiple audio and video files. These files can also be located on the syncing computer. There is album artwork located at the **/mobile/Media/iTunes_Control/Artwork** folder which contains more .ithmb files that can be opened with Keith's iPod Photo Reader. As discussed in Chapter 14, locate the Keith's iPod Photo Reader settings table and look for settings for the First-generation iPhone, but check the box for "Flip Indian." Another subfolder of the **iTunes_Control** folder is called **iTunes**. Within that folder are several text files and .plist files that refer to playlists, Podcasts, TV shows, and movie rentals as shown in Figure 16.59.

Figure 16.59 iTunes Folder

After the **iTunes** subfolder is the **Music** subfolder, which is similar to the **Music** subfolder on an iPod.

iPhotos

Next is another image folder at **/mobile/media/Photos**. This folder contains images that are synced through iTunes from the Mac's iPhoto library. Again, these pictures reside in *.ithmb* format. Again Keith's iPod Photo Reader will be needed to view these images. The way to view these files using Keith's iPod Photo Reader is discussed in Chapter 14. The settings are the same as those on the First-generation iPhone. This concludes the examination of the **Media** directory.

Bash History

Before leaving the mobile user domain, there is one last file to consider, the *.bash_history* file, as shown in Figure 16.60. This file shows all command line activity from a jailbroken iPhone.

Figure 16.60 *.bash_history* File

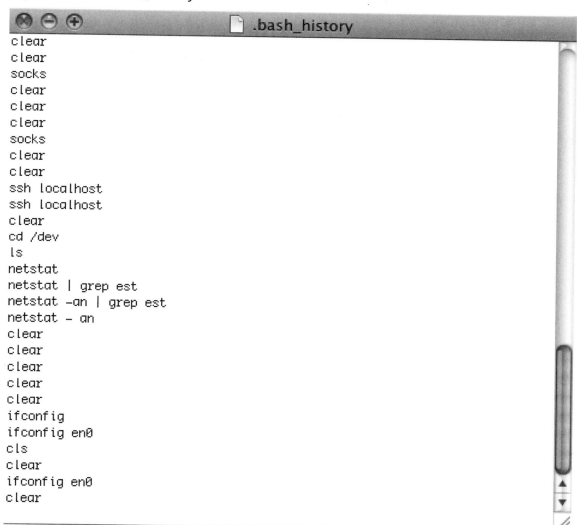

Root

The **root** folder has some of the same data that you can find in the Mobile user domain. The root/ Library folder, as shown in Figure 16.61 shows all its subfolders.

NOTE

Do not confuse the root of the drive, or "/", with the root folder, which is often referred to as "root's home directory." Root is another user on the iPhone, that also contains data.

Figure 16.61 /root/Library/ Folder

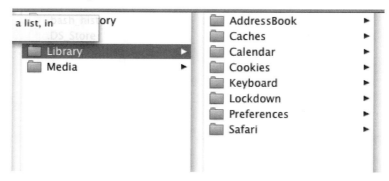

Now let's examine some of the subfolders within the root folder.

Address Book

Within the **Library** subdirectory, there is a folder called **AddressBook. AddressBook** also has an address database file. This database file has the same structure as seen in the previous file, but the database is empty.

Caches

There is a *cache.plist* file that contains the last GPS fix along with date and time stamps. The *cells.plist* file contains a date and time for last purge. Next there is a *clients-b.plist* that contains black listed applications. There is also a WiFi folder that contains .dat files that don't contain any readable text.

Calendar

The **Calendar** folder within the **Library** subfolder of **root** also contains an empty database.

Lockdown

The **Lockdown** folder has the public and private keys to activate iPhones through iTunes in the *data_Ark.plist* file. A user must activate an iPhone through iTunes; the activation information is held in this *.plist* file, as shown in Figure 16.62.

Figure 16.62 iPhone Activation Information

Property List	Class	Value
-DeviceName	String	mobile iPhone
-FirmwareVersion	String	iBoot-320.20
-ProtocolVersion	String	1
-SBLockdownEverRegisteredKey	Boolean	No
-SIMStatus	String	kCTSIMSupportSIMStatusReady
com.apple.mobile.iTunes.store-AccountKind	Number	0
com.apple.mobile.iTunes.store-AppleID	String	feverwilly@yahoo.com
▶ com.apple.mobile.iTunes.store-downloaded-apps	Array	13 ordered objects
com.apple.mobile.iTunes.store-DSPersonID	Number	89316629
▶ com.apple.mobile.iTunes.store-KnownAccounts	Array	1 ordered object
com.apple.mobile.iTunes.store-PreferHQTracks	Boolean	Yes
com.apple.mobile.iTunes.store-PurchaseTypes	Number	4
com.apple.mobile.iTunes.store-Storefront	String	143441
com.apple.mobile.iTunes.store-UserName	String	wally barr
com.apple.mobile.lockdown_cache-ActivationState	String	WildcardActivated
com.apple.mobile.restriction-ProhibitAppInstall	Boolean	No

Preferences

The **Preferences** folder within the **/root/Library** directory does not contain any evidentiary information. Neither does the **Safari** directory in the **/root/Library folder**.

Run

Let's now look at the **run** directory which is on the root of the second partition. There are several files there which don't contain noteworthy information.

Stash

Earlier we discussed the **stash** folder. This folder holds all the applications that are on the iPhone.

Tmp

The **tmp** folder has a folder called **UpdatedSnapshots**. These are actually .jpgs of screenshots. Some may be of evidentiary value.

This concludes the examination of the second partition, which is the data partition of the iPhone. Next we will discuss how some forensic tools can aid in the examination of the iPhone.

Carving

Since the release of Firmware 1.1, each time a user goes from one screen to the next, or from one Web page to another the iPhone periodically takes screenshots. These can be carved from unallocated space.

SubRosaSoft's MacForensicsLab

SubRosaSoft's MacForensicsLab, as shown in Figure 16.63, is a good carving tool on the Mac platform. MacForensicsLab can view the complete file structure of the slices of the iPhone. The Salvage feature in this application can help you examine a lot of images.

Figure 16.63 Viewing the Second Partition/Slice 2 Image with MacForensicsLab

Name	Size	Cr...	Type	Header	CRC	Re...	UID	GUID	Fin...	Pe...	Created	Modified
▶ MacDrive	(32)	MACS	disk			2	501	501	0000	000	8/30/08	9/11/08
▼ Data	(26)	MACS	disk			2	501	501	1000	000	7/27/08	8/28/08
▶ Keychains	(2)	MACS	fold			18	501	501	1000	755	6/16/08	8/26/08
▶ Managed Preferences	(1)	MACS	fold			19	501	501	1000	755	6/16/08	6/16/08
▶ MobileDevice	(2)	MACS	fold			21	501	501	1000	755	6/16/08	8/28/08
▶ backups	(0)	MACS	fold			22	501	501	1000	755	7/27/08	7/27/08
▶ cache	(2)	MACS	fold			23	501	501	1000	755	7/27/08	7/27/08
▶ db	(3)	MACS	fold			28	501	501	1000	755	6/25/08	7/27/08
▶ empty	(0)	MACS	fold			31	501	501	1000	755	6/16/08	6/16/08
▶ folders	(0)	MACS	fold			32	501	501	1000	755	6/16/08	6/16/08
▶ lib	(4)	MACS	fold			33	501	501	1000	755	7/27/08	7/27/08
▶ local	(0)	MACS	fold			93	501	501	1000	775	7/27/08	7/27/08
▶ lock	(0)	MACS	fold			94	501	501	1000	755	7/27/08	7/27/08
▶ log	(4)	MACS	fold			95	501	501	1000	755	6/25/08	8/28/08
▶ logs	(4)	MACS	fold			99	501	501	1000	755	6/25/08	8/28/08
▶ mobile	(7)	MACS	fold			101	501	501	1000	750	6/16/08	8/18/08
▶ msgs	(2)	MACS	fold			118	501	501	1000	755	6/16/08	8/28/08
▶ preferences	(2)	MACS	fold			120	501	501	1000	755	6/16/08	8/28/08
▶ root	(4)	MACS	fold			121	501	501	1000	750	7/27/08	9/21/08
▶ run	(11)	MACS	fold			129	501	501	1000	775	7/27/08	8/27/08
▶ spool	(0)	MACS	fold			132	501	501	1000	755	7/27/08	7/27/08
▶ stash	(8)	MACS	fold			9051	501	501	1000	755	7/27/08	8/18/08
▶ tmp	(4)	MACS	fold			133	501	501	1000	777	6/16/08	8/27/08
▶ vm	(0)	MACS	fold			134	501	501	1000	755	6/16/08	6/16/08
.DS_Store	12292	....	....	...Bud1	803650CF	122...	501	501	5000	644	8/28/08	8/28/08

MacForensicsLab : Test Case #1

Access Data's Forensic Tool Kit

FTK is an outstanding file carving utility. However, the FTK tool was written for a Microsoft Windows platform. You can still use FTK on your Mac if you have Windows installed in Boot Camp or you are using VMware Fusion or Parallels. See Appendix A for more information.

FTK, as shown in Figure 16.64, cannot parse out the file system. However, FTK interprets the two partitions and unallocated space. If you use VMware Fusion, install FTK, and bring in the full raw/Slice0 and carve for images. Here you will find screenshots for maps, e-mail, Web pages, SMS, and just about any service that is viewable to the user.

Figure 16.64 FTK within VMware Fusion Showing Results from Data Carve

Non-Jailbreaking Method of iPhone Analysis

On any Mac there is a plethora of information from the iPhone. This information is located at **/[Username]/Library/Application Support/MobileSync/Backup**. This is where all the data is stored when an iPhone is backed up, when a firmware version is installed, and if the user manually backs up the iPhone to the Mac via iTunes.

In order to force a backup of an iPhone to a Mac take the following steps:

1. Open **iTunes8**.
2. Select **iTunes > Preferences**, as shown in Figure 16.65.

Figure 16.65 Navigating to iTunes Preferences

3. Click the **Devices** tab in the Preferences Settings dialog box.
4. Check the box that disables the automatic syncing for iPhones and iPods, as shown in Figure 16.66.

Figure 16.66 Devices Tab

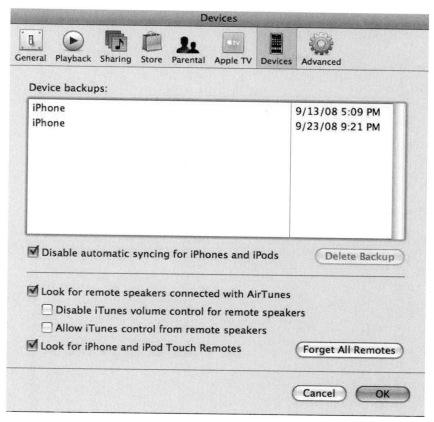

5. Click **OK**.

6. Quit **iTunes**.

7. Attach the iPhone to the Mac forensic workstation.

8. Restart **iTunes**.

9. ctrl-click the iPhone icon when it appears within **iTunes** and select **Back Up** from the pop-up menu, as shown in Figure 16.67. This will force a backup of the iPhone to the Mac.

Figure 16.67 Showing a Forced Backup
of the iPhone to the Mac Forensic Workstation

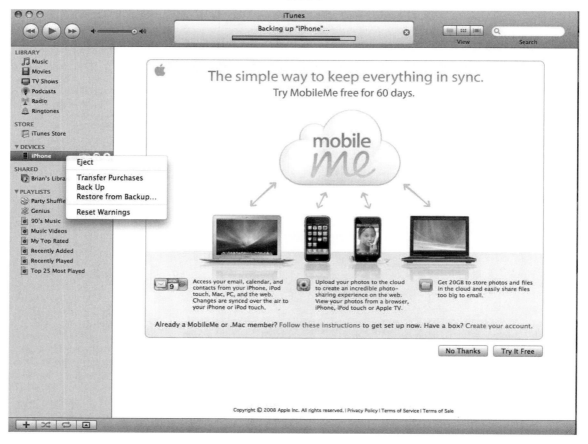

From here we can use our tools to examine the MobileSync data.

When the iPhone is backed up, the information is placed in a folder with a filename that is a hash value. If you use **Get Info** from the Finder, you will see the created or backup dates from the iPhone. Within these folders are numerous files that have the extension *.mdbackup*. This is further demonstrated in Figure 16.68. Each of these files can be viewed with the **Property List Editor**, and have information from images to databases to *History.plist*. Everything that was on the iPhone appears to be here in these files. The data in these files are in binary format, and some, like the SMS database can be viewed using "strings" from the command line. There are two applications that can parse this information.

One tool that can be used to parse the information, which was created by Vaughn Cordero, called MobileSyncBrowser (MSB) can be downloaded from http://homepage.mac.com/vaughn/msync/.

There is both a Mac and a Windows version of this application. This tool is great for viewing some of the data from the MobileSync directory. That data is the following:

- Call Logs
- Contacts
- SMS
- Notes

The following is a procedure for using the MobileSyncBrowser:

1. From your suspect's locked .dmg file, or from your forensic machine, navigate to **/[*username*]/Library/Application Support/MobileSync/Backup**, as shown in Figure 16.68.

Figure 16.68 MobileSync Backup

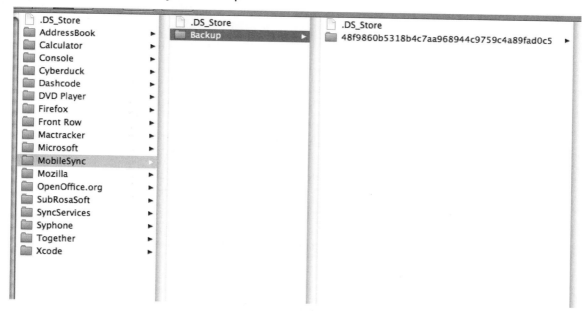

2. Within the **Backup** folder, you will see the actual backup file with the hash value filename. Copy the complete **MobileSync** folder.

3. From your forensic workstation, paste the **MobileSync** folder in the same location as it was retrieved from.

If you force a backup to your forensic workstation you can skip steps 2 and 3.

4.   Start the **MobileSyncBrowser**. The application will scan and locate the backup, as shown in Figure 16.69.

Figure 16.69 MSB Scanning MobileSync Data

When the scan is complete you will see the screen depicted in Figure 16.70.

Figure 16.70 MSB Collecting MobileSync Data

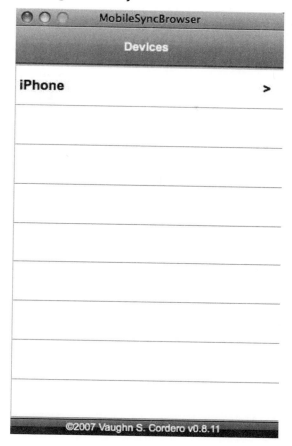

5. Double-click on **iPhone** to call up the screen shown in Figure 16.71. This will show the data retrieved by this application—SMS, Calls, Notes, Contacts.

Figure 16.71 MSB Main Data Screen

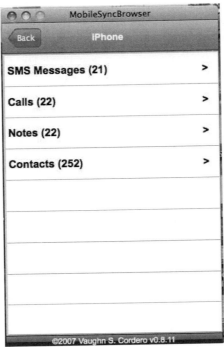

When you click on **SMS Messages**, the next field will give you the names of individuals that have been sent text messages or who have sent text messages themselves.

6. Double-click on one of the names in the next screen and you will see the complete stream of texts that had been sent back and forth from the iPhone user to other individuals or the reverse. As you will notice, the application uses the same iChat–like format to show the messages, as shown in Figure 16.72.

Figure 16.72 MSB Text Message Output

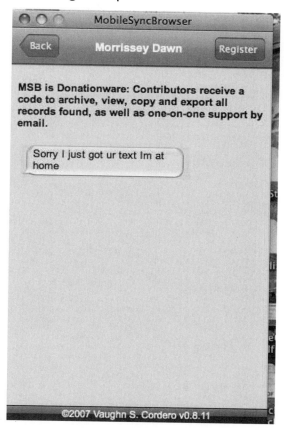

7. Double-click on **Calls** and the following log is shown: Names, numbers, date, time and duration of calls made or received, as shown in Figure 16.73.

Figure 16.73 MSB Call Log

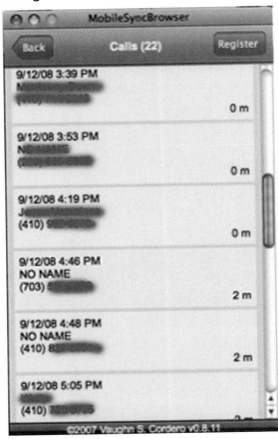

8. Double-click on **Contacts** and a list of contact names will appear.

9. Click on any name and the information from that contact will be shown, as seen in Figure 16.74.

Figure 16.74 MSB Contact Info

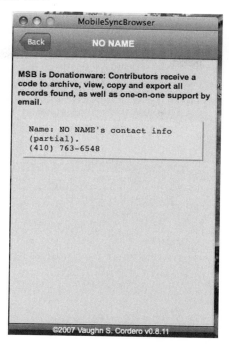

MobileSyncBrowser

Back   NO NAME

MSB is Donationware: Contributors receive a code to archive, view, copy and export all records found, as well as one-on-one support by email.

Name: NO NAME's contact info (partial).
(410) 763-6548

©2007 Vaughn S. Cordero v0.8.11

10. Double-click on **Notes** and a list of notes will appear.

11. Click on a note and the contents of the notes will be shown, as seen in Figure 16.75.

Figure 16.75 MSB Note Contents

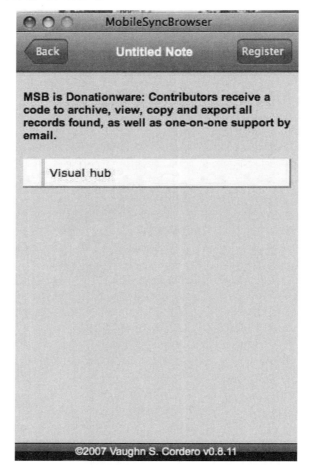

MobileSyncBrowser's export function is not available for free download. For a small donation to the developer the export function can be enabled. There is a new version under development that will enhance the operation of this tool.

A second tool that goes farther but doesn't have the graphical interface of MSB is the iPhone Parser, available for download at www.macosxforensics.com. This tool can only be used on a Mac, and parses all the information that you need from the MobileSyncBackup. This tool puts out everything from all the .plists, images, databases, SMS, contacts, and call logs. These steps will show you how to parse the MobileSync data from either a forced backup or a suspect's image.

1.   Force a backup of the iPhone.

or

2.   Copy out the **MobileSync** folder from the suspect's image.
3.   Paste the **MobileSync** folder to the same location on your Mac forensic workstation.
4.   Double-click on the iPhoneParser.app icon, as shown in Figure 16.76.

Figure 16.76 iPhone Parser Icon

5.   Click **OK** to start the application, as shown in Figure 16.77.

Figure 16.77 iPhone Parser Startup

6.   The parser will ask if you want the output to your desktop. Again click **OK**.
7.   The output file by default is named **iPhone_backup**.

Within the **iPhone_Backup** folder there is another folder named with the phone number of the iPhone. Within that folder is a plethora of information that will aid any investigator. The results of the parsed data are seen in Figure 16.78. The items can be viewed using many of the procedures discussed in this chapter.

Figure 16.78 iPhone Parser Results Example

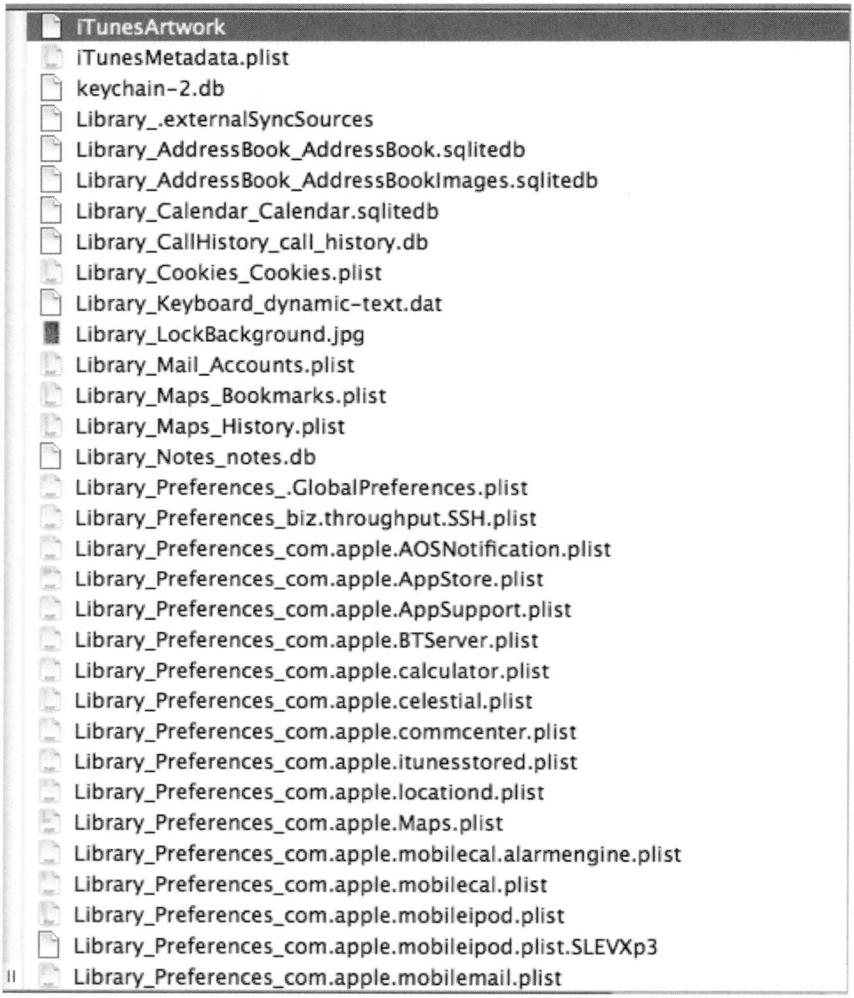

Property Lists From the Suspect's Mac

Within the **/[username]/Library/Preferences/com.apple.iPhoto.plist** file there is an entry of the location for importing images from the iPhone, as shown in Figure 16.79.

Figure 16.79 iPhoto Property List

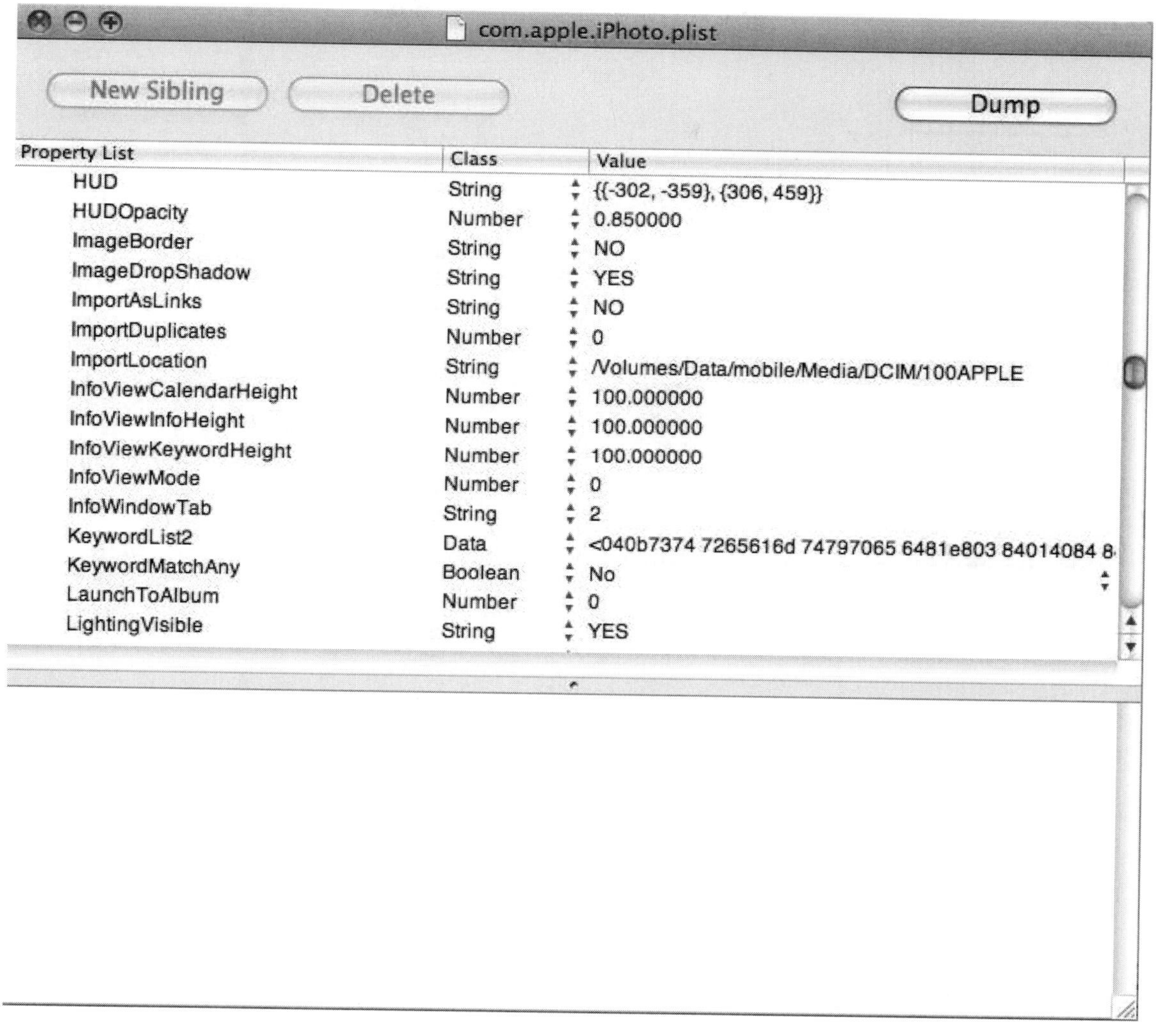

If you want more information about the iPhone connected to the host computer, you can look at the **/[*username*]/Library/Preferences/com.apple.iPod.plist** file. In this *.plist*, as shown in Figure 16.80, there is an IMEI number (International Mobile Equipment Identity Number –A number that is unique and identifies the iPhone), serial number, firmware version, how many times the iPhone was connected to the Mac, and the date of the last time the iPhone was connected.

Figure 16.80 iPod Property List

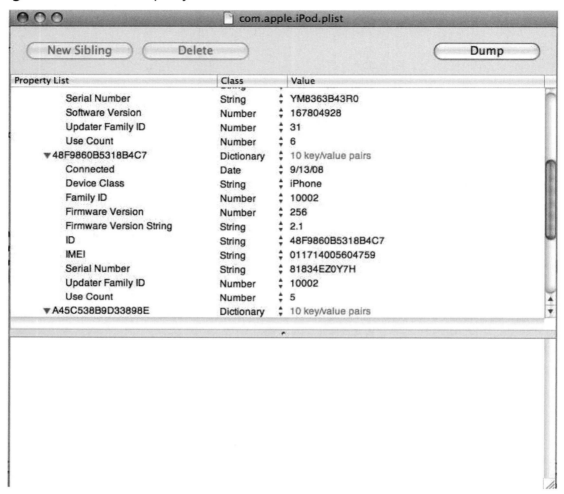

Other Non-Jailbreak
Methods of iPhone Forensics

There are other forensic tools that are presently in development from companies such as Paraben, Cellebrite, Six Legion and RTL. Most of these companies claim to get data from Contacts, Call Logs, SMS, and Calendars. You can also acquire artifacts by taking screenshots of the iPhone. This is a tedious process; but it is safe and can get almost everything off the iPhone. There are two manufacturers for taking screenshots of an iPhone: Project-a-Phone and ZRT.

iPhone SIM Card

The iPhone sim card can be examined with many different tools. For example, one tool is Paraben's SIM Card Seizure. The results from this application are the last ten numbers dialed from the phone.

Nmap the iPhone

Figure 16.81 shows the Nmap output of the iPhone. There seems to be one open port that is listening: port 62078.

Figure 16.81 iPhone Nmap

```
PORT        STATE    SERVICE    VERSION
1126/tcp    filtered unknown
8649/tcp    filtered unknown
32782/tcp   filtered unknown
62078/tcp   open     iphone-sync?
```

You can see several other ephemeral ports, one open port (62078), and the protocol is TCP (TCP wrapped). The service that is running is iPhone-Sync. This is apparently how the iPhone connects to the App Store and iTunes. Just by coincidence, this is the same port number used by XBOX360 and Playstation3.

Summary

The iPhone is a fascinating product from Apple and has presented many hurdles for investigators and examiners to deal with in retrieving artifacts from it. It is important not to forget the canons of forensics by using nonforensic methods like jailbreaking. It's better to wait until Apple gives law enforcement an ethical way to get at the phone or some other method that does not touch or stomp all over the iPhone. Jailbreaking is being used for expedience, when the investigator does not have the patience that science will prevail. Resorting to tactics used by bad guys to do our job is just not the right way to go. This chapter showed the examiner what the file system looks like and where the information is. This is not a validation of jailbreaking. There are tools that are close to being developed that will yield an effective method of iPhone forensics.

Solutions Fast Track

iPhone Functions

☑ The second partition or slice has the information important to the investigator.

☑ The first slice has operating system files.

☑ AppleTV and iPhone have similar partition breakdowns.

Carving

☑ FTK is a good carving tool.

☑ SubRosaSoft's MacForensicsLab is a good carving tool that runs on the Mac platform.

☑ FTK and SubRosaSoft's MacForensicsLab are proprietary tools.

Non-Jailbreaking Methods of iPhone Analysis

☑ The MobileSync Browser can be used to Pull Data from an iPhone without resorting to jailbreaking methods.

☑ The MobileSync Browser was created by Vaughn Cordero.

☑ The MobileSync Browser is a free tool.

Frequently Asked Questions

Q: What is a jailbreak?

A: A method used to alter the firmware of an iPhone.

Q: What tools are good for data carving?

A: FTK and SubRosaSoft's MacForensicsLab are good carving tools.

Q: Is jailbreaking a forensically sound method?

A: Absolutely not!

Q: What tools are available besides jailbreaking?

A: The MobileSync Browser and iPhone Parser.

Q: How is the iPhone like AppleTV?

A: AppleTV and iPhone have similar partition breakdowns.

Q: Which iPhone partition has the good stuff?

A: The second partition or slice 2 has all the data that is of evidentiary value.

Q: Which iPhone partition has the operating system?

A: The first partition or slice 1.

Using Boot Camp, Parallels, and VMware Fusion in a MAC Environment

Solutions in this appendix:

- Boot Camp
- Parallels
- VMware Fusion
- VirtualBox

☑ Summary

☑ Solutions Fast Track

☑ Frequently Asked Questions

Introduction

In January 2006, Apple produced the first Intel-based Macs. Overnight, people were able to natively install (through various hacks) operating systems such as Microsoft Windows XP Professional, Vista, and SUSE, Red Hat, Debian, Fedora Core, Mandriva, Xandros, and flavors of FreeBSD, OS/2, eCommStation, Solaris, and OpenBSD 3.8 on their Macs. Prior to the release of the Intel-based Mac, installing Windows on a Mac was a feat that required hardware emulation. With the necessity for a multiboot solution came the subsequent birth of Boot Camp. Initially released as a beta for Tiger (at the time, Leopard was available only to a select few developers), Boot Camp is a feature of Leopard that allows users to dual-boot their Mac systems to either their Mac OS or Microsoft Windows (or some flavors of Linux, such as Ubuntu, Red Hat, and Gentoo, among others, though not officially supported). It is a popular feature, mainly because it's free and requires no third-party utility, such as Parallels or VMware Fusion, and one you need to be aware of as a computer forensic investigator because you may see it in the field.

> **NOTE**
>
> The only versions of Windows that will work using Boot Camp are 32-bit versions of XP Home, XP Pro, and Vista Home Basic, Home Premium, Business, and Ultimate. There are ways around some of those requirements, and we'll get to that later in the appendix.

Parallels and VMware Fusion allow you to run an OS in a virtual environment. Virtualization is different from emulation because it doesn't have to mimic hardware that is not actually there (such as mimicking Intel architecture on IBM's Power PC architecture). Thus, virtualization speeds up the user experience tremendously (reportedly running on an x86 OS at 95 percent speed versus dual-boot scenarios). Emulation is painfully slow, sometimes as bad as 30 percent to 50 percent slower than running the OS on its native hardware, and therefore it is not typically used unless the end-user has some Windows application he or she cannot do without (typically in a business environment). Virtualization on Macs has become more popular because it allows people to run Windows and Linux on a virtual machine (VM), without having to quit what they're doing on their Macs in OS X to reboot into Windows (or Linux) using Boot Camp. This allows them to use programs on those systems that might not be available for the Mac platform. Products such as Parallel's Coherence and VMware Fusion's Unity further blur the line between the operating systems by allowing other OS applications to seemingly interact with the Mac desktop environment as though they were "native" OS X apps.

In this appendix, we will introduce you to the two commercial solutions (and one free solution) available that allow you to install other operating systems on Intel-based Macs. We will also walk you through the process of installing Windows, Ubuntu Linux and OS X Leopard Server, in a step-by-step fashion using Parallels as an example.

Boot Camp

Let's face it: Nobody wants to start learning a completely new and alien OS out of the blue (unless you're a geek, like I am). Boot Camp is Apple's answer to users who fear that buying a Mac means not being able to run applications they have been using for years in Windows. With Boot Camp, you don't have to give anything up (besides some free space on your hard drive). You get all the benefits of Apple's famed style and quality with the familiarity of Microsoft's Windows XP or Vista (if you have to)—the best of both worlds, if you will. Apple even supplies you with drivers for Windows XP or Vista. These drivers are written for the specific configuration in the specific Mac on which you are installing them. Rarely do you get an install of Windows in which the exact collection of hardware you are using has actually been tested for compatibility with each other *and* with the OS you have installed.

NOTE

As of this writing, Apple has retired the Boot Camp beta program on Tiger (10.4.x) and no longer supports its use. As a matter of fact, if you happen to have Boot Camp installed on Tiger and you try to start the Boot Camp Assistant (Apple's Boot Camp wizard), you will get an error on launch stating that the beta has expired and that Apple recommends that you upgrade to Leopard (10.5.x). This does *not* mean any existing Windows or Linux installations will cease to function. You just will not be able to set up *new* partitions and install a new Windows instance using Boot Camp Assistant.

The benefits of using Boot Camp are that you get full use out of your hardware without having to share resources (again, aside from some hard drive space) with another running OS. In my experience, you also get the benefit of external hardware (such as printers, scanners, digital cameras, USB-to-serial port converters, etc.) running natively, without a host OS as the middleman running interference on the guest operating system's behalf. The more complicated the setup the more things can go wrong. Virtualization is no exception to that rule. When something doesn't work quite right you have the host OS, guest OS, virtualization application, virtual drivers, and actual hardware to troubleshoot, just to find the culprit.

Scores of simple tutorials on installing and configuring Boot Camp are available, scattered around on the Internet but they are not always complete and some miss a step or two and end up leaving you hanging. We'll run through the steps in layman's terms. We'll go over the prerequisites first.

WARNING

Remember that anytime you alter your hard drive's partitions, you should back up your data first. These tutorials are designed to get you through the use of Boot Camp, step by step, *without* data loss. However, you can never be too careful. Apple recommends that you make sure you back up your data before you start, and then frequently while you're using Windows installed on a Boot Camp partition.

If you've already partitioned your hard drive with a beta of Boot Camp, you don't need to do anything to the partition. All you have to do is upgrade the drivers in Windows on your Boot Camp partition. You'll find the updated drivers on the Leopard install disc. Just boot to the Windows partition in Boot Camp and pop in the DVD; your Windows OS will see it as a 400MB CD, and if you haven't disabled AutoRun it will automatically start the setup.exe file and initiate the driver update. Select the **Repair** option to upgrade the existing drivers. You must also be running Leopard (OS X 10.5.x or later). Apple strongly recommends that you use the latest version of its OS when using Boot Camp.

To review, when creating a new partition using Boot Camp Assistant, make sure you adhere to the following rules of thumb:

- You must have access to a local account with administrative privileges in OS X Leopard.

- You must start with a hard drive formatted in the HFS+ file system with no more than one partition.

- You will need to have your OS X install media (disc 1) on hand.

- Apple recommends at least 10GB of free hard drive space (much more if you want to install anything in Windows).

- Apple also recommends that you have at least 2GB of RAM if you plan to install Windows Vista on your Boot Camp partition.

- You also require installation media for your favorite operating system. If you are going to install Windows you must own a copy of a fully licensed Windows installation disc. No upgrade CDs will work. You'll need the *full* installation discs. If you are planning to use Windows XP (Home or Pro) the installation media *must* have Service Pack 2 (no less!). You cannot (according to Apple) install Windows XP SP 1 in Boot Camp and upgrade it later.

Dual-Booting Mac and Windows

There are three basic steps to installing Windows using Boot Camp on your Mac. The first step is to navigate to the /Applications/Utility folder in Finder. You must be using an account with administrative privileges to create or resize a partition on your hard drive; therefore, you must have administrative privileges to run Boot Camp Assistant. Find Boot Camp Assistant and double-click the app to start it. You'll get a window such as the one shown in Figure A.1.

Figure A.1 Boot Camp Assistant Introduction

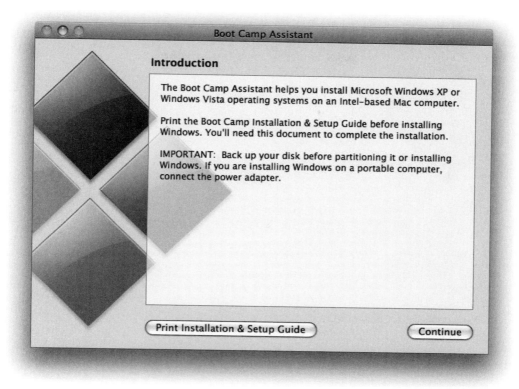

One of Apple's endearing traits is its ability to take complicated and sophisticated technology and wrap it in a simple yet elegant user interface so that anybody, regardless of his or her tech savvy, can use it. Boot Camp is no different. Boot Camp Assistant removes all of the work involved in partitioning your hard drive by displaying your hard drive in a simple graphical user interface (GUI), with a slider enabling you to slide your way to any size partition without losing existing data (also known as non-destructive repartitioning, as shown in Figure A.2). Buttons are also available for you to make the partition 32GB or divide the partitions equally.

Figure A.2 Creating a Partition for Windows

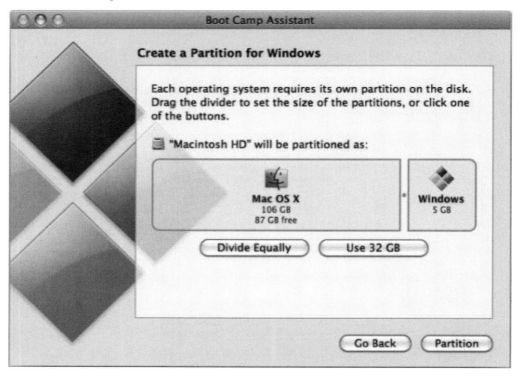

Just remember that the smaller you make the Windows partition the fewer applications you will be able to install, and the slower your system will run over time as Windows runs out of free space (5 GB and 20 GB to 40 GB are the smallest that Microsoft recommends you make your partitions for Windows XP and various Vista versions, respectively). You must also remember to leave at least 5 GB free on your Mac OS X partition for the same reasons.

NOTE

Windows operating systems may react erratically; sometimes displaying the Blue Screen of Death (BSOD) during boot on a FAT32-formatted partition if the boot partition is larger than the maximum size of 32 GB. If you are going to use NTFS, however, the sky is the limit, as NTFS supports booting off a partition up to 2 TB (terabyte).

After Boot Camp Assistant finishes repartitioning your hard drive, you'll move on to step 2. Pop in your favorite version of Windows (XP SP 2 through Vista) and follow the on-screen instructions, as shown in Figure A.3).

Figure A.3 Starting Windows Installation

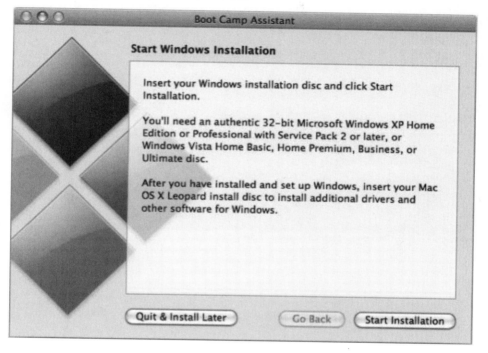

After you click the **Start Installation** button in Boot Camp Assistant, your Mac will boot into the newly created partition and will start the Windows installation.

You will see the standard Windows installation screen. Although it is blue in Windows XP, it's not the dreaded BSOD (see Figure A.4).

Figure A.4 Windows XP Pro Setup

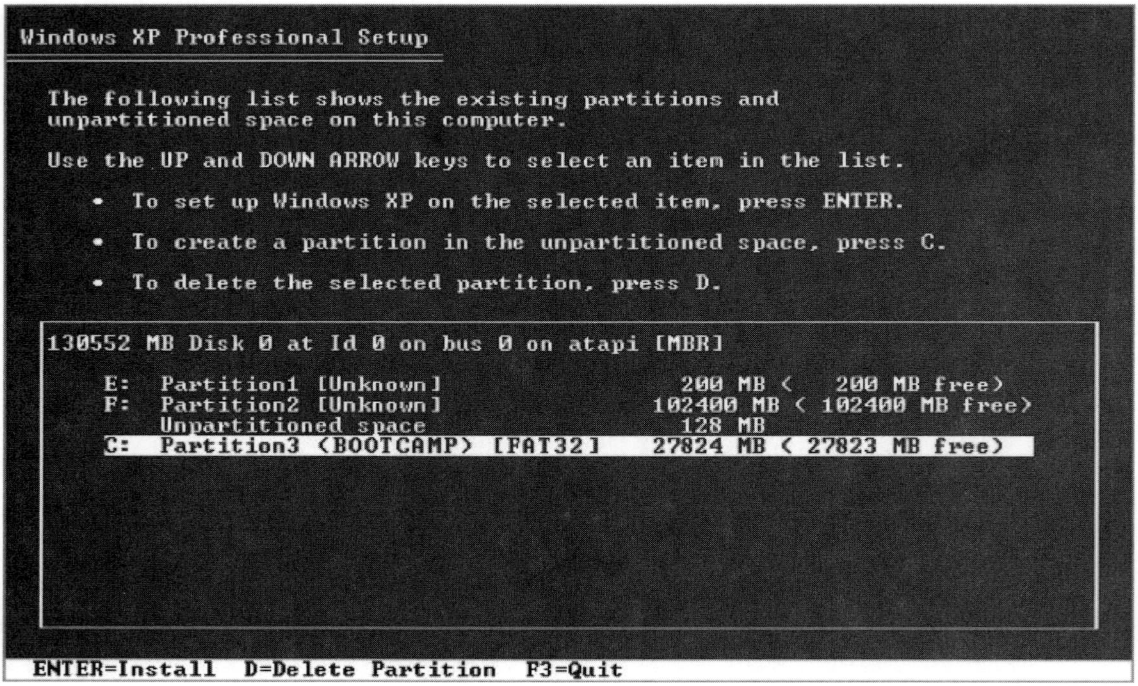

```
Windows XP Professional Setup

    The following list shows the existing partitions and
    unpartitioned space on this computer.

    Use the UP and DOWN ARROW keys to select an item in the list.

       •  To set up Windows XP on the selected item, press ENTER.
       •  To create a partition in the unpartitioned space, press C.
       •  To delete the selected partition, press D.

   ┌────────────────────────────────────────────────────────────────┐
   │ 130552 MB Disk 0 at Id 0 on bus 0 on atapi [MBR]                 │
   │                                                                  │
   │    E:  Partition1 [Unknown]              200 MB <    200 MB free)│
   │    F:  Partition2 [Unknown]           102400 MB < 102400 MB free)│
   │        Unpartitioned space               128 MB                 │
   │    C:  Partition3 <BOOTCAMP> [FAT32]    27824 MB < 27823 MB free)│
   │                                                                  │
   └────────────────────────────────────────────────────────────────┘

  ENTER=Install   D=Delete Partition   F3=Quit
```

In Windows Vista, your screen will look a little more polished, as shown in Figure A.5. Here you will select the partition created by Boot Camp Assistant (typically named **<BOOTCAMP> [FAT32]**).

One of the first choices you have in a typical Windows installation is a choice between formatting your boot partition (and any subsequent partitions, for that matter) using NTFS or using FAT32. Here you must be mindful to choose the appropriate file system to suit your needs. NTFS, introduced in 1993, is Microsoft's latest file system and boasts many improvements over FAT. Among its many features are improved support for metadata, the use of advanced data structures for better performance, more reliability than FAT32, and better utilization of available disk space. It also has access control lists (ACLs) to define user access, and limited file journaling. That being said, due to Microsoft licensing restrictions, Apple OS X is only partially licensed for NTFS use and therefore cannot write to an NTFS partition. Because of this limitation, you might consider using the "format using FAT" option during the Windows install to facilitate the sharing of files between your Windows and Apple OS X partitions. Remember that if you choose FAT32 the partition *must* be smaller than 32 GB. Otherwise, it will be unbootable.

NOTE

There are workarounds if you want the benefits of NTFS but still want the ability to write data to your NTFS partition while booted to your Leopard OS X partition.

Paragon NTFS for Mac OS X is a commercial utility that enables transparent read/write support for NTFS in OS X (www.paragon-software.com/home/ntfs-mac/).

An open source solution to the NTFS write issue is NTFS-3 g (http://macntfs-3g. blogspot.com/), a full-featured NTFS plug-in for MACFuse (you must have MACFuse installed to make use of this plug-in). MACFuse is a Mac version of FUSE (File-system in USErspace) from Linux, ported over by the fine folks at Google Code. You can find more information and a download link from http://code.google.com/p/macfuse/.

Figure A.5 Windows Vista Install

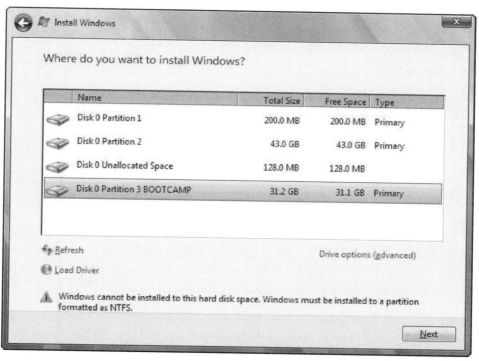

WARNING

You must take extra care to install Windows on the correct partition. You don't want to accidentally install Windows on the wrong partition and overwrite OS X. Do not delete or create any partition. Boot Camp Assistant takes care of everything for you. Install Windows only on the partition that Boot Camp Assistant creates for just that purpose (typically called Partition3 <BOOTCAMP> [FAT32]).

After you've selected the correct partition, the Windows XP installer will ask you whether you want to format your drive or leave the current file system intact. Do *not* choose the latter, as it will render your Windows XP installation unbootable. You may choose from any of the other options, as shown in Figure A.6.

Figure A.6 Windows XP Pro Partition Setup

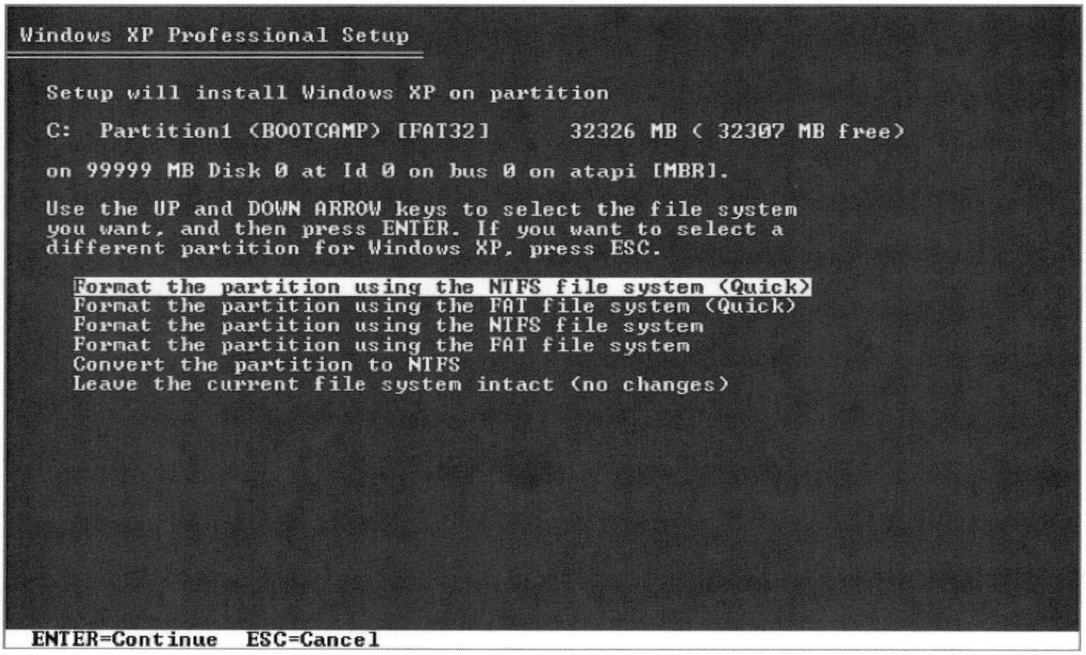

For Windows Vista, click **Drive options (advanced)**; then select **Format**, click **OK**, and then click **Next**. After formatting the partition, the Windows installer copies all the files needed to complete the setup to the new partition and reboots into Windows. Windows will continue the installation, stopping occasionally to ask you your preference on some setting or other. Once the Windows installation is complete you are ready for step 3, installing the Apple drivers for your Mac's hardware in Windows.

Boot to Windows, as shown in Figure A.7 (if you aren't already there), and then insert your Leopard DVD to install the Windows drivers included there.

Figure A.7 OS X Boot Choice

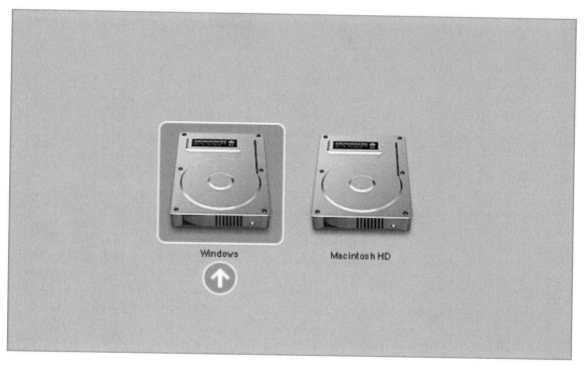

Don't be alarmed; Windows will see your DVD as a CD-ROM. The installer should run automatically (unless you've disabled AutoRun; if so, navigate to the CD-ROM in My Computer and double-click the **setup.exe file**). You might get a message window stating that the software you are installing has not passed Windows Logo testing (as shown in Figure A.8). You can disregard that and click **Continue Anyway**.

In Windows XP, you will get a window (the Found New Hardware Wizard) prompting you that new hardware was found. Just follow the instructions found in that wizard and any other wizards that may appear.

Figure A.8 XP Driver Install Warning

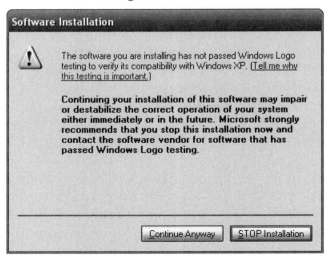

That's it! You have successfully set up a Windows and Mac OS X dual boot. At this point, you can choose which OS you would like to boot to by default. On OS X, just click the little **Apple logo** in the top left of your monitor, and then select **System Preferences** and click **Startup Disk**. Now select the OS you want as your default. In Windows, just click the **Boot Camp System Tray icon** (next to the time at the bottom right corner of the screen) and choose **Boot Camp Control Panel**, as shown in Figure A.9. If you want to select a different OS during boot, just hold down the **Option** key until the disk icons appear and then click the one you wish to use, as was shown in Figure A.7.

Figure A.9 Boot Camp Control Panel

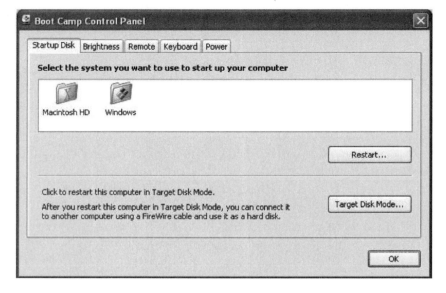

Dual-Booting Mac and Linux

One of the many changes Apple made when it switched to the Intel architecture was to drop the archaic Master Boot Record (MBR) and employ the new Extensible Firmware Interface (EFI), an illustration of where EFI comes in relation to the OS is shown in Figure A.10. EFI, originally developed by Intel in the mid-1990s, is now maintained by the Unified EFI Forum (officially known as UEFI). EFI is a considerable improvement over MBR, replacing the old legacy BIOS firmware interface traditionally used by all IBM PC-compatible computers. EFI can use the standard PC disk partition scheme, MBR, and adds support for a GUID Partition Table (GPT), which does not suffer the same limitations as MBR does (i.e., support for only four partitions and only 2TB per partition at most). EFI is a pre-OS environment (known as the *EFI Shell*) that can run applications, transfer files, load a complete TCP/IP stack, or load and unload drivers, and it supports full graphical menus. It can also load extensions, adding supplementary functions to the EFI.

Installing Linux using Boot Camp is actually just as easy as installing Windows. However, because Apple does not officially support Linux, you need to follow the instructions for dual-booting Mac and Windows and insert your Linux CD when Boot Camp prompts you to insert your Windows disc.

Figure A.10 EFI Stack

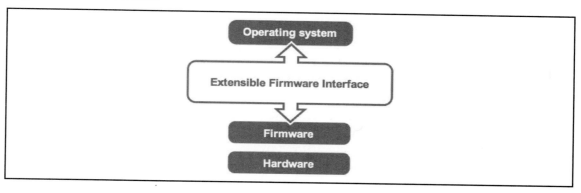

Even though Linux has had the ability to support EFI natively using ELILO (EFI Linux Loader), a standard Linux boot loader for EFI-based PC hardware, or EFI versions of GRUB (Grand Unified Bootloader), the Linux requirement to create a separate "swap" partition messes with the OS X partitioning scheme, rendering your OS X partition unbootable. Other issues included the requirement of a specially prepared kernel to run on Apple's EFI, and the fact that not all the features worked (such as accelerated graphics). That's where rEFIt comes in. rEFIt is a boot menu for Apple Macs. (It also has a maintenance toolkit). You can use it to dual-boot operating systems easily. With a little tinkering you can even triple-boot operating systems with Boot Camp. The installation is completely automated and thoroughly documented. You can download rEFIt at http://refit.sourceforge.net/#download.

Parallels

Initially released in July 2006 as Parallels Workstation for Mac OS X, Parallels Desktop for Mac was the first VM solution for the Intel Mac. Parallels uses hypervisor-based virtualization technology on Apple Mac computers with Intel VT-x hardware virtualization support to map the host's existing hardware to the VM. This enables a VM to think it's a stand-alone machine with its own CPU, hard drive, network card, video card, modem, floppy drive, USB controllers, and so forth. You can download a free 30-day trial of Parallels Desktop for Mac from www.parallels.com/en/download/desktop/.

NOTE

One of the benefits of using a VM is that the virtual hardware and drivers in the VM are identical. The application hosting the VM actually has to deal with whatever unique hardware you may have. This makes the VM highly portable, meaning you can copy the VM image and run it on another machine running the same VM application. There are even converters written to convert one company's custom VM image to work with another's (such as converting a Parallels image to work with VMware Fusion, and vice versa).

Configuring Parallels

Once you've downloaded the latest version of Parallels (as of this writing, the latest version is the current private beta 4.0, Build 4.0.2928, released in September, 2008), just mount the **.dmg file** by double-clicking it, and then double-click the **install.mpkg file** the start the installation. You *must* install this app using an account with administrative privileges. To install Parallels you need a Macintosh computer with an Intel processor that supports hardware virtualization. (To run 64-bit operating systems in VMs, you need an Intel Core 2 or later processor.) Additional requirements include at least 1 GB of memory (at least 2 GB is recommended), at least 300 MB of disk space on the boot volume for the Parallels Desktop installation, and about 15 GB of disk space for each VM. Follow the on-screen instructions to complete the installation.

Once the install completes, navigate to your Applications folder in Finder. There you will find the Parallels folder; double-click the **Parallels Desktop app** therein. To run Parallels Desktop you will need to activate it with an activation key. If you purchased the box version of the program in a retail store, you can find the activation key printed on the installation CD sleeve. If you downloaded it from the Parallels Web site, you should have received the activation key via e-mail. If you downloaded an evaluation copy of Parallels Desktop, you can get a trial activation key, usually with a 30-day window until expiration. An install of Parallels Desktop that is not activated will not work. After you activate your copy of Parallels Desktop, you'll receive full rights to create and manage VMs, edit their configuration, and install operating systems.

Installing an Operating System

The first time you run Parallels Desktop for Mac (hereafter called Parallels) you'll get the Add Virtual Machine Assistant, as shown in Figure A.11. The Assistant is pretty simple. Parallels was written for the layman; therefore, it hides all the nuts and bolts under the hood, wrapped in a pretty GUI.

Figure A.11 New Virtual Machine Assistant

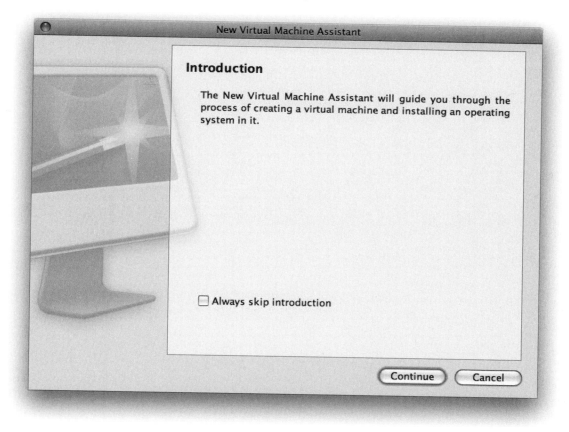

Windows

If you're going to install a flavor of Windows, Parallels can even script it for you using the Express installation option, as shown in Figure A.12.

Figure A.12 New VM Express Windows

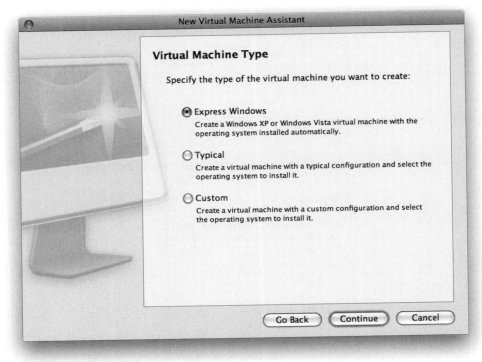

All you have to do is answer a few simple questions, including your username, organization name, and CD key, as shown in Figure A.13.

Figure A.13 New VM Express Windows Key

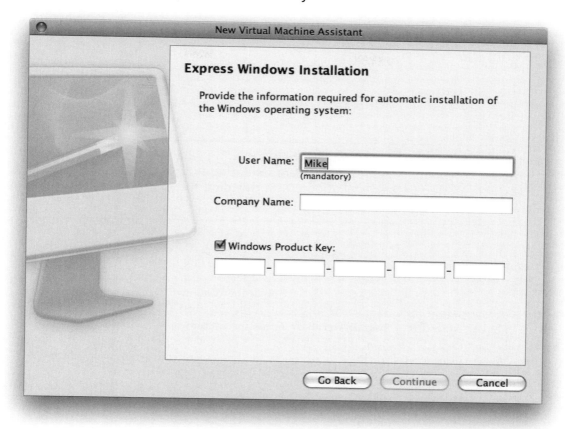

If you mistyped any of the answers in the Express Windows Installation wizard, the Windows installation will stop and will prompt you to correct your input. Once the installation completes, you should be looking at the Windows Desktop in Parallels. The next step is to install Parallels Tools.

Parallels Tools is a collection of exclusive tools, utilities, and drivers that tell Windows how to interact with the unique collection of hardware and features in a Parallels VM install. Parallels Tools includes the following features:

- Mouse synchronization
- Time synchronization
- Clipboard synchronization
- The Dynamic Resolution tool
- The Shared Folders tool
- The Coherence tool

- The Shared Profile tool

- The Shared Applications tool

- The Shared Internet Applications tool

- Parallels Compressor (Windows only)

TIP

For more information about Parallels Tools, including what each tool does and its respective compatibility with the different operating systems, check out the Parallels User Guide located in the installation CD, or the .dmg file you downloaded from the Parallels Web site.

Parallels Tools are available for most Windows and Linux operating systems (e.g., Windows 2000/2003/XP/Vista, Red Hat Enterprise Linux 4, Red Hat Enterprise Linux 5, Ubuntu, and many others). The installer should start automatically as soon as the Windows installation completes. If it does not, don't panic; just make sure you're logged in to the guest OS (Windows in this case), and go to the **Virtual Machine | Install Parallels Tools** menu item in the Parallels menu bar. This actually mounts a CD image in the Parallels virtual CD-ROM and will AutoRun the installer from there. An installation wizard will pop up. Follow the on-screen instructions to finish the Parallels Tools installation.

NOTE

Just some nomenclature to remember: The OS you have Parallels installed on is called the *Host* and the OS you have installed in Parallels is called the *Guest*.

Linux

I chose Ubuntu as the Linux distribution (also called a *distro* in geek slang) that we'll use for this demonstration because it has become the most widely used distro by professionals and laymen alike, due primarily to its ease of installation and compatibility with most hardware configurations. You can download a free copy from the official Ubuntu Web site, www.ubuntu.com/getubuntu/download. You can even request an Ubuntu CD shipped to you free of charge!

First, you'll want to navigate to the Parallels folder located within the Applications folder in Finder. Double-click the **Parallels Desktop app** therein. If this is a new installation of Parallels and you have not created any VMs yet, you'll be greeted with the New Virtual Machine Assistant. If this is not your first VM, just click the **plus sign** icon on the bottom left of the Parallels Virtual Machines Directory window, as shown in Figure A.14.

Figure A.14 Parallels VM Directory

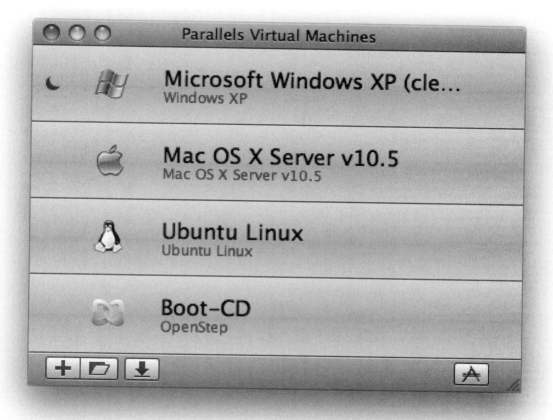

Click the **Continue** button on the New Virtual Machine Assistant window. You will now see two drop-down option fields: one titled "Type:" and the other "Version:" Here you get to select what OS you wish to install (you must, of course, have the media). These choices let Parallels know what you are attempting to do so that it can configure the VM properly. For our purposes, we will choose **Linux** in the **Type: field** and **Ubuntu Linux** in the **Version: field**, as shown in Figure A.15. (Notice how many flavors of Linux Parallels has presets for in that list!) Click the **Continue** button, leave the default VM type as **Typical**, and click the **"Continue"** button to (you guessed it!) **Continue** again. The next screen will ask you what you would like to name your VM. You can name it whatever you like. In this case, we'll just use the default name. This time instead of the **Continue** button you get to click the **Create** button.

Figure A.15 Parallels OS List

Red Hat Enterprise Linux
Red Hat Enterprise Server 3
SUSE Linux Enterprise
SUSE Linux Enterprise Server 9
Debian GNU/Linux
Red Hat Linux
Fedora Linux
CentOS Linux
OpenSUSE Linux
Mandriva Linux
Xandros Linux
✓ Ubuntu Linux
Other Linux kernel 2.4
Other Linux kernel 2.6
Other Linux

Next, pop in the Ubuntu CD and start up your newly created Ubuntu VM.

TIP

You don't have to burn the ISO (CD image) you downloaded earlier to a CD in order to use it. Parallels can mount the image as a virtual CD-ROM. Just click the little **triangle** next to More Options on the last page of the New Virtual Machine Assistant. A few more options will drop down in the window. Select the **CD/DVD image** option, and click the **Browse** button to browse for the CD image on your hard drive.

As soon as the new VM starts up you'll notice the virtual BIOS dialog, just like what you'd see in a real, physical PC. GRUB will kick in and the Ubuntu CD will come to life (see Figure A.16). The Ubuntu CD is what is known in the Linux world as a Live-CD because you can run the full GUI OS right off the CD without installing it on the hard drive.

Notes from the Underground…

Live-CD

The first Linux-based Live-CD was Yggdrasil Linux; it did not function well because of the slow speed of the CD-ROM drives at that time, and it went out of production in 1995. The Debian-derived Linux distribution Knoppix was released in 2003, and it became popular as both a rescue disk system and a primary distribution. Since 2003, the popularity of Live-CDs has increased, partly because of Linux Live scripts and remastersys which made it easy to build customized systems (check out http://en.wikipedia.org/wiki/Live-CD for more information).

Live-CDs are also used in the hacker community to run an OS that has been precompiled with all the necessary drivers, software, and dependencies to run various cracks against password files, wireless and wired networks, encrypted files, and so forth

Figure A.16 Parallels Ubuntu Live-CD Start Menu

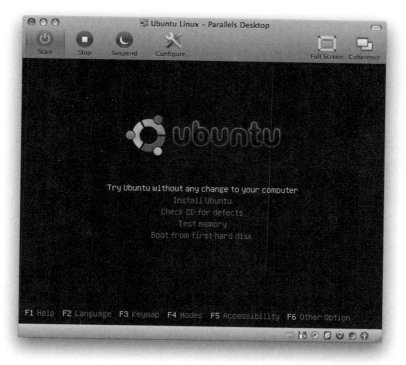

The first prompt asks you what language you want the OS to use, as shown in Figure A.17. We'll leave it on the default (English) for now, so we'll all be on the same page. Press the **Enter** key.

Figure A.17 Parallels Ubuntu Install Language

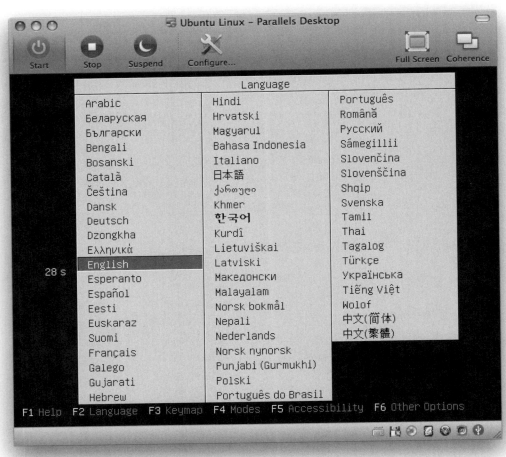

Once you get to the Ubuntu desktop, you'll see that there are only two icons, as shown in Figure A.18. One of those icons is a shortcut to install Ubuntu on your hard drive, and is simply called "Install". Go ahead and double-click the **Install icon** to get the installation going.

Figure A.18 Parallels Ubuntu Live CD Desktop

The first prompt in the installation again asks you what language you want the OS to use, as shown in Figure A.19. Leave it on the default and click the **Forward** button.

Figure A.19 Parallels Ubuntu HD Install Welcome

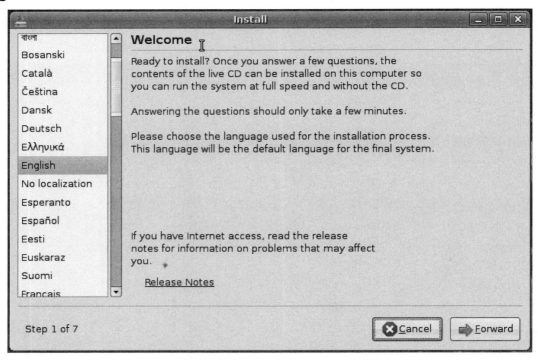

The next prompt is for the time zone (the default is New York, as shown in Figure A.20). Choose the appropriate time zone for your area and click the **Forward** button again. Do the same for the Keyboard Layout prompt. Just choose a suitable layout (the default is USA) and click **Forward**.

Figure A.20 Parallels Ubuntu HD Install Time Zone

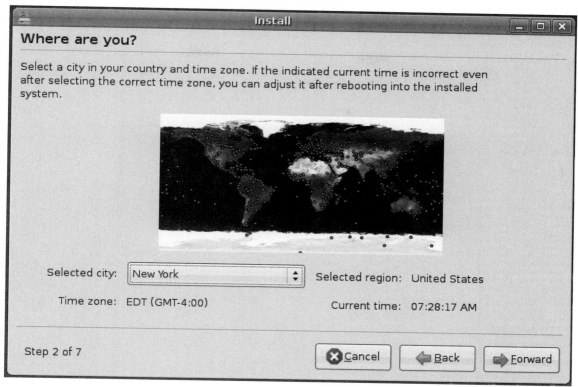

Next, you'll be asked how you want to proceed with partitioning the hard drive, as shown in Figure A.21. Just leave it at the default choice and click **Forward**.

Figure A.21 Parallels Ubuntu HD Install Partition

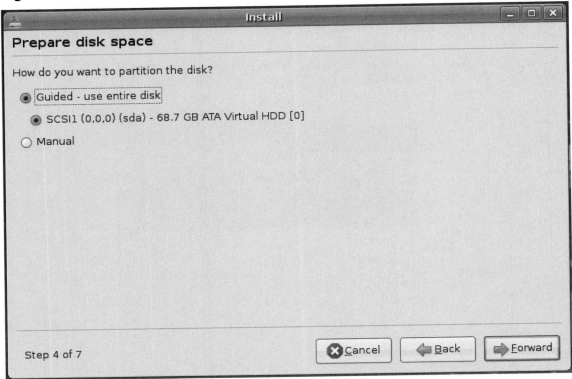

Now you'll be asked for a little personal information, as shown in Figure A.22, such as your name, what username you'd like to use as a logon, a password, and what you would like to name your computer (remember, Ubuntu doesn't know it is not installing itself on a real physical machine).

Figure A.22 Parallels Ubuntu HD Install Who Are You

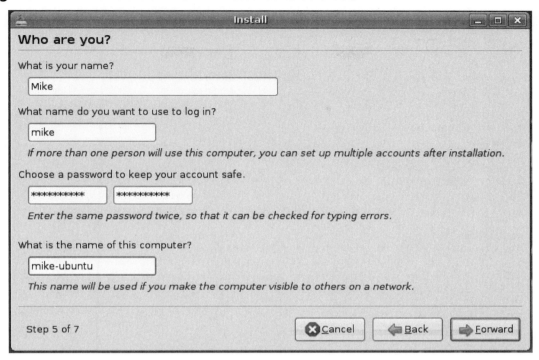

Now that you've answered all the necessary questions, you are ready to install Ubuntu. Actually, Ubuntu will do all the work for you; just review the last screen to make sure you typed all your answers correctly (see Figure A.23) and click **Install**.

Figure A.23 Parallels Ubuntu HD Install Review

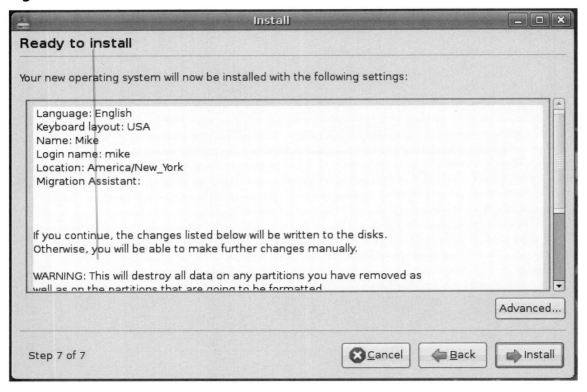

The next thing you'll see is a progress bar (similar to the one in Figure A.24).

Figure A.24 Parallels Ubuntu HD Install Progress Bar

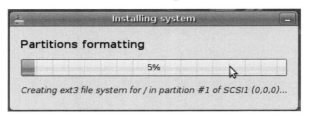

When the install is done you will see an Installation Complete window prompting you to either continue using the Live-CD or restart and use the new installation you've just completed off the hard drive (see Figure A.25). Just click the **Restart Now** button. Don't forget to take out the installation CD (or disconnect the image) at the prompt or you will boot back into the Live-CD. Right-click the **CD icon** on the bottom-right side of the Parallels window (make sure you're in Single Window mode) and click **Disconnect** in the menu.

Figure A.25 Parallels Ubuntu Install Restart

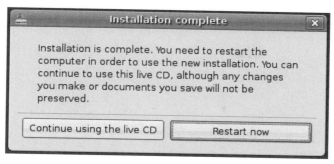

OS X 10.5.x Server

Leopard Server includes iCal Server, Wiki Server (a Wiki server), Spotlight Server, and Podcast Producer for turnkey podcasting. Leopard Server also introduces updates to many other services, such as Apache 2.2, MySQL 5, Apache Tomcat 6, QuickTime, Streaming Server 6, iChat Server 2, Xgrid 2, and Open Directory 4.

Unlike previous versions of OS X Server, Leopard Server now includes three install configurations: Standard, Workgroup, and Advanced. The Standard server configuration is intended for small businesses or small workgroups. The Workgroup server configuration is similar to Standard, but allows the server to connect to existing directory services (Open Directory, Active Directory, etc.). The Advanced server configuration allows for more granular and advanced installations. For more information on Apple Mac OS X Leopard Server check out Apple's Web site at www.apple.com/server/macosx/.

The ability to install OS X 10.5.x Server is a brand-new feature that, until the release of Parallels Desktop 4.x.x, was reserved for Parallels Server 3.x.x. The addition of this feature is, no doubt, in response to VMware's decision to include support for OS X Server in the 2.0 release of VMware Fusion, a free update for 1.x registered users (don't you just love competition?).

As of this writing, Apple has ended its free trial program for Leopard Server, so you'll have to get the disc by some other means. Assuming you have the installation DVD for Leopard Server, we'll start the VM image creation.

First, navigate to the Parallels folder located within the Applications folder in Finder. Then double-click the **Parallels Desktop app** therein. If this is a new installation of Parallels and you have not created any VMs yet, you'll be greeted with the New Virtual Machine Assistant. If this is not your first VM, just click the **plus sign** icon on the bottom left of the Parallels Virtual Machines Directory window, as shown in Figure A.26.

Figure A.26 Parallels VM Directory

Click **Continue** on the New Virtual Machine Assistant window. You will now have two drop-down option fields: "Type:" and "Version." Choose **Mac OS X** in the Type: field and **Mac OS X Server v10.5** in the Version: field (see Figure A.27). Click **Continue**, leave the default VM type as **Typical**, and click **Continue** again.

Figure A.27 New VM Assistant OS X

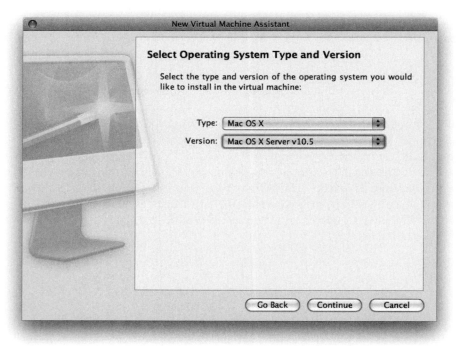

The next screen will ask you what you would like to name your VM; just use the default name, and then click **Create**.

TIP

You don't have to burn a DVD image in order to use it. Parallels can mount the image as a virtual DVD-ROM. Just click the little **triangle** next to More Options on the last page of the New Virtual Machine Assistant. A few more options will drop down in the window. Select **CD/DVD image** and click **Browse** to browse for the DVD image on your hard drive.

Make sure you have the installation media connected (DVD in the DVD-ROM or the DVD image mounted) in Parallels, and start up the VM.

The first screen you'll get is the virtual BIOS in Parallels trying to detect the boot device, as shown in Figure A.28. Since the verbiage in Apple's licensing explicitly forbids Leopard client to be installed in a VM, Parallels has included scripts that verify the OS you're attempting to install is indeed Leopard Server, and not the client.

Figure A.28 Parallels OS X Install Boot Screen

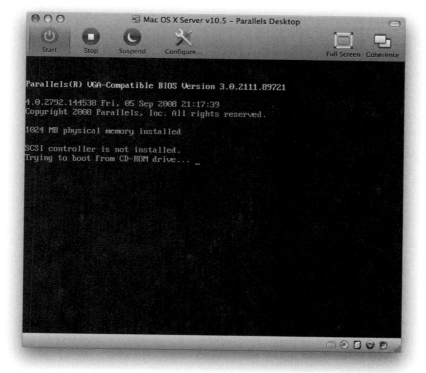

If all goes well and the installation media is verified, the next screen you will see is a gray screen with the Apple logo in the middle of it (see Figure A.29).

Figure A.29 Parallels OS X Install Initialization

The next few windows will prompt you with the basic questions required to complete the installation. The first window will prompt you to select the language you want to use (the default is English). Once you've made your selection, just click the **round button with the right pointing arrow** on the bottom right of the installation window.

The next window will be the Welcome window; just click on through. Next, read the Service License Agreement (SLA) and click **Agree** (if after reading it you indeed agree).

The installer will next ask you where you want to install the OS. Click the **icon** that looks like a hard drive labeled "Macintosh HD" and a green downward-pointing arrow will appear over it. Then click the **right arrow** to continue.

The last window is the review page. Look over the settings to make sure they're correct before clicking **Install**.

TIP

This last window of the install is where you may customize the installation. Just click the **Customize** button and a new window will fold out of the Installation Wizard bar. I like to remove the components I know I won't be using from the installation to save some hard drive space. You may safely remove Language Translations, Printer Drivers (you won't need these in a VM anyway, since Parallels proxies the printing for you), and X11. This will save you about 4 GB of hard drive space!

Once you've clicked the **Install** button, a little window will appear with a progress bar. That's a media check verifying the installation media against defects. If you have never used this media before, I suggest that you go ahead with the check. If you have successfully used the media in the past, you can click the **Skip** button. It normally takes about thirty minutes to finish this verification. After that, just sit back and enjoy the installation progress bar. Don't forget to eject the DVD (or disconnect the DVD image) once the installation is complete.

Now that the initial installation is complete, you're ready for the hard part of the installation. That's right, the first boot configuration (it's not really hard; it's just involved). The first window you'll see is the Welcome window. Just click **Continue** and you'll be on your way. The following window will be the Server Configuration window. Apple simplified the installation by giving you three options that install the most common components for the type of install you choose, as shown in Figure A.30. Make your choice and click **Continue**.

Figure A.30 Parallels OS X Server Configuration Options

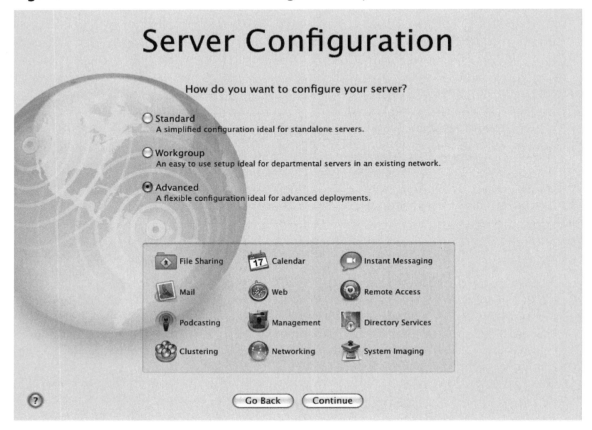

On the following window you will be asked for the keyboard language. Select the appropriate one from the list (the default is English) and click **Continue** (you can click the **Show All** box to see many more languages to choose from).

In the next window, shown in Figure A.31, you'll need to install your Mac OS X Server installation serial number and your License Information. Click **Continue** once you've completed this step.

Figure A.31 Parallels OS X Registration Information

Registration Information

Please enter your company/personal information. This information is used to register your Apple product.

Company/Organization
`Sparq Technology Consulting`

Email Address
`mike@sparqteq.com`

First Name
`Mike`

Last Name
`Chasman`

Area Code
`443`

Phone Number
`6707122`

To learn how Apple safeguards your personal information, please click the Help button to review the Privacy Policy.

Address
`2833 Smith Avenue, Suite 122`

City
`Baltimore`

State/Province
`MD`

Zip Code
`21209`

Country
`United States`

☑ Stay in touch! Keep me up to date with Apple news, software updates, and the latest information on products and services.

The warranty for your Apple product does not require you to register the product.

(Go Back)   (Continue)

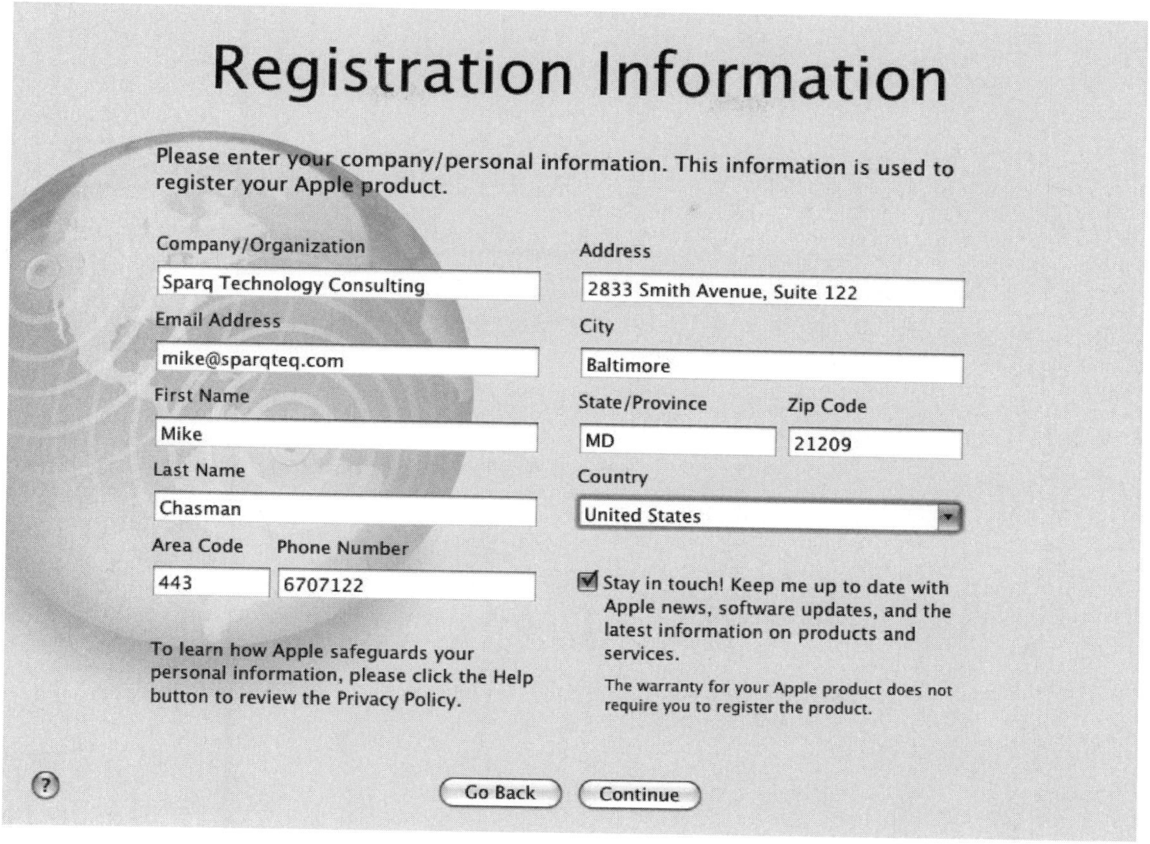

The next two windows are optional, as shown in Figure A.32. You can leave them blank or you can enter all of your company information, and register the installation.

Figure A.32 Parallels OS X AFMQ

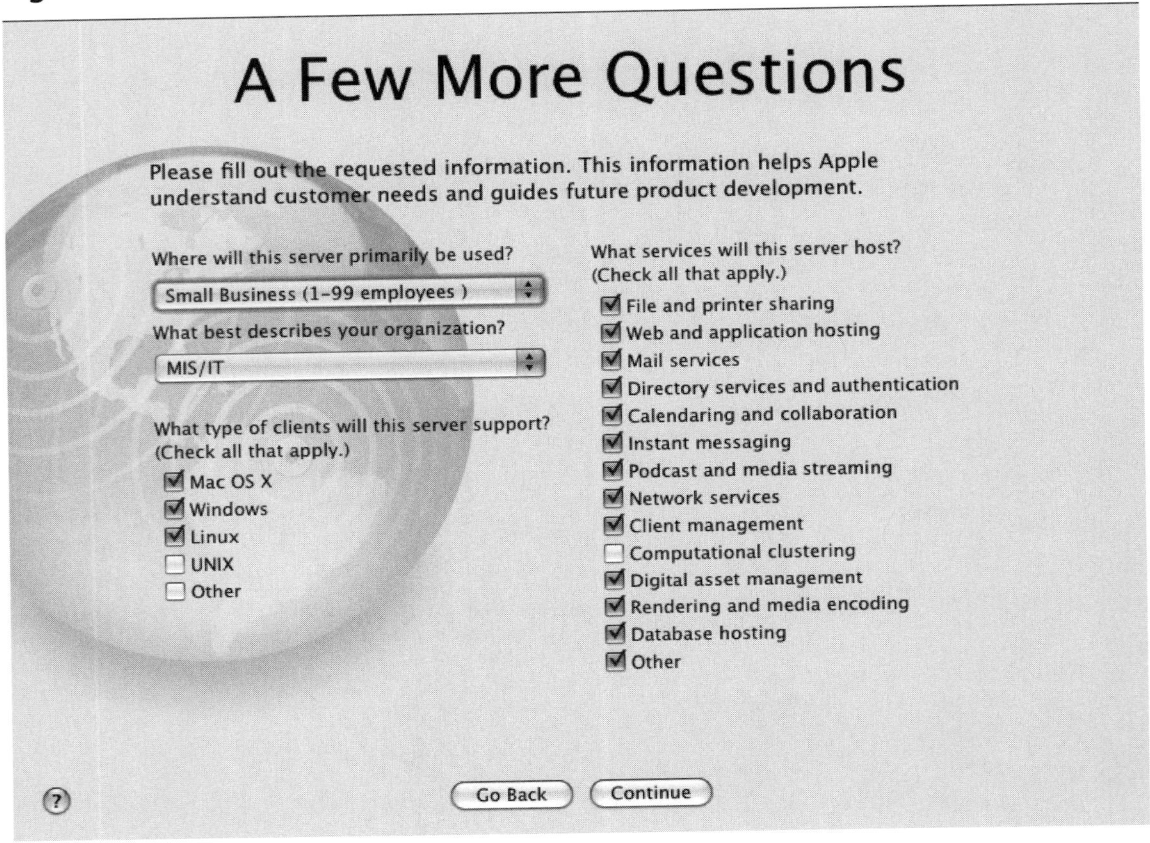

Now you get to set up your first user account in this fresh, newly installed OS (see Figure A.33): the Administrator account—the king of kings in the server world; the first; the top of the hierarchy; the user account holding all the power to change anything on the server (I don't know about you, but I have shivers running down my spine).

Figure A.33 Parallels OS X Administrator Account

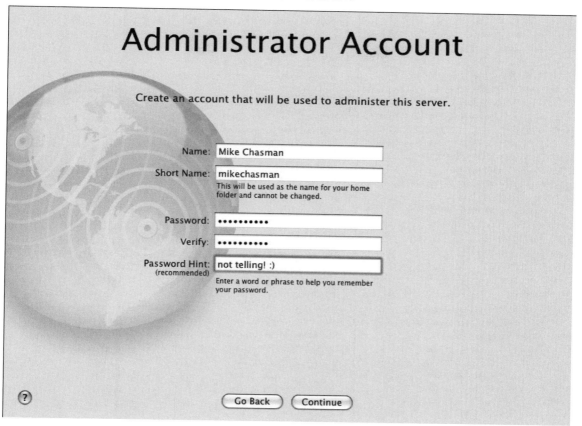

The Network Address window is next. Just leave the default settings—it's getting an Internet Protocol (IP) address from the virtual network interface card (NIC) in Parallels—and click **Continue**.

In the Network Names window you'll want to name your new server (something fun, no doubt), or you can just leave the default name and click **Continue** when you're done.

The Time Zone window is next. Find the nearest major city to you and click **Continue**.

Next, in the Directory Usage window, just leave the default setting (Standalone Server) and click **Continue**.

The next window is the Confirm Settings window. Look over the list of settings to make sure there are no crazy spelling mistakes and click the **Apply** button. A progress bar will drop down (see Figure A.34) and then slide up when the settings are applied, and OS X will prompt you to restart.

Figure A.34 Parallels OS X One moment please...

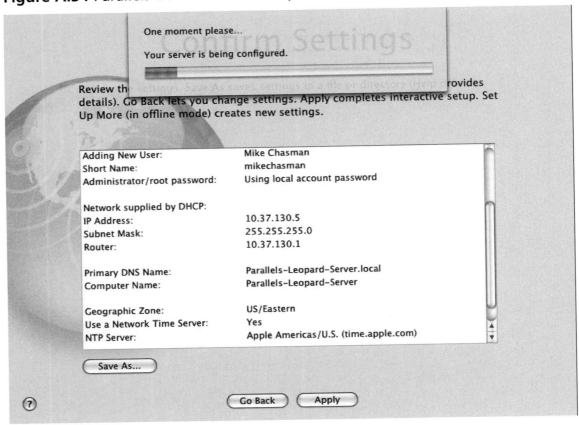

You should now have a working Leopard Server installation in a Parallels VM. All you have left to do is install Parallels Tools.

When you fist start up OS X Leopard Server you will be prompted to configure services (Leopard assumes you installed it to function as a server). Just click the **Choose Configured Services** button (see Figure A.35). You don't actually have to choose anything at this point.

Figure A.35 Parallels OS X First Boot

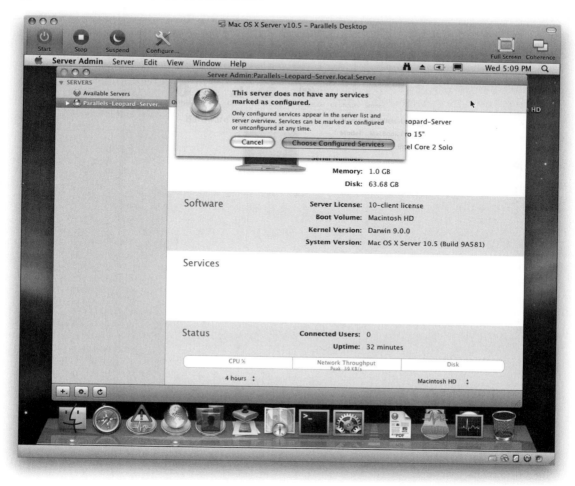

Now you can go ahead and install Parallels Tools. Click the **Virtual Machine | Install Parallels Tools** menu item in the menu bar. You will notice that Finder has a dmg called Parallels Tools mounted. Navigate to it and run the installer by double-clicking the **Install.mpkg** file. The install is pretty straightforward, and you will have to restart when it's done.

That's it, you've done it! Apple OS X 10.5.x Leopard Server is installed and ready for work (or ready for messing around with; your choice).

Boot Camp in Parallels

Parallels also has an option to mount a Boot Camp partition instead of a VM image, as shown in Figure A.36.

WARNING

If you installed any OS on your Boot Camp partition other than Windows XP (SP 2) or Windows Vista/SP 1, you may damage that installation trying to mount it in the Parallels Desktop as a VM. Also remember that if you mount a Boot Camp partition running Windows in Parallels Desktop it will install Parallels Tools, installing new drivers for virtual hardware. Windows sees this as changing hardware, which most likely will require you to reactivate Windows XP or Windows Vista.

Figure A.36 Parallels HD Settings

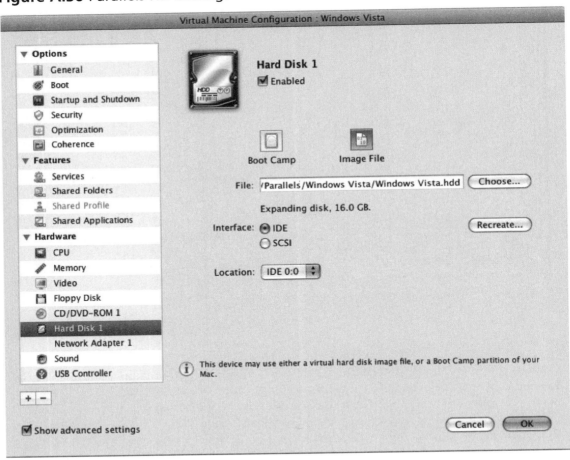

There are a few limitations to using Boot Camp partitions over native VM images. For instance, the OS cannot be suspended; you can't use the snapshot feature in Parallels; you can't boot into "safe mode"; and the compacting or compression functions of Parallels cannot be performed on a Boot Camp partition. The benefits are that you can boot to Windows in Boot Camp for extra speed and game compatibility utilizing the full DirectX 10 capabilities in Windows (Parallels has support for DirectX 9.0). Additionally, you can access your Windows-only application from your Boot Camp partition without rebooting. It's like having two Windows installations that synchronize your installed application and settings.

Coherence

Version 2.5 of Parallels Desktop was officially released in February, 2007. One of the groundbreaking features included in that release was Coherence. Coherence further blurs the line between the Mac OS and Windows installed in a Parallels VM. When you change a running VM (with one or more applications running in it) into Coherence mode, you will see the applications windows running on your Mac OS X desktop side by side with the Mac OS X applications windows (see Figure A.37). By default, both the Windows taskbar and Mac OS X Dock are present on the screen.

Coherence mode is available (through the installation of Parallels Tools) for Windows 2000/XP/2003/Vista guest operating systems.

Figure A.37 Parallels Coherence

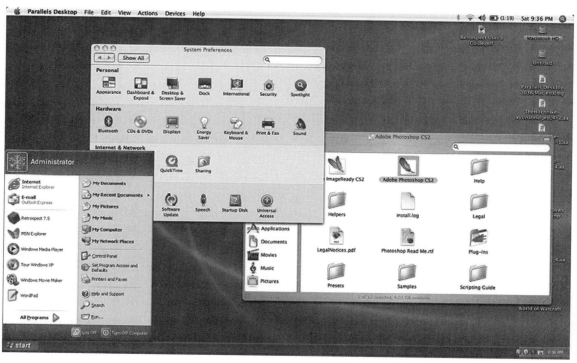

Parallels Desktop can provide close integration between guest OS applications and Mac OS X depending on what security setting you choose in the Parallels preference: You can access Windows file systems from Mac OS X and vice versa. You can set file associations in both systems for applications regardless of the OS running them; doing so will let you open Windows files in Mac OS X applications and Mac OS X files in Windows applications. You can choose a default browser and e-mail client no matter what OS runs it. The Dock can display both Windows and Mac OS X application icons. You can even access the Windows Start menu from the Mac OS X Dock.

VMware Fusion

VMware has proven itself to be an established player and global leader in the virtualization market. Founded in 1998, the company came into the Mac virtualization market a little late, trailing Parallels by a full 15 months. However, right out of the gate, in August, 2007, VMware stepped up with a strong 1.0 release.

VMware Fusion, although in public beta for a while before its official release, felt like a release candidate from the start. Using the beta, you could tell the maturity of the company. VMware released version 2.0 of Fusion in September, 2008 and made it a free update to 1.x registered users. Included in the 2.0 release are a few new features, most notably the option to install Leopard Server, forcing Parallels to scramble to include this feature (previously reserved for its server edition of Parallels) in the upcoming 4.0 version of its desktop virtualization software.

Since Parallels Desktop and VMware Fusion are neck to neck as far as feature set and ease of use, it would be unnecessary to include a thorough tutorial on Fusion VM creation and OS installation.

VirtualBox

I would be remiss if I were to leave out Sun Microsystems' excellent free virtualization solution, VirtualBox (available from their Web site at www.virtualbox.org/wiki/Downloads). Although not as easy to set up as Parallels and Fusion, it's still a stable alternative (as you can see in Figure A.38) that doesn't take up a lot of space on your hard drive (when compared to Fusion and Parallels).

Figure A.38 VirtualBox Comparison Chart

VirtualBox vs. VMware vs. Parallels

Feature	VirtualBox	Parallels Workstation / Desktop	VMware Server / Workstation
Supported host operating systems	Windows 2000, XP, 2003, Vista, Linux, Mac OS X, Solaris 10U5, OpenSolaris, FreeBSD (under development)	Windows 2000, XP, 2003, Vista, Linux, OS X	Windows 2000, XP, 2003, Vista, Linux (32bit and 64bit), Mac OS X
Supported guest operating systems	DOS, Windows 3.1, 95, 98, NT, 2000, XP, Vista, Linux, OpenBSD, FreeBSD, OS/2, Solaris, OpenSolaris, others	DOS, Windows 3.1, 95, 98, NT, 2000, XP, Vista, Linux, OS/2	DOS, Windows 3.1, 95, 98, NT, 2000, XP, Vista, Linux, FreeBSD, Solaris
64bit host OS support	yes	no	yes
64bit guest OS support	no (planned)	no	yes
Intel VT-x support (CPU virtualization extensions)	yes	yes	limited
AMD-V support (CPU virtualization extensions)	yes	yes	limited
Virtual network cards	up to 4	up to 5	up to 4
Virtual Disk Controller	IDE or SATA (up to 32 disks in a guest)	IDE (up to 4)	IDE or SCSI
USB support	yes	yes	yes
iSCSI support (VMs can directly access storage servers over iSCSI)	yes	no	no
Serial ports	up to 4	up to 4	yes
Parallel ports	no	up to 3	yes
CD/DVD writing	yes	no	no
3D acceleration	no	no	limited
Support of VMware images	yes	no	n/a
Headless operation	yes	no	yes
Remote VM access	Integrated RDP server	no	limited
Remote USB support	Yes, arbitrary devices	no	no
Seamless Windows	yes	yes	yes
Shared Folders	yes	yes	yes
Guest power status reporting	yes	no	yes
API	Full API, 100% scriptable	no	yes
Open source	yes (dual licensed, some enterprise features are closed source)	no	no
Customizations	yes, upon request	no	no
License costs	Free	Workstation for Windows/Linux - $49.99, Desktop for Mac OS X - $79.99	Workstation for Windows/Linux around $189, Fusion for Mac - $79.99, Server free for end users, not redistributable

Summary

Once Apple released the Intel Mac, it was only a matter of time before users decided to put Windows on their MacBook. Unbelievably, putting Microsoft Windows on your MacBook is actually supported by Apple, as long as you are running Leopard. Windows XP and Vista are both fully supported. Linux isn't, but you can still utilize it. Apple's Boot Camp gives users the ability to dual-boot their systems between Microsoft Windows and Mac OS X Leopard.

If you do not feel like messing with partitioning or repartitioning your disk, you have other options, such as Parallels, VMware Fusion, and VirtualBox. Of these three virtualization solutions, Parallels and VMware Fusion are the most widely used, although they are not free solutions. VirtualBox is a free solution for those of you with restrained budgets. Regardless of what you use, as you can see the advent of the Intel Mac has allowed Microsoft Windows to intermingle with OS X.

Solutions Fast Track

Boot Camp

- ☑ A solution written by Apple that enables the dual booting of Mac OS X and Windows.
- ☑ Boot Camp is no longer available in Tiger.
- ☑ You need Leopard to use Boot Camp.
- ☑ Apple strongly recommends that you back up your system before setting up Boot Camp.

Parallels

- ☑ Windows installations are supported.
- ☑ Linux installations are supported.
- ☑ Free Trial, Not a Free Product Though

VMware Fusion

- ☑ Windows installations are supported.
- ☑ Linux installations are supported.
- ☑ Free Trial, Not a Free Product Though

VirtualBox

- ☑ Windows Installations are Supported
- ☑ Linux Installations are Supported
- ☑ Open Source (Free)

Frequently Asked Questions

Q: What is Boot Camp?

A: Boot Camp is a way to boot your Mac between OS X and Microsoft Windows or Linux.

Q: What versions of Windows are supported with Boot Camp?

A: Boot Camp supports Windows XP Service Pack 2 or greater and Windows Vista.

Q: What version of OS X do I need to use Boot Camp?

A: You need Tiger to utilize and upgrade an existing Boot Camp installation and you need Leopard to run Boot Camp Assistant to create a new partition or upgrade an existing installation.

Q: What should I do before setting up a dual boot in Boot Camp?

A: Apple strongly recommends that you back up your system before setting up Boot Camp. Make sure you have administrative credentials for your Mac.

Q: What if I want to run Microsoft Windows and OS X, but I do not want to use Boot Camp?

A: You can use Parallels, VirtualBox, or VMware Fusion. You can also use rEFIt.

Q: Are any of the virtualization products free?

A: VirtualBox is free. Parallels and VMware Fusion offer trial versions, but are not free products.

Q: What operating systems can I run in VirtualBox, Parallels, and VMware Fusion?

A: Microsoft Windows, Linux, and other operating systems can be utilized.

Appendix B

Capturing Volatile Data on a Mac

Solutions in this appendix:

- **Volatile Data Collection**

☑ **Summary**

☑ **Solutions Fast Track**

☑ **Frequently Asked Questions**

Introduction

A good investigator will collect as much evidence as possible to build a strong case. Traditional forensic techniques often involved unplugging the suspect system, taking it back to the lab, and analyzing it, a process commonly referred to as *dead box forensics*. But technology continually emerges and changes and investigative procedures must adapt to deal with these changes.

Pulling the plug may have been a good technique to use on older computers running older operating systems, but starting with OS 10.3 (Panther) and later, FileVault could be implemented on the system you are seizing. If FileVault is being utilized and you decide to pull the plug, you may not see the suspect's data again, including network settings, disk information, and user account information. As such, volatile data collection has become more important in recent years and will most likely become a more critical component in the data collection process in years to come.

Volatile Data Collection

In general, your computer's random access memory (RAM) is volatile. In plain language, this means that items stored in RAM will be lost shortly after the machine is powered off. How quickly that occurs is the subject of some debate. Many experts always believed that everything in RAM was lost immediately. However, in February of 2008 researchers at Princeton, including Seth Schoen and Jacob Appelbaum, demonstrated that memory loss fades gradually. Schoen, Appelbaum, and their fellow researchers also demonstrated techniques to make memory chips fade even more slowly by cooling the chips using liquid nitrogen. For more information regarding the research at Princeton, visit http://citp.princeton.edu/memory/. We highly suggest that anyone working in the field watches the five-minute video on that Web site. Using techniques such as those demonstrated in the video, it is possible to capture items such as the 128-bit FileVault Advanced Encryption Standard (AES) key even if the machine is left in a password-protected state.

Volatile Data Collection on an Unlocked System

Collecting some of the volatile data from a system you are seizing might be a good idea if you have open access to the suspect's unlocked desktop. Some agencies have their investigators collect data that will be lost when the computer is shut down, such as applications that are running and open network connections. Many times the data is collected using a trusted tool set which is usually a set of executables that are known good files from the operating system. Agencies do this to avoid using executables that could have been altered on the suspect's machine. Make a note of what commands you are running and the output of these commands. Many times an investigator will send the output to an external source, such as a different computer placed on the network. It is important to follow the guidelines of your agency and remember that commands are being used to capture volatile data, not to alter the system you are examining.

If an OS X system is left up and running and you have unrestricted access to the user's desktop, you should strongly consider examining the user's Home folder to determine whether FileVault is implemented. If FileVault is implemented, as shown in Figure B.1, you will likely see a black-and-white lock icon.

Figure B.1 FileVault Implemented on the User's Home Folder

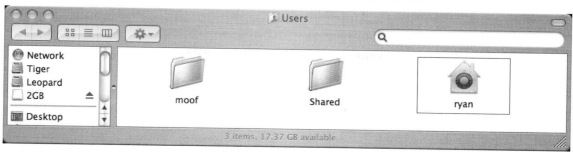

If you see the lock icon shown in Figure B.1, you should collect all of the data from the user's folder and send it to an external device because while the user is logged in, his Home folder is unencrypted, as shown in Figure B.2. Also, keep in mind that once the user's system is shut down his Home folder will be encrypted with 128-bit AES encryption. If the computer is turned off, you will need the password or keys to restore the encrypted sparse image (or sparse bundle for Leopard).

Figure B.2 The User's Home Folder
in an Unencrypted State While the User Is Logged On

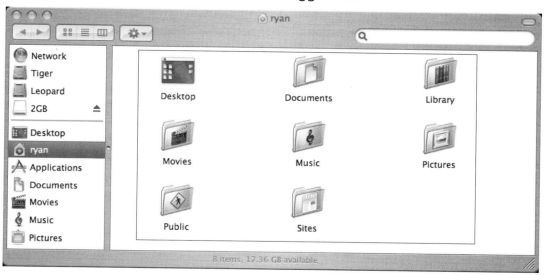

WARNING

If a user has implemented FileVault and you have unrestricted access to the user's unlocked desktop, copy the contents of the user's Home folder to an external source while the desktop is in its unencrypted state. If you choose to turn the system off without obtaining the user's Home folder, you will need the user's password or keys to decrypt the encrypted sparse image.

When approaching a FileVaulted Macintosh system, consider making a logical copy of the user's Home directory as part of your initial response. Otherwise, you will be extremely disappointed when you take the drive to your lab and find out that the data was encrypted and cannot be read. Do not attempt to turn off FileVault, even if the suspect gives you the password. Doing so could overwrite valuable data in the hard drive's unallocated space as the decryption process takes place. Instead, image the entire drive after completing the logical copy of the user's Home directory to ensure the most complete data capture possible. In summary, never turn off encryption, because the space used to unencrypt may overwrite important data.

With some encryption methods, such as Microsoft's BitLocker, you can actually turn encryption off without authenticating. On a Windows Vista system, if you attempt to turn off BitLocker and the account you are using has administrative privileges, you will likely only need to click Allow to enter the BitLocker applet to turn off the encryption for the drive. Mac OS X, however, is not so lax on security, and you would need to authenticate with a password, as shown in Figure B.3.

Figure B.3 Password Required to Turn Off FileVault

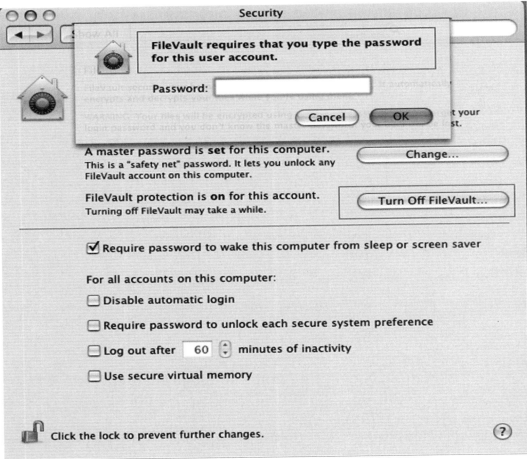

The master password will also allow you to unlock any FileVault account on the computer. However, once again Mac OS X proves to be security-conscious and will not allow you to change this password without providing the current password, as shown in Figure B.4. So, without the password, turning off FileVault is not an option. You could ask the user for the password if he is present. But even without the password, you can copy the user's Home folder in its unencrypted state. The benefit of the master password is that it will allow you to recover all of the encrypted Home folders on the disk. So, if you can convince a suspect to give you this password, you will be in good shape. Also, you will not be risking erasing any data, as you might if you turn off FileVault.

Figure B.4 Mac OS X Disallowing a Master Password Change Unless the Current Master Password Is Provided

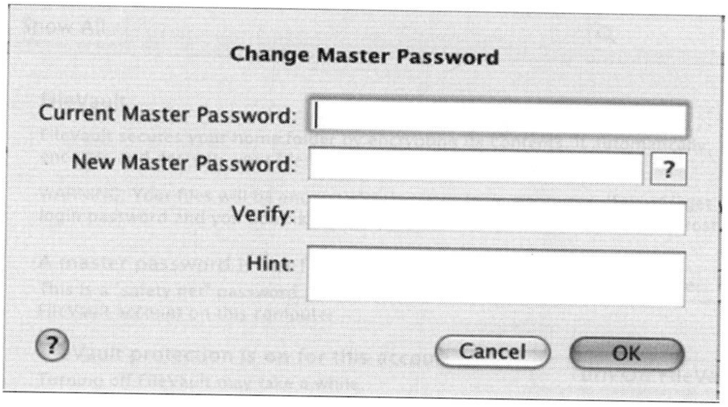

Volatile Data Collection on a Locked System

Collecting the volatile data off a system with a trusted tool set may work fine if a user's system is in an unlocked state and you have access to the user's desktop. However, sometimes you may encounter a user's system in a password-protected state, as shown in Figure B.5. You could ask the user for the password if he is present, but many users with something to hide are not willing to surrender this information. If you are unable to get the password, you need to consider alternative methods, such as using the FireWire attack or the msramdmp program.

Figure B.5 A Locked System That Needs a Password

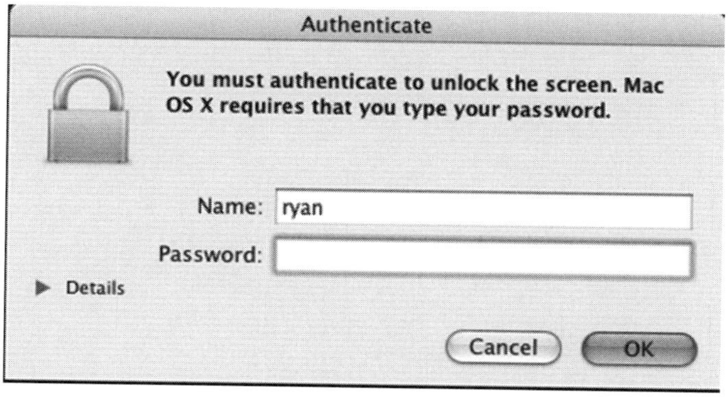

The FireWire "Attack"

You can use a variety of techniques to try to access the user's volatile data when the screen is in a locked, password-protected state. One technique involves connecting a Linux machine running a direct memory access program to the Mac's FireWire port. Adam Boileau developed this technique and he describes it in the paper "Hit by a Bus: Physical Access Attacks with FireWire." Using this technique, one researcher wrote a tool to extract the user logon name and password from a system running Tiger. You can read more about it here:

- http://blog.juhonkoti.net/2008/02/29/automated-os-x-macintosh-password-retrieval-via-firewire

Keep in mind that the FireWire specification calls for direct memory access and these researchers are using FireWire to directly access and read the Mac's memory. Although these techniques may provide valuable information to the on-goings in RAM, they are somewhat invasive and involve tricking the system into thinking an iPod is being connected to the system. Consult with your legal department if this is the way you plan to capture volatile data on a system in a locked or password-protected state.

Msramdmp

Developed by researcher Wesley McGrew, the msramdmp program will capture and write the contents of a system's RAM to a USB drive. This technique is much less invasive than other techniques of volatile RAM collection, such as the FireWire technique discussed in the preceding section. Unlike other techniques, which often involve connecting to the system and running commands or programs, this technique does not involve doing anything to the suspect's system other than turning it off while it's in a password-protected state. Once you do that, hold down the Option key and insert the msramdmp_cd and USB stick into the machine; the memory will automatically be written to the USB device. Then, after an image of the USB device is created, you can analyze the image with a hex editor or scripts to extract the data from the captured memory.

Several steps are involved in this process, including burning the msramdmp_cd.iso image, wiping the thumb drive, and creating a thumb drive with a Linux type 40 Venix 80286 partition. In Exercise B.1 you will create a dd of the RAM image and then use a hex reader to view the dd image.

Configuring & Implementing...

Exercise B.1: Burning the msramdmp_cd.iso Image

This exercise will walk you through the process of forensically wiping a disk. This process will zero out all data at the physical layer so the disk will be ready to store digital evidence.

1. Download the msramdmp_cd.iso file from:

    http://www.mcgrewsecurity.com/tools/msramdmp/msramdmp_cd.iso.

2. From the menu bar, select **Go | Utilities** and open the **Disk Utility.app**.

3. From the File menu, choose **Open Disk Image** and select the **msramdmp_cd.iso** image from the desktop, as shown in Figure B.6.

Figure B.6 Selecting the msramdmp_cd.iso Image

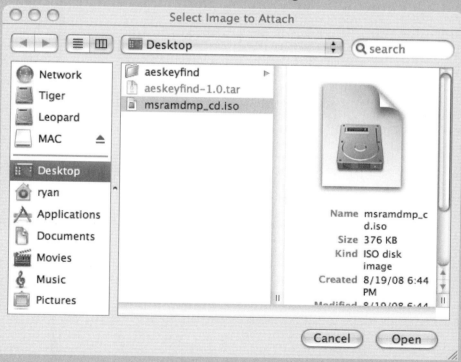

Continued

4. Select the **msramdmp_cd.iso** image from the **Disk and Volume** pane and click the **Burn** button, as shown in Figure B.7.

Figure B.7 Burning the
msramdmp_cd.iso Image with the Mac OS X Disk Utility

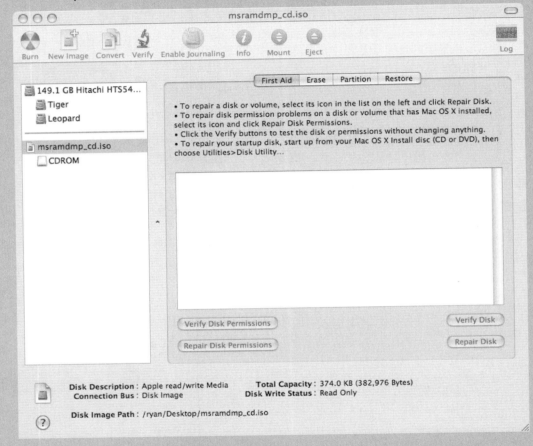

5. Click the **Burn** button again. You should see the message that the burn was successful (and hear a cool noise)!

End of Exercise

Configuring & Implementing...

Exercise B.2: Wiping the USB Media

In this exercise, you will prepare the destination media by wiping the drive.

1. Insert into the drive the USB media stick to be wiped. Your USB stick should have as much as or more RAM than the system you are working with. Warning: All data will be destroyed!

2. From the Menu bar, select **Go | Utilities** and open the **Disk Utility.app**.

3. Select the **USB disk** from the **Disk and Volume** pane and click the **Erase** button from the menu bar, as shown in Figure B.8.

Figure B.8 Wiping the Destination Media to Avoid Any Type of Contamination

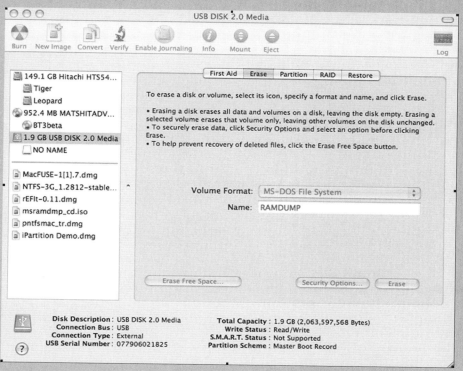

Continued

4. In the **Volume Format** pull-down menu select **MS-DOS File System**, as shown in Figure B.8. Enter **RAMDUMP** as the name of the volume, also as shown in Figure B.8.

5. Click the **Security Options** button shown in the bottom of Figure B.8. Choose **Zero Out Data**, as shown in Figure B.9. Click **OK**.

Figure B.9 Wiping the Destination Media

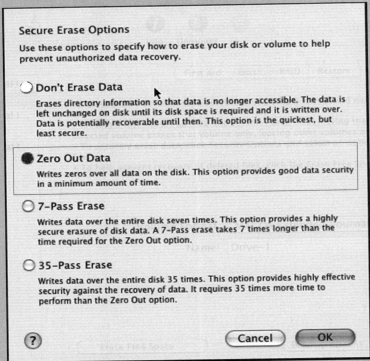

6. Click the **Erase** radio button next to Security Options. Confirm that this is the drive you are attempting to erase and click **Erase** again. Warning: All data will be destroyed!

7. Close the **Disk Utility.app** when the secure delete has finished and eject the media, properly selecting the USB device, holding down the **Control** key, and selecting **Eject**.

End of Exercise

Configuring & Implementing...

Exercise B.3: Burning the BackTrack ISO

This exercise will walk you through the process of burning the BackTrack 3 Final CD.

1. Download the BackTrack ISO from http://www.remote-exploit.org/cgi-bin/fileget?version=bt3-cd.

2. From the menu bar, select **Go | Utilities** and open the **Disk Utility.app**.

3. From the File menu choose **Open Disk Image**, and select the **bt3-final.iso** file from the download location.

4. Select **bt3-final.iso** from the **Disk and Volume** pane, and click the **Burn** button.

End of Exercise

Configuring & Implementing...

Exercise B.4: Creating a Venix 80286 Partition

This exercise explains how to create a Venix 80286 partition using the BackTrack Live CD.

1. Make sure the BackTrack 3 CD is in the drive.

2. Restart your Mac. Hold down the **Option** key.

3. Accept the default boot option from the BackTrack menu.

4. Open a terminal and type **fdisk –l**.

5. Note the Mac EFI partitions that have been recognized by the BackTrack distribution as /dev/sda1, as shown in Figure B.10.

Continued

Figure B.10 The fdisk-l Command Recognizing the Disk with GPT/EFI

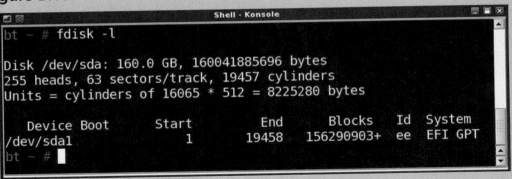

You should see an EFI and GPT, as shown in Figure B.10. In this Mac, there is only one physical disk. If you have additional disks in your system, they will be recognized as sdb, sdc, and so forth. Insert your USB stick (or FireWire) into the drive. If a window opens and asks you what you want to do, click **Do Nothing**.

6. Type **fdisk –l** again. Notice the recognized drive, most likely /dev/sdb1. You should see this disk listed as a FAT32 partition, as shown in Figure B.11.

Figure B.11 The fdisk-l Command
Recognizing the Added Thumb Drive Device

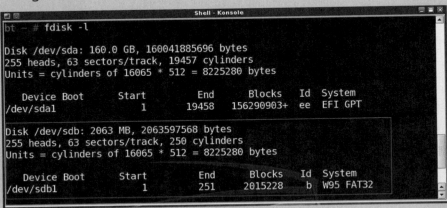

7. Type **fdisk /dev/sdb**. Note that if your drive designation was different, replace /dev/sdb1 with the letters assigned to your USB drive. Be very careful to follow these directions or important data might be destroyed!

Continued

8. Type the following sequence of commands in the fdisk submenu:

- **m** (to display the Help menu)
- **d** (to delete the existing partition)
- **n** (to add a new partition)
- **p** (to make the partition the primary partition)
- **1** (to number the partition as 1)
- **Enter** (to accept the default for the first cylinder)
- **Enter** (to accept the default for the last cylinder)
- **t** (to change the partition type)
- **L** (to list all the partition types)
- **40** (to change the partition type to 40, Venix 80286)
- **p** (to print the partition table)
- **w** (to write the partition table)

9. Type **fdisk –l**. /dev/sdb1 should be listed as a Venix 80286 partition.

10. Type **shutdown –r** at the terminal and reboot into Leopard or Tiger.

End of Exercise

Configuring & Implementing...

Exercise B.5: Using the msramdmp Program

In this exercise, you will use Wesley McGrew's msramdmp program on a Mac. The exercise requires a bit of practice to get the timing down, before you try it out in the field. If you come across a situation where a computer running Mac OS X Tiger or Leopard is at a password-protected screen, turn off the power and turn it back on immediately while holding down the **Option** key.

1. Hold down the **Option** key while you insert your CD immediately, then your USB drive with the Venix 80286 partition.

2. If the steps were completed properly, your screen will look like Figure B.12.

Continued

Figure B.12 Wesley McGrew's msramdmp Program

```
ISOLINUX 3.61 2008-02-03  Copyright (C) 1994-2008 H. Peter Anvin

---------------------------------------------------------------
msramdmp - McGrew Security Ram Dumper - v 0.5.1
http://mcgrewsecurity.com/projects/msramdmp/
Robert Wesley McGrew: wesley@mcgrewsecurity.com
---------------------------------------------------------------

Found msramdmp partition at disk 0x81 : partition 1
Partition isn't marked as used.  Using it.
Marked partition as used.
Writing section from 0x00000000 to 0x0009FFFF
Writing section from 0x00100000 to 0x10000000
_
```

End of Exercise

Configuring & Implementing…

Exercise B.6: Creating a dd of the PPC PReP Boot Type 41 Partition

In this exercise, you will create a dd image of the RAMDUMP Type 41 partition.

1. Open a terminal on your Mac by selecting **Go | Utilities | Terminal**.
2. Type **sudo su**, and then enter your root account password.
3. **ls /dev/disk?**
    This lists all of the disks that are presently connected to the Mac.
4. Insert the USB device.
5. Type the command **ls /dev/disk?** and note which is the newly listed disk, as shown in Figure B.13.

Continued

Figure B.13 Viewing the Added USB Device with ls /dev/disk?

```
Welcome to Darwin!
mac:~ ryan$ ls /dev/disk?
/dev/disk0          /dev/disk1
mac:~ ryan$ ls /dev/disk?
/dev/disk0          /dev/disk1        /dev/disk2
```

6. One the new disk is displayed, use that disk as the source in the if= statement. An example is provided below:

   Enter **dd=if/dev/disk2 of=RAMCAPTURE.DD** (where **disk2** is the number assigned to the disk).

End of Exercise

Now you can download any hex editor program and open the RAMCAPTURE.DD file. You can find all types of interesting information from RAM, including usernames, passwords, and keys. Have fun!

Summary

If you come across a system that is not password-protected, you may want to make logical copies of items such as the user's Home folder, in case encryption mechanisms such as FileVault are in place. However, when you take this approach, it is important that you always document your steps and follow the guidelines of your agency. If you come across a locked system, you may want to consider using the msramdmp program to try to obtain information from RAM, such as usernames, passwords, and keys. Practice the techniques associated with using this technique before you attempt to use it while performing an acquisition. Once again, be sure to document your actions and follow the guidelines of your agency. Consult with your legal point of contact before using the msramdmp program.

Solutions Fast Track

Volatile Data Collection

- ☑ Copy the user's Home folder if FileVault is in use.
- ☑ Follow the guidelines of your agency.
- ☑ Document your actions.
- ☑ If you can get the master password, you can recover all encrypted Home folders.
- ☑ If you have unrestricted access to the user's desktop, collect volatile information such as the Internet Protocol (IP) address and network connections.
- ☑ If the user's screen is locked, you can use the msramdmp program.
- ☑ Dumping the RAM requires a Venix 80286 partition.
- ☑ You can use the disk utility to burn the msramdmp_cd.iso image.
- ☑ Make an image of your RAM dump with dd and open it with a hex editor.
- ☑ Turning off FileVault is never an option because doing so may erase vital evidence.
- ☑ If the user's screen is locked, you can perform a FireWire attack.

Frequently Asked Questions

Q: What is msramdmp?

A: Msramdmp is a program you can use to capture volatile data when the computer is in a password protected state.

Q: Should I make a logical copy of the user's Home directory if the user is using FileVault?

A: Yes.

Q: Where can I find out more information about the msramdmp program?

A: Wesley McGrew's website: http://www.mcgrewsecurity.com/tools/msramdmp/

Q: My agency says not to use the msramdmp program, but it might help me retrieve artifacts from a suspect's system. What should I do?

A: Follow the guidelines of your agency.

Q: Should I ever turn off FileVault?

A: Never.

Q: What will the master password do?

A: The master password will unlock all FileVault images.

Index